Gender and Rock

Gender and Rock

MARY CELESTE KEARNEY

OXFORD
UNIVERSITY PRESS

Oxford University Press is a department of the University of Oxford. It furthers
the University's objective of excellence in research, scholarship, and education
by publishing worldwide. Oxford is a registered trade mark of Oxford University
Press in the UK and certain other countries.

Published in the United States of America by Oxford University Press
198 Madison Avenue, New York, NY 10016, United States of America.

© Oxford University Press 2017

Library of Congress Cataloging-in-Publication Data
Names: Kearney, Mary Celeste, 1962– author.
Title: Gender and rock / by Mary Celeste Kearney.
Other titles: Gender and rock
Description: New York, NY : Oxford University Press, [2017] | Includes index.
Identifiers: LCCN 2016055604 | ISBN 9780199359516 (pbk. : alk. paper) |
ISBN 9780190688660 (hardcover : alk. paper)
Subjects: LCSH: Rock music—Social aspects. | Sex role in music.
Classification: LCC ML3918.R63 K42 2017 | DDC 781.66081—dc23
LC record available at https://lccn.loc.gov/2016055604

Gender definitions are an imposition.
I grew up in a world where I assumed that women can make noise,
and that noise should be put on a shelf
right next to the noise that men make.

Ani DiFranco,
Trouble Girls: Rolling Stone's Book of Women in Rock

Although an account of rock cannot ignore its musical effectivity,
it is also the case that rock cannot be defined in musical terms.

Lawrence Grossberg,
We Gotta Get Out of This Place:
Popular Conservatism and Postmodern Culture

CONTENTS

PART V Rock's Other Players: Consumers and Critics

LIST OF ILLUSTRATIONS

ACKNOWLEDGMENTS

SERIOUS RESPECT AND PROFOUND gratitude to Mavis Bayton for leading the way in feminist rock scholarship: Your work is beyond essential. Special thanks to Sheila Whiteley, who supported so many of us who study gender and popular music. Lots of grrrl love to Norma Coates, Cynthia Fuchs, Donna Gaines, and Lori Tomlinson, who together with me created Clitlist, an inspiring and supportive online space for exploring the gender politics of rock culture and our own complicated relationships with them. Much admiration and big hugs to Carla DeSantis Black for creating *Rockrgrl* and fighting to keep its spirit alive. Feminist fist bumps to Pamela Chandran for loaning me her L7 and Bikini Kill albums way back when. Mucho gracias to David Uskovich, with whom I have spent untold hours talking about rock's cultural politics over good beer at the Spider House.

Major thanks also to students in my Gender and Rock Culture and Feminist Popular Music Criticism classes at the University of Southern California, the University of Texas at Austin, and the University of Notre Dame. I so appreciate your brains, your creativity, and your brave challenging of my assumptions about both gender and rock. I am forever grateful for how your knowledge of and experiences with rock and other music cultures helped to shape my thinking and this book.

Buckets of gratitude to Peter LaBella for his enthusiasm for this book from the start and his guidance during its early development at Oxford University Press. I'm also super grateful to Norm Hirschy, for his support and patience during the final steps needed to get this thing between covers. Sincere thanks to Oxford's anonymous reviewers, who helped make this a much better and more useful book. Heartfelt thanks also to my awesome research assistants and mutual feminist rock fans, Morgan Blue and Jessalynn Keller.

It is impossible for me to dedicate this book to just one person since the spirit that kept me going when writing it came from many sources. I dedicate it first to my siblings—Christy, Terry, and Tom—whose musical tastes and record collections profoundly shaped my own from a very young age. Second, to my favorite guitarist and gearhead, Michael, who helped me buy my first guitar . . . and keeps encouraging me to play it. Thank you for teaching me most of what I know about musical gear, and even more for your patience during all those weekends and summers interrupted by my work on this book. And finally, to musicians everywhere who defy rock's boys' club, especially Chrissie Hynde, Poly Styrene, and Annie Lennox, who first sparked my curiosity about rock culture as an important site of gender trouble.

You all are the rock and roll that saved this girl's life.

INTRODUCTION

Power Chords and Groupie Chicks

LISTEN/WATCH: JOAN JETT and the Blackhearts, "I Love Rock 'n Roll" (*I Love Rock 'n Roll*, Blackheart, 1981). *A thoroughly infectious anthem for rock fans worldwide, this cover of The Arrows' song and its accompanying video should inspire you to immerse yourself in rock culture while thinking critically about gender. Consider how the lyrics alter the traditional romantic narrative of boy pursuing girl. In the video, Jett's creative power, bad-girl attitude, and gender nonconformity are on full display, demonstrating that rock culture is a compelling site for the subversion of social norms (as shown in Figure I.1).*

Power chord: A loud and heavy sound produced on an electric guitar by playing concurrently a root note and its fifth interval and then magnifying and diversifying that sound by channeling it through an amplifier. Popularized by male rock guitarists, power chords are often considered displays of musical virtuosity and technical prowess and have long been used to express mastery, strength, virulence, and rebellion. As a result, they are commonly affiliated with masculinity, regardless of their performer's gender identity.

Groupie chick: A young female fan who seeks out intimate relations with rock musicians. Emerging in the late 1960s, this term is commonly shortened to "groupie." Although repudiated by many feminists and rockers, self-identified groupies argue that they are creative muses for musicians and that their sexual agency is evidence of their liberation from gender norms.

Power chords and groupie chicks are two phenomena stereotypically associated with rock music. They are featured regularly in representations of rock culture, including movies, like *School of Rock*. Simultaneously popularized in the late 1960s, when rock music became more popular and standardized, power chords and groupie chicks bolstered a unique identity in rock culture that was associated with youthfulness, rebellion, authenticity, and white heterosexual

Figure I.1   Joan Jett and the Blackhearts, "I Love Rock 'n Roll"
Boardwalk Records, 1981

masculinity. This identity has remained dominant in **rock culture** for over sixty years, a remarkable track record given its emergence alongside the women's and gay liberation movements, which have fought to subvert the gender norms that benefit heterosexual men.

Power chords and groupie chicks have helped to define and reinforce rock culture's regressive gender norms over many years. Nevertheless, as suggested above, both of these phenomena, like many others in rock culture, are imbued also with a sense of transgression that complicates their association with just conservative ideologies. In other words, the meanings and values of power chords and groupie chicks are not neat and clean. Neither solely conservative nor solely progressive, they have been defined via both of these perspectives by different people in different times and in different places.

Power chords and groupie chicks are not the only examples we can use to discuss the tension between conservatism and nonconformity that characterizes rock culture. Rock is a complex formation with numerous instances of such contradictory perspectives, and, as such, it is a compelling site of analysis for those interested in how power functions in popular culture. This book introduces readers to these unstable and often messy operations of cultural power via a particular focus on **gender**, a social system wherein people, objects, practices, and numerous other things are categorized as "masculine" or "feminine," or both, based on qualities conventionally associated with men and women. As the chapters that follow will show, rock culture is defined by gender in both regressive and progressive ways. By drawing on previous scholarship in both gender studies and popular music criticism, this book aims to facilitate readers' understanding and application of the primary theories and methods used in gender-based analyses of popular music culture.

Rock culture is the larger social formation that has **rock music** at its central, binding feature. A form of Western popular music, rock has roots in both white country music and various black musical forms, including jazz, the blues, gospel, and R&B (rhythm and blues). Rock music, as a commonly mediated and commodified form of cultural expression, walks a delicate balance between art and commerce through its affiliations with authenticity and rebellion and oppositions to superficiality and commercialism. First created by American youth in the 1950s, rock music is now a global phenomenon appreciated by members of multiple age groups and backgrounds. Indeed, over the second half of the twentieth century, rock music became so popular that the "rock" label was often used to describe popular music in general. Although rock's sonic dominance has been significantly challenged since the 1980s by rap's prominent role in popular culture, it has been impacted most recently by digital technologies. Nevertheless, rock music remains ubiquitous in our cultural soundtrack, and many people still invest heavily in its production and consumption.

Rock music has been an academic subject for several decades in a variety of disciplines. Yet critical attention (like public attention) to the gendered aspects of rock culture is a relatively recent practice. Only since the turn of the twenty-first century has a significant number of feminist scholars and critics turned their analytical gaze toward rock, thus helping to construct a vibrant intellectual community focused on the study of gender in rock culture. This development can be connected to a variety of other social transformations during the late twentieth century, especially the popularization of feminist ideologies, the development of feminist and queer musicology and popular music criticism, the media's increased attention to women and queer musicians, and the greater visibility of fan discourse as a result of the Internet.

When I taught my first course on gender and rock culture in 1997, I had a difficult time drawing from academic research to build my syllabus. As I write today, almost two decades later, a dearth of scholarship on gender and rock is no longer a problem. Indeed, a primary challenge for both my teaching and this book is what scholarship *not* to include, since so much work has been published in this area. This book is in part the result of that collective effort to keep critical discourse about gender loud, rebellious, and center stage in the much larger and more cacophonous milieus of rock criticism and rock culture.

Approach

As Lawrence Grossberg suggests in one of the epigraphs that begins this book, rock culture cannot be analyzed using only musical theory, since it is made up of not just musical texts but also numerous other objects, practices, roles, and institutions related to musical performance, recording, commodification, consumption, and criticism. In other words, rock culture is a complex formation with multiple dimensions. Therefore, this book does not have rock music and lyrics as its only objects of study. Rather, it uses a multiperspectival approach to explore gender in rock's numerous sites, including performance, music videos, fandom, and the recording business.

As multiple discourses of gender influence the development of rock culture, each site of activity in that culture deserves critical attention, given its contributions to rock's broader **gender politics**, that is, the ongoing struggles over ideas about and values related to women and men, femininity and masculinity, and cisgender and transgender people. (**Cisgender** people are those whose gender identity and presentation align with the sex category assigned to them at birth. **Transgender** people's gender identity and presentation do not align with the sex category assigned to them at birth.) Although musicians, fans, critics, and business people do not experience rock culture in this fragmented way wherein their activities are confined to just one site, this book hopes to facilitate an informed perspective on rock culture as a whole by exploring individual sites most significant to its gender politics.

To examine these multiple sites in rock's gendered culture, this book adopts an **interdisciplinary** approach that draws on theories and methods used in musicology, popular music criticism, cultural studies, media studies, literary analysis, performance studies, and sociology, as well as feminist and queer scholarship. As discussed in Chapter 2, **feminism** has a variety of forms and meanings, but it can be summed up as a movement aimed to end gender oppression and to bring about gender equality. **Queer** is used in this book both as an umbrella term for members of the **LGBTQI community**—i.e., lesbian, gay, bisexual, transgender, queer/questioning, intersex people—as well as to signal an antinormative view on gender and sexual politics.

Contemporary **gender theory** is a key component in this book's critical approach and significantly informs the analyses of rock that it contains. This book argues that gender is socially constructed and contested in numerous sites in rock culture rather than inherent in individual bodies, objects, practices, or institutions. Yet this book departs significantly from the gender-specific focus of most previous analyses of gender and rock culture. Since the mid-1980s, numerous scholarly articles and books focusing on women and rock have appeared, including Mavis Bayton's *Frock Rock*, Sheila Whiteley's *Women and Popular Music*, Lori Burns and Mélisse Lafrance's *Disruptive Divas*, Marion Leonard's *Gender in the Music Industry*, and Helen Reddington's *The Lost Women of Rock Music*. Such texts have importantly drawn attention not only to the previously silenced history of women in rock music but also to the dynamic ways women are changing rock culture. In doing so, these texts participate in troubling the traditional male domination of both rock music and rock scholarship.

Nevertheless, the women-centric approach of most feminist rock studies has resulted in a fairly lopsided body of literature, not to mention a reproduction of gender as a binary system (male/female, masculine/feminine). Despite feminist arguments that rock culture is dominated by **patriarchal ideology** (the belief that males are superior to females and thus should have the most power), relatively few analyses of gender and rock have moved beyond women and femininity to interrogate patriarchy and its effects in rock culture. Robert Walser's *Running with the Devil*, Matthew Bannister's *White Boys, White Noise*, Freya Jarman-Ivens's collection *Oh Boy! Masculinities and Popular Music*, and Peter Lehman's *Roy Orbison* are important exceptions here. Hopefully, such work will inspire more scholars to critique men and masculinity in rock culture. More attention must be paid to the wide variety of gender discourses circulating in this culture if we are to comprehend fully how it offers not only men but also women and transgender people various opportunities for experimenting with gender identities.

Like many previous feminist analyses of rock culture, this book pays close attention to the roles women have played in the production, performance, consumption, and criticism of rock music. Nonetheless, this book does not reproduce the common conflation of "gender" and "women" wherein the two terms are seen as naturally interchangeable and men thus escape critical inquiry. Much like the essays in Sheila Whiteley's collection *Sexing the Groove,* this book is grounded in the understanding that all human beings "do" gender. Therefore, men and masculinity must be explored alongside women and femininity, just as transgender people must be explored alongside those who are cisgender, if we are to understand fully how gender works in rock culture. In addition to being feminist, the gender politics that ground this book are also queer. The binary sex/gender system that privileges cisgender bodies is understood as constructed rather than natural. Moreover, all those belonging to the LGBTQI community are included with straight people in the spectrum of gendered identities and performances. By approaching gender broadly, this book hopes to elicit greater comprehension of how rock functions as a site for both the affirmation and the subversion of gender norms.

As a result of the difficulties of language and this book's reliance on other scholarship, this book risks reproducing the binary, cisgender logics of heteronormativity by employing unqualified terms, like "men," "women," "male," and "female." (**Heteronormativity** is the belief that heterosexuality is the best and most natural form of sexuality.) Nonetheless, the gender politics at the heart of this book are more in line with the fluid, nonbinary values central to contemporary feminism and queer culture and on display in other feminist/queer rock studies, like Mimi Schippers's *Rockin' out of the Box*. This book also adopts Ani DiFranco's logic about gender in rock, which appeared in Barbara O'Dair's *Trouble Girls* and is reprinted here as this book's first epigraph. DiFranco argues that gender categorization is an imposition in rock culture, closing down rather than opening up opportunities. This book argues that gender is always constructed relationally, and I encourage readers to consider how masculinity and femininity, as well as patriarchy, feminism, and queerness, always operate interdependently across and through rock culture. Both conservative (patriarchal, heterocentrist) and progressive (feminist, queer) ideologies of gender inform rock's various texts, practices, participants, and institutions, making it a truly exciting site for both cultural engagement and critical inquiry.

Critical Principles

Several principles constitute the backbone on which the analyses in this book rest. They are important to keep in mind when reading this book.

Gender is central to rock culture. Exploring the gender politics of rock does not mean looking in marginal places or for subtextual meanings. It is a foundational assumption of this book and feminist rock criticism that gender is one of the primary forces shaping rock culture. Indeed, the idea that gender is not important in rock culture is itself grounded in a particular ideological perspective that is strongly gendered: patriarchy. This ideology privileges boys and men not only by placing them above girls and women but also by affording them a certain blindness to gender politics. As this book explores, gender impacts *all* of rock culture.

The term "gender" is not equivalent to "women." It is an unfortunate effect of patriarchal ideology that many people assume gender to be an issue for women only. Yet *all* human beings are gendered. This book explores gender politics in rock culture through investigations of masculinity, femininity, and nonbinary **genderqueerness**, which mixes in one body traits traditionally associated with masculinity and femininity and thus troubles the historic equation of masculinity with males and femininity with females. Human beings are not the only things that are gendered, however. Because we use language to create order out of the chaos of our everyday realities, we categorize the numerous phenomena that make up those realities so as to understand and communicate about them quickly and efficiently. As this book explores, virtually everything in rock culture is gendered, from musical instruments to musical sounds, from video techniques to lyrical styles, from musician roles to rock criticism. This does not mean, however, that such gendered meanings are stable or unchangeable. If they were, **heteronormative patriarchy** would have always ruled this culture, and women, queer people, and those who identify as nonbinary or genderqueer would have never found a place, much less success, in it.

Men have dominated and continue to dominate rock culture. Male readers, fear not! This book's purpose is not meant to denigrate men, manhood, or masculinity. Nonetheless, rock's male dominance, patriarchal values, and privileging of hegemonic masculinity are facts that are readily seen in the awards shows mentioned above, as well as the Rock and Roll Hall of Fame, which to date has never inducted an all-female rock band and whose 205 inducted acts include only 34 (16.6 percent) that have women members. Rock's masculinism has been well established also via analyses of live performances, record charts, music videos, and popular criticism, as well as ethnographic studies of particular rock scenes. Such research demonstrates that women musicians continue to be marginalized in concert tours organized around rock music, to get less radio airplay and print media attention, and to have fewer recording contracts than all-male or male-dominated bands. Fewer music videos are produced featuring women rock musicians, and far fewer women musicians appear in books, films, audio recordings, and museum exhibits celebrating the history of rock music. This book contributes to the critique of rock culture's historical domination by men, while also exploring the complexity of maleness and masculinity in rock culture and thus being mindful of the frequent subversion of gender norms by some of its male participants.

Rock's patriarchy is socially constructed and therefore can be deconstructed. The dominance of rock culture by males is not natural. It is socially produced and yet precarious, since other gender ideologies also circulate through this community. One of the aims of this book is to expose the various roles, practices, and institutions where male hegemony is actively maintained. Only by recognizing these sites of patriarchy's insecurity in rock culture can we envision possible mechanisms for deconstructing it, which will ensure more access and opportunities for those who have been historically marginalized in this community.

Girls and women have participated in rock culture since its emergence. Despite the overwhelming presence of males in rock culture, and the regular tokenism of a few talented female performers, which suggests women's general absence, girls and women have always constituted a significant part of this community, and not only as consumers. Thus, women have long posed a challenge to rock's patriarchal values, structures, and practices. Without eliding or subordinating the male and masculine aspects of rock culture, this book aims to reclaim female participation for rock history, while also insisting on the importance of rock culture for girls' and women's history.

Binary gender politics are still prevalent throughout rock culture. While rock culture has long been considered a legitimate space for gender subversion, individuals are regularly required to identify as men or women in it, just as they are in the rest of society. Most research on rock culture, even that which is feminist, replicates this binary, typically by not calling it into question and not exploring the experiences of genderqueer rock musicians and fans. This book is guilty of this charge also, in part because it condenses many previous studies on gender in rock, but also because resisting the ease of the **gender binary** is difficult, especially when discussing a culture in which that binary is so intrinsic. Prior to 2010, the nonbinary genders associated with transgender and intersex people were not discussed widely.

Yet genderqueer people and gender-neutral terminology have become more prominent in popular discourse in the past several years, in part due to the greater promotion of transgender and intersex rights as well as the increased visibility of celebrities with such identities. Although few rock musicians have identified publicly as nonbinary, genderqueer, transgender, or intersex, it is necessary for anyone studying gender politics in rock culture to consider the numerous ways the gender binary impacts this community.

The gender politics of rock culture are inherently contradictory. Rock culture is a complex, dynamic mix of both conservative and transgressive social forces. As a result, repugnant instances of both misogyny and homophobia coexist in rock culture alongside utopic moments of gender parity and sexual equality. It is the copresence and fluidity of these conflicting forces that makes rock an exciting cultural site for its participants, including those who study it.

Gender always intersects with other identities. By focusing on gender in this book, I do not mean to suggest that other modes of identity are not important to human identity or rock culture. This book takes as a given that gender is always interconnected with other identities, such as race, class, age, sexuality, and ability. In particular, this book considers the centrality of heterosexuality, whiteness, youthfulness, and working-classness to rock's conventionally masculinist politics, while also exploring how that structure is bolstered through its resistance not only to femininity but also to queerness, nonwhiteness, adulthood, and middle-classness. This is an **intersectional** approach to identity.

Black culture is central to rock. Since the mid-1960s, rock culture has been defined primarily in the global north by white British and North American musicians, consumers, critics, and industry professionals. Rock's whiteness is perhaps most noticeable when the media focus on the talented people of color in this culture, such as Prince, Slash, or Brittany Howard, since, as exceptions, they prove the rule. Yet, as demonstrated by Kandia Crazy Horse's collection *Rip It Up*, rock 'n' roll would never have emerged, nor would rock culture be what it is today, without the participation of black people, not to mention white people's inspiration by, mimicry of, and, in too many cases, exploitation of them. Nonetheless, many white people have ignored, marginalized, or rejected rock's blackness while affirming this musical form as for white people only. This book resists that reductive and offensive narrative by approaching race and ethnicity as modes of identity that intersect with gender and powerfully shape people's opportunities and challenges in rock culture.

Queerness and nonnormative sexualities have always been a part of rock culture. Despite their presence in rock culture, members of the LGBTQI community have been denied and marginalized in it as a result of the homophobia and transphobia that shore up rock's heteronormative masculinist politics. In turn, queer sexualities and politics have been subordinated to those that are homonormative. This book aims to reclaim queerness and nonnormative sexualities for rock while also relying on queer theories for its analyses of gender in this culture.

Mainstream corporate rock culture is just part of a much larger rock culture. Like all forms of contemporary popular music, rock culture is significantly structured by the recording business and thus the values and practices of capitalist commerce. Nevertheless, rock has never been shaped solely by them. The rock community has always included individuals who have resisted the corporatization of culture and attempted to remain independent of it, whether through alternative practices of production or consumption or both. Many of these people have been at the forefront of promoting gender and sexual equality in rock culture. Thus, many of this book's examples of progressive gender politics come from rock's independent sector.

Organization

This book is organized according to five primary concepts that create a structural logic for analyzing gender in rock culture. Part I provides readers with the basic knowledge needed for comprehending material presented in the rest of the book. Chapter 1 offers a brief survey of rock criticism while also exploring its connections to cultural studies and distinguishing it from traditional musicology. In addition, the first chapter presents some of the primary theoretical and methodological approaches used in rock criticism today. Chapter 2 provides a survey of feminist and queer music scholarship, as well as an overview of contemporary gender theory, the key lens through which this book explores rock culture.

Part II delineates the main structures that characterize and organize rock culture while also exploring gender's impact on these structuring elements. Chapter 3 examines the ideological roots of rock by surveying the various musical cultures and other sociocultural phenomena that have most informed it. This chapter covers much of rock's prehistory yet also maps the values that have shaped its social politics. Chapter 4 considers the role of commerce in this arts-based culture and examines the intersections of capitalism and patriarchy, looking in particular at the impact of gender politics on rock business, including in the independent sector. Focusing on rock's various genres, Chapter 5 considers those that have had the most impact on rock culture's gender politics, while also examining how gender participates in the construction of these genres.

While the chapters in Part III critically analyze rock culture as a creative formation, they also adopt a sociological approach in their examination of gender in rock musicians' everyday practices. Chapter 6 explores how gender norms impact musician roles in rock culture, as well as musical training and band formation. Chapter 7 analyzes the gendering of rock's musical instruments and technologies, especially the electric guitar. Also discussed in this chapter are the gender dynamics of rock's "gearhead" culture, whose members are passionate about the equipment used to create rock music. Chapter 8 focuses on the roles, practices, and spaces involved in live music performance and the impact of gender politics on the experiences of gigging and touring.

Part IV considers the role gender plays in the primary artifacts created and consumed in rock culture. It also exposes readers to the various approaches used in analyses of rock's cultural forms. Chapter 9 explores the expression of gender in rock lyrics. Chapter 10 examines gender's relation to rock's musical sounds. Chapter 11 concerns the representation of gender in rock's print media, focusing on still imagery in magazines and album covers. Chapter 12 explores gender in rock music videos.

Part V looks beyond the creative worlds of rock musicians to investigate the gender politics structuring the two other primary groups involved in rock culture. Chapter 13 focuses on rock fans by examining the role of gender in rock consumption, taste patterns, fan stereotypes, and star/fan relations. Chapter 14, the book's last chapter, examines rock critics and the gender politics of rock criticism.

Each chapter of this book begins with a recommended song to get readers in the mood for that particular subject and to expose unfamiliar readers to new music and musicians. Each chapter ends with exercises and suggested readings meant to stimulate further thinking on the subjects addressed.

Caveats

A few caveats are necessary before reading further. First, readers should not be surprised to find only a minimal number of references to current rock songs, performers, and events. I have provided examples from across rock's many decades to demonstrate long-term patterns in this culture's gender politics, as well as to highlight periodic disruptions and inconsistencies in those patterns. Yet, despite my desire for historical inclusivity, it is impossible for this (or any other) book to be up-to-date now and always. It is my hope that readers will feel motivated to apply the forms of analysis addressed here to the rock culture contemporary to their own experience. Moreover, because many of the gendered patterns discussed here do not appear in rock alone, I hope that readers will draw connections to other musical cultures as well as nonmusical formations, such as other communities where men have long dominated.

My second caveat is that I have defined rock music somewhat narrowly in this book by focusing on the version most common in popular discourse. Although rock music in its first decade was quite eclectic in sound, lyrics, and performance, since that time it has been understood as an up-tempo style of popular music that privileges the distorted sounds of the electric guitar. In addition, rock music has long been defined as created by small groups of musicians who perform their own songs and who value youthfulness, rebellion, and authenticity. As a result of this popular definition, a considerable amount of music that might have once been defined as "rock" is now excluded from this culture, including virtually all music labeled as "pop" as well as most music made by women and people of color. (Think here of songs by Michael Jackson or Lady Gaga, for example.) This valuing of some forms of rock over others is commonly referred to as **rockism**, and such exclusions have worked to maintain rock as a straight white male enclave in the face of the genre's potential transformation via its influence by other musical forms, such as disco, hip-hop, and electronica. I support this critique of rock's exclusionary values, and I encourage readers to keep it in mind when reading this book. At the same time, it has been necessary for me to create some artificial boundaries around rock music to keep this text manageable and avoid confusion. Therefore, I hope you will see this book as a starting point for discussions of gender and popular music, rather than a text that offers the final word.

In addition to expanding stylistically, rock is now a musical form with a broad geographical reach. Yet to date most rock scholarship and criticism has focused on the United States and, to a lesser extent, Great Britain and Canada. This is not surprising, since U.S. American and British bands have dominated rock culture for decades. My third caveat is I am guilty of the same charge: Most of the research and rock examples included here are specific to these two national contexts. I regret this ethnocentric perspective, but it is my hope that readers will find easier access to the musical texts discussed here because of their place on rock's global stage. At the same time, I hope that my future work and that of others will upset the Anglo-American dominance of rock culture and research. This book should provide a useful structure for the study of gender dynamics in other countries where rock has flourished.

My fourth caveat is that numerous aspects of rock culture have changed since I began research in this area in the early 1990s. With regard to gender, perhaps the most noticeable changes are that fewer women-powered rock bands are on major labels today, yet female-designed musical equipment is now available from companies, like Daisy Rock Girl Guitars. Meanwhile, *Rockrgrl* has ceased publication, yet *She Shreds* and *Tom Tom Magazine* are going strong. Much could be said about the gender politics responsible for these contradictory trends, and this book offers tools for unpacking this situation.

The most far-reaching development in rock culture in the past two decades has been digitization. Indeed, it has thoroughly upended the production, distribution, and consumption of rock music. Via digital media, bands can self-distribute their music more easily and with more profit by uploading it to services like Spotify and Bandcamp. Meanwhile, rock consumers can use such services to download or stream music via their mobile devices, and the size of album covers has shrunk to a half-inch or less as a result. Far fewer people buy music today than in the past, and if they do, most rock consumers buy MP3 singles rather than full albums (either digital or analog). In addition, many people listen to rock via smartphones rather than home stereo systems. Music videos are consumed most often via websites like YouTube, which has become a primary site for discovering new music. Barely in existence a decade ago, social media platforms, like Facebook, Twitter, and Instagram, have become the primary means for publicizing and communicating about rock music, even though plenty of rock magazines and blogs exist online. Nevertheless, as much as digital technologies have reshaped rock culture, it is important to keep in mind that the vast majority of rock's cultural artifacts were produced in analog form, and those artifacts still exist. Therefore, this book's explorations of rock music production, distribution, reception, and criticism are not written with only digital media in mind.

My final caveat, and one related to others above, is that no book can be comprehensive and satisfy all readers' needs and desires. This limitation is especially true for a textbook, which is meant to light a spark of cultural curiosity and critical ambition rather than build a bonfire that exhausts both. I have made no attempt, therefore, to analyze fully the role that gender plays in every site, practice, and relationship in rock culture across its long history and numerous geographic locations. In other words, this book is not meant to have all the answers or the final say on how gender operates in rock culture. Those would be impossible projects anyway, given the length of this culture's history, the breadth of its international expansion, and its constant change across time, as well as space, not to mention the spatial constraints on this book. It is my hope, therefore, that you will be inspired enough by what you read and learn here to extend your critical thinking, writing, and discussions about gender in rock to your own life and other communities. Rock on!

Further Reading

Bannister, Matthew. *White Boys, White Noise: Masculinities and 1980s Indie Guitar Rock*. Burlington: Ashgate, 2006.

Bayton, Mavis. *Frock Rock: Women Performing Popular Music*. Oxford: Oxford University Press, 1998.

Burns, Lori, and Mélisse Lafrance. *Disruptive Divas: Feminism, Identity and Popular Music*. New York: Routledge, 2001.

Crazy Horse, Kandia, ed. *Rip It Up: The Black Experience in Rock 'n' Roll*. New York: Palgrave Macmillan, 2004.

Grossberg, Lawrence. *We Gotta Get Out of This Place: Popular Conservatism and Postmodern Culture*. New York: Routledge, 1992.

Jarman-Ivens, Freya, ed. *Oh Boy! Masculinities and Popular Music.* New York: Routledge, 2007.

Lehman, Peter. *Roy Orbison: Invention of an Alternative Rock Masculinity.* Philadelphia: Temple University Press, 2010.

Leonard, Marion. *Gender in the Music Industry: Rock, Discourse, and Girl Power.* Burlington: Ashgate, 2007.

Mahon, Maureen. *Right to Rock: The Black Rock Coalition and the Cultural Politics of Race.* Durham: Duke University Press, 2004.

O'Dair, Barbara, ed. *Trouble Girls: The Rolling Stone Book of Women in Rock.* New York: Random House, 1997.

Reddington, Helen. *The Lost Women of Rock Music: Female Musicians of the Punk Era.* Burlington: Ashgate, 2007.

Reynolds, Simon, and Joy Press. *The Sex Revolts: Gender Rebellion and Rock 'n' Roll.* Cambridge: Harvard University Press, 1995.

Schippers, Mimi. *Rockin' out of the Box: Gender Maneuvering in Alternative Hard Rock.* New Brunswick: Rutgers University Press, 2002.

Walser, Robert. *Running with the Devil: Power, Gender, and Madness in Heavy Metal Music.* Middletown: Wesleyan University Press, 1993.

Whiteley, Sheila, ed. *Sexing the Groove: Popular Music and Gender.* New York: Routledge, 1997.

Whiteley, Sheila. *Women and Popular Music: Sexuality, Identity and Subjectivity.* New York: Routledge, 2000.

Gender and Rock

I

Foundations

Rock and Gender

1 NOT JUST MUSIC
Studying Rock Culture

LISTEN: THE VELVET UNDERGROUND, "Rock & Roll" (*Loaded*, Cotillion, 1970). *A popular rock anthem for generations, this song celebrates rock music as a salvation for alienated youth. Consider the gender of the child saved by "rock & roll" and compare the roles, activities, and spaces open to others like her in the 1970s versus today.*

Where should we begin a study of gender and rock culture? As with all scholarship, perhaps the best place to start is by looking to the larger social context of the object of analysis. When most people hear the term "rock," they think of one thing: music. This is not surprising, for rock is first and foremost a musical style. More specifically, **rock** is a form of **popular music**, a broad field of musical styles that emerged from rural American **folk musics**, such as the blues. Most popular music is not just artistic expression, but also commercial product; it is recorded and distributed for profit via the recording and broadcasting industries. In addition to rock, contemporary popular music styles include pop, jazz, country, R&B, rap, and EDM (electronic dance music).

The study of rock is typically located in **popular music studies**. This interdisciplinary academic field has largely developed outside **musicology**, the traditional discipline for music studies. Because popular music differs in several ways from the music studied by traditional musicologists, scholars interested in analyzing popular music forms, like rock, have relied on methods of analysis associated with other disciplines, including literary studies, sociology, media studies, and cultural studies. Knowledge of these approaches can help us understand the various ways rock music might be analyzed.

A key component of popular music studies, and a chief way it differs from musicology, is that music is often not the only or primary object of analysis. Popular music scholars understand music as enmeshed in human communities, and see analyses of such communities' practices, institutions, and discourses as crucial for understanding the musical texts created and consumed in them. In addition to introducing readers briefly to musicology, this chapter examines the primary **theories** (critical interpretive and explanatory frameworks) and **methodologies** (the means by which scholars perform research and analysis) associated with popular music studies. In addition, this chapter will introduce the **Cultural Studies**, an interdisciplinary field that emerged in Great Britain during the 1970s and has had a tremendous impact on popular music studies.

In taking a cultural studies approach, this book aims to help readers understand rock as a complex cultural phenomenon that involves not only cultural **texts**, like songs and music videos, but also systems of cultural **production**, such as songwriting and record distribution, as well as practices of cultural **consumption**, like listening and dancing. Rock is a **culture** or way of life developed and sustained by a group of people who share a common set of values, and who have developed particular roles, relationships, discourses, practices, artifacts, technologies, and institutions in relation to those values. Yet, as the book will show through its explorations of gender, **rock culture** is not easy to pin down. It is complex and often contradictory, and not only because this culture's participants and their practices have changed over its sixty-some years of existence. Rock culture is always in a dynamic state because of its larger cultural, social, economic, and political contexts. Yet, as much as these factors make it difficult to define rock culture, they also make it an exciting object of study.

The Study of Music

In musicology the primary type of music studied has been European **art music**, seventeenth- through nineteenth-century orchestral and operatic compositions that elites have long understood as making the best artistic use of music's unique qualities. Scholars in this field have traditionally been categorized into two groups: historians, who focus on the historical facts associated with a particular piece of music or its composer, and theorists, who develop scientific explanations for sound components and structures, such as pitch and meter. As a result of their particular focus, musical historians and theorists have typically avoided **musical criticism**, the interpretation and contextualization of music and its effect on listeners. (The subfield **critical musicology** has taken up this project. Meanwhile, **ethnomusicology**, a subfield of musicology focusing on musical cultures, involves analyses of audience reception.)

Although the field of musicology now embraces popular forms of music, traditional musicological approaches posed several difficulties early on for popular music scholars that limited how popular musical styles could be analyzed. First, early musicologists had class-based tastes that encouraged them to understand popular music styles as unsophisticated because of their roots in working-class culture. (Art music has its origins in religious compositions and later developed as an art form appreciated by nobility and members of the upper class.) Unfortunately, as a result of the reproduction of this elitist mindset, many musicologists working prior to the 1990s deemed popular music unworthy of analysis. As a result, popular music scholars had difficulty being taken seriously by other musicologists.

The second factor contributing to the difficulty of incorporating popular music into musicology is related to methodology. In musicology, the score—a written or printed musical composition that includes the notes for vocal and instrumental parts—is often the primary object of study. Yet few popular music songs are transcribed as scores (for reasons discussed later). Moreover, of those songs that are, few share the specific notational style associated with art music. Indeed, vast discrepancies exist in the various informal forms of transcription developed for popular music (e.g., guitar tablature or "tabs"), thus making standardized methods for analyzing such notations virtually impossible.

Third, because few art music forms are similar to popular music styles, it has been difficult to apply theories developed by musicologists to the sounds and structures of popular music. No lexicon or common vocabulary exists for the sonic phenomena associated with popular music. Many individuals use impressionistic terms to describe the musical sounds they create or hear (e.g., heavy, twangy, mushy, bright, dark); however, no consensus has formed around the appropriateness of such terms as musical descriptors. Moreover, the meanings of such terms are often too subjective and imprecise for most scholars' use in criticism. Thus, musicologists interested in popular forms still rely on theories developed for art music to understand the formal qualities of popular music, even though these theories typically cannot explain the particularities of such sounds and structures. (We will return to musicology in Chapter 9, which explores the sonic qualities and formal structures associated with rock music.)

The fourth factor contributing to the difficulty scholars had incorporating popular music into musicology was that popular music is a primarily performative medium. In contrast to the strategies of art musicians, who often attempt to reproduce a piece of music exactly as notated by its composer, popular musicians emphasize creativity, originality, and authenticity in each performance. As a result, no one performance of a particular popular song can be understood as representative of them all. A song's meaning changes with each iteration, making its transcription onto paper a somewhat futile exercise. (Nevertheless, commercial music publishers perform this practice to profit from amateur musicians interested in learning popular songs.) Thus, while musicologists studying art music often confine their analyses to the notes in a score, musicologists interested in popular music argue that music's meaning can be understood only in relation to its social context. For such musicologists, music is a social practice. Therefore, they pay attention to the multiple aspects involved in musical performance, including song lyrics, performers' gestures, musical equipment, and audience behavior.

Despite these four challenges, since the mid-1990s, an increasing number of musicologists have embraced popular music as their primary object of study, helping to form a field now known as **popular musicology**. Its primary difference from popular music studies is that musical sounds are the focus of its critical analysis rather than other aspects of musical culture.

Popular Music Studies

Because of the difficulties associated with applying musicological theory to popular music, scholars wanting to make sense of popular styles in all their permutations—including lyrics, performance, reception, and videos—have relied on modes of interpretation associated with other academic disciplines. For example, literary theory has been employed to analyze the words and lyrical structures of popular songs, and theories from theatre have been used to study musical performances. In turn, scholars interested in audiences have drawn from the fields of sociology, anthropology, ethnomusicology, and cultural studies. Since the rise of music videos in the early 1980s, scholars have used film and television theories to explore the visual representation of songs and performers.

As a result of the need to look beyond musicology for modes of analysis, the study of popular music today is interdisciplinary and dispersed throughout numerous academic fields. Several problems have developed from this eclectic field, however. As noted, popular music scholars are typically not trained in either musicology or musical performance. Therefore, most avoid studying musical sounds and instead conduct research that privileges other aspects of music culture, such as lyrics, technology, business, or audiences. As a result, many studies of popular music are often limited to a singular object of study and a singular method of analysis. For example, scholars who focus on the lyrics of popular songs tend to exclude from their analyses the other aspects of music that give it meaning and listeners find most compelling, such as beat and distortion. Moreover, since not all popular music privileges lyrics, and plenty of popular songs have none (e.g., "Team" by Bon Iver, "Silver Wheels" by Heart), literary theories and methods are not always useful for studying this form of music.

Studies of popular music by scholars in the disciplines of literature, theatre, media, and sociology have contributed significantly to this field's development. However, a one-dimensional approach limits our understanding of the rich complexity of popular music. In light of these problems, several scholars have argued for a more holistic approach for studying popular music that can better account for its multiple components and modes of affect.

Today, the field of popular music studies is typically situated not in musicology but in cultural studies. Scholars who adopt a cultural studies approach are interested in everyday life and focus on forms of popular culture traditionally devalued by intellectuals and deemed unworthy of academic analysis, such as television, fashion magazines, and popular music. Cultural studies scholars are influenced by **critical theory**, which focuses on social, political, and economic systems of **power** (agency, influence, and authority). Because of their political commitment to exploring the cultural practices of marginalized groups, cultural studies scholars often focus on issues of **identity**, such as gender, race, and sexuality. The pleasures of consumption and nonhegemonic or alternative practices have also been given attention by cultural studies scholars. As discussed in Chapter 2, **poststructuralist theories** related to discourse, power, representation, and identity have become essential to cultural studies, and thus popular music studies also.

Influenced by sociology and cultural anthropology, cultural studies scholars are interested in the **articulation** or connection of cultural phenomena to their specific **sociohistorical contexts**, that is, the place and time of their occurrence. In turn, those engaged in cultural studies emphasize a multiperspectival approach that takes into consideration any culture's three primary sites: **texts** (e.g., recorded music, performances, videos, celebrities), the **production** of such texts, and the **reception** of such texts by consumers. Although it is difficult to engage with all of these sites in one study, cultural studies scholars are expected to attend to at least two and to be critically aware of how these sites relate to one another.

With regard to **textual analysis**, cultural studies scholars typically use **qualitative** approaches to interpret the meanings of particular cultural texts and their relation to society. (**Quantitative** analyses involve the scientific measurement of observable phenomena.) Most qualitative textual analyses begin with **content analysis**, during which researchers examine the most superficial characteristics of the text or phenomenon being analyzed (e.g., images, sounds, printed text) to get a general impression. Yet qualitative textual analyses rarely stop there. Most involve other, more sophisticated forms of study, such as **narrative analysis** (plot, genre, character), **formal analysis** (style), **performance analysis** (character, blocking, set design), **semiotics** (signs or symbols), **psychoanalytic theory** (processes of the human psyche), **ideological analysis** (values and power struggles), and **discourse analysis** (conceptual frameworks and their relation to power and knowledge). Each of these methodological approaches is based on particular critical theories, and they are discussed in detail in later chapters where appropriate to the cultural phenomenon being considered.

Cultural studies scholars also analyze processes involved in the **production of culture**. Today, such studies commonly entail interviews with creative producers, such as musicians, as well as those involved in the commercial side of culture, such as industry executives. Such production studies can also involve analyses of discourses used to represent creative work and cultural producers, as in trade journals, as well as technologies used to produce creative work, such as musical instruments. Some scholars engage in **political economy analyses**, focusing on particular political and economic conditions impacting cultural production, including government regulation and ownership of the means of production, marketing, and distribution. Cultural production is never situated just in industries and governments, however. As is clear from popular music history, independent producers have always been part of this larger field. We will engage with studies of rock's political economy by focusing on both the mainstream and independent sectors of the recording business.

Perhaps the most significant contribution of cultural studies to date has been analyzing practices of cultural reception. Rather than understanding consumers as passive and uncritical in their relationships to texts, cultural studies scholars argue that it is through the practices of reading, viewing, and listening that cultural texts ultimately have meaning. **Reception studies** are indebted to sociology and cultural anthropology, which have long traditions of studying human communities via **ethnography** (human observation, interviewing, questionnaires). Yet literary scholars have also been important contributors to this type of cultural study. This book includes explorations of both rock consumers and the larger realm of rock fandom. In addition, we will examine popular and academic forms of rock criticism, which are also part of the larger field of cultural reception.

The Study of Rock Culture

Strongly influenced by cultural studies' multiperspectival approach, several rock scholars have argued against the traditional method for studying popular music—that is, analyzing the development of specific musical styles. Rather, they argue that popular music is made up of many different components that are not specifically categorizable as music. For instance, David Shumway encourages us to understand rock as a **cultural practice** (or rather a set of practices) that includes not just the composition and performance of music but also the recording, promoting, and hearing of music. Moreover, he suggests that rock is more than the sum of those practices, since it includes a wide variety of other activities, roles, texts, events, technologies, institutions, spaces, and ideologies. In other words, Shumway argues for understanding rock as a **culture**, a way of life. While not all rock musicians, consumers, critics, or recording industry professionals are immersed in this life on a daily basis, the collective activities of such individuals help to construct it as a unique site of cultural practice. The primary rock practices this book considers are related to musical performance, recording, criticism, and consumption. Yet we will also examine the particular roles, spaces, objects, and institutions related to each of these. (A list of rock culture's various practices appears at the end of this chapter.)

While Shumway made an important contribution to popular music studies by encouraging scholars to looks *inside* rock culture to understand its complexity, Lawrence Grossberg urges us to looks *outside* this culture to understand its relationship with the rest of society. In other words, he argues for an understanding of rock as a **social formation**, a group of articulated practices forming a structure of unity that in turn exists in relation to other social formations that share some of those practices. Two of the social formations with which rock culture are most linked are youth culture and the mass media; without these, rock as we know it would never have emerged. However, other social formations are also significant to rock culture, including fashion and bar culture, for example.

As a social formation, rock culture is situated both geographically and temporally, specific to a place and time. As Grossberg notes, for example, it is impossible to study the emergence of rock without considering U.S. society after World War II, a time of considerable cultural change, as a result of the emergence of radical social movements, the expansion of consumer capitalism, the development of television, and the birth of the baby boom generation. Richard Peterson adds several other factors, including transformations in music copyright law and radio station licensing, as well as the introduction of transistor radios and 45 rpm records. To study the rock formation of the early twenty-first century, we must pay attention to the rise of neoliberalism, the expansion of globalization, the introduction of digital technologies, and the birth of millennials or Generation Y. Nevertheless, not everything contributing to contemporary rock culture is novel. What has held this culture together as a somewhat unified social formation for over sixty years is the reproduction of particular practices, roles, and values in it. Before we delve into those, it is necessary to explore the concepts of ideology and discourse, which are necessary to examining gender in rock culture.

Ideology

As noted, cultural studies scholars are concerned with issues of power. This is true also for researchers studying popular music forms, like rock. One of the primary lenses through which scholars analyze power is **ideology**, an idea, value, or belief commonly agreed on by a group of people, though not always consciously. Many people today associate ideology only with political values; however, every sector of society has ideologies associated with it, and the majority of individuals in each society share those values.

The process of achieving ideological **hegemony** or dominance is complex. Although the ideologies of those groups with the most power are typically dominant, because societies are made up of many different groups, many ideologies exist, and they are always in competition with each other. Thus, **counter-hegemonic** ideologies are always competing with those that are hegemonic. For example, the dominant political ideology in the United States is democracy (rule by the people); yet, other political ideologies compete with democratic ideals, including oligarchy (rule by a small minority group), theocracy (rule by religious leaders), and anarchism (a belief that all forms of political governance are undesirable). In rock discourse, the terms "mainstream" and "alternative" are typically used to describe what scholars refer to as "hegemonic" and "counter-hegemonic."

In most societies, an ideology achieves dominance not because individuals are physically forced to believe it (although this has happened) but because most people have consented to that ideology and unwittingly reproduce it by acting as if it is true. Ideological hegemony is achieved when people who are not in power understand their value system to be the same as that of those in power, even if it does not ultimately benefit them. For example, conspicuous consumption has been a primary value of middle-class Americans since the end of World War II. Many poor people help to reproduce this ideology by using credit cards to shop for items that help them to be seen as fashionable, despite the fact that they have little disposable income for nonessential items and cannot afford to pay the total balances on their credit cards each month. Instead, they accrue interest on their debt, which makes it more difficult to pay off such balances. Therefore, the ideology of conspicuous consumption does not ultimately serve the interests of poor people.

Ideologies become dominant when a large number of people consent to them. With mass acceptance over a long period of time, ideologies become understood as "natural," "true," or "common sense," and individuals ascribing to them do not question their validity—a process called **naturalization**. Thus, while ideologies may seem true, in actuality they have been socially constructed, produced collectively by human beings and circulated by social institutions, such as the media, government, religious organizations, and the educational system. Naturalization was once achieved through the circulation of religious texts, such as the Bible. As Western societies have become increasingly secularized, science has been the primary institution used to support ideological hegemony. For example, the Bible constructs men as superior to women, and thus many Christians believe this ideology to be true. Yet science has also reproduced such **patriarchy** by providing empirical data on women's inferiority to men, such as smaller brains. (Eugenics advocates have similarly used scientific data to demonstrate the inferiority of homosexuals and people of color.)

Most studies of ideology focus on values associated with social institutions, such as religion and government. Consider these social ideologies that have circulated in the United States.

Social institutions	Dominant/mainstream ideology	Competing/alternative ideologies
politics	democracy/republicanism	monarchy, fascism, anarchy
economics	capitalism	socialism, communism
religion	Christianity	Judaism, Islam, atheism
culture/ethnicity	Western/European	Non-Western/non-European, multicultural

In addition to social/institutional ideologies, societies produce values associated with personal identities, such as gender, race, and class.

Components of personal identity	Dominant/mainstream ideology	Competing/alternative ideologies
gender	patriarchy	feminist, queer
race	white supremacy	racial pride, diversity
sexuality	heterocentrism	LGBTQI pride
class	upper-middle-classness	working-classness
age/generation	youthfulness	respect for elderly

Individuals whose identities entirely or mostly align with dominant ideologies (e.g., white straight rich men) have the most power in society, while failure to achieve any one of them usually results in a person being disadvantaged and sometimes oppressed. As Audre Lorde argues, those with ideal identities come to represent a **mythic norm** to which others are encouraged to aspire. Yet this norm is mythic because those with ideal identities are not in the majority; they are exceptional. To survive socially, members of deprivileged groups must develop what Teresa de Lauretis calls **double vision**, knowledge of both dominant and competing ideologies of identity. For example, women are knowledgeable about both femininity and masculinity—the first because they are encouraged to identify with it, and the second because it is the ideal form of gender. In other words, deprivileged individuals live as the Other yet also must understand what it is like to be **normative**. This concept is related to W. E. B. DuBois's theory of **double consciousness**, wherein deprivileged people understand their own identities as well as how others with power perceive them (often via stereotypes).

In contrast to deprivileged people's double vision and double consciousness, those in power have the privilege of being ignorant about the ideologies of personal identity that contribute to their social dominance. For example, white people often ignore race, men often ignore gender, and straight people often ignore sexuality. Yet it is important to remember that individuals who are part of a dominant social group may not always be in situations where that dominance is operable. Our individual relations to dominant ideologies shift with different social contexts. For example, while men are dominant in many public spaces, women far outnumber men in most gender studies classes.

Many ideologies exist in rock culture. Yet patriarchy has been one of its most dominant ideologies, despite the broad influence of feminism and the increasing number of women musicians over the past half century. Chapter 2 explores various feminist ideologies of gender that have emerged over the past century in response to patriarchy, and the remainder of this book explores how members of rock culture either invest in or resist rock's patriarchal ideology.

Discourse

A primary approach scholars use to study rock culture is **discourse analysis. Discourses** are conceptual frameworks people use to create and organize meaning for social phenomena and abstract concepts. The term "discourse" commonly means written and spoken language, but scholars use it for a range of communicative forms, including images and sounds. Discourses are produced by social institutions via specialized forms of knowledge, such as the fashion industry's discourse of beauty. Nevertheless, discourses are neither static nor singular in definition; they change over time and are **polysemic** (having multiple meanings). By attending to the ideologies that inflect discourses, scholars can understand the development of these conceptual frameworks and their possible effects on identity and social relations.

Discourses are arbitrarily constructed by people, yet they are also constitutive, producing that which they attempt to represent. In his studies of discourse, Michel Foucault explored how social institutions (e.g., education, religion, government) produce and circulate particular discourses that affect how the individuals associated with those institutions come to know themselves as well as how they come to be known and treated by other people. In particular, he was interested in how institutional discourses produce knowledge and assertions of truth about specific groups of people and practices that can then be used as a means to power.

For example, one of the discourses operating in rock culture is that of the groupie (discussed more in Chapter 13). This discourse developed in the late 1960s with the rise of hard rock bands and their adoring female fans. Because of the gender and sexual politics of that time period, musicians, music critics, and other fans often understood the groupie as a young woman seeking male rock stars' affirmation through sexual relations. One prominent effect of the media's broad circulation of groupie discourse since the late 1960s is that female rock fans at large came to be understood (including by many feminists) as sex toys for male rockers rather than as serious listeners, or performers, of the music.

Nevertheless, groupie discourse has not remained stable over time, as a result of new ways of thinking about female sexuality as well as better understanding of the limits of female agency in the 1960s. Several groupies of that period, including Pamela des Barres, have complicated the patriarchal ideology that impinges on the discursive construction of their fandom, arguing that groupies were not passive and exploited but sexually empowered women on whom male rock stars depended. By sharing their experiences publicly, these fans have altered the discourses of both the groupie and female rock fandom.

Because rock culture is made up of many different institutions, social roles, and practices, the discourses circulating in it are quite numerous. This book will pay primary attention to discourses of gender, that is, the concepts of male and female, masculinity and femininity, as well as cisgender, transgender, and genderqueerness. Chapter 2 looks more at theories of gender, which are essential tools for any study of gender in rock culture.

Summary

This chapter introduced the study of rock culture by addressing its disciplinary legacy and primary methodological approaches. At the heart of rock culture is rock music; therefore, much research on rock culture has focused on this musical style and the musicians who play it. Yet rock analyses differ from musicological analyses in several ways. In contrast to art music, the style most studied by musicologists, rock is a performance-based form that does not follow written compositions. Thus, the strategies long used by musicologists are typically not employed by scholars who study rock. Moreover, because many researchers of popular music have little training in music theory or experience in musical performance, they have often avoided traditional musical analyses. Instead, such scholars tend to study other components of music, such as lyrics, performance, and reception, which necessitates their reliance on other approaches of critical inquiry. This phenomenon has resulted in an interdisciplinary field of popular music studies that now encompasses theories and methodologies affiliated with other disciplines, including literary studies, theatre, sociology, and media studies.

The transdisciplinary field of cultural studies has been a primary force in popular music studies since the 1980s. Advocating a multiperspectival approach to cultural analysis, scholars associated with this field typically perform qualitative, sociohistorically specific analyses of culture that include not just cultural artifacts but also cultural production and reception practices. Researchers of rock culture have adopted this holistic, integrated approach, moving beyond music to study rock as a social formation that involves numerous sites and intersects with other social formations. Key objects of study for cultural studies scholars are power, ideology, and discourse. These concepts are of particular interest to those researching identity, because the categories societies use to label people and regulate their behavior have commonly worked to limit human experience, especially for individuals who do not conform to society's notions of the ideal citizen or subject, such as women, youth, the poor, people of color, and members of the lesbian, gay, bisexual, transgender, queer, and intersex (LGBTQI) community.

The Elements of Rock Culture

The following lists summarize the main components of rock culture in order to familiarize readers with the many sites in this culture that are available for critical analysis.

Rock Roles

songwriters

musicians (vocalists and instrumentalists)

consumers and audiences

managers and agents

artists & repertoire (A&R) agents

record label employees

record producers

recording engineers

disc jockeys

tour agents

concert venue employees

stage crew and roadies

sound engineers

wardrobe and make-up

music video producers, directors

MTV/VH1 programmers

marketers

music critics

music scholars

Rock Practices

write lyrics and/or music

perform music

consume music products, make fan texts

represent performers

find and secure new talent for record labels

facilitate production, distribution of music

manage recording process

operate recording equipment

play and promote music on the radio

organize performers' tours

manage concert venues

carry and maintain equipment

monitor sound during performances

dress and groom performers

facilitate the production of music videos

schedule broadcasting of music videos

promote performers in mass media

critique music and interview performers for popular press

analyze music, performers, fans, industry

Rock Texts

live performances

gigs (performances by individual acts)

concerts (performances by multiple acts)

festivals (multiple-day concert events)

sheet music

recorded music (vinyl, tape, CD, mp3)

singles

albums

compilations with various performers, groups

music videos

promotional singles (aired on TV and in bars and malls)

compilations (sold for purchase by individual consumers)

music magazines

for consumers about rock music, culture (paper, online)

for musicians (paper, online)

for the recording industry (trade journals)

Rock Roles	Rock Practices
films about music	documentaries (concerts, tours, biographical, historical)
	docudramas (fictionalized films about real musicians)
	fictional films
books about music	popular histories, biographies of performers, styles, industry
	critical analyses of history, styles, performers, fans, industry
other music-related texts	articles in nonmusic newspapers, magazines
	TV reports on music performers, styles, fans, industry
	advertisements (print, audiovisual)
music-related paraphernalia	clothing, posters, stickers, websites

Rock Technologies

musical instruments (guitars, drums, basses, keyboards)

amplification equipment (microphones, amplifiers, effects pedals)

recording equipment

manufacturing equipment

equipment associated with live performances, video production, radio, journalism

Rock Spaces

rehearsal spaces
performance venues (bars, clubs, arenas)
recording studios
tour buses, airplanes
retail outlets for recorded music and musical equipment
consumers' homes, cars, workplaces

Rock Institutions

recording industry (labels, studios, distributors, marketers)
broadcast industry (radio and television)
film industry
publishing industry

Rock Ideologies

bohemianism
libertarianism
patriarchy
whiteness
youthfulness

Further Exploration

1.   Compare interpretations and transcriptions of a rock song.

Listen to a rock song. First, consider a musicologist's interpretation and a popular music scholar's interpretation of the song's musical sounds. How do these interpretations compare? Second, review a musical transcription of the song (its composition) and several different guitar tablatures for it. Consider what knowledge is required to understand these interpretations and transcriptions. Also consider why they differ and what consequences such differences have for interpreting music.

Example: Hole's "Violet" from *Live Through This* (Geffen Records, 1994).

A musical transcription, musicological analysis, and popular music critique of the song can be found in Lori Burns and Mélisse Lafrance's *Disruptive Divas: Feminism, Identity & Popular Music* (New York: Routledge, 2002). Guitar tablatures for this song can be found online.

2.   Watch Cameron Crowe's film *Almost Famous* (2000).

Discuss the various roles, practices, texts, spaces, technologies, institutions, and ideologies the film represents as associated with rock culture. How does gender impact these different sites in rock culture? What changes have occurred for women in rock since the time period depicted in this film? How have men's roles changed?

Further Reading

Grossberg, Lawrence. "Rock Cultures and Rock Formations." *We Gotta Get Out of This Place: Popular Conservatism and Postmodern Culture.* New York: Routledge, 1992. 131–35.

Kellner, Douglas. "Cultural Studies, Multiculturalism, and Media Culture." *Gender, Race, and Class in Media: A Text-Reader.* Eds. Gail Dines and Jean M. Humez. Thousand Oaks: Sage, 1995. 5–17.

McClary, Susan, and Robert Walser. "Start Making Sense!: Musicology Wrestles with Rock." *On Record: Rock, Pop, and the Written Word.* Eds. Simon Frith and Andrew Goodwin. New York: Pantheon Books, 1990. 277–92.

Peterson, Richard A. "Why 1955? Explaining the Advent of Rock Music." *Popular Music* 9.1 (1990): 97–116.

Shepherd, John. "Musicology and Popular Music Studies." *Music as Social Text*. Cambridge: Blackwell, 1991. 189–212.

Shuker, Roy. *Understanding Popular Music*. New York: Routledge, 1994.

Shumway, David. "Rock & Roll as a Cultural Practice." *South Atlantic Quarterly* 90.4 (Fall 1991): 753–69.

2 REFUSING SILENCE
Gender Studies and Rock Criticism

LISTEN: JAYNE COUNTY AND the Electric Chairs, "Are You a Girl or Are You a Boy?" (*Let Your Backbone Slip*, RPM Records, 1995). *While listening to this cover of the Barbarians' song, consider the singer's main question. Why are there only two options? How do we know what "girls" and "boys" are? How do people who do not fit neatly into one of these categories define themselves? How does society treat those people? How does the singer's status as transgender impact your understanding of the song?*

Most academic analyses of music have been conducted by men who have focused their attention on male performers and composers and, to a lesser extent, audiences and critics. Nevertheless, feminist scholars (some of whom are men) have increased in number and become more vocal in this field since the 1990s, offering critiques of male dominance and women's subordination not only in musicology and popular music criticism but also in music cultures at large. Concerned with how these patterns of privilege and exclusion are developed and sustained, feminist researchers have formed a unique approach to popular music studies that foregrounds gender politics. Yet feminists' critical approach is not just negative. Fortified with theories of gender as socially constructed, feminist music scholars are also examining instances where hegemonic gender politics are challenged and subverted in music cultures. Therefore, this scholarship is imbued with hope for change and strategies for a more progressive future.

To understand the development of and approaches in feminist music studies, it is necessary to be familiar with feminist scholarship and theories of gender, the roots of which are located in feminist politics. Multiple feminist ideologies have developed over the two-hundred-plus years of feminist activism, and these values have had a direct impact on the directions of feminist research. This chapter provides readers with a basic foundation in feminist history (both political and scholarly) and contemporary theories of gender, as well as an overview of feminist music studies, including scholarship examining rock culture's gender politics.

Feminist Music Studies

The diffusion of feminist ideologies and rise of feminist scholarship during the late twentieth century has transformed both musicology and popular music studies. Beginning in the 1980s, feminist scholars called attention to the dearth of women-centered research in these two fields. In part, this phenomenon resulted from men's and women's different social status during much of academic history. Until the late twentieth century, women were primarily confined to the domestic sphere (either in their own homes or as domestics living in the homes of others) and thus had little access to the worlds of public musicianship and scholarship. In contrast, men have had considerable presence in these two spheres historically. Nevertheless, this situation does not explain male music scholars' traditional inattention to women composers and musicians. In fact, women's increased presence as composers and musicians since the early twentieth century did not lead to a rise in research on women's music. Clearly, then, other dynamics are involved in the historical marginalization of women in music research.

In particular, we might consider how the male dominance of academic research has contributed to the reproduction of **patriarchal ideology** and thus the construction of males as superior as well as the marginalization of women. This pattern persists in many forms of research, despite the dramatic increase of feminist scholars and the rise of women's and gender studies as an academic discipline during the late twentieth century. Nevertheless, since the 1980s, several feminist scholars have brought critical attention to, and attempted to redress, music studies' traditional patriarchy, and this work has importantly shaped feminist musicology and popular music studies.

Susan McClary is one of the first feminist scholars to address how the interpretive concepts and procedures used in musicology historically are gendered. In her book *Feminine Endings*, McClary notes that while musicologists traditionally ignored the gendered aspects of music, they nevertheless routinely reproduced patriarchal rhetoric and codes with little consideration of their social effect. For example, she notes that musicologists have long categorized cadences (the endings of musical phrases and compositions) according to traditional **gender norms**, with "masculine" cadences valued because they are understood as strong, normal, and objective. Meanwhile, "feminine" cadences have been deprivileged because they are considered weak, abnormal, romantic, and excessive. Moreover, McClary argues that while music has been considered feminine because of its association with the body, many male musicologists have worked to subvert this gendered coding and to bolster music's masculinity by defining music as the ideal art form, overemphasizing its rational dimension, insisting on its objectivity, universality, and transcendent power, and restricting female participation in musical training, composition, performance, and scholarship.

Several feminist musicologists have attempted to rebalance music history and the classical music canon by reclaiming such women musical composers as Maria Teresa Agnesi, Vittoria (Raffaella) Aleotti, Amy Beach, Hildegard von Bingen, Cécile Chaminade, Élisabeth Jacquet de La Guerre, Kassia, Francesca Lebrun, Ethel Smyth, and Barbara Strozzi. Such feminist historical work has been crucial to the legitimation of both female composers and women's compositions. Previously most male historians ignored women composers, whose work, via circuitous illogic, was then deemed unworthy of study by other musicologists because the absence of these composers from musical history allegedly signaled their lack of innovation and greatness.

Suzanne Cusick has critically assessed the gendered history of musicology so that contemporary scholars might subvert such patriarchy and sexism. Using the story of American composer Ruth Crawford (Seeger) as a starting point, she demonstrates how women were discouraged from participating in the formation of the American Musicological Society because of male music scholars' desire to distance musicology from other men's accusations that its status was that of "women's work." To bolster the masculinity of musicologists, the male founders of the society also emphasized their work as rigorous, objective, scientific, and universal to gain legitimacy alongside other academic disciplines.

Because these practices persisted well into the 1990s, Cusick, like many other feminist music scholars, has called for musicology's reconstruction, arguing that musicologists, in addition to paying more attention to the gendering of music and music studies, must no longer have a pretense of objectivity and detachment. They must stop valorizing musical studies that are detached from performance and rationalized through scientific analysis. Instead, much in line with ethnomusicology and cultural studies, Cusick proposes that musicologists recognize that music is a historically specific cultural formation that is neither divorced from the rest of society nor comprehensible only through the human mind. To make sense of music as a social practice that profoundly shapes identities and communities, musicologists must seek out other forms of academic study. Such feminist calls for change have contributed to a significant transformation of musicology as a discipline and, more specifically, the development of critical musicology as a subfield. Feminist scholars of popular music have similarly critiqued the patriarchy that has persisted in their field.

Feminist Rock Studies

Since the early 1990s, several feminist scholars have examined the patriarchy of rock criticism, a realm of popular music studies where analyses of gender were absent historically. This phenomenon has resulted from the assumption that rock is a "boys' club" and therefore men, not women, have the right to critically examine it. At the same time, many feminist scholars have understood rock as a "bad object," a site of patriarchy not worthy of feminist analysis. (Instead, such scholars have focused on **women's music**, a style grounded in the singer-songwriter tradition and developed by feminists in the 1970s.)

One notable exception to the feminist avoidance of rock analysis prior to the 1990s is the article "Rock and Sexuality," first published by Simon Frith and Angela McRobbie in 1978. Following on the heels of feminist music critic Ellen Willis, Frith and McRobbie pioneered academic work in this area by theorizing the gender (or what they called "sexual") politics of rock culture. Exploring the genres of "cock rock" and "teenybop," they argue that the first is identified exclusively with males and masculinity and the second with females (especially girls) and femininity. Although groundbreaking in their examination of music as gendered, Frith and McRobbie's argument was undermined by their gender essentialism and **heteronormative** perspective (i.e., that heterosexuality is the only or most natural form of sexuality). Moreover, they failed to critique rock's gender politics as socially constructed. (Frith responded to such criticisms, and raised a few of his own, in a later piece, "Afterthoughts.")

Building from Frith and McRobbie's work, Mavis Bayton helped to galvanize feminist popular music criticism in the early 1990s by critiquing the dearth of such scholarship and arguing for more of it. In "Out on the Margins," she outlines reasons feminists were not participating in popular music studies. For instance, feminist scholars had focused primarily on other forms of popular media created for and enjoyed by women, particularly film, television, and magazines. Moreover, popular music had historically been devalued by musicologists in comparison to classical music. Yet it is also crucial to remember that the study of popular culture (of which popular music criticism is part) is relatively new, given that academics interested in culture have traditionally privileged the fine arts. The historical disparagement of popular culture forms by elites has made it difficult for feminist popular music scholars to have their work deemed legitimate. Bayton advocates a cultural studies approach that analyzes gender at multiple levels of music culture: texts, production, and reception. In particular, she encourages more ethnographic studies so as to better understand musicians and consumers, as well as to challenge the rational, abstract theories traditionally valued by musicologists. Her book *Frock Rock* (see Figure 2.1) is exemplary in this regard and has inspired more recent feminist ethnographies of rock musicians, such as Mimi Schippers's *Rockin' out of the Box*.

As Bayton's work reveals, despite feminist opposition to rock during much of the late twentieth century, several feminist scholars have shown recent critical interest in this music and its associated culture. Most of these researchers are interested in studying rock culture because they understand it as another influential and historically male-dominated site where women should be treated equally—as musicians, consumers, critics, and businesspeople. Gillian Gaar's

Figure 2.1 Mavis Bayton, *Frock Rock*
Oxford University Press, 1998

book *She's a Rebel* (see Figure 2.2) helped to launch the project of feminist **historical revisionism** by drawing attention to the many women involved in rock history to date.

This work was built on the pioneering efforts of Sue Steward and Sheryl Garratt, who in *Signed, Sealed, Delivered* provide a comprehensive view of women's involvement in popular music cultures as performers, consumers, critics, and businesspeople. Such projects are revolutionary, for in foregrounding women's achievements in rock culture, they subvert the numerous historical accounts that focus only or primarily on men. Moreover, these historical

Figure 2.2 Gillian G. Gaar, *She's a Rebel*
Seal Press, 1992

accounts are essential for feminist scholars interested in women's involvement in the development of rock music.

Another part of this feminist reclamation process is research on the role of female rock consumers, a project undertaken by scholars like Sue Wise, Susan Fast, and Arlene Stein. Meanwhile, Evelyn McDonnell and Ann Powers have reclaimed women's engagement in rock criticism by republishing significant pieces of such writing in their collection *Rock She Wrote*, a project undertaken also by Liz Evans in *Girls Will Be Boys*.

Other popular music scholars, such as Sara Cohen, Norma Coates, Theodore Gracyk, Mimi Schippers, and Sheila Whiteley, find rock culture intriguing because they see in this social formation not a stable privileging of masculinity and male dominance but a continual negotiation of gendered roles and practices. As Cohen argues, rock's identity as a masculine culture is not inherent; it is socially produced through the privileging of activities, relationships, technologies, spaces, and forms of knowledge typically associated with men. (Bayton's ethnographic work in *Frock Rock* affirms Cohen's findings.) With Cohen's argument in mind, this book explores the primary sites in rock culture where gender is constructed, noting in particular where norms are reaffirmed, negotiated, and subverted. Yet before we proceed with those analyses, it is necessary to have a foundational knowledge of feminist political history and contemporary theories of gender.

Feminist Politics and Ideologies

Because feminist scholarship emerged from feminist politics, the history of feminism provides a roadmap of the ideas that have shaped this community's development. The feminist movement is over two hundred years old. Hence, many different ideologies are associated with it, and they, in turn, have produced multiple forms of feminist activism and scholarship. Nevertheless, we can roughly define **feminism** as a social movement whose primary concern is women's lack of equality in comparison to men. Yet feminists disagree about the causes of such inequality, as well as the most effective means for eliminating it.

Many historians trace the origins of Western feminist activism to women's social reform of the mid-nineteenth century, a community composed primarily of wealthy women whose goal was to improve the lives of poor women through volunteerism and charitable acts. This community grew out of the larger social reform movement that emerged in Great Britain and the United States in the early 1800s in response to the social transformations caused by industrialization and urbanization. Through their involvement with widows, prostitutes, unmarried mothers, and other deprivileged women, women social reformers began to understand themselves and other women as members of a sex category, a concept that was crucial for the development of a social movement organized for the betterment of women.

Feminist philosophies about women's inequality emerged well before the nineteenth century, however. Mary Wollstonecraft's *A Vindication of the Rights of Women*, one of the foundational texts for early feminism, was published in the late eighteenth century. Nevertheless, feminists didn't begin to organize formally until the mid-1800s, when industrialization's transformation of gender roles and women's unfair social treatment became clearer. Women's subjugated social status during this historical period was similar to that of children, criminals, and nonwhite people. Women were not allowed to vote or to own property; their lives were largely confined to the **private** or **domestic sphere**. Very few attended school, and all were discouraged from having nondomestic jobs. When married couples divorced, women had no rights to their offspring. Children, like women, were the property of men. In an effort to improve women's experiences, members of the mid- to late-nineteenth-century **woman movement** advocated women's equality with men in the **public sphere** (e.g., education, business, and politics) and the elimination of legal barriers to women's civil rights. Such activism was often led by white, wealthy women. However, they—along with women of color and poor women—were also involved in raising feminist issues in abolition politics and the labor movement.

Eventually, women's right to vote became the primary goal of feminists, bringing both conservatives and radicals together, yet causing rifts with African American abolitionists with whom they had previously joined forces. Although the term **suffragism** connotes more broadly any movement to secure the right to vote, it is the label commonly used to distinguish this period of feminist history from others. New Zealand instituted women's suffrage in 1893, yet it wasn't granted in the United Kingdom until 1918 and in the United States until 1920.

While the feminists who made up the woman movement largely advocated a **reformist** perspective that privileged the gradual improvement of certain aspects of women's lives (e.g., education, health), the suffragists had a **liberal** approach that located the cause of gender inequity in law and thus advocated legal reform to improve women's freedom, particularly in the public sphere of work and education. Yet, rather than advocating systemic social change, liberal feminists envisioned politics primarily on an individualist basis. An additional criticism is that liberal feminism fails to interrogate its construction of men, especially wealthy, white, Western men, as the ideal form of citizen to which women should aspire. Moreover, liberal feminism tends to focus solely on gender and thus fails to understand identities as multiple and interdependent.

Following the success of the suffragist movement, feminist sentiment declined in the United States and Britain during the 1920s through 1940s, largely as a result of common struggles experienced by both males and females during the Great Depression and World War II. While many women were liberated from the domestic sphere as a result of the need for more laborers during the war, returning veterans displaced the majority of women workers, and the idea that "a woman's place was in the home" gained popular acceptance again. Yet, as the economy moved toward advanced capitalism after the war, the expenses associated with the consumerist middle-class lifestyle forced many married women into work outside the home, a situation that was contradicted by the housewife ideal prevalent in popular culture during this time. Eventually, women's discontent with the suburban lifestyle and the traditional roles of housewife and mother fueled the reemergence of feminist sentiment. Yet it was not until the 1960s that a movement for the improvement of women's status and rights received broad-based support again.

The **women's liberation movement** of the 1960s and 1970s advocated women's full social and economic equality with men. Many feminists involved in this movement had been radicalized to a critical understanding of systems of social oppression via their involvement in the civil rights movement and the New Left. Those influenced by Marx's theory of economic oppression reconfigured it by arguing that society is primarily divided not by class but by sex via a patriarchal ideology that valorizes men and oppresses women. In particular, these feminists emphasized the gendered division of labor at that time, where men's work was largely public and paid and women's work was largely private and unpaid. Because of their leftist leanings, their interest in exploring the primary cause of gender inequity, and their advocacy for a revolution that would eliminate the division of society based on sex, these feminists became known as **radical feminists**. In the mid-1970s, black feminists, such as Audre Lorde and those in the Combahee River Collective, began to argue that gender should not be dealt with separately from other forms of identity, such as race, class, and sexuality, which led to a reconfiguration in identity politics and scholarship. In the 1980s, this concept was labeled **intersectionality**.

As radical feminism declined in the early 1970s, it made way for two other feminist ideologies to become dominant. The first, **liberal feminism**, continues to be the dominant form to this day, perhaps because it requires the least change by men. Liberal feminism has been referred to as **equality feminism** because of its emphasis on women achieving the same rights as men. Some of the policies liberal feminists in the United States worked on during the 1970s include Title IX, which prohibits gender discrimination in federally funded educational institutions, and the Equal Rights Amendment to the U.S. Constitution, which has not yet been ratified by all states.

Once several liberal feminist battles were won and feminist sentiment began to circulate more broadly in the mid-1970s, many feminists began to advocate a different ideology known as **cultural feminism**. Unlike liberal feminists, who conceive of men and women as equal under the law, cultural feminists believe that women are biologically and psychologically different from men (which resulted in this ideology being referred to as **difference feminism**). Moreover, rather than understanding men as the norm to which women should aspire, as liberal feminists do, cultural feminists value females and femininity so as to counteract years of their disparagement under patriarchy. Many cultural feminists of 1970s and early 1980s argued that women should form a culture separate from men and patriarchal society where women could feel safe, legitimate, and supported. Although cultural feminism has been much critiqued for its essentialist perspectives on gender, its profemale perspective has been diffused broadly, helping to bring light to women's many accomplishments and to legitimate character traits traditionally associated with women and femininity, like caring and collaboration. The emergence of women's studies as a discipline would not have been possible without cultural feminism.

The term **third wave feminism** is often used to refer to the current period of feminist activism. (Despite feminist activism prior to the late nineteenth century, women's suffragism is commonly understood to be the first wave of feminism, and the women's liberation movement is referred to as the second wave.) Third wave feminism includes a critique of earlier forms of feminism, particularly those that understood all women to be the same and thus privileged attention to gender over other identities, like race and sexuality. Third wave feminists have also attempted to reclaim for women two aspects of life they see as ignored or disparaged by earlier feminists: sexuality and popular culture. Most feminists today differentiate third wave feminism from **postfeminism**, a contemporary sensibility that asserts that women can "have it all" (i.e., be equally successful in the public and private realms) despite evidence to the contrary. As Angela McRobbie and Rosalind Gill have argued, postfeminist rhetoric is primarily a commercial discourse that takes feminism and women's equality with men for granted while repudiating feminist struggles against gender oppression. Privileging the notions of choice and empowerment alongside the neoliberal values of individual responsibility and wealth, postfeminism demands a performance of hyperfemininity from agential women to lessen their threat to men and heteronormative patriarchy. Postfeminism thus reproduces **gender dimorphism**, the distinction between males and females.

Feminist Scholarship

The establishment of women's studies as an academic field in the 1970s was rooted in liberal feminist goals. In an effort to balance intellectual inquiry and human knowledge, women's studies research during that period raised awareness of women's contributions to society that had been ignored previously. Thus, it was primarily a recuperative practice. As with the majority of feminist activists during the 1970s, many feminist scholars demonstrated their allegiance to liberalism. As a result, they rarely questioned how their assumptions about female identity led them to recuperate primarily privileged women (i.e., white, middle-class, heterosexual, able-bodied, Western) under the large category of "women." Nevertheless, liberal approaches to feminist scholarship have contributed greatly to women's studies by calling attention to women's unequal treatment and representation in history, law, culture, education, business, and politics. Through analyses of women's subjugation in these social realms, liberal feminist scholars have effectively argued for women's increased presence and improved treatment in public practices and spaces long dominated by males.

Rather than trying to insert women into male-dominated realms of academic thought and society, cultural feminist scholars began to explore women's uniqueness in the mid-1970s. In the humanities, the cultural feminist call to foreground women's difference from men led some feminist scholars to theorize about feminine aesthetics, such as Hélène Cixous's theory of *écriture feminine* (feminine writing). The women-centered approach has been used successfully by feminist scholars to analyze those roles, practices, and institutions historically identified with women and femininity, thus expanding knowledge about human beings and legitimating women's experiences. For example, without the cultural feminist approach to research, little would be known about the domestic arts, motherhood, or shopping, or about the ways women have challenged patriarchy by developing their own forms of culture, education, business, and politics. Yet, by positing women as inherently different from men, cultural feminist scholars typically homogenized women as a monolithic social group whose primary identity was feminine, and thus failed to address the broad diversity of women's identities and experiences.

For much of the last three decades, liberal and cultural feminist ideologies have dominated women's studies scholarship. Nevertheless, since the late 1960s, such universalizing perspectives have been challenged by women of color and non-Western women who have denaturalized the terms "woman," "women," "sisterhood," and "feminism" by foregrounding **difference**. Moreover, such feminists have called attention to the multiple, **intersectional** components of identity (including gender, race, class, age, and sexuality). Affiliated primarily with **women of color feminism (womanism)**, **postcolonial feminism**, and **Third World feminism**, these concepts have subverted the one-dimensional perspective on identity commonly held by feminists who have the privilege of being able to isolate gender and ignore other modes of identity.

Poststructuralist theories have transformed feminist scholarship also, helping feminist researchers to realize more fully the project Simone de Beauvoir started with *The Second Sex* in the 1940s: understanding the social construction of gender. Poststructuralism formed in response to **structuralism**, a group of theories that explore the structures or frameworks on which human experience is built, such as language, economics, and government. Poststructuralists often refer to structuralist theories as "master narratives," for they are presented as true, natural, and universal and thus have been overwhelmingly significant in how human beings perceive reality. One of the main criticisms of the structuralist approach is that contradictions in the structures must be ignored in order for scholars to arrive at generalizable theories about society. As a result, a vast amount of material reality has been left out of structuralist schemas. Poststructuralists argue that we need to challenge generalized theories about people and society that are presented as true, natural, and universal by paying close attention to the specific **sociohistorical contexts** (geographical and temporal location) of social phenomena, for meaning shifts with changes in such contexts.

Two primary ways poststructuralist theory has altered feminist scholarship is that it posits reality as relative and socially constructed, and resists oppositional forms of meaning making. First, our sense of reality is also understood as socially constructed, because the only way to understand and communicate about reality is to process it via language, which is a human construct. Reality, then, is not solely determined by nature. In addition, reality is understood as **relative,** because the meaning of any human experience depends on the identity and background of the individual experiencing it, as well as the social context of that experience. For example, your reading of this book may be different from that of others, depending on your gender and the degree to which you are familiar with music criticism and feminist scholarship. At the same time, your reading of this book may change, depending on where you are and whom you are with.

Second, poststructuralists have challenged the **dualistic** form of meaning-making dominant in Western society for centuries. Westerners have long made sense of the world by categorizing concepts and social phenomena into two different groups, or **binary opposites**, such as good and evil, black and white, men and women, straight and gay. Poststructuralists argue that such binary opposites are never equally balanced: one term is always more privileged than the other. For example, men are opposed to yet superior to women, heterosexuals to gays and lesbians, rich people to poor people. Poststructuralists argue that we have to get rid of dualistic and binary forms of meaning making because reality is rarely composed of such absolute opposites. Moreover, binary opposites limit our knowledge of the world, since they fail to acknowledge diversity. Instead, poststructuralists argue that all social phenomena and human experiences are multiple and complex. For example, the possibilities for gender are not just masculine and feminine, those for race are not just white and black, those for sexuality are not just straight and gay. The poststructuralist challenge to dualism and binarism has been important for feminists because one of the primary goals of feminism is to subvert traditional definitions of gender, since they limit the options both women and men have in terms of roles, practices, appearance, and relationships.

Third wave feminist scholars have been influenced by both poststructuralist theory and Third World feminism, and thus understand gender to be socially constructed and intersected by other components of identity, including sexuality, class, and race. Another characteristic of third wave feminist scholarship is the greater attention to males and masculinity, which has challenged the historically female domination of feminism. Feminist attention to masculinity has resulted in part from gay, lesbian, and queer studies, which have examined alternative forms of masculinity and manhood.

In differentiating these forms of feminist ideology I do not mean to suggest that individual feminist researchers are committed to only one ideological approach. Most feminist scholarship demonstrates the convergence of multiple feminist ideologies. For example, a feminist historian researching a woman musician's career might reveal her investment in cultural feminism by adopting a female-centric perspective, and her investment in liberal feminism by drawing attention to this musician's success in a male-dominated culture. Moreover, that scholar might rely on poststructuralist and Third World feminist approaches to analyze the musician's gendered performance strategies and their relation to other components of her identity, such as race. All of these approaches to rock's gender politics will be explored in this book.

Sex and Gender

Before examining gender in rock culture, it is necessary to consider how human beings are differentiated in society. Two of the primary methods for such differentiation are sex and gender. Along with other demographic identities, such as race, the concepts of sex and gender were developed ages ago to categorize human beings, to communicate about them, and to ease social interactions. Most of us unconsciously use such categories as a means of quickly understanding other people so as to determine how to engage with them. Since dualism has long structured Western meaning-making processes, these categories of identification are often constructed through binary opposites (e.g., male/female, masculine/feminine).

Sex is an identity category that historically has been determined upon birth by midwives' or doctors' attention to physiological characteristics. If a penis is present, the baby's sex is determined as male. If a penis is absent, the baby is determined to be not-male, or female. Today medical technicians are able to determine sex before birth through ultrasound, a procedure wherein sound waves show images of the fetus, or through amniocentesis, a process used to study the fetus's chromosomes, which appear in amniotic fluid. In most societies, only two sex categories are used, affirming the traditional heteronormative perspective that reproduction is the only objective of sexual relations. This binary system of classification constructs the male as the norm (a perspective referred to as **phallocentrism**), produces the not-male/female as subordinate, and ignores **intersex** people, who are born with a mixture of biological characteristics traditionally classified as "male" and "female."

Given that medical science divides human beings into male and female, gender scholars now conceptualize sex as a socially constructed category. Moreover, sex is thought to be one and the same as gender, which has always been understood as a social construct. Nevertheless, understanding the differences between sex and gender is important for those who desire a better comprehension of the ways human beings distinguish themselves, and are distinguished, from one another as well as how those processes of differentiation are linked to systems of power.

In everyday society, human beings rarely proclaim their identity as male or female by displaying their genitalia, the most explicit way to do so. Instead, as

Candace West and Don Zimmerman argue, we often deduce a person's membership in a **sex category** based on the presentation of their other physical traits. As a result of patriarchy, male physiology is considered the norm, and nonmale/female physiology is understood as its opposite, and often its inferior.

Physical Traits Associated with Sex Categories		
	Male	Nonmale/female
genitals	penis	no penis, vagina
height	tall	short
build	large	small
	muscular	nonmuscular
	flat-chested	full-breasted
body hair	hairy body and face	minimal body and facial hair
voice	low	high

A person can make claims to a sex category by foregrounding physical traits associated with that category and downplaying those associated with the opposite category. For example, a person can claim the female sex category by exaggerating traits associated with females, such as breast cleavage, or by removing or hiding male traits, such as body hair. Another way human beings can make claims to a specific sex category is through particular bodily movements. For example, those people who want to be read as male often take up considerable physical space when sitting, while those who want to be read as female are encouraged to take up as little space as possible by crossing their legs. Observe the difference between people's body comportments the next time you fly or go to a movie theater. Vocal pitch is another way humans make claims to sex categories. Those individuals wanting to be understood as female often raise the pitch of their voices, while those who are male often lower theirs.

Note that *all* people can make claims to either sex category, even if it does not match the one assigned at birth. Claiming membership in a particular sex category is not dependent on one's genitals, hormones, or chromosomal make-up. For example, an individual categorized at birth as male can claim membership in the female sex category by raising his vocal pitch and taking up less space with his body. **Cisgender** people are comfortable with the sex category assigned to them as a baby and thus regularly make claims to that category. **Transgender** people are not and do not. If a transgender person wants to make claims to a sex category different from the one assigned to them at birth, they will sometimes take hormones or have genital reconstruction surgery. People who consider themselves **nonbinary** or **genderqueer** reject sex categories for being too limited for describing their gender identity.

Sex is one of the main categories human beings use to understand ourselves and other people, and it is often the first thing we notice when interacting with someone the first time. For example, if you get a phone call from a stranger, one of the first things you do is listen to the pitch of the caller's voice to categorize the caller by sex. Most of us do not do this consciously, but it is one of the primary ways we begin to make sense of who the caller is. When we meet someone in person, we unconsciously do the same thing. We look at their body to see if their physical presentation and comportment matches our society's norms of how male and female bodies look and act. As West and Zimmerman argue, we hold other people accountable for how well they exhibit characteristics of their desired sex category.

Of course, a person's ability to make successful claims to a sex category has everything to do with genetics. Hence, it is difficult for short, small, nonmuscular, hairless men with high voices to claim maleness, just as it is difficult for tall, large, muscular, hairy women with low voices to claim femaleness. Such individuals sometimes cause confusion or aggression among others who depend on sex categories to make sense of other people. The reason for such negative reactions is that those individuals who defy the binary system of sex categorization require us to think beyond our society's norms of identity, a practice many people find confusing if not disturbing. Thus, when an intersex person displaying both types of genitalia is born, doctors often encourage the parents to have surgery performed on the baby so that one sex becomes dominant and the person can more easily make claims to just one sex category.

In addition to making claims to particular sex categories, human beings use another social system of sexual categorization commonly referred to as **gender**. The concept of gender was developed by feminists to foreground the constructedness of human categorization. Gender is often defined as a particular set of roles, behaviors, or personality traits commonly understood as socially appropriate for each sex category. In heteronormative patriarchal societies, only two gender options are considered valid: Males should display **masculine** characteristics, while females should display those that are **feminine**. Gayle Rubin named this convergence of sex and gender as the **sex/gender system**.

Those individuals whose gender performances align with those considered "appropriate" for their birth sex are referred to as cisgender. "Cis" means "on this side of." The privileging of cisgender identities in most societies is connected with heteronormative ideology, in that heterosexuality demands the coming together of two different bodies. Nonetheless, gay men, lesbians, and bisexuals can present as cisgender also, and many straight people do not present as purely masculine or feminine.

Many transgender people align their gender presentation with their gender identity, which differs from the sex assigned to them at birth. Nevertheless, as suggested by the collective term **trans***, a great variety exists among transgender people's presentations of gender due to their differing desires, abilities, and actions. People who prefer to be called genderqueer or gender nonbinary often exhibit a mix of gendered traits and reject the dualistic sex/gender system. The increased visibility of transgender and genderqueer people in contemporary society has led to the greater use of gender-neutral pronouns, such as "ze" and the singular "they."

The process of constructing a person's gender typically begins when parents find out their child's sex. Indeed, gender is done to us by parents and doctors before we begin doing it ourselves. Parents often select gender-specific names for their children, as well as gendered toys, clothing, and bedroom decorations. These objects become part of a child's life in an attempt to communicate their sex. Yet, because gender is socially constructed, it is also sociohistorically specific. For instance, it was only after World War II that the color pink was associated with femininity and blue with masculinity. In addition to families, all other social institutions participate in the construction of gender, including school, work, religion, and politics. This book is specifically concerned with the construction of gender in rock culture.

A primary site where gender is expressed is via personality traits. Traditionally masculine and feminine traits have been considered opposites.

Personality Traits	
Masculine	**Feminine**
strong	weak
active	passive
independent	dependent
autonomous	relational
rational	irrational/emotional
smart	dumb
technological	technophobic
productive	consumerist
cultural	natural

The traits identified as stereotypically masculine help to construct what R. W. Connell refers to as **hegemonic masculinity**, a form of heteronormative masculinity that has achieved social dominance as a result of its subordination of other forms of masculinity (e.g., gay masculinity) as well as its opposition to and superiority over femininity. Connell argues that there is no feminine equivalent to hegemonic masculinity because no equivalent power structure exists among women and women's performances of femininity vary so greatly across society. Nevertheless, Connell finds a strong pattern of **emphasized femininity**, wherein women are compliant in their subordination to men and accommodate male desires and interests.

Traditionally in patriarchal societies, masculine traits have been most valued, and feminine traits have accumulated negative connotations. For example, since rationality is privileged in our culture, emotionality has been construed as negative. While liberal feminists have encouraged girls and women to adopt masculine traits (e.g., assertiveness, confidence) to succeed in school and work, cultural feminists have privileged feminine traits, for example, by noting that relational subjectivities as better suited for productive social interactions, including work environments.

Gender is often communicated through the occupations and roles we take on. Historically, men have had greater access to the public sphere, and to this day they continue to dominate the most privileged roles in most social institutions, including education, business, religion, politics, and media. In comparison, women have historically been allowed little access to the public sector and therefore have mostly occupied roles associated with the home, such as mother and homemaker. A considerable number of women have entered the public sphere over the past century. Yet women's first paid jobs were those that privileged feminine traits, such as teacher, nurse, and domestic worker. Some women, especially white and wealthy women, have risen to great heights in their professions. Nevertheless, most women's opportunities for work remain far more restricted than those for men, a form of subordination that is reflected in salaries as well. Indeed, with the exception of wage disparities among men and women, perhaps no better evidence demonstrates patriarchy in the public sphere than women successful in historically male-dominated fields being referred to first by their gender and second by their job title: woman doctor, lady pilot, female guitarist. Such job titles are rarely qualified by the adjective "man," since the male domination of these positions remains the norm and is therefore understood as "natural."

Gender categories are constructed also via the leisure practices historically associated with males and females and thus considered off-limits to the opposite sex. For example, men have long been thought to value such activities as hunting, sports, and tinkering with technology. Therefore, such practices have been gendered masculine. In contrast, women are thought to most enjoy cooking, handicrafts, shopping, and beautification projects. Thus, those activities have been gendered feminine.

As noted, a strong connection exists between the sex/gender system and a heteronormative perspective, which privileges heterosexuality above all forms of sexuality and has reproduction as sexuality's primary objective. Adrienne Rich's concept of **compulsory heterosexuality** is helpful in explaining how all individuals are encouraged to reaffirm binary cisgender norms to maintain the dominant system of sexual desire and interaction. Heterosexuality by definition requires two different sex categories; thus, straight males and females are encouraged to present themselves differently from each other so no confusion exists between sexual partners. Perhaps nowhere are claims to particular sex categories more obvious than in places where heterosexual men and women congregate to "hook up," such as bars and clubs.

Because of the dominance of the binary sex/gender system, individuals with a heterocentric perspective often erroneously assume that a person's nonnormative gender expression is related to nonnormative sexual identity, particularly homosexuality. Thus, women who are muscular, are athletic, have short hair, have small breasts and hips, have low voices, and do not engage in typical feminine activities (e.g., shopping, taking care of children) are often assumed to be lesbian. Indeed, this is the dominant stereotype of lesbians. Similarly, men who are not muscular, are nonathletic, have high voices, and do not participate in typical male activities (e.g., sports, technology) are often assumed to be gay, and the stereotype of gay men is associated with an effeminate **gender display**. Yet in reality lesbians and gay men display just as broad a range of gender identities as straight people, from cisgender to gender nonbinary.

One of the primary goals of feminists as well as queer people has been the dismantlement of the binary sex/gender system. This goal has emerged because the sex/gender system has produced norms that have limited the range of roles, behaviors, practices, and personality characteristics available to human beings. This is true for all people, not just women. Confined to one set of gendered characteristics, human identities, experiences, and relationships have been severely limited. Thus, feminists' attempts to subvert the sex/gender system are related to increasing the liberty of all human beings.

As Judith Butler argues, it is helpful to think of gender as a **performance**, an act that we play out, as if we were in a theatrical production. Yet gender is typically not produced through conscious decision-making; most of us perform gender unconsciously. Nor is gender performed in isolation; it is constituted through our social interactions. Like theatre, gender demands an audience. We learn gender roles, behaviors, and personality traits from older people at an early age as ways to express our identities and desires, as well as to facilitate communication and relationships. Different social situations require different gender displays. For example, a male business owner may display primarily masculine qualities, such as assertiveness, mastery, and leadership, when he is at work. But at home with his family he may display primarily feminine qualities, such as nurturance, emotional sensitivity, and relational conversation. Importantly, not all of us have the same access to the broad array of gender performances because of the constraints imposed by our physical bodies, our other identities (e.g., age, race, sexuality, class), and larger social structures, including compulsory heterosexuality.

Like all human constructs, gender is never stable or assured. Gender norms can change over time, so they must be continually performed to achieve coherence. In other words, our gender identity gets constructed via repetition in the roles we occupy, the practices in which we engage, and the personality characteristics we display. For those who find traditional gender norms oppressive, knowledge of this phenomenon should elicit hope. For if gender requires repetition to secure coherence, gender norms can be subverted by refusing to repeat characteristics traditionally associated with masculinity and femininity.

Another key theory in feminist scholarship today is gender's construction through various social technologies. Teresa de Lauretis first theorized

technologies of gender in the late 1980s. Borrowing the concept of social technologies from Michel Foucault, she proposed that various cultural phenomena—popular discourse (e.g., journalism), cultural artifacts (e.g., films), and social institutions (e.g., religion)—function like tools, working together to produce particular power relations. Technologies of gender are those used to construct the sex/gender system and to maintain traditional gender relations between men and women. De Lauretis's theory has been useful for understanding how gender is produced beyond human bodies. Like Butler, she is interested in understanding systems that reproduce the sex/gender system and conceptualizing the means by which heteronormative patriarchal ideology might be challenged.

Many of us have witnessed some transformation in gender norms in our lifetime. For example, most Western women today (especially middle-class women) are required to display both masculine and feminine qualities. This phenomenon is largely the result of the broad diffusion of liberal feminism, which positions men as the norm to which women should aspire. It is due also to women's increased presence in traditionally male-dominated realms that privilege masculine traits, like competitiveness. Historically, Western men have not been encouraged to display feminine traits, such as emotional sensitivity, except when engaged in the role of lover or parent. Yet today many men (primarily middle-class men) display feminine attributes, such as a focus on style, without reprisal, thus leading to the "metrosexual" stereotype. This transformation is related to our society's increasing emphasis on physical appearance, the further legitimation of queer culture, and men being appealed to as consumers in much the same way women have been.

In addition to having numerous technologies of gender impinging on it, rock culture is an extremely interesting site of gender performance. While many individuals associate rock with men and displays of aggressive, virulent masculinity, the history of this culture demonstrates that nonnormative gender expression has often been present, if not celebrated. As Butler might put it, rock culture is a site of significant feminist and queer **gender trouble**. Indeed, if we think about the some of the most interesting and influential rock performers—Little Richard, Elvis Presley, Tina Turner, Mick Jagger, Janis Joplin, Jimi Hendrix, Robert Plant, David Bowie, Patti Smith, Iggy Pop, Freddie Mercury, Steven Tyler, Joan Jett, Annie Lennox, Robert Smith, Prince, Björk, Kurt Cobain, Marilyn Manson, Beth Ditto—it seems that many have blurred the boundaries of masculinity and femininity via their lyrics, sounds, performance styles, and representational strategies and thus challenged the binary sex/gender system supported by heteronormative patriarchy. By doing so, many of these rock musicians have been embraced by members the feminist and LGBTQI communities, who read them as potentially feminist or queer even if they do not identify publicly that way. Indeed, Alexander Doty has argued that such performances of gender trouble and queerness are central rather than subtextual within popular culture. Thus, we do well to consider what that might mean for rock culture.

Why and how rock culture remains a dominant location for such gender trouble, particularly when that culture so overvalues heteronormative masculinity, is one of the primary questions underlying this book and feminist rock studies. The chapters that follow will explore how gender norms are produced, negotiated, and subverted in each of rock culture's primary sites. At the same time, however, we will pay close attention to how the gendering of rock's various sites is complicated by the shifting discourses of other intersecting modes of identity, including race, age, class, and sexuality.

Summary

This chapter has explored feminist scholarship and gender studies, with a particular eye toward feminist music criticism. This field developed in response to the male domination of musicology and popular music studies and the related silencing of women's musical accomplishments and scholarship. Feminist rock criticism emerged in the 1980s and owes a great deal to journalists who have reviewed women's music and written histories of female musicians and consumers. Such work has expanded rock history and complicated rock culture in significant ways. Key to understanding the concerns and approaches of feminist music scholars are the larger history of feminist activism and, within it, the ideologies of gender that have been developed by different groups of feminists. Thus, this chapter also surveyed feminist politics, theories of gender, and the development of gender studies so as to provide a foundation for the analyses elsewhere in this book. One of the most important contributions to feminist rock criticism is Judith Butler's theory of gender as performative, for it offers a means for understanding how gender norms are socially produced at different sites in rock culture, as well as how they might be subverted. In the next chapter we will explore the sociocultural roots of rock and the primary ideologies associated with this particular musical culture.

Further Exploration

1. Watch Cameron Crowe's film *Almost Famous* (2000).

Discuss how the film represents the gender politics of rock culture. Pay particular attention to how gender norms impact the roles, practices, spaces, technologies, and institutions the film represents.

2. Watch Stephanie Bennett's film *Women in Rock* (1986).

Discuss the experiences of women rock musicians explored in this film. What gender politics have these women experienced? How have some of these women musicians negotiated the patriarchy of rock culture and the recording industry? How have women musicians' experiences in rock culture changed since this film was released?

3.   Watch Pratibha Parmar's film *The Righteous Babes* (1998).

Discuss the various experiences of women rock musicians explored in the film. What forms of sexism have these women experienced? How have some of these women musicians negotiated the patriarchy of rock culture and the recording industry? How have women musicians' experiences in rock culture changed since this film was released?

Further Reading

Bayton, Mavis. *Frock Rock: Women Performing Popular Music*. New York: Oxford University Press, 1998.

Bayton, Mavis. "Out on the Margins: Feminism and the Study of Popular Music." *Women: A Cultural Review* 3.1 (1992): 51–9.

Butler, Judith. *Gender Trouble: Feminism and the Subversion of Identity*. New York: Routledge, 1990.

Coates, Norma. "(R)evolution Now? Rock and the Political Potential of Gender." *Sexing the Groove: Popular Music and Gender*. Ed. Sheila Whiteley. New York: Routledge, 1997. 50–64.

Cohen, Sara. *Rock Culture in Liverpool: Popular Music in the Making*. Oxford: Clarendon Press, 1991.

Connell, R. W. *Gender and Power*. Stanford: Stanford University Press, 1987.

Cusick, Suzanne G. "Gender, Musicology, Feminism." *Rethinking Music*. Eds. Nicholas Cook and Mark Everist. New York: Oxford University Press, 1999. 471–98.

De Lauretis, Teresa. *Technologies of Gender: Essays on Theory, Film, and Fiction*. Bloomington: Indiana University Press, 1987.

Doty, Alexander. *Making Things Perfectly Queer: Interpreting Mass Culture*. Minneapolis: University of Minnesota Press, 1993.

Evans, Liz. *Girls Will Be Boys: Women Report on Rock*. London: Pandora, 1997.

Frith, Simon. "Afterthoughts." *On Record: Rock, Pop, and the Written Word*. Eds. Simon Frith and Andrew Goodwin. New York: Routledge, 1990. 419–24.

Frith, Simon, and Angela McRobbie. "Rock and Sexuality." *Screen Education* 29 (1978): 3–19.

Gaar, Gillian G. *She's a Rebel: The History of Women in Rock & Roll*. Seattle: Seal Press, 1992.

McClary, Susan. *Feminine Endings: Music, Gender, and Sexuality*. Minneapolis: University of Minnesota Press, 1991.

McDonnell, Evelyn, and Ann Powers, eds. *Rock She Wrote: Women Write about Rock, Pop, and Rap*. New York: Delta, 1995.

O'Brien, Lucy. *She Bop: The Definitive History of Women in Rock, Pop and Soul*. New York: Penguin, 1995.

Schippers, Mimi. *Rockin' out of the Box: Gender Maneuvering in Alternative Hard Rock*. New Brunswick: Rutgers University Press, 2002.

Stein, Arlene. "Rock against Romance: Gender, Rock 'n' Roll, and Resistance." *Stars Don't Stand Still in the Sky: Music and Myth*. Eds. Karen Kelly and Evelyn McDonnell. New York: New York University Press, 1998. 215–27.

Steward, Sue, and Sheryl Garratt. *Signed, Sealed, Delivered: True Life Stories of Women in Pop*. Boston: South End Press, 1984.

West, Candace, and Don H. Zimmerman. "Doing Gender." *The Social Construction of Gender*. Eds. Judith Lorber and Susan A. Farrell. Newbury Park: Sage, 1991. 13–37.

Whiteley, Sheila. *Women and Popular Music: Sexuality, Identity and Subjectivity*. New York: Routledge, 2000.

Wise, Sue. "Sexing Elvis." *On Record: Rock, Pop, and the Written Word*. Eds. Simon Frith and Andrew Goodwin. New York: Pantheon Books, 1990. 390–98.

II

Rock's Sociocultural Contexts

Values, Commerce, Distinctions

3 ROLL OVER BEETHOVEN
Rock's Discursive and Ideological Roots

LISTEN: CHUCK BERRY, "ROLL Over Beethoven" (*After School Session*, Chess, 1956). *Written during rock's first decade, this rebellious song helped to usher in a new form of music that would prove to be as much an anthem for post-war teenagers as it was anathema to many adults.*

Rock culture did not emerge in a void, nor did it emerge fully formed or as we know it today. It originated in a particular place during a specific historical moment and therefore is the result of a convergence of many different cultural and social phenomena that gave it its unique character. Necessary to rock's development was the hybridization of Anglo and African American musics into a style that was widely enjoyed by young people, particularly members of the baby boom generation. Yet also key were the adult **cultural intermediaries** who connected that music with this particular youth audience, as well as advancements in media technologies and racial politics.

This chapter pays close attention to the context of rock 'n' roll's emergence and the various sociocultural elements that contributed to its development. We will also explore the primary ideologies associated with rock culture as well as analyze how those ideologies have impacted rock's social politics. In particular, we will examine how specific ideologies related to race, gender, and generation are embedded in rock's value system, as well as how rebellion and authenticity came to be celebrated by rock musicians and fans. This chapter serves as a foundation for the rest of this book, as it facilitates a better understanding of how rock's values have shaped the roles, practices, objects, and institutions associated with this community.

Rock Culture's Primary Ideologies

As a result of rock 'n' roll's musical hybridity, relation to youth, and emergence in the United States during the mid-1950s, rock culture necessarily inherited the values of the musical scenes, youth cultures, and larger social context of which it was originally part. In particular, rock musicians and fans have privileged expressive authenticity, bohemianism, rebelliousness, and youthfulness in their community.

Many contemporary artists, writers, and other cultural producers value **expressive authenticity**—the communication of one's innermost feelings and thoughts via the creative arts—as a result of the lingering values associated with **Romanticism**, an artistic movement that emerged in the late eighteenth century in response to the Industrial Revolution. For folk artists such expression emerges in its truest form via immediacy and improvisation, as well as a lack of excessive mediation and commercialization. Many popular music cultures, including those that contributed to rock's development (e.g., the blues, jazz, gospel, country), have expressive authenticity as one of their primary goals. Nonetheless, folk culture's forms of authentic expression have been difficult to achieve in industrial, capitalist societies.

The opposition of artistic authenticity and commodified, industrialized entertainment is one of the primary ideological projects in rock culture. As Deena Weinstein explains, many individuals in rock culture work constantly, albeit often unconsciously, to negotiate this tension. Musicians struggle to be understood as artists rather than exploited laborers, fans to have their tastes and identifications with artists affirmed rather than ridiculed, and journalists to be understood as art critics rather than commercial shills. Yet ultimately it is the recording industry that benefits from the efforts of all the others who invest in this mythic opposition of art and commerce. **Modernism**'s celebration of novelty and embrace of technology is evident in rock culture also, however, and thus participates in these ideological struggles.

Bohemianism is an ideology that was first associated with the Roma (gypsies), who were assumed to have come from Bohemia (now the Czech Republic). It is now predominantly associated with artists, writers, and intellectuals who have unconventional views about culture and society, as well as nonconformist lifestyles. Bohemianism has typically emerged in urban environments and under socioeconomic conditions that can support individuals' regular pursuits of artistic activity as well as **voluntary poverty**. One of bohemianism's main peaks in Western societies occurred in the mid-twentieth century, the era of rock's emergence. Indeed, rock culture became a primary site of bohemianism for the remainder of that century.

Although commonly associated with political radicals, **rebelliousness** is a sensibility that has developed also outside formal politics among individuals dissatisfied with their immediate lives and the society in which they live. Often such individuals do not have direct political engagement, or access to economic structures of power, and thus use the realm of culture to resist the status quo and perform their utopian visions for a progressive future. The site of rock's emergence, the United States in the mid-twentieth century, was a place and time of considerable social upheaval, and many movements were launched during that period to rebel against social oppression and to secure more rights for marginalized groups, particularly women and people of color. Contributing to what has come to be known as the "**generation gap**," many adolescents and young adults felt alienated from mainstream society during the post-World War II era and searched for new identities and ways of being that were meaningful to them. Resisting mainstream values, these youthful rebels participated in various forms of cultural transgression, including rock 'n' roll.

Originating in the late nineteenth century with the development of adolescence, **youthfulness** is a sensibility that most values teenagers and young adults, as well as older adults with a youthful perspective. As an ideology, youthfulness contrasts with the generational values of traditional societies, which revere older people. While many people have associated youth with problems plaguing society, youthfulness is a celebratory perspective that understands young people as a progressive social force. Once associated only with youth, youthfulness has been available to older adults since the mid-twentieth century as a result of the juvenilization of popular culture, as well as adults' greater opportunities to behave, dress, and surgically reconstruct the body in ways that signify youth. Rock culture inherited an ideology of youthfulness from Beat culture as well as earlier age-specific music trends, particularly jazz's **swing** culture of the 1940s.

The Great Depression and World War II

To understand rock culture's privileging of rebellion, bohemianism, youthfulness, and expressive authenticity, it is necessary to examine the sociohistorical context of this culture's emergence, for the ideologies in play during its early years shaped the values of rock performers and consumers for decades to come. Rock music emerged in the United States in the mid-1950s. Yet its ideological and aesthetic roots go back further, particularly to the previous two decades, a time of considerable social transformation as a result of the Great Depression and World War II. These two events altered U.S. society and popular culture in such significant ways that their effects were felt for many years.

The Depression began in 1929 and impacted millions of Americans over the next decade as businesses failed, wages fell, and unemployment skyrocketed. The administration of President Franklin Delano Roosevelt attempted to alleviate this crisis via relief programs for the poor and a reform of the U.S. financial system, a project referred to as the New Deal. One result of this process of socioeconomic renewal was that the federal government, as well as artists, writers, and other cultural producers of that time, brought more attention to poverty than ever before.

During the Depression, many musicians galvanized support for rural, working-class Americans, renewing appreciation for the authentic forms of artistic expression associated with folk culture. While Delta blues musicians, such as Robert Johnson, expressed both the heartbreak and hope of African Americans suffering from racism, some white musicians, particularly Woody Guthrie, drew inspiration from poor Americans and channeled that into a politicized folk style. Meanwhile, gospel musicians, such as Thomas Dorsey and Sister Rosetta Tharpe, lifted Americans' spirits through upbeat spiritual tunes that, like the blues, would help to form the foundation for R&B and, later, rock 'n' roll. Interestingly, these musical styles gained popularity at a time when the U.S. recording industry was experiencing one of its worst economic slumps, as a result of the Depression and the development of radio and talking pictures.

Roosevelt's New Deal helped Americans cope with the Depression during the 1930s; however, it was the United States' involvement in World War II that eventually rescued the nation's economy. Mobilization for that conflict required an increase in industrial output, which in turn meant more jobs and greater spending than in previous decades. Once the United States declared war on Japan and Germany in 1941, numerous adolescents and middle-class women entered the workforce to replace the millions of adult men who were fighting abroad. With newfound status and income as laborers, these two groups developed considerable consumer power, a factor that was not lost on the culture industries. Indeed, **teen culture** blossomed during this period, as the entertainment industries attempted to attract adolescent consumers to their products, and teenagers used such commodities to build their own age-specific, peer-based culture. The emergence of this niche market in the 1940s was crucial to the development of rock culture in the next decade. Meanwhile, the culture industries' privileging of women consumers during the war was somewhat curtailed afterward, as returning veterans pushed many women out of jobs and left them with less cash to spend.

Jazz, a musical style that emerged in the early twentieth century, was the most privileged form of popular music during World War II. With roots in both African and European music as well as performers and fans spanning the racial continuum, jazz helped bridge the historic divide between white and black Americans. Jazz was also instrumental in the development of age-based musical tastes, as teenagers of the 1930s and 1940s were more interested in swing's energetic sounds than those of the "**standards**" preferred by adults. Improvisation is intrinsic to jazz's expressive authenticity, and it has been championed by other musical forms influenced by jazz, including rock 'n' roll.

The Postwar Era

Following World War II, the U.S. economy continued to improve, as technologies and industrial practices developed for the war effort were harnessed for rebuilding the nation. Postwar social transformations were considerable, particularly the drive toward **consumer capitalism** and credit card purchases, which facilitated the transition from living within one's means to living beyond them. In addition, the postwar boom led to increased construction of buildings, roads, and other infrastructure, as well as manufacture of consumer products, including automobiles, which, like new housing, contributed to middle-class migration from cities to suburbs. Moreover, the development of the interstate highway system and the expansion of commercial airlines increased opportunities for travel. These latter developments had important consequences for musicians, who must travel regularly to promote their art outside their home communities.

Also significant for the dissemination of music, television was introduced to consumers after the war and quickly replaced radio as the primary mass medium, even as the number of new radio stations increased. The expansion of stations and the turn to recorded music as a primary source of programming content provided space on the dial for emergent forms of music, like rock 'n' roll. The introduction of portable **transistor radios** was also crucial to rock's development, for such technology increased young people's opportunities for music listening, particularly outside their homes.

Top 40 radio, a programming style that features popular hits, is another development significant in rock 'n' roll's emergence. Unlike earlier programming that was focused on standards and pitched to an undifferentiated, "general" audience, Top 40 shows privileged novelty and helped to diversify music during the postwar era. Such programming was also facilitated by the introduction of the **45 rpm single**—a record format that features only one song per side and is cheaper to produce than the **long-playing (LP) album** format. Easily affordable for youth and a perfect medium for Top 40 programs featuring the latest hits, singles were essential in early rock culture. Also important was the development of programs featuring **crossover** artists—that is, African American musicians performing for white audiences and white artists performing up-tempo R&B numbers created by black musicians.

As in other time periods following major conflicts or natural disasters, a family-oriented perspective permeated U.S. society after World War II. Various social institutions, including the mass media, urged men to identify with the **breadwinner ideal**, the ideal of the sole household wage earner, while women were encouraged to emulate the **housewife ideal** by caring for their children and home and not working outside it. With this focus on the family, the average age of newlyweds dropped to an all-time low during this period, while the birthrate skyrocketed. Meanwhile, new compulsory education and child labor laws kept young people out of the full-time workforce, which further solidified their school-based orientation and thus peer cultures.

The 1950s is a decade known for social conservatism, as the ideological conflicts associated with the previous two decades were ignored in an attempt to construct a sense of normalcy and to reconstitute the United States as a powerful global force. Nevertheless, tensions lurked just beneath the surface. As the Cold War between the United States and the Soviet Union continued, Americans were encouraged to see communists as dangerous threats to the nation. The reemergence of a "Red Scare" during the Cold War contributed to a general unease with liberal and socialist values and agendas, as well as widespread fears of political dissent and anything else deemed "un-American." Nonetheless, many individuals' frustrations with dominant ideologies festered during this period, eventually leading to several initiatives to end social inequality, including the civil rights movement, the women's liberation movement, and the gay liberation movement.

The Baby Boom

The first group of American adolescents to be widely referred to as "**teenagers**" were born during the 1930s and created a unique peer culture during World War II. Yet the generation born after the war contributed most to the expansion of teen culture and the development of rock music. Composed of those born between 1946 and 1964, this demographic group was so large it became known as the **baby boom** generation. Indeed, so many children were born during the postwar era that by 1964, the year the Beatles broke, 40 percent of Americans were under the age of twenty.

Since its emergence, the baby boom generation has been encouraged to see itself as unique and special. Born after the Great Depression and the worst war in global history, "boomers" were the best-fed, best-dressed, and best-educated generation to that point in U.S. history and thus were commonly represented as symbols of American progress and promise. Moreover, as a result of this generation's size and thus buying power, its members were made the darlings of the consumer industries, and savvy businessmen, like "Colonel" Tom Parker (Elvis Presley's manager), developed creative strategies to attract their attention. Many scholars trace the "juvenilization" of U.S. culture to this period when the media industries began to cater to the tastes of adolescents more than those of adults.

Nevertheless, many teenagers felt repressed during the Cold War era. In contrast to the war years, when youth had considerable agency in both the workforce and the consumer market, postwar adolescents were still minors without political power and often felt restricted by adults' rules. Widespread moral panics about juvenile delinquency after World War II led to parents' increased supervision and disciplining of their children. Moreover, as a result of mandatory education requirements, more adolescents were enrolled in school than ever before, and educational institutions became an additional place of adult control of youth. The widespread xenophobia and conformity of the early Cold War era further exacerbated teenagers' sense of constant surveillance and regulation.

Baby boom teens responded to such social pressures via three primary practices: first, further developing a peer-based culture largely facilitated by schools' age-based structure; second, socializing in nondomestic spaces (e.g., schools, record shops); and, third, if they were white, by turning to African American culture, which was more accessible as a result of developments in broadcasting and transportation. In particular, many white teens used black music, especially R&B and doo-wop, as a symbol of resistance and a mechanism for liberation from their parents' repressive lifestyles.

Black, Latino, and other nonwhite teenagers, who were beholden to the white culture that dominated U.S. entertainment, already had exposure to white musicians and thus did not benefit from the racial crossings happening in music during this period in the same way white youth did. Nonetheless, because it was constructed as a music of *teenagers*, rather than one affiliated with a singular race, rock 'n' roll became a site of identity and investment for all youth during the 1950s and 1960s and thus, like the civil rights movement, contributed to the further deconstruction of racial barriers in the United States.

Beat Culture

In the midst of postwar social upheaval in the United States, some young people began to question the dominant ideologies associated with American identity and to articulate new values and lifestyles. One group that had a significant impact at that time was made up of mostly white, middle-class young male artists and writers who expressed their uneasiness with U.S. traditions and a desire for alternatives. Jack Kerouac—author of *On the Road* (1957)—dubbed this community of nonconformists the **Beats**, a term that contradictorily suggested both a downtrodden (beaten down) sensibility and an energetic (upbeat) perspective. The Beat lifestyle and value system had strong connections to nineteenth-century bohemian culture in Europe. As Mel van Elteren demonstrates, the primary ideologies of Beat culture were defiant masculinity, narcissistic male bonding, Romanticism, primitivism, and expressive authenticity. These values are important to explore here, given that they have had a profound, enduring effect on the values associated with rock culture.

Primarily associated with Greenwich Village, New York's bohemian center, Beat culture also found a home in San Francisco during the early Cold War era. Other popular male writers and artists involved in Beat culture included William S. Burroughs, Neal Cassady, Gregory Corso, Lawrence Ferlinghetti, Allen Ginsberg, and Peter Orlovsky. Although numerous women participated in Beat culture as artists and writers (e.g., Diana di Prima, Joyce Johnson, Hettie Jones, Joanne Kyger), not to mention as friends and partners of male artists, the gender politics of this community privileged a form of **defiant masculinity** traditionally associated with adolescent boys. Alienated from the middle-class version of the American Dream, Beat men considered themselves rebels who desired freedom from convention and thus derided the breadwinner role, white-collar careers, and suburban family lifestyle held up as ideal. Developing an anti-domestic sensibility, the young men of Beat culture also valorized masculinity and bonded primarily with other young men, a pattern van Elteren calls **narcissistic male bonding** and one that contributed significantly to their marginalization of women. For some male Beats, this behavior was in keeping with traditional heteronormative patriarchy, while for others such homosociality facilitated homosexual identities and relationships.

As a result of their rejection of the middle-class adult lifestyle, as well as their valorization of freedom, spontaneity, and play, Beat men were often understood as having a **Peter Pan complex**, a syndrome long associated with bohemian artists who resist conformist adulthood. Various social transformations contributed to the Beats' privileging of youthfulness. Most Beats were adolescents during the late 1930s and early 1940s, a time when teenagers emerged as a distinct demographic group and consumer market. Young people growing up during that era were the first large group of Americans who were continuously encouraged to privilege their common age and generational identity by subordinating their individual differences. Nevertheless, teenage girls of that era did not have the same access to the freedoms of adolescence as boys had. The housewife ideal was so valued in U.S. society that fewer work opportunities were made available to women, and most girls found it almost impossible to imagine a life without marriage and motherhood.

Rather than capitulating to the stable bourgeois lifestyle modeled by their parents and privileged in popular culture, the Beats were antidomestic and valued the **nomadic** practices associated with troubadours, seasonal hunters, and the Roma people, believing that a mobile lifestyle would allow for greater exposure to new people, places, and ideas and thus better facilitate their spiritual growth and artwork. Ironically, to live the bohemian life, Beat men often relied on women for financial support, an oddly gendered economy also typical of many music cultures, including rock.

The Beats' tendencies of **Romanticism**—a sensibility that privileges emotion and aesthetics, in contrast to the Enlightenment's valuing of rationality and science—were primarily rooted in American **transcendentalism**, a philosophy that values the spiritual over the physical realm. The Beats sought such transcendence or "beatitude" via their engagement in Eastern forms of spirituality as well as sex, drugs, travel, and non-Anglo cultures—all of which led to experiences that deviated from conventional white middle-class ways of being. The Beats developed a populist mentality and lifestyle that also included voluntary poverty. The primary model for this way of life was the urban poor, for their lifestyle was seen as more natural and spiritual than that of middle-class white people.

The Beats valued originality and authenticity in art and felt these aspects were achieved best through spontaneous execution and exposure to unconventional experiences. The Beats romanticized African Americans because of their "natural" ways of being and expressive cultural tendencies, thus continuing a tradition of **primitivism** in earlier white-dominated bohemian cultures. Using black musicians as their barometers of coolness and improvisational, authentic art, the Beats created a community of nonconformist "hipsters" who opposed mainstream "squares" focused on the American Dream. Later the Beats added white rock 'n' rollers, such as Elvis Presley, to their list of cultural icons.

Postwar Racial Politics

Given the importance of the Beats' romanticization of black masculinity to Beat culture, and the rock culture that was influenced by it, more attention needs to be paid to that romanticization. Eric Lott's research is useful here, for it helps us to understand the historical fascination that young white males have had with black men and the resulting impact of that fascination on culture. As Lott argues, white American male identity is constructed in relation to black manhood because of the United States' legacy of slavery. It is a relationship imbued with both rivalry and desire, with white men simultaneously competing with and being attracted to black males, and black culture more broadly. In this complicated dynamic, white men see black manhood as animalistic, dangerous, and hypersexual as well as cool, dynamic, and potent.

Lott theorizes that some white men negotiate such contradictory emotions (including potential homoerotic desire) by attempting to embody black manhood, a process that entails the internalizations of a historically abject form of identity yet continues the oppressive racial dynamics associated with slavery and imperialism. In other words, while white males have pursued the project of conquering the black "Other" via politics, economics, science, and culture, such desires for control often happen internally also: mastering the Other in oneself by "blacking up."

Many cultural critics understand white men embodying black masculinity as evidence of racism and white supremacy. For example, bell hooks refers to such practices as "eating the other," linking such appropriations to black culture's consumption by white people, who retain power in these unbalanced interchanges. According to Lott, however, practices of **racial cross-dressing** primarily occur when the division between races seems intractable yet a collective, albeit often unconscious, desire aims to bridge that gulf. He traces this phenomenon in U.S. culture back to **blackface minstrelsy**, a performative musical style that involved white (and later black) young men blackening their faces to appear African. Nineteenth-century white minstrels were typically urban northerners with political ties to then conservative and often white supremacist Democratic elite. Minstrelsy is often critiqued for its stereotyping of black people, not to mention its cultural and economic exploitation of people of color. Yet for Lott blackface allowed young white men to explore an identity they linked to freedom, play, and pleasure. By performing fantasies of black men, these young performers were able to exist, at least temporarily, outside the Victorian bourgeois norms expected of them. Moreover, as touring performers, they lived an unstable, nondomestic lifestyle that facilitated freedom from convention and involvement in alternative experiences, while exposing audience members to the concepts of racial crossing and hybridization.

The Beats alienated from white middle-class society a century later adopted many of the same values as blackface minstrels, particularly a romanticization of black masculinity and privileging of a nomadic, bohemian lifestyle. Later, these values were taken up by many white performers associated with rock culture. Important to consider, therefore, are the racial dynamics of 1950s U.S. society and their impact on many young Americans. In general, deep divisions still existed between white and black people during the postwar period, and Americans of color faced considerable discrimination and violence by whites. Many African Americans, along with Latinos and Native Americans, became politically active during the 1950s in response, thus leading to the development of the civil rights movement. (Such racial politics were evident also during this period in the United Kingdom—another site of early rock culture—due to an influx of black British from the West Indies after World War II.)

Despite such tensions, racial integration increased in significant ways during the postwar era. This social transformation was due to the convergence of several social phenomena, in particular a new wave of African American migration to the northern United States (which was historically more white), the growth of the black middle class, and the increased power and influence of white liberals, particularly in popular culture. Indeed, as the history of both minstrelsy and rock 'n' roll suggest, racial integration has often happened in culture before the rest of society, and music is often a primary catalyst for such crossings.

Racial Musical Crossings

During the early 1950s, young Americans who weren't listening to standards produced for the general audience primarily listened to two forms of popular music: **R&B** and **rockabilly**. Each of these two musical styles is affiliated with a specific racial group in the United States, as well as a particular form of American **folk music**, that is, traditional music created for expressive rather than commercial reasons. (Chapter 9 explores the heritage and characteristics of rock's musical sounds.)

Emerging in the late 1940s, R&B has roots in African American slave songs and gospel music and developed as a variation of urban blues and boogie-woogie, two high-energy styles produced through electrification, fast-paced rhythms, and frenetic showmanship. Some popular early R&B artists who influenced rock music include Delores LaVern Baker, Ruth Brown, Sam Cooke, Fats Domino, Louis Jordan, Willie Mae ("Big Mama") Thornton, and Big Joe Turner.

Also fast and raucous yet affiliated primarily with white Southerners, rockabilly (a merging of "rock 'n' roll" and "hillbilly") emerged as an energized and modern form of country music in the mid-1950s. As a musical style, rockabilly has roots in Celtic folk music as well as Appalachian bluegrass, Western swing, and honky-tonk; it is influenced also by gospel, jazz, boogie-woogie, the blues, and R&B. Early rockabilly stars who most influenced rock 'n' roll music include Johnny Cash, Bill Haley, Roy Orbison, and Carl Perkins. With the exception of Brenda Lee, most female rockabilly performers of this period, including Janis Martin and Wanda Jackson, did not achieve the success of their male peers.

While white musical styles were privileged across the postwar media landscape, R&B—like other forms of black music—was largely confined to African American communities prior to the mid-1950s. Anglo Americans had little access to this new style via live performances, record stores, and mainstream media, although those living near black communities had some exposure via black churches and radio stations. As U.S. culture grew increasingly racially mixed after World War II, not all U.S. citizens celebrated racial integration. Nevertheless, the greater mixing of black and white people during this period produced interesting experiments in popular music that were soon enjoyed by many Americans.

Most significant for this discussion, in the mid- to late 1950s several popular musicians, including Buddy Holly, Elvis Presley, and Chuck Berry, began to merge rockabilly with R&B, thus transgressing traditional racialized music boundaries and developing a style that came to be known as rock and roll or **rock 'n' roll**. It was these musicians who borrowed R&B's **band** structure (a guitarist, bass guitarist, drummer, and, to a lesser extent over time, pianist), as well as its privileging of a twelve-bar chord structure and a backbeat. In turn, they sped up the pace of the music and increasingly privileged the role of the lead guitarist, much as rockabilly groups did. And, in keeping with both R&B's and rockabilly's lyrical styles, they sang about the good times more than the bad. (Chapter 10 explores the lyrical roots of rock music.) Unlike many other popular musicians at that time, many of these early rock 'n' rollers performed music and lyrics they had composed themselves.

This traditional portrait of early rock 'n' roll privileges its up-tempo roots and upbeat character while ignoring the influence of slower, ballad-oriented music, such as that associated with **doo-wop**, a form of R&B that privileges vocal harmonies (similar to barbershop quartets). Developed in the 1940s, doo-wop had considerable influence on early rock 'n' roll via all-male groups, like Frankie Lymon and the Teenagers, as well as "girl groups," like the Chantels. Although less popular in later decades, doo-wop continued to have an effect on rock in the 1960s via such groups as the Beach Boys.

While musicians were at the forefront of rock culture's racial crossings during the 1950s, they were not alone. **Cultural intermediaries**—those who connect producers with consumers—were crucial to this process. For example, white independent record label owners, like Sam Phillips of Sun Records and Ahmet Ertegün of Atlantic, songwriters, like Jerry Leiber and Mike Stoller, and radio disc jockeys and concert promoters, like Alan Freed and Pat DiCesare, who were attracted to both white and black musics helped bridge the gulf between the two by promoting performers of both races. (Freed is commonly credited with naming this hybridized style of "rock and roll.") Because of the limited presence and economic power of female and black entrepreneurs at that time, the development of rock 'n' roll as a popular, commercially viable genre must be understood as dependent on such white male influence.

Many individuals have understood white people, including these cultural intermediaries, as unethical appropriators of African American culture. This perspective has been affirmed in rock culture through numerous stories of white managers', record producers', label owners', and concert promoters' financial exploitation of black musicians, many of whom were young and had little knowledge of business matters. The then-conventional practice of record label executives employing white performers to cover black-authored music to profit from white consumers is further evidence of such economic exploitation, not to mention cultural appropriation. Increased public awareness of such incidents, as well as the increased power of black historians and cultural producers, during the late twentieth century led to a profound rewriting of rock 'n' roll's early history that downplays the significance of white performers, like Elvis Presley and Jerry Lee Lewis, and foregrounds the innovations of black musicians, such as Muddy Waters, Bo Diddley, Little Richard, and James Brown.

Nevertheless, as discussed previously, Lott encourages us to think about racial cross-dressing not just in relation to economics but also in the context of sociohistorically specific racial relations and cultural progression. Thus, just as white minstrels attempted to move outside their normal circles through blackface performances and helped to ameliorate the racial divide during the nineteenth century, so, too, have later generations of liberal white males tried to find new means of cultural expression and identity through dialogues with black culture. At the same time, Karl Hagstrom Miller's research demonstrates that such racial crossings have long happened the other way also, with African Americans performing music identifiable as "white," largely to secure a living by playing for Anglo and European American audiences. Although black musicians have rarely been able to financially exploit their interests in white musical styles to the degree that the opposite has occurred, the music of several early R&B performers, including Hank Ballard, Chuck Berry, and Bo Diddley, reveals how much white country forms influenced black performers, and thus the development of rock 'n' roll.

Yet it was not just musical performers, DJs, songwriters, and record industry executives who transgressed the historical divide between white and black America during the postwar era. Many consumers contributed to this phenomenon also. The primary listeners of early R&B and rockabilly were members of the baby boom generation, a consumer market with considerable buying power and thus appeal to the culture industries. In fact, it was largely because of white adolescents' consumption of black music during the 1950s that more white DJs, concert promoters, recording industry executives, and retailers decided to make investments in it, eventually leading to the hybrid style known as rock 'n' roll. Following the popularity and commercial success of several white rock 'n' roll performers in the mid-1950s, such investments surged, as record producers like Don Kirshner, Phil Spector, and Dick Clark rushed to create the next musical sensation for the lucrative boomer market. (Chapter 5 explores the development of rock's various musical styles after the 1950s.)

Rock 'n' Roll and Postwar Gender Politics

As noted, postwar teenagers were encouraged to see themselves as a unique demographic group with a common generational identity and thus to ignore issues of difference in their identities and experiences. But not all teenagers experienced early rock 'n' roll in the same way. Despite the racial progressiveness often attributed to this period of rock culture, race-based barriers made it more difficult for youth of color to succeed as performers and participate as consumers. In addition, the traditional gender dynamics that reemerged after World War II meant that teenage boys had much more access to rock culture, as both consumers and producers, than adolescent girls did. Discounting class disparities, on average the teenage boy earned more for paid work than did his female peer (despite girls' dominance of babysitting, a new lucrative cottage industry). Thus, boys had greater access to the technologies used to make and consume rock 'n' roll music. Moreover, boys had more license to partake in social activities outside the home. Girls had far less freedom, as they were encouraged to aspire to the housewife ideal, placing marriage and motherhood above other goals. Girls' formation of a **bedroom culture** during this period facilitated their confinement to the domestic sphere, yet it also enabled their transgression of it via pop star idolatry.

A considerable number of teenage girls rebelled against the staid life of middle-class housewives during the postwar era, yearning instead for the carefree and exciting experiences traditionally afforded male youth. Some girls sought out alternative lifestyles, particularly those associated with the creative world of cultural production. While some became involved in Beat culture, a significant number of teenage girls—white, Latino, and African American—gained entry to the recording industry as performers as a result of the experimental climate of early rock 'n' roll. Indeed, the popularity of **girl groups,** like the Exciters and the Shangri-Las, in the late 1950s and early 1960s contributed to the largest influx, and success, of young female performers in rock until the 1990s.

Yet, of the female adolescents who gained popularity as rock 'n' rollers during this period, many—including Janis Martin and Laurie Collins—had their careers disrupted or cut short by early marriages and pregnancies. Because the emerging rock culture of that era increasingly privileged youthfulness over adulthood, such "mature" young women were marginalized, making way for younger, single female adolescents, like Brenda Lee and Veronica "Ronnie" Bennett (later Spector), who could better project the teen spirit associated with rock 'n' roll. Perhaps because of her high energy and her husband Ike's musical ambitions, Tina Turner is one of the few young female performers associated with early rock 'n' roll whose musical career was not significantly disrupted by her domestic roles.

Young female performers enlivened early rock culture. Yet their success is often explained not by the quality or popularity of their music but as a result of the void left by the loss of Elvis Presley to the U.S. army, Chuck Berry to jail, Little Richard to religion, Jerry Lee Lewis to his marriage to his teen cousin, and the Big Bopper, Buddy Holly, and Ritchie Valens to death. Indeed, using similar criteria developed by rock critics in the late 1960s to dissociate pop from rock, particularly the privileging of music performed by those who compose it, many scholars exclude girl groups from the history of rock 'n' roll and ignore the impact of their music on male groups, like the Beatles and the Ramones.

Rock culture became increasingly masculinized during the late 1960s and 1970s via the popularity of male-centered bands, like the Rolling Stones, as well as the development of harder, more aggressive styles, like heavy metal. As Sheila Whiteley demonstrates, rock's privileging of a Beat-like fraternity during this period relied not only on the exclusion of female musicians but on conservative notions of woman as either maternal nurturer or sex object, the virgin/whore dichotomy to which female rock consumers were relegated also. Although female musicians did find some access to rock via folk and, later, punk, it would take women and girls until the end of the twentieth century before they approached the same level of involvement in rock's production and consumption they had during the early days of rock 'n' roll. In the meantime, many of the young males who have dominated rock culture since the 1960s have continued to champion many of the values and practices of Beat culture, as can be seen in the classic rock mantra "Sex, drugs, and rock 'n' roll," as well as the privileging of youthfulness. And although the black man has been replaced periodically by other mythic figures idolized by young white men as expressively authentic (e.g., the white folk singer-songwriter, the white working-class laborer), defiant masculinity, often shored up by a misogynist sensibility, has remained a primary component of the rock ethos.

The Legacy of Rock Culture's Traditional Gender Politics

Despite rock culture's dominance by men during the later decades of the twentieth century, its gender politics were anything but stable during this period as plenty of nonconformist male performers and fans challenged rock's hegemonic masculinity while female musicians and consumers refused to be left outside rock's "boys' club." Nonetheless, rock's privileging of a rebellious, youthful masculinity as performed by white young men has remained strong to this day. One of the primary questions guiding research on rock culture's gender politics is how and why this particular form of masculinity has remained hegemonic despite the legacy of progressive ideologies and practices in this community.

Challenging the notion that the male orientation of rock's culture is natural or predetermined, several feminist scholars have shown how rock's gender politics are socially produced in this culture. Sara Cohen, one of the first, conducted an extensive ethnographic study during the late 1980s of Liverpool's rock scene (home to the Beatles, Echo and the Bunnymen, and Ladytron). Cohen's findings are telling since they reveal the multiple activities and individuals that contribute to the maintenance of rock's male-dominated structure. For instance, Cohen demonstrates that men held almost all of the most valued roles of cultural production in the Liverpool scene. This included everyone from musicians to club owners to customers. She found that roles involving technology and property ownership were especially off limits to women. Men's dominance of these roles helped to construct females in the scene as interlopers.

Cohen's research also demonstrates that males in Liverpool's rock scene privileged homosocial relationships and engaged in conversational styles marginalizing of women. Training and band formation contributed to such homosociality and exclusion since the male musicians learned to play their instruments from other males and created bands through preexisting friendship groups (a finding supported by Mary Ann Clawson's later research). In addition, male musicians and other rock scene entrepreneurs (e.g., show producers, zine editors) participated in what Will Straw has defined as a culture of connoisseurship, wherein detailed knowledge about bands, technology, musical styles, and business practices is exchanged among men to display cultural capital, gain power, and affirm status in the scene. This discursive and relational style worked to maintain the gendered boundaries of this largely homosocial community.

In a later study, Cohen explores how rock scenes like Liverpool's develop as male-dominated in part because of the gendered aspects of their physical locations and the time of day when those spaces are occupied by rockers. She notes that the bars and clubs where rock musicians perform are typically frequented during the late evening hours and located in marginal areas deemed unsafe due to minimal street traffic as well as the prevalence of alcohol, illegal substances, and delinquent behavior. Females have long been socialized to avoid such spaces, particularly at night, to protect themselves. Meanwhile, younger men, especially those aspiring to hegemonic masculinity, may feel brave and powerful after successfully navigating such spaces at night.

Because of these interconnected phenomena, rock scenes tend to be male-dominated and to privilege a masculine sensibility. It is no surprise, therefore, that females have found it difficult to be involved in such scenes, a point Mavis Bayton demonstrates also through interviews with women rock musicians. Cohen found that females are often excluded from male rockers' social networks, even as girlfriends and wives. Yet male musicians frequently rely financially on their female partners. In addition, many women, particularly those with children, find it difficult to adjust their domestic responsibilities and schedules to the nomadic and nocturnal world of rock culture. In contrast, men historically have not been expected to help out with children and therefore often had more free time than women. As a result of these various elements, the traditional female role in rock scenes has been that of a male musician's companion and thus is fairly conservative in terms of gender norms. When women have broken such gender barriers, the creative positions they have occupied most legitimately have been restricted to those that do not undermine their femininity or threaten male power (e.g., backup singers, costumers, public relations agents).

Norma Coates has added to Cohen's project and our own understanding of rock's masculinist orientation through attention to poststructuralist theories of gender. As discussed in the Chapter 2, these theories offer useful ways of thinking critically about how gender is socially constructed through discourse and performance. In particular, Coates draws attention to how rock's patriarchy rests on the **abjection** of femininity. She notes that this Othering and rejection occurs in the rock press's gendered opposition of rock and pop: the former is constructed as emotionally honest, expressively authentic, artful, and valuable, traits that are then construed as masculine, while the latter is represented as superficial, prefabricated, commodified, and illegitimate and thus feminine. In turn, Coates demonstrates that the rock press has historically grouped all female rock musicians together, foregrounding their gender over their music while also suggesting their contingent status in a culture assumed to be male. Meanwhile, she notes that male rock musicians reproduce a mythic form of rebellious phallic masculinity to which women have no access while regularly incorporating femininity into their acts as a means of lessening its threat to rock culture.

The feminist studies noted above, which demonstrate rock's patriarchy and sexism, hold up fairly well when used to analyze contemporary rock scenes, not to mention rock culture at large. In turn, data from recent industry-produced reports, such as *Billboard*'s sales and radio-play charts, as well as the presentation of prestigious music awards, such as the Grammys or the Brit Awards, substantiate scholarly claims about rock's historical domination by males. (Chapter 6 includes a detailed gender-based study of the Grammy nominees and winners.) Nevertheless, beyond the world of rock, gender politics have changed considerably in the past few decades, a development which in turn has impacted rock culture.

Such progressive transformations are largely a result of the dissemination of feminist thinking, the rise in female education, and the increased presence of women in roles historically associated with males. In comparison to previous decades, more girls today, especially those of the middle class, socialize with male peers outside the domestic sphere and feel entitled to participate in historically male-dominated arenas related to school, leisure, and work. As a result, female youth are more familiar and comfortable with the social dynamics of such milieus. Moreover, more young women feel confident performing historically masculine activities, such as sports.

In rock culture, such changes in gender politics have meant that more female instrumentalists are involved in rock music, and women have greater control over their art and representation than in the past, even if they still have difficulty achieving cultural legitimation. Moreover, more women musicians demonstrate feminist values and rely on them when creating their music and developing their public personas. Transformations in the gender politics of society at large have also meant that women have more access to technical and executive positions in the recording industry, as well as more senior writing and editorial positions in the rock press.

Transformations in gender norms have not just happened for females, however. In many countries, more men, particularly middle-class men, now share childcare and household duties with their partners. In addition, more men today feel comfortable interacting with women in the workplace than in previous decades, perhaps because there are more women in such spaces, including in positions of authority. In turn, a considerable number of young men are less invested in hegemonic masculinity, and some practice gender equality in their everyday lives even if they do not support feminism outright. The feminist and LGBTQI communities' numerous struggles to raise critical consciousness about gender are at the heart of these transformations.

Such changes in rock's gender norms seem particularly evident in independent music scenes where both men and women are engaged in identity performances that undermine the sex/gender system. This is evidenced by the Grammy's "Best Alternative Rock Album" award, for which over 31 percent of the acts include at least one female, in comparison with only 12 percent for the "Best Rock Album" award. In addition to more male rock musicians being welcoming of female performers than in the past, so, too, are more male engineers, producers, critics, executives, and consumers.

Yet such transformations in rock's gender norms do not mean that this culture is now an egalitarian place. Just as many women and men in it are attempting to undo traditional gender politics, many others continue to be invested in regressive gender norms that reify patriarchy and heteronormativity. The remainder of this book explores the various sites in rock culture where such norms are reasserted and challenged to demonstrate the complexity of rock's gender politics, as well as this culture's significance as a space for exploring gender.

Summary

This chapter has examined the roots of rock's primary ideologies via a survey of the complex sociohistorical context that gave rise to rock 'n' roll as a unique form of music. One of the most significant cultural trends to emerge out of the social upheaval of the mid-twentieth century, rock 'n' roll structured itself according to the values of the music and youth cultures from which it evolved. Such historic events as the Great Depression, World War II, and the postwar baby boom encouraged American youth, particularly teenage boys and young men, to seek new forms of community and creative expression that valued freedom while also foregrounding rebellion, youthfulness, and expressive authenticity. The privileging of these ideologies contributed to the appreciation of African American culture and black masculinity among alienated white youth, at the same time that it led to a reaffirmation of patriarchy and male homosociality at the expense of girls and women. Most closely aligned with the Beats, these values eventually informed the development of rock culture in the 1950s.

In addition to surveying some of the musicians and cultural intermediaries significant to rock 'n' roll's early development, this chapter has considered postwar identity politics, which allowed many young males—both white and black—to succeed in this new musical style yet restricted the involvement of girls and women. Although some female musicians became successful via "girl groups" in the late 1950s and early 1960s, rock culture became an exclusive community of predominantly white young males by the end of the 1960s. Rock culture has largely remained that way until this day, with the exception of the 1990s, when a large number of females asserted their musical tastes and talents, and more men worked alongside them to shift rock's gender politics in a more progressive direction. Unfortunately, rock culture has not yet experienced the racial diversity of its first two decades. People of color continue to be somewhat anomalous in this community today. In Chapter 4, we will explore the rock business, whose politics of both race and gender have long shaped what music reaches the public and becomes popular.

Further Exploration

1. Explore minstrelsy.

Watch the film *Bamboozled* (2000). Discuss the major components of blackface minstrelsy and its effects on American popular culture, especially music, as represented in this movie.

2. Examine racial music crossings.

Watch the film *Hairspray* (1988) and Time-Warner's *The History of Rock 'n' Roll,* part 1, "Rock 'n' Roll Explodes" (1995). How does each text explore racial music crossings? Discuss any differences or similarities in how these two films construct these phenomena.

3. Analyze Beat culture.

Watch the film *The Beat Generation: An American Dream* (1987), and discuss the primary ideologies associated with the Beats. In particular, discuss their gender politics.

4. Explore youthful masculinity as an identity.

Read and listen to the lyrics of Tom Waits's song "I Don't Want to Grow Up" (1992, also covered by the Ramones) and Blink 182's "What's My Age Again?" (1999). How is youthfulness presented in these songs? Discuss the gender politics of the lifestyle represented in these songs. Compare the youthful masculinity referenced in these songs to the form of masculinity on display in the documentary *The Other F Word* (2011). What points of similarity or contrast do you see?

5. Examine women musicians' experiences in early rock culture.

Watch the film *Welcome to the Club: The Women of Rockabilly* (2004) and *Girl Groups: The Story of a Sound* (1994). Discuss how dominant ideologies of gender and generation affected the careers of young women associated with these two forms of popular music. In addition, discuss the intersections of racial and gender identity experienced by the girls in each film.

Further Reading

Chapple, Steve, and Reebee Garofalo. *Rock 'n' Roll Is Here to Pay: The History and Politics of the Music Industry*. Chicago: Nelson-Hall, 1977.

Coates, Norma. "(R)evolution Now? Rock and the Political Potential of Gender." *Sexing the Groove: Popular Music and Gender*. Ed. Sheila Whiteley. New York: Routledge, 1997. 50–64.

Cohen, Sara. "Men Making a Scene: Rock Music and the Production of Gender." *Sexing the Groove: Popular Music and Gender*. Ed. Sheila Whiteley. New York: Routledge, 1997. 17–36.

Cohen, Sara. *Rock Culture in Liverpool: Popular Music in the Making*. Oxford: Clarendon Press, 1991.

Friedlander, Paul. *Rock and Roll: A Social History*. 2nd ed. Boulder: Westview, 2006.

Keightley, Keir. "Reconsidering Rock." *The Cambridge Companion to Pop and Rock*. Eds. Simon Frith, Will Straw, and John Street. New York: Cambridge University Press, 2001. 109–42.

Lott, Eric. "White Like Me: Racial Cross-dressing and the Construction of American Whiteness." *Cultures of United States Imperialism*. Eds. Amy Kaplan and Donald E. Pease. Durham: Duke University Press, 1993. 474–95.

Medevoi, Leerom. *Rebels: Youth and the Cold War Origins of Identity*. Durham: Duke University Press, 2005.

Peterson, Richard A. "Why 1955? Explaining the Advent of Rock Music." *Popular Music* 9.1 (1990): 97–116.

van Elteren, Mel. "The Culture of the Subterraneans: A Sociological View of the Beats." *Beat Culture: The 1950s and Beyond*. Eds. Cornelis A. van Minnen, Jaap van der Bent, and Mel van Elteren. Amsterdam: VU University Press, 1999. 63–92.

Warwick, Jacqueline. *Girl Groups, Girl Culture: Popular Music and Identity in the 1960s*. New York: Routledge, 2007.

4 ART AND COMMERCE
Rock Business

LISTEN: CONSOLIDATED, "MUSIC HAS No Meaning" (*Friendly Fa$cism*, Nettwerk, 1991). *Delivering a didactic message while inspiring us to bop along with its beat, this song moves us to reflect critically about the relationship of art and commerce, meaning and power.*

Since the late 1960s, many rock musicians, fans, and critics have privileged authentic expression as one of this community's primary values, often via oppositions of rock and pop, the second of which is constructed in comparison as superficial, overproduced, and thus inauthentic. In fact, for most rock aficionados, "sell out" is the worst criticism any band can receive, and many rock performers work strenuously to avoid that label. Yet rock music did not emerge as an art form only; almost always it has been a commodity also. While mass-produced material goods, such as records and CDs, have been the most obvious evidence of rock's commercialization and industrialization (at least until the digital era), even live performances of rock music are typically organized as products meant to generate consumers and profit. Moreover, if we consider which bands are most celebrated and most represented in rock history, it is clear that commercial success matters just as much, if not more than, artistic quality. Thus, members of the rock community have long had to negotiate this tension between rock as art and rock as commerce.

Due to their nonconformist values and privileging of Romantic ideals, many rock performers have been uneasy with the involvement of commodification and corporate industrialism in music scenes, since they see these mainstream forces as nefarious pollutants of authentic creativity. Yet few musicians are able to gain popularity and financial success without promoting their music via live shows where listeners pay a fee. Moreover, since popular music today is largely recorded music, very few musicians are able to operate outside the recording industry without risking their viability, not to mention longevity, as professional musicians.

Negotiating a balance between art and commerce has become even more difficult for rock musicians in an era of **late capitalism** and **conglomeration**. Rather than deal with stand-alone recording companies, many musicians now sign contracts with transnational media conglomerates, like BMG, which maximize their revenue streams by producing multiple commodities based on a common theme, commodities that together create a singular cultural experience for consumers. This practice of transmedial exploitation has existed in rock as far back as Elvis Presley's time. Yet today's media conglomerates focus far less on a band's music than its image, which can be affixed like a brand to a variety of products that operate apart from music. Indeed, rock culture's overall reputation as rebellious, which was considered anathema to mainstream business for several decades, is now regularly harnessed to appeal to consumers invested in youthfulness and independence. How else to explain the use of the Stooges' raucous "Lust for Life" to advertise a cruise package, the Ramones' "Blitzkrieg Bop" to sell soft drinks, or the Beatles' "Revolution" to sell sports shoes?

As much as the terms "business" and "commerce" are associated now with corporate capitalism, the reproduction and distribution of rock music is not the conglomerated culture industries' purview alone. Rock culture has long included individuals who value art more than commerce, and many have created alternative mechanisms for the circulation of rock music and related products. Hence, since its emergence as a controversial musical form, rock has a complicated commercial history that involves both corporate industry and independent companies.

This chapter focuses on half of rock's art/commerce relationship by analyzing the business side and what might be called its **culture of production**. With a focus on workers' identities, we will explore how gender politics have influenced employment practices and working conditions in the rock business. At the same time, we will consider how some rock business professionals marginalized by their gender or sexual identities have responded to such challenges by creating their own companies. In turn, we will examine the changes that have occurred in this business because of the dispersion of feminist ideologies and the rise of digital technologies.

Rock Business's Roles and Practices

Howard Becker has described communities that sustain practices of creative production as **art worlds**. In this chapter we will explore those workers who facilitate the recording, manufacture, promotion, distribution, and retailing of rock music and its associated products—an amalgam of individuals and companies that collectively make up the **rock business.** (Chapter 8 will explore workers who assist live rock performances.) As with those who labor on behalf of live rock performances, those who work on the production and distribution of rock recordings help to maintain rock culture as a site of both commerce and art. In the rock business's recording and manufacturing sector, such workers include band managers, A&R (artists & repertoire) scouts, label executives, producers, session musicians, and recording engineers. Those who promote, distribute, and sell rock recordings include public relations agents, disc jockeys, record store retailers, music video directors, and, on the Internet, those who market and distribute MP3 files. Yet this business also includes nonmusic roles traditional in other forms of business, such as accountant, attorney, administrative assistant, and executive officer. Today, most of these roles are affiliated with the **culture industries**, since many record labels that were once independent companies, like Columbia, are now affiliated with media conglomerates, like Sony, which engage in numerous forms of cultural production, not just music.

Today's rock business is vast and complicated by media conglomeration. Nevertheless, as Geoffrey Hull, Thomas Hutchison, and Richard Strasser argue, the practices performed by those working with music and musicians can be grouped into three basic categories or "streams": music publishing, live entertainment, and recordings. Attention to each stream provides a broader understanding of the rock business's culture of production, since practices associated with these three streams take place in both the mainstream and alternative sectors of the music business. Nonetheless, *the ways* these tasks are accomplished (their **modes of production**) often differ significantly because of the contrasting values and perspectives associated with the mainstream/corporate and independent sectors.

Over the past sixty years, the individuals and companies that produce, reproduce, distribute, market, and sell rock music have developed specific practices and strategies to function as an organized, efficient, and profitable field of cultural production. Yet since the larger music business has been in existence since the eighteenth century, when sheet music was first commercialized, many of its practices were developed well before rock 'n' roll emerged. Some of those practices have been reconfigured, however, because of the specific needs and values of rock musicians. For example, since the mid-1960s, most rock musicians write their own music and no longer require music publishers to hire songwriters. In turn, because rock musicians often do not notate their compositions, the publishing of sheet music for rock songs does not happen to as full an extent as it does with other musical genres. Hence, most of the business dealings that are rock-specific are related to live entertainment and recordings. While commercial recordings of music were introduced in the late nineteenth century, live musical performances have been commoditized for over two hundred years. Thus, old traditions about how musicians turn live performances into money persist and are often inflected with traditional gender politics.

To become popular and commercially successful, a rock band must develop its fan base by performing in public. This topic is explored in greater detail in Chapter 8, but the role of **band manager** must be discussed here also, since those individuals are often involved in the production of rock recordings as well. The band manager has historical roots in a field known as **talent management**. A manager operates as both an adviser and representative of musicians. In a band's early days, the manager role is often informally performed by a friend or companion who does not expect or require payment. As a band secures more gigs and rises in popularity, it will typically contract with a professional manager familiar with the recording industry who can help in defining the band's creative and commercial objectives. (Often, however, band managers are superseded by record producers at the time of actual recording.) In turn, band managers negotiate relationships among band members, serving as mediators in difficult situations. Some managers also function as personal assistants to individual band members. Many managers work independently; however, numerous companies offering band management services are part of the larger music industry.

The third stream of music business practice is that of recordings and involves the reproduction of musical performances for sale as commodities. For much of the twentieth century, music was recorded and reproduced materially as analog **records** made of varying materials, diameters, and rotations per minute (rpm). The standard for the first half of the twentieth century was 78 rpm records with just one song per side. In 1948, **33 1/3 long-play (LP) records** or **albums**, which can hold multiple tracks of about sixty minutes total, were introduced and quickly became the standard for "serious" music, such as jazz, and by the late 1960s, rock. Meanwhile, **45-rpm records,** or **singles**, became associated with pop and commercialism. As magnetic cassette tape and digital CD technologies were introduced, the recording industry adopted the length of LP records as their standard for cassette and CD albums also. Even with digital formats, which do not have the material constraints of shellac, vinyl, or tape, the sixty-minute album remains the standard format of recorded rock music. Nevertheless, singular songs are more easily produced and distributed today than in the past because of digital technologies, such as the MP3 file.

Record labels are companies with which musicians contract for the recording, distribution, and promotion of their music. The music industry typically divides record labels into **majors** and **independents** (or "indies"). Most major labels today are subsidiaries of multimedia conglomerates that include numerous companies related to different forms of cultural production. Indie labels are typically owned by individuals or companies that object to the corporate culture industries' economic motives and thus utilize different strategies of business that privilege creative expression over financial gain.

Record label companies include **artists and repertoire** (A&R) divisions that work on finding and contracting new musicians. **Talent scouts** in such divisions are often young people knowledgeable about the latest trends in music culture. They listen to aspiring bands' **demos** (demonstration recordings) and search for new talent in local rock scenes. (Meanwhile, other A&R staff members mine the label's catalog of previously marketed music for further commercial exploitation, such as "greatest hits" compilations.) Once a band signs with a record label, they are responsible for abiding by the contract's terms, which often includes recording requirements as well as royalty specifications over a specific time period. New bands have very little leverage to negotiate such contracts, which often make them responsible for much of the expenses required to produce, distribute, and market their work. Many of those working in the music business's independent sector oppose such exploitative contracts and attempt to return more profit to musicians.

Record labels are responsible for manufacturing, distributing, and marketing the products associated with their musicians. Thus, they typically employ numerous individuals responsible for transforming music into commodifiable products, including those who produce and record music, design album covers, manufacture records, tapes, and CDs, create music videos, manage websites, and advertise musicians and their music. Large media conglomerates, like Time Warner, host multiple companies involved in these various components of the music business. In contrast, smaller independent labels often must work with several unaffiliated companies to transform recording sessions into products. Successful musicians are often able to negotiate with labels for control over their recordings (if not their promotion). Yet all artists must participate in recording sessions alongside **producers**—who provide expert advice on instrumentation and sound quality— and **recording engineers**—who record musicians' performances and manipulate sound to achieve desired effects. Largely absent from public view and thus music history, **session or studio musicians,** who perform instrumental or vocal music for recording sessions, are crucial to most rock recordings also.

In addition, record labels are responsible for the marketing of the musicians with whom they have contracts. **Public relations** staffs engage in promotional activities for rock bands via the arrangement of press reviews and interviews, the circulation of press kits, and the production of music videos. Lawyers work on behalf of record labels in negotiating royalties, licensing, and other copyright issues with music publishers and performing rights organizations, such as ASCAP (American Society of Composers, Authors, and Publishers) and BMI (Broadcast Music, Inc.).

Prior to the twenty-first century, most rock musicians were highly dependent on the music industry for the recording of their music, as well as its distribution and promotion via retailers, radio, and other forms of media. In contrast, many contemporary rock musicians are now able to promote and disseminate their music on their own, and often to much larger audiences, than in the past because of the development of digital media technologies.

A Brief History of the Music Industry

The music industry has recently received much attention for being an unstable, if not deeply troubled, commercial enterprise, primarily because digital technologies have reconfigured the recording, commodifying, and consuming of music. This description of industrial instability is accurate and not just for today. The music industry's efficacy has fluctuated continuously since its emergence due to competition between major and independent labels, technological developments, and changing legal and economic conditions. Because of its appeal to younger people, the rock business in particular is beholden to the size, disposable income, and buying power of youth, as well as their shifting entertainment interests.

Roy Shuker observes that the recording industry alternates between periods of stability, when musical output is homogeneous in form and commercially predictable, and instability, when output is diverse and less predictable. Industry homogeneity results from **oligopolistic** conditions, where a few companies control the market and restrict the growth of independents. Periods of diversity, competition, and instability occur because of consumer desires for innovation that is unmet by homogeneous products and an increase in independent labels. While the rise of new indies necessarily decreases the majors' power over the music business, smaller labels (along with independent radio stations) have often found the new talent the industry needs to remain culturally interesting and commercially viable. Despite such fluctuating circumstances, the majors bring stability to the industry through **consolidation**, buying up smaller, independent labels to increase their contact with innovative musicians, to update their rosters, and to appear more exciting to consumers.

The 1990s is commonly thought to have been a peak period for independent record labels specializing in rock. Because of a simultaneous decrease in the cost of recording technology and increase in recording efficiency, numerous small labels—often owned by musicians themselves—sprang up at that time. The **do-it-yourself (DIY) ethos** of punk also permeated rock culture to a greater extent than it had previously, encouraging musicians to record themselves to remain independent of mainstream rock. Nevertheless, the history of independent rock labels goes as back to the emergence of rock 'n' roll, as small labels, like Sun and Atlantic, recorded many of the genre's pioneering performers before the majors understood this new music as lucrative. Independent labels that have achieved notoriety (if not always commercial success) in U.S. rock culture more recently include Alternative Tentacles, Dischord, Epitaph, K Records, Kill Rock Stars, Righteous Babe, and SubPop (see Figures 4.1 and 4.2).

New musical genres have often emerged when independent labels have gained considerable ground. This was the case in the 1950s, when rock 'n' roll developed, as well as in the 1960s, after the "British Invasion" (rock culture's domination by white British bands) and hard rock's development, and again in the 1970s, with the rise of heavy metal, punk, and hip-hop. Some scholars have argued that shorter periods of stability/homogenization and instability/diversity in the music business have occurred since the late 1980s. Homogenization

Figure 4.1   Kill Rock Stars logo
Kill Rock Stars

Figure 4.2   Righteous Babes Records logo
Righteous Babes Records

has increased largely because of consolidation and a drop in the number of conglomerates controlling the industry. For example, in the 1990s, six conglomerates dominated the business via their **music holding groups**: Warner, EMI, Sony, BMG, Universal, and Polygram. BMG is now part of Sony, and EMI and Polygram are owned by Universal. These conglomerates own many formerly independent record labels, which has created some debate as to which labels really count as indie today.

Since the 1990s, the music business has been transformed considerably because of digital technologies. Because of composing software, the Internet, and **MP3s** (compressed digital audio files shared easily online), musicians are no longer dependent on professionals to record, distribute, and promote their art. (Such technologies have posed new challenges also for retailers and **disc jockeys**, those cultural intermediaries who have long facilitated relations between musicians and consumers by broadcasting, promoting, and selling recorded music.) Of primary importance to this scenario are digital music formats, particularly MP3S, as well as the broad expansion of the Internet and the increased proliferation of online radio platforms, **peer-to-peer (P2P) sharing sites,** and **social networking sites**, like Pandora, Jango, Last.fm, SoundCloud, Bandcamp, Facebook, and YouTube. The convergence of such technologies and platforms allows more ease and speed in gathering and sharing music. In turn, online fundraising sites for creative work, like Kickstarter, are now used by musicians wanting to produce and distribute their work independently. Such technological developments have not only expanded the ways in which musicians can now distribute their music; they have also increased consumers' ability to access music and interact with it in new ways. Chief among the industry's concerns is illegal copying of musical files, which returns no profits to the corporations that invested in such recording's production. Hence, digital technologies and practices have required the rock business to reinvigorate its standard practices, such as live performances, and to increase its involvement in new ventures, such as music streaming services.

Gender and Labor

Feminists have been interested in labor and business due to capitalism's historical privileging of male workers and mistreatment of women, especially through unequal wages as well as limited training and advancement. Several scholars have conducted quantitative analyses of women's labor in different national media industries since the 1990s. Their work demonstrates only incremental improvements in gender equity over the past four decades, despite female gains in many other professional fields during that same period.

Quantitative studies of gendered labor in the U.S. music industry are rare. Yet several studies conducted recently in the United Kingdom have been useful for mapping the gender politics of this global business. For instance, the 2012 membership survey for the Association of Independent Music showed that only 15 percent of the British record labels it supports are majority-owned by women.[1] In turn, a 2013 study by Creative & Cultural Skills revealed that 67.8 percent of workers in the U.K. music industry is male.[2] According to a 2009 study by the same organization, that amount increases to 77 percent when only managers are considered.[3] Anecdotal information offered by those who work or have worked in the music business supports such reports, indicating that most jobs in the record business—particularly those offering considerable agency, visibility, and financial gain—have been occupied by men. Even in the allegedly progressive world of independent music, men have occupied most positions of power and control, while women have been contained in subordinate positions, such as administrative assistant, and afforded little opportunity for advancement, wealth, and recognition.

A primary reason for the sexism and male domination associated with the music business is heteronormative patriarchal ideology, which has privileged the **sexual division of labor** so as to maintain men's power and women's subordination. **Capitalism**—a profit-driven economic system—has worked alongside traditional gender politics to maintain men's socioeconomic dominance over women. Men's labor has commonly been constructed in relation to the public sphere, while historically "a woman's place was in the home." Prior to the late nineteenth century few women were educated; therefore, women were deemed not to have the mental capacity and skills necessary for business. This is not to say that women didn't labor. They did. But few worked in public or for wages, as "women's work" was confined to the domestic sphere via housekeeping and childcare. Moreover, without voting rights, women had few avenues for improving their labor opportunities, advancement, and pay.

Over the last forty years, patriarchal capitalism's sexual division of labor has been significantly challenged by feminist activists and working women advocating women's equal access to the public labor force and equal pay for work equal to men's. Such values have led to women being integrated into men's existing business structures and to businesses adopting policies that make work environments less harmful for women (such as those prohibiting **sexual harassment**). By the early twenty-first century, the **sexual segregation** of labor was undone in most developed nations. Women have become a substantial part of the paid labor force and regularly work alongside men without being labeled outsiders or treated as interlopers.

Nevertheless, the gender dynamics of labor are still out of balance in numerous occupations today, because of men's desires (conscious and unconscious) to maintain control of products and profit-earning ventures, as well as women's limited power to make change. Moreover, wage and promotion gaps continue to be gendered, with men earning more and having more opportunities for advancement than women. According to the U.S. National Committee on Pay Equity, for example, American women's earnings in 2016 were 79.6 cents to every male dollar on average. In other words, for every dollar a woman makes, a man earns $1.26. To make up this wage gap, over the course of her life in paid labor, a woman would have to work an extra twelve years longer than a man. Because of sexism's convergence with racism and classism, this situation is worse for nonwhite women and those without high school degrees.

The gendered imbalances of labor begin long before girls are old enough to seek nondomestic jobs. In patriarchal societies, female youth are socialized to develop knowledge and skills in self-beautification and childcare, while boys are encouraged to develop talents useful in the paid workforce. Despite feminist activism, the emphasis on female beauty has increased in the current postfeminist era. Now girls and women are encouraged to invest in hyperfeminine fashion and beauty regimes to lessen the threat they pose to male power via aspirations for success and independent wealth. Meanwhile, schools often reinforce the sex-based division of labor by suggesting that some occupations, such as nursing and the military, are inherently gendered. Both males and females are subject to this pattern, but women have faced more challenges than men when trying to break into fields dominated by the opposite sex. Many women find it difficult to get training or advance in jobs traditionally occupied by men because the associated tools and practices are understood as masculine.

Gender differences are sometimes reinforced in the workplace through practices discriminatory to women, such as receiving less pay and benefits than men working the same job, as well as the devaluing of historically feminine practices, such as expressing emotion. Some employers show little concern for their employees' household and childcare obligations, which are still largely the responsibility of women and constitute the "second shift" for those women who work outside the home.

Unconsciously reproducing stereotypes of subordinate, domestic femininity, many male bosses and coworkers have asked women employees to do traditionally female practices, such as serving coffee, taking notes, or organizing meetings. More insidious, numerous women have reported harassment in maledominated fields, from sexual overtures to accusations of being "bitchy" when asserting opinions and to the destruction of work. In addition, many women have been subordinated by men who take credit for their work, while many others have had difficulty being promoted to positions of authority, a phenomenon known as the **glass ceiling effect.** Constructing women as unworthy interlopers, these practices attempt to contain the threat female workers pose to male homosociality, advancement, and power. Because of the increasing number of women in the paid workforce, many men today have little problem working with or being supervised by women, and a good number even prefer that situation to working with or reporting to men. Nevertheless, numerous men still find it hard to be peers with or subordinate to women and thus undermine female coworkers and managers.

Men are not entirely to blame for the unequal treatment many females experience at work. Numerous women perpetuate gender inequality at work as a result of beliefs they hold about the sex/gender system, gender-specific work, and the different capabilities of males and females. Indeed, while a large number of women still avoid historically male-dominated work altogether, others avoid advancement in their fields because taking on more power and authority is often conflated with being aggressive and masculine, qualities that undermine a woman's achievement of heteronormative femininity.

Feminist scholars and activists have struggled against labor-based gender inequality to provide women and men with equitable training, pay, work conditions, and advancement opportunities. Socialist feminists have called for greater recognition of the relationship of patriarchy and capitalism, which results in female workers earning lower wages and advancing at a slower rate than their male peers. Liberal feminists have fought for women's equal wages and opportunities in the workforce. Cultural feminists advocate women's mentoring and training of other women and girls as well as the establishment of feminist businesses as a means of subverting the sexism historically aligned with patriarchal capitalism and improving women's lives and the products of their labor. As more women gain agency and authority in our current neoliberal late capitalist system, some feminists have called for more analyses of postfeminism's enticing myth of "having it all" while others advocate reworking earlier socialist/materialist critiques of economic power and privilege via theories of intersectionality.

Gender Politics in the Recording Industry

Traditional ideologies of gender and labor have impacted the gender politics of the recording industry's culture of production, with far fewer women than men being involved at both the creative and executive levels. (Chapter 8 explores the gendered labor of rock performance specifically.) This ongoing problem has had a profound effect on the success of women musicians and other female music professionals. An important yet difficult question to answer is why the music industry has maintained such unequal gender politics—even with the naturalization of liberal feminism and greater gender equity in other lines of work. In addition to patriarchy and sexism, one probable reason is that great fame and financial gains are possible in the record business, and the men who benefit from positions of creative and economic power do not want to give them up. In addition, as the 2015 Twitter storm inspired by music journalist Jessica Hopper revealed, male homosociality, cronyism, and nepotism ensure that female newcomers to the business have difficulty breaking in, finding support, and achieving legitimacy (see Figure 4.3). When we add the intersecting dimensions of

Jessica Hopper
@jesshopp

Following

Gals/other marginalized folks: what was your
1st brush (in music industry, journalism, scene)
w/ idea that you didn't "count"?

RETWEETS   LIKES
364   578

10:16 AM - 24 Aug 2015

364   578   •••

Figure 4.3 Jessica Hopper Twitter post
Jessica Hopper, 2015

race and sexuality to gender, we can understand better how straight white men
have historically outnumbered other social groups in the recording industry.

Women Musicians and the Industry

Marion Leonard argues that the recording industry's masculinist gender politics have long worked in favor of both male musicians and the male-
dominated corporations involved in this business. As the industry seeks to
maximize profits, its talent scouts minimize financial risk by focusing on bands
that are understandable and accessible to consumers. Once a band has achieved
significant commercial success, it is determined to be "established" and "important." This process has contributed to a canon of rock artists to which other
bands are compared—by the industry, critics, and fans. Because rock stars, since
at least the late 1960s, have been most promoted when male, the stereotype of
the rock musician is male, and all-male rock bands have been sought after, promoted, and celebrated to a greater extent than those that feature women. This
problem has been exacerbated by the industry hiring more male than female
talent scouts and label executives, and the historical tendency for males in these
positions to undervalue women musicians and their art. Leonard's analysis of
rock guides and encyclopedias published between 1977 and 2001 shows that
only 8–22 percent of the bands featured included a female artist or a band with
more than one woman. Other listings of canonical rock bands, including many
histories and textbooks on rock music, similarly privilege male bands.

Many of the elements that keep girls from learning rock instruments and
engaging in rock performance (discussed further in Chapter 6) deter women
from becoming interested in working professionally as recording artists. The
rock business has a reputation for being both patriarchal and sexist, a kind
of "boys' club" where women are often understood and treated as interlopers.

Female rock musicians regularly tell stories of male label executives creating virtually no space for the development of female artists. For example, musician Elaine Summers reported: "One thing that I keep seeing and makes me laugh is when a label says they can't sign you because 'We just signed two female singers and we'll see how that does first' or 'We just signed someone just like you.'"[4] In turn, Kathleen Hanna argues, "I hate that attitude of 'We already have a Lydia Lunch, so we don't need a Bikini Kill.' Well, there's like two hundred million all-male bands all writing 'baby, baby I love you let me drag you around on my ankle.' Is that enough already? Duh!"[5]

In the 1990s, the major labels appeared quite interested in signing women performers and female-centered rock bands, like L7, Hole, Babes in Toyland, and the Breeders. Nevertheless, such groups were often promoted via labels, like "women in rock," that continued to make gender primary and musicianship secondary. As Donita Sparks from L7 argues, "it belittles women to lump them all together. . . . We rock hard. That's all there is to it. But we always get the girl-band bullshit. We don't rock hard for women; we just rock hard."[6] Many female rockers have argued something similar, often in the face of being rejected or ridiculed for engaging in a "male" practice. Meanwhile, other women rock performers have taken advantage of being understood first as females and second as musicians since they see their gender as helping to create possibilities they may not get otherwise in this male-dominated cultural practice. For example, Sara Watts of Treacle has argued: "if you're a male band you're ten a penny, but if you're a female band, as soon as somebody who books gigs hears that you are a female band, without even listening to the tape, 90 per cent [*sic*] of the time they'll offer you a gig."[7]

Like many male rock musicians, numerous female rockers have found managers, producers, and executives supportive of their vision and willing to take risks, including letting the musicians call the shots. As Lori Barbero of Babes in Toyland argued in the early 1990s, "rock 'n' roll has been run by men, but that's changing. Always women were just there as a front, but now we're playing the music and writing it too."[8] Yet many women artists have struggled with recording industry professionals who either see such artists as women first and make sexual advances toward them or discount their musical knowledge and skills because they are female. Hence, there is a long history of male executives, producers, and managers attempting to exert control over women's music, performance styles, and public images. For example, Judy Parsons of the Belle Stars reports: "We hate [our producer] because he makes you feel really low and inferior. And it might just be to do with being female, that he can't handle women. But I'll never know. He just makes you feel that you are a shitty musicians and if only he could replace the whole band with [male] session players and computers it would be much better."[9] It's not just women's musicianship that is at stake for such controlling producers and other industry professionals. As Kim McAuliffe of Girlschool recalls, "we did have a bit of a problem when we signed to this American record company. They wanted us to change our image and be more glamorous and all that sort of thing. And we actually got a 'front' singer in then—a blonde front singer! . . . It was a total disaster."[10] When women musicians assert themselves with industry professionals to maintain control over their image or sound, they often get criticism meant to keep them in line. For example, Lauren Wood recalls: "I had a reputation for being a really nice person but a pain in the butt—meaning I was involved and interested and good at being a producer."[11]

Once a female-centered band gets signed, one of the primary forms of sexism they must deal with is how their label promotes them visually. Many companies continue to rely on the idea that "sex sells," and women musicians far more than their male peers are regularly encouraged to heighten their sex appeal to attract consumers to their products. This has proven to be a conundrum for female rock artists who want to be understood foremost as musicians in a culture that privileges masculinity. As Terry Hunt of Jam Today notes, "you find you have to keep up your feminine girly thing and that doesn't particularly go with being in a hard, slaggy job, which is what [rock] music's all about."[12] As discussed in Chapters 11 and 12, heterosexualized femininity is the primary form of display for women rock musician. This tension seems to be resolved in the current postfeminist era, where aspirational women are encouraged to believe that hypersexualization is the form of power in which they should most invest. Indeed, many established female artists, like Jewel, who achieved success without going this route but are now aging, find it necessary to use their sexuality to promote their products. Nevertheless, this form of hyperfeminine display rarely increases women's power outside the realm of sexuality; it works mostly to lessen their potential threat to male control.

Women Laborers in the Recording Industry

Prior to the increase in women's higher education, few females who were not songwriters or musicians were able to find work in the recording industry. Female employees working in the business prior to the late 1980s were typically relegated to subordinate positions, and only a few were able to advance to executive positions. As with female musicians, some women who did break through the glass ceiling were perceived as a threat by male coworkers and were harassed to impede their progress, including accusations about sexual services being exchanged for promotions. Some women may have gotten ahead via their relationships with men in the business, and this is not surprising, given that cronyism and nepotism are rampant in the culture industries. Nevertheless, other women's success in the recording industry came through their involvement in less popular and less profitable genres. For example, several women managed early punk bands before that genre was considered commercially viable, including Nicole Panter (the Germs). Nevertheless, as Caroline Coon, who worked with the Clash, recalls, her gender caused problems in her business dealings as manager: "whatever I did was sabotaged by the fact that I had tits."[13] Indeed, even her legacy is compromised by her gender, as she and other female managers are typically ignored in conventional rock histories, which celebrate only male managers, like Colonel Tom Parker (Elvis Presley), Brian Epstein (the Beatles), and Andrew Loog Oldham (the Rolling Stones).

Meanwhile, some female employees' successful sexual harassment lawsuits against record labels demonstrate that some men working in the industry understand women primarily as sexual beings. Penny Muck's highly publicized lawsuit against Geffen Records in the 1990s confirmed many women's fears about working in this business, just as it raised some public awareness of sexism in the recording industry.

In addition to the traditional gender politics informing the mainstream record industry, rock's privileging of rebellious machismo has precluded many women from becoming involved in this culture's business side. Some administrative jobs allow women to work at a distance from the masculinist world of rock musicians. Yet many positions, from band manager to talent scout to producer to recording engineer, require direct interaction with such performers and require workers to be comfortable with the rebellious and machismo world in which they circulate. Women are at a disadvantage when understood only in sexual terms. As Moira Sutton, the manager of Red Tape Studios in Sheffield, recalls, "one of the studios actually specifically said they wouldn't have women engineers or studio managers, because artists would feel that they couldn't behave naturally in front of them."[14] Jill Sinclair, cofounder of the SPZ Group, explains: "women have a civilizing influence, and a lot of rock groups don't wish to be civilized."[15] Given these dynamics of the business, it is not surprising that employees often discuss how female workers have to play at being "one of the boys" if they want to be treated as legitimate and achieve success. Even well-respected female session musicians, such as bass player Carol Kaye, have reported as much.

Women's roles in the music industry were still largely restricted through the end of the twentieth century. As Diana Graham, formerly of Arista Records, recalled, "women are allowed to excel in publishing, human resources and the International department—all jobs that men don't want, and that don't lead to running major corporations."[16] Yet since that time the business has been accommodating a greater number of women in positions of power. More women have become band managers, talent scouts, and producers, including for male musicians, like Keith Richards (Jane Rose) and Henry Rollins (Gail Perry), as well as presidents and CEOs of major record labels. In turn, according to Lorraine Ali, by the early 1990s, women were six to eight times more likely to reach senior management in the music industry than in older, more established industries (although they tend to earn far less than men in those same positions).[17]

Women's recent rise in the music industry is due in part to the broad dispersion of feminist ideologies and increased acceptance of women in historically male-dominated work fields. Moreover, the music industry is first and foremost a business, and this field is becoming less masculinized via women's increased education in formal managerial programs and involvement in business administration. Yet the influx of women into the music business is due also to the perseverance and role modeling of assertive female industry professionals who have carved paths other women could follow. For example, Ethel Gabriel, who became a vice president at RCA after years in A&R, convinced her company to financially support her training program for women wanting to be label executives. One of the women she mentored is Nancy Jeffries, who served as an A&R scout for RCA, A&M, and Virgin US before becoming senior vice president of A&R for Elektra. A similar mentoring relationship took place between Mimi Joran, CEO of London Records, and Helene Blue, now general manager of MPL Communications, Paul McCartney's publishing company.

Despite the importance of female mentoring relationships, we must be mindful also of the men who have supported female workers, for progressive gender politics do not develop only through women's involvement. Mentorship by well-respected men in the music business has been particularly important for women aspiring in areas with too few women. For instance, acclaimed music executive Sylvia Rhone was mentored by Doug Morris, who helped to promote her at Atlantic Records, Warner Music Group, MCA Records, and Universal Motown Records.

As the aforementioned women's careers suggest, many who become successful in the music business begin, or get a major break, in A&R, a field that requires not only musical expertise but also considerable "people skills," as much of the work of contracting and recording musicians is the responsibility of A&R scouts. One of the most successful female A&R scouts in rock culture was Karin Berg, who worked at Elektra before heading up the A&R department for Warner's East Coast division. She signed numerous bands associated with punk, new wave, and alternative rock in the 1980s and 1990s, including the Cars, Television, the B-52s, and Hüsker Dü. Today some of the most successful female A&R scouts (some of whom head their labels' A&R divisions) include Jane Baintel (Atlantic), Renee Bell (RCA), Nancy Brennan (SBK Records), Kim Buie (Capitol, Lost Highway), Susan Collins (Virgin), Laura Hill (Atlantic), Paige Levy (Warner).

The tide has changed considerably during the past two decades for women occupying senior executive positions in the recording industry. Sylvia Rhone was the first woman and first African American to become head of a major record label when she was appointed chairman and CEO of Elektra in 1994. (She served as president of Universal Motown Records and executive vice president of Universal Records until 2011. She is now CEO of her own label, Vested in Culture.) In the late 1990s, Rhone and Sheila Shipley Biddy of Decca Records were the only women heading major record labels in the United States. Today several women hold top executive positions at such labels, including Michele Anthony (Universal Music Group), Julie Greenwald (Atlantic), Evelyn Shriver (Bandit), Ethiopia Habtemariam (Motown), and Michelle Jubelirer (Capitol). Other significant female executives to break the glass ceiling for women in the music industry include Marilyn Bergman (chair and president of ASCAP), Judy McGrath (chair and CEO of MTV Networks), Christina Norman (president of MTV), Sue Peterson (former head of the National Association of Recording Merchandisers), Frances Preston (former president and CEO of BMI), and Hilary Rosen (former chair and CEO of Recording Industry Association of America).

Billboard introduced its annual "Power Players: Women in Music" series in 2005. Individuals occupying upper management positions in various sectors of the industry are nominated by colleagues and *Billboard* readers. Based on those nominations, the magazine's editors select the annual honorees. The series highlights the success of such female music executives as Rhone, Greenwald, and McGrath. Given the music industry's historical privileging of men over women, these efforts are surely to be commended. Nevertheless, *Billboard*'s annual acknowledgment of a few dozen executives who happen to be women obscures the marginalized status of the thousands of other women working in the industry.

While women have made some gains in the music industry, one place where their numbers are still marginal is in producing. While recent attention to the few women at the top of this field, like Sylvia Massey and Linda Perry, signals to girls that producing is not just for men, it also obscures the disproportionate number of men occupying this position and the challenges many other female producers have in gaining legitimacy. Women-run organizations like Female Music Producers and the Female Producers Association are working to change this paradigm by creating an infrastructure that supports women in this field.

As Keith Negus reports, female recording engineers were practically nonexistent prior to the 1990s, and in 1998 James Dickerson called engineering the "last bastion" of male domination in the music business. Recording engineers are responsible for not just knowing about and using technology but also lifting it and repairing it when necessary. (This field grew out of mechanical engineering, another reason it has historically been male-dominated.) And as with the learning of rock instruments, training in recording equipment often happens informally in male homosocial groups, thus lessening the opportunities for female involvement.

Boden Sandstrom offers another explanation for the dearth of female engineers by relating the male domination of the recording process to the power engineers have over how music sounds and thus their important role in mediating between musicians and listeners. As Sandstrom notes, some male engineers are unwilling to give up this control, even to musicians, a problem that becomes exacerbated in a climate of gender inequality. (Similarly, the most acclaimed record producers in rock culture are men with reputations for excessive control of the mixing process, such as Phil Spector.)

Sandstrom cites several individuals who believe that female engineers have greater sensitivity to both sound and human relations and thus mix music better than men. These claims are controversial and may reproduce stereotypes of women and reify the sex/gender system. Yet they encourage consideration of the social contexts that might produce gendered listening habits. With an increase in the number of women enrolled in record engineering programs, it is likely that their knowledge if not skills in recording will supersede those of the men (and women) who learn more informally about this practice. In the meantime, male students learning alongside female students are more likely to be accepting of women in this profession.

Many of the reasons that keep women from engaging in sound engineering also preclude women's interest in being radio disc jockeys. A position requiring familiarity with not only cultural trends but also technology, DJ-ing is a practice imbued with radio culture's gender politics. In the early 1920s, women made up a significant portion of amateur radio operators. Yet once broadcasting went commercial, women's voices were deemed unsuitable for most programming because of their high pitch. This belief still circulates today, as few radio stations employee female disc jockeys. In the smaller niche of rock stations the problem is worse because of the patriarchal ideologies of this genre and the rebellious, machismo performances required of its most public members, DJs included. (Some of rock's most influential, and colorful, characters have been male disc jockeys, including Alan Freed, Casey Kasem, Wolfman Jack, and John Peel.)

Noncommercial radio stations, part of the independent sector of the music business discussed below, are not as exclusionary with regard to gender. Many—including numerous college radio stations, which have had a huge influence in rock culture since the 1980s—have regularly employed female disc jockeys and station managers. Numerous female DJs—including Lois Maffeo, a musician who worked at KAOS—have created shows that feature the music of women artists, thus helping to rebalance the gender dynamics of rock broadcasting. Meanwhile, other women have gone one step further, founding their own independent radio stations so as to stay clear of the sexism they feel still permeates broadcasting culture and to remain in control of their mission to promote women's culture.

Yet for many women in the music business, the mainstream industry is still a significant site of feminist activism and potential social change. In an effort to support and promote female workers in this business, some have founded such organizations as Women in Music (WIM), which was launched in 1985 in New York. Women in Music includes workers at all levels of the record business. It provides training sessions to educate women on various jobs and practices in the industry, while also hosting award shows to honor those who have been successful and to inspire others. After folding *Rockrgrl*, Carla DeSantis Black founded Musicians for Equal Opportunities for Women (MEOW), an organization that was similarly devoted to improving the working conditions for women in the music business by providing mentorship, coaching, and education at its conferences, which were similar to those DeSantis Black had hosted via *Rockrgrl*. With a similar mission to MEOW's, the Women's International Music Network (WIMN) was founded by Laura B. Whitmore and produces the annual Women's Music Summit, bringing together female musicians and industry professionals for support and training. The Women's International Music Network also hosts the She Rocks Awards, which celebrate, promote, and inspire women's achievements throughout the recording industry.

Gender Politics in Independent Music Culture

As in many other fields, women's assimilation in the corporate music industry has not been the only means of transforming gender politics in this line of work. Many women have sought legitimacy, community, and success in the independent realm of the music business, often because of their poor experiences in the mainstream industry. For example, Regine Moylett formed a public relations company after years at Island Records: "I just got tired of their company, having to readjust, translate everything in my mind, work with male methods. I was continually being told my methods were ridiculous."[18] Working in the independent sector of the music business has been especially attractive to those interested in punk and other forms of rock aligned with progressive politics and anticorporatism. Fortunately, the indie scene is as diverse as the commercial music industry, thus offering such workers numerous opportunities for involvement, from scouting and engineering to disc jockeying, label ownership, retail merchandising, and even music video production.

Although the gender politics of the owners and staff members of early, postwar independent rock labels were fairly conservative, since the 1980s more women have become actively involved in this line of work. Many indie labels advocate women's involvement in all aspects of the recording process, and numerous women have been mentored by and collaborated with male owners of independent labels, like Dischord Records and Kill Rock Stars. Other women have carved out a space for themselves by founding their own indie labels, like Righteous Babe and Thrill Jockey. Punk's DIY ethos is often given credit for the success of independent labels since the 1980s. However, equally important, especially for women, has been the influence of feminist **women's music** culture. Because of the recording industry's patriarchal values and sexism, many cultural feminists have argued for the separation of "women's music" from mainstream music (including rock) and have created a separate commercial infrastructure to support women's musical endeavors. Recalls Judy Dlugacz of Olivia Records (the most successful of such ventures): "I think separatism was necessary, because the male-dominated rock thing was so exclusionary anyway, you needed to form something that you could say 'Hey, this is ours, we're claiming it. This is our territory, this is our pride, and we're going to provide a safe space of ourselves to be creative and learn how to do it.'"[19] Developing alternative models for the performance, recording, promotion, and distribution of women's music, such feminists have been important role models for younger generations of musicians seeking different paths of exposure, community, and success.

In the 1990s and early 2000s several women influenced by cultural feminist values and Riot Grrrl (a punk feminist community) started their own female-run labels, including Tinuviel's Villa Villakula, Donna Dresch's Chainsaw, Liz Naylor's Catcall, Kaia Wilson and Tammy Rae Carland's Mr. Lady, and Sarah Dougher's Cherchez La Femme (see Figures 4.4 and 4.5).

Although not a label owner, Kathleen Hanna of Bikini Kill and Le Tigre sums up the values at the heart of this "girl power" practice: "what [some] bands

Figure 4.4 Mr. Lady Records logo
Mr. Lady Records

Figure 4.5 Cherchez La Femme Records logo
Cherchez La Femme Records

do is go, 'It's not important that I'm a girl, it's just important that I want to rock.' And that's cool. But that is more of an assimilationist thing. It's like they just want to be allowed to join the world as it is; whereas I'm into revolution and radicalism and changing the whole structure. What I'm into is making the world different for me to live in."[20]

Some women label owners have helped others learn how to get records produced, distributed, and promoted. For example, Jenny Toomey and Kristen Thompson of Simple Machines created *An Introductory Mechanics Guide to Putting Out Records, Cassettes and CDs*, which was published in 1991 as part of Dischord Records' larger guide to independent music production, *You Can Do It* (see Figure 4.6). Over eight years, Toomey and Thompson printed over ten thousand copies of their guide, eventually publishing it on the Internet for aspiring independent record producers. The Internet has facilitated other DIY training in record production via such sites as freqControl.com, which features how-to tips and videos of bands recording their music and talking about the creative process.

Like many other institutions developed by progressive individuals, independent record labels typically have values opposed to those associated with the corporate music industry. Such businesses typically privilege process-oriented means (emphasizing mutual respect, open communication, and emotional expression) and value-driven ends (a socially responsible end product), as well as consensus decision-making, a deemphasis on hierarchy and specialized roles, and understanding workers as people with needs. They are also often anticapitalist, privileging creative expression over financial gain. They funnel whatever profits are earned onto musicians and back into the business.

Nevertheless, as Cynthia Lont has demonstrated through her study of Redwood Records, a commitment to progressive politics does not always result in a well-managed business. For example, although involving all staff members in decisions is a noble goal based on democratic ideals, it is difficult and time-consuming to run an efficient, successful company via consensus decision-making. Many such organizations go out of business quickly. Thus, some independent labels that started with an alternative business structure, like Redwood, have moved closer to a traditional, hierarchical structure, albeit without sacrificing their progressive values of providing their employees with reasonable pay and a safe work environment. Independent labels run by women seem especially considerate of female employees' needs due to pregnancy and childcare.

Recognizing the gender disparity that has prevented many women from participation and advancement in the music industry, several organizations associated with independent music, such as MEOW and the Association of Independent Music, have created opportunities for better networking among women in the business. Via workshops and conferences, female musicians, label employees, critics, and, at times, scholars come together to collectively support one another and work on improving the status, advancement, and wages of

Figure 4.6 Simple Machines' *An Introductory Mechanics Guide to Putting Out Records, Cassettes and CDs*

Simple Machines, 1993

women musicians and other female employees in the music business. Such meetings have happened also on a smaller scale in female-dominant music ventures, such as Riot Grrrl and Ladyfest, both of which have expanded beyond their U.S. origins (see Figure 4.7).

Because collaboration is a premium value in the independent music business, the individuals and companies associated with it have created a viable network on which they can depend. Hence, this community has provided many

Figure 4.7 Shanghai Ladyfest 2016 poster
Shanghai Ladyfest 2016

women, queer people, and other marginalized individuals with a supportive structure for their engagement with rock culture.

Summary

This chapter has explored the recording business, a primary site in rock culture mediating between musicians and consumers. With gender as our primary lens, we have considered the numerous jobs, practices, and values that compose the rock business. This investigation looked at both the history of the music industry and the various sectors where the commercialization of rock takes place, including the independent sector, which functions somewhat autonomously from the mainstream industry.

Like most other sites in rock culture, the music business has long been male dominated. Nevertheless, women have always been involved in this sphere of cultural production, primarily in administrative roles. Because of shifts in the economy, gender politics, and women's education and employment, an increasing number of female record label executives have advanced in recent years, thus upsetting the male hold on power in this cultural business. Meanwhile, many rock producers and musicians work outside the commercial recording industry because of their opposition to capitalism and other systems of social oppression. Frustrated by the sexism and homophobia that continue in the mainstream industry and inspired by the DIY philosophy associated with punk and women's music, several women have created their own labels to promote their art and support that of other female musicians. With the broad penetration of the Internet and other digital technologies, such independent production and promotion has become all the easier, thus radically changing the ways popular music is made and heard. In Chapter 5, we will examine the gender politics of rock's various music styles, which are used by the record business, as well as consumers, to distinguish its numerous products.

Further Exploration

1. Analyze the gender dynamics of record production.

Determine the primary individuals responsible for creating your favorite musicians' albums by perusing their websites or CDs. Make a list of jobs and the number of males and females occupying each. Which jobs seem to be dominated by men? By women? Are any jobs equally occupied by men and women? Why do you think that is?

2. Study women's record labels.

Research the history of women-owned record labels. How many are there? What type of women founded them (e.g., race, age, sexuality)? What kinds of music do these labels primarily promote? How many of these labels are rock-specific? How are these labels advertised?

3. Examine the career of one male and one female head of a record label.

Research the careers of these two people. How did each enter into the music business? What jobs has this person held? How does this person account for her or his success? Has this person worked with any famous musicians or any famous record industry people? When did this person become head of the record label? How has their success been handled by the press?

4. Study the gender dynamics of a radio station.

Choose a radio station that plays rock music. Research the employees currently working for this station. Make a list of jobs and the number of males and females occupying each. Which jobs seem to be dominated by men and by women? Are any jobs occupied in equivalent amounts by men and women? Consider the playlists of male and female DJs over the course of a few days. Who plays more female performers—men or women?

5. Analyze gender in engineering training.

Peruse a few issues of a contemporary trade magazine for musicians, such as *Guitar Player*. For advertisements promoting educational programs in sound or record engineering, note the gender dynamics of the verbal discourse and images used. In your opinion, who is the targeted market for such programs?

If possible, visit one of these programs and observe the gender politics of its administrative and teaching staff as well as its classrooms. (Be sure to check with your instructor first about your institution's guidelines for human subjects research.)

Further Reading

Albini, Steve. "The Problem with Music." *Maximumrocknroll* 133 (June 1994). http://www.arancidamoeba.com/mrr/.

Dickerson, James. *Women on Top: The Quiet Revolution That's Rocking the American Music Industry.* New York: Billboard, 1998.

Frith, Simon. "The Industrialization of Popular Music." *Popular Music and Communication.* Ed. James Lull. Newbury Park: Sage, 1987. 53–77.

Hull, Geoffrey P., Thomas Hutchison, and Richard Strasser. *The Recording Industry.* 3rd ed. New York: Routledge, 2011.

Leonard, Marion. *Gender in the Music Industry: Rock, Discourse and Girl Power.* Burlington: Ashgate, 2007.

Lont, Cynthia. "Redwood Records: Principles and Profits in Women's Music." *Women Communicating: Studies of Women's Talk.* Eds. Barbara Bate and Anita Taylor. Norwood: Ablex, 1988. 233–50.

Negus, Keith. *Producing Pop: Culture and Conflict in the Popular Music Industry.* London: Arnold, 1992.

Sandstrom, Boden. "Women Mix Engineers and the Power of Sound." *Music and Gender.* Eds. Pirkko Moisala and Beverley Diamond. Chicago: University of Illinois Press, 2000. 289–305.

Schmutz, Vaughn, and Alison Faupel. "Gender and Cultural Consecration in Popular Music." *Social Forces* 89.2 (2010): 685–707.

Shuker, Roy. *Understanding Popular Music.* New York: Routledge, 1994.

Weinstein, Deena. "Art versus Commerce: Deconstructing a (Useful) Romantic Illusion." *Stars Don't Stand Still in the Sky: Music and Myth.* Ed. Karen Kelly and Evelyn McDonnell. New York: Routledge, 1999. 56–69.

5 ROCK 'N' ROLL EXPLODES
Rock Genres

LISTEN: XTC, "THIS IS POP?" (*White Music*, Virgin, 1978). *Recuperating a style disparaged by many rock aficionados, this new wave song reveals the practices of cultural distinction, taste, and genre formation.*

The practice of distinguishing types of recorded music via **genre labels**, such as classical or folk, was developed in the early twentieth century by the recording industry to rationalize product and make the business more efficient. Musicians, critics, and consumers have sustained such labels' relevance by using them to differentiate and evaluate music styles. Yet genre labels are utilized to categorize much more than just sounds. They are used also to communicate about patterns in lyrics, performance styles, representational strategies, commercial activities, and consumption practices. Thus, genre labels help to distinguish communities of cultural practice.

Many scholars have debated genre's usefulness for understanding popular music, including rock. Nevertheless, most individuals in rock culture utilize genre on a regular basis, including when answering this community's most basic questions: "What kind of music do you listen to?" and "What kind of music do you play?" When responding, rock aficionados name their preferences, define their identities, and establish connections with other people with similar tastes. In doing so, they reaffirm their musical community and the territorial boundaries used to understand specific forms of rock music and segments of rock culture. (Because of this process, many rock genres have been instrumental in establishing music **scenes**, which are discussed in Chapter 8.)

This chapter considers genre as a system of meaning making in rock culture and thus also as a system imbued with gender politics. When analyzing a specific genre, scholars typically examine its development and explore the characteristics associated with it, especially in regard to sound, lyrics, performance, and reception. Therefore, performing feminist rock genre analysis requires familiarity with the concepts and terms used elsewhere in this book. In this chapter we will explore four genres of rock music to demonstrate this particular approach.

Many rock genres have emerged over this culture's long history, often through interactions with other genres. It is difficult, therefore, to establish consensus on a specific rock genre's primary characteristics, particularly if it has persisted over many years. (Consider, for example, the changes in metal since its emergence in Great Britain in the 1960s.) Because of this, readers are encouraged to remember that although genres provide a productive framework for understanding patterns and variations in rock's various practices and products, the definitions of rock genres are always in formation and thus contestation.

Genres and Their Uses

Because our external and internal realities are complex, chaotic, and thus potentially confusing, human beings have developed mechanisms for organizing, understanding, and communicating about the different things that exist in those realities. One of the most basic systems for such practices is **classification**, which involves grouping similar elements together and distinguishing those elements from others that are different (e.g., us and them). What remains outside the group is just as important to defining it as what is included in it.

In the arts, the primary form of classification produces **genres**, categories of artworks that share similar stylistic (form) or narrative (content) features. Such systems of classification do not exist in nature. Rather, they are human constructs produced through subjective perspectives that make such categories vague and unstable. Moreover, genres are necessarily impacted by the historical moments and geographical locations in which they circulate. In other words, genres are not ahistorical, universal, or ideology-free.

Musicologists studying genre have largely paid attention to aesthetic classification, particularly sound quality and structure. Yet popular music is a style with significant relations to both audiences and industry that cannot be ignored. Thus, popular music genres cannot be discerned by focusing on musical texts alone. The numerous sites of meaning making in rock culture require that we look broadly to understand the differences between rock genres.

Simon Frith has analyzed the numerous individuals and institutions that collectively produce popular music genres and has outlined the uses of those genres, as well as their points of creation and negotiation. For instance, because popular musicians typically do not have training in musical theory and composition, they use genre discourse to discuss musical styles, as well as their identities as performers. In turn, musicians in search of gigs will commonly seek out clubs specializing in genres they understand themselves as playing. Performing in such clubs helps to construct those musicians' generic identities.

Frith also describes the ways consumers utilize genre labels to organize the listening process. All consumers use genres to discuss their musical preferences. Yet most consumers do not find new musical acts and recordings on their own. Cultural intermediaries help to facilitate these interactions by using genre labels. For example, club DJs will sometimes label a new genre to distinguish the various styles they play. That label is then appropriated by radio DJs, critics, and the recording business, which in turn draws more listeners and performers to that style and helps it cohere into a genre.

In addition, Frith focuses on the use of genres to organize the sales process, which includes musical reproduction, distribution, exhibition, and promotion. For example, record companies and concert promoters employ genre formulas to create commodities (albums and band tours) that will attract large audiences and thus produce a profit. Music magazines often specialize in particular genres to attract specific consumer groups to the commodities advertised. *Spin*, for example, caters to rock consumers, while *Vibe* caters to hip-hop consumers. Similarly, radio stations organize their programming schedules according to different genres (e.g., jazz at 9 p.m.). Record stores, including those that are virtual, like iTunes, use the genre labels created by record labels and radio stations to more easily facilitate consumer purchases.

Musical Genres

Three genres are currently used to classify Western music: art, folk, and popular. Each is commonly divided into subgenres. Although the boundaries between these genres are blurry, they have been used to distinguish styles that differ in aesthetic qualities as well as instrumentation, producer, audience, performance, reproduction, commodification, and mediation.

Art music, also known as serious music or classical music, has roots in Christian liturgical music. It is typically performed by symphony orchestras composed of professional musicians playing string, brass, and woodwind instruments. Voices are used also in opera and art song. Art musicians play notes transcribed by professional composers, and improvisation has been valued less than in other genres. The original audience for art music outside religious institutions was European royalty and other wealthy Westerners, who were expected to listen quietly rather than participate actively in the performance. Sheet music eventually provided opportunities for nonelites to engage with such music outside church. Like other genres, art music has been mass distributed via radio and recordings since the early twentieth century.

Folk music is often contrasted with art music particularly because of its secularism, its affiliation with amateur performers from the peasant or working classes, its privileging of voice and oral transmission, and its involvement of audience and community. In addition, folk music relies on lyrics and tunes passed down through generations, created by composers whose identities are often unknown today. Because folk music is often affiliated with forms developed before the twentieth century and the introduction of mass media technologies, it is sometimes referred to as traditional or old-time music. During some historical periods, such as the 1930s and the 1960s, folk music was associated with leftist movements, such as the labor and antiwar movements.

Popular music has roots in folk music and thus continues the tradition of performance by individuals or small groups for the general public. In turn, improvisation is highly valued, vocals are often dominant, performers do not play from sheet music, and groups typically include only one instrument of each type. Yet, unlike folk music (prior to the twentieth century), popular music is recorded, commodified, and mass-mediated. Contemporary popular music also usually involves the playing of amplified instruments, such as the electric guitar.

A century ago, popular music genres were often delineated in the United States by the racial identities of performers. For example, music created by black people was placed in the **race records** category regardless of aesthetic qualities. Since the 1950s, explicit racial classification has not been used. Nevertheless, racial politics still impact the labeling of popular music genres. For example, rap and R&B are commonly understood as genres rooted in African culture and performed, if not consumed, primarily by black people. In turn, country is understood as a genre rooted in Anglo culture and performed and consumed by white people.

Today, Western popular music is commonly subdivided into several subgenres, including blues, jazz, gospel, country, R&B, rock, pop, hip-hop, and Latin American music. In turn, each of these subgenres is further divided into subsubgenres. As we will explore in this chapter, rock has many different subforms, whose number has grown substantially since the emergence of its original style— rock 'n' roll—in the mid-1950s.

Defining Rock as a Musical Genre

Rock music developed from the convergence of several forms of American popular music. In particular, the blues, country, and R&B have contributed significantly to rock, each bringing rich aesthetic histories because of its own development from previous popular forms, especially African American and Anglo American folk musics. (This heritage is discussed in Chapter 9 when considering rock's unique sonic style.) Yet rock was influenced also by the other streams of American music, including pop, jazz, folk, and gospel, whose differences make rock a difficult genre to classify. From the blues, rock inherited various stylistic features associated with African American musics, particularly the backbeat, twelve-bar chord structure, and instrumentation (although keyboards and brass instruments have not always been important in rock). From country, rock inherited an array of aesthetic features associated with Anglo folk musics, including vocal styles, lyrical themes, and instrumentation (although the fiddle, mandolin, and banjo are not used as much in rock). From both R&B and country, rock inherited an upbeat tempo and small band structure (guitarist, bass, drums). Yet rock music also inherited jazz's privileging of improvisation and syncopation, as well as gospel's call-and-response structure and impassioned vocals. Since its emergence, rock has adapted to new genres also, such as rap and electronic music, which makes differentiating between them difficult.

Although rock songs can be classified via their common sonic qualities, rock music has never been defined solely by its aesthetics. In the Western tradition of meaning making, rock has also been distinguished through opposition, that is, by describing what it is not. In particular rock has been defined in opposition to **pop**, a process that began in the 1960s and is discussed below. As rock critics, musicians, and consumers have articulated these oppositions, rock has been constructed as authentic and meaningful since it allegedly springs from the expression of personal experience and a rebellious spirit. In contrast, pop has been disparaged as superficial and valueless since it is understood as commercially driven and highly mediated. In turn, rock musicians are valued for creating songs that carry a consistent theme across an entire album, while pop performers allegedly produce only autonomous singles aimed at becoming radio hits. Thus, rock is presented as progressive, moving culture and society forward, and pop is constructed as conservative, helping to maintain the status quo. Gender ideologies have been mapped onto this rock/pop binary, with rock constructed as masculine and pop as feminine. Buried in such gendered constructions is the sex/gender system's conservative politics, which have contributed to the difficulties faced by female and gay male rock musicians.

Yet, as many popular music scholars have noted, these binary definitions of pop and rock do not hold up well when the histories and commercial characteristics of these two musical styles are considered closely. Plenty of rock musicians have made overproduced hits without political messages for economic profit, while numerous pop artists have created conceptual album tracks authentically expressing their ideological values. Thus, both rock and pop reveal discursive tensions between art and commerce.

Rock Genres

Franco Fabbri argues that musical genres develop in relation to rules agreed to by their users, particularly musicians, consumers, and industry professionals. First, the *formal and technical rules* of genre are related to aesthetic styles, sound quality, and the types of instruments used in songs. Second, genres are governed by *semiotic rules*, which pertain to how music makes meaning. (In popular music, lyrics are often understood as the heart of a song's meaning.) Third, *behavioral rules* pertain to the practices of on- and offstage performances. For example, musicians often develop personas and stage antics that add another layer of meaning to their music and thus align them with specific genres. Fourth are *ideological rules* pertaining to the social norms of the musical community to which musicians belong. Finally, *commercial and juridical rules* refer to the practices involved in the commercial production, distribution, and exhibition of music, as well as to those pertaining to ownership and copyright.

Fabbri's schema reveals the multiple sites involved in constructing genre categories, each of which has its own gender politics. Rather than analyzing every rock genre from a feminist lens, this chapter will focus on just a handful, attending to the specific characteristics that have produced each as a unique musical style and community. In particular, we will consider sound, lyrics, performance, and reception and explore how ideas of gender have impacted these different sites. The analyses offered here should serve as a template for your own studies of other rock genres.

Rock 'n' Roll

The original rock genre is referred to as rock and roll or **rock 'n' roll**. The phrase "rocking and rolling" has a much longer history than rock music, however. It has been used to describe the upbeat music of early gospel performers, like Sister Rosetta Tharpe, and has been employed as slang to refer to intimate sexual relations. Disc jockey Alan Freed first used the term "rock 'n' roll" in 1952 to describe the up-tempo songs he was playing on the radio at that time.

As discussed in more detail in Chapter 9, the sonic style of rock 'n' roll developed because of the merging of country music and the blues in the early 1950s. Yet, because this was a period of great sonic experimentation, not all music that became categorized as rock 'n' roll sounded the same. Nevertheless, the genre quickly became identified with several artists associated with the southern United States, specifically Chuck Berry, Buddy Holly, Jerry Lee Lewis, Elvis Presley, and Little Richard. Such musicians privileged loud, boisterous, song-based music with a distinctive backbeat that was performed by small bands, typically a guitarist, bass player, drummer, and vocalist, yet sometimes also a piano player or brass instrumentalists. (Although Berry and Holly became famous in part because of their guitar-playing skills, the valorization of the electric guitar as the instrument most important to the rock sound did not happen for almost another decade.)

Like race and class, gender was not a considerable barrier for performing rock 'n' roll. Many girls were enthralled with this music as much as boys were, although most young women who performed it sang and did not play an instrument. Unfortunately, most rock histories have constructed rock 'n' roll as a primarily male genre, especially with regard to musicians. Hence, white women who performed this type of music, like Laurie Collins, Wanda Jackson, and Janis Martin, are typically associated with rockabilly and country music, while black female performers, like Ruth Brown, LaVern Baker, and "Big Mama" Thornton, are regularly described as R&B artists.

The lyrics of rock 'n' roll songs focus mostly on good times, although early rock musicians sometimes performed romantic ballads also. As the name of this genre suggests, sexual innuendo appears in some early rock 'n' roll lyrics, such as Little Richard's "Tutti Frutti." Such lyrics were sometimes "cleaned up" and performed by musicians constructed as wholesome so that those songs would appeal to a broader audience and become hits. During this same period, Ritchie

Valens pioneered a form of rock 'n' roll infused with Spanish lyrics, thus expanding the genre's lyrical style beyond its roots in the English language.

Since rock 'n' roll was an experimental form, and one largely associated with African Americans, most of its original artists were contracted with independent labels. Such cultural, social, and commercial marginality helped to construct rock 'n' roll as deviant, a connotation some performers of this genre relished and worked hard to promote. Borrowing an energetic performance style from both gospel and R&B, rock 'n' roll musicians—especially Lewis, Presley, and Little Richard—became well known for their high-spirited onstage movements, although female performers had less liberty. Suits and ties were standard for male entertainers of that period, yet early rock musicians often added a flamboyant, youthful spirit to such costuming via modern hairstyles and stylish accessories. The black women artists of this period, particularly when performing for a white audience, often contained their bodily movements and dressed in the upscale evening wear associated with wealthy adults so as to assimilate into mainstream culture. White female rockers had greater flexibility in terms of both performance style and costuming.

As with other forms of popular music, rock 'n' roll was originally promoted through live performances. Yet as the genre became more popular and more artists recorded songs, radio stations and movies helped to disseminate it also. Television, still a relatively new medium in the early 1950s, was crucial to rock 'n' roll's promotion nationwide. Like its performers, rock 'n' roll's consumers crossed every identity line but generation, as it was embraced by youth across the United States (and eventually around the globe) and was understood as unwholesome by many adults. As a result, rock 'n' roll was one of the first musical genres specifically identified with young people, thus contributing to youthfulness as one of the primary ideologies of rock culture.

Folk Rock

In the midst of the **girl groups** and the "invasion" of white male British bands, both of which achieved tremendous popularity by the mid-1960s, rock fans were exposed to a new wave of folk musicians. With origins in the simple traditions of folk culture, folk music attempts to speak directly to audiences about everyday life via acoustic instruments and message-oriented lyrics. With vocals privileged over instrumental sounds, the genre has long been associated with social movements opposing commercial culture and dominant political ideologies. The costuming and performance strategies of folk musicians are similarly unglamorous and "natural"; performers often wear street clothing rather than costumes.

Folk music became a recorded, commercial form of music in the early twentieth century. Its first revival among American urban youth occurred in the 1930s and 1940s via performers like Woodie Guthrie and Pete Seeger. Another revival happened in the 1950s via "purist" (some ethnic, most political) folk musicians, like Odetta and Pete Seeger, as well as commercial groups, like the Kingston Trio and the New Christy Minstrels. As the United States experienced more social upheaval in the 1960s, the period's zeitgeist changed from innocence to rebellion, and once again folk music became the soundtrack of such activist initiatives as the antiwar movement. The clear vocals, stripped-down acoustic sounds, and political views of early folk performers strongly influenced young folk musicians of this period, including Bob Dylan, Joan Baez, and Richie Havens.

Known for his poignant, well-crafted lyrics, Dylan became a role model for numerous musicians in the 1960s, including rockers, encouraging them to compose their own songs rather than simply cover those written by others. Moreover, he modeled a mature, politically invested lyrical style. In 1965, Dylan shook the folk world by performing with an electric guitar at the Newport Folk Festival. While many folk fans understood his use of an electrical instrument and engagement with rock aesthetics as producing offensive noise, that act worked to align Dylan with many of the period's most prominent rock musicians, including John Lennon and George Harrison of the Beatles. Indeed, many critics have noted that the dramatic transformation of the "Fab Four" from pop-oriented performers to serious musicians was the result of Dylan's influence.

Separating themselves from the escapist fantasies of commercial pop, many other 1960s rock musicians became more serious about their craft, their image, and their public role via their adoption of the folk aesthetics privileged by Dylan and other young folk musicians. Indeed, during the late 1960s, **folk rock** developed into a popular genre as it became the medium of choice for a new generation of political activists. While Dylan continues to be the musician most associated with the style, many other folk rockers were popular during this period, including Simon and Garfunkel, the Byrds, the Mamas and the Papas, and Crosby, Stills, Nash, and Young. Folk rock also influenced the work of many **singer-songwriters** of this period, including Donovan, Cat Stevens, Joni Mitchell, James Taylor, and Jackson Browne. Mostly white, these musicians contributed to the whitening of rock culture during this period. In turn, they continued the privileging of casual, everyday attire for performances as a means of communicating their **authenticity** and alliance with working-class people as well as their objections to mainstream consumer culture.

Interestingly, as the rock world became more male and patriarchal in the late 1960s, many feminist musicians repudiated rock sounds, identifying more with the values and aesthetics of folk music. Wanting to separate from the sexism they felt permeated the recording business, these musicians worked to develop a style of folk outside mainstream rock culture that came to be known as **women's music**. Contemporary solo female rock musicians who compose and play their own music, such as Sarah McLachlan, are often associated primarily with the folk/singer-songwriter style, a rhetorical strategy that works to marginalize them in rock culture.

Blues Rock and Hard Rock

By the late 1960s, the most privileged form of rock music was **blues rock** or electric blues, a style that developed because a new generation of young musicians tapped into the deep cultural roots of rock 'n' roll's rich heritage. Several groups associated earlier with the "British Invasion" form of rock music, in particular the Rolling Stones and the Yardbirds, loved blues standards and were influential to this development. Indeed, as a result of such groups' popularity, a bluesy sound came to dominate rock music during this period. For example, most guitar-based groups associated with psychedelic rock—another rock genre to emerge around that time—fit into the blues rock category, such was their privileging of blues aesthetics. A particular version of early blues rock came to be known as the "Muscle Shoals sound" because several recording studios located in that Alabama town were popular among rock musicians.

During the late 1960s and early 1970s, several new blues rock bands emerged, including Cream, Led Zeppelin, the Animals, and the Jeff Beck Group, that would substantially influence other rock bands, not to mention rock culture in general. Much like the Rolling Stones, these new bands commonly covered the songs of famous blues musicians, including Willie Dixon, Howlin' Wolf, Muddy Waters, and Robert Johnson. Such bands are well known for their privileging of musical aesthetics associated with the blues, including a particularly deep and passionate vocal style and lyrics associated with authenticity. Yet blues rock bands are also important for ushering into rock culture virtuosic and improvisational moments, especially those centered on the electric guitar. Powerfully influenced by the technical mastery and creativity of Jimi Hendrix, a guitarist associated with psychedelic rock, blues rock guitarists worked hard to develop a particular overdriven sound via distortion and volume that became standard in hard rock. Via virtuoso performances displaying their mastery of the equipment, blues rock guitarists gave rise to the notion of the **guitar hero** and were essential to the electric guitar's solidification as the primary symbol of rock music and culture. For many male and some female fans, blues rock's heightened attention to the electric guitar contributed to their own pursuit of technical and musical expertise. For those who didn't play, the miming of such virtuosity by playing "air guitar" was always a possibility.

In contrast to the majority of performers associated with psychedelic rock, the most famous blues rock musicians were British, most of whom—including Eric Clapton, Jeff Beck, and Jimmy Page—had some relationship to one of two early blues rock bands: the Yardbirds and John Mayall and the Bluesbreakers. Moreover, unlike most psychedelic bands, the blues rock bands were exclusively male, a factor that contributed to the increased masculinity, patriarchy, and sexism associated with rock culture during the 1970s. Indeed, blues rock is sometimes referred to as "cock rock," given its overprivileging of phallic masculinity in lyrics and performance styles.

As bands performing this harder-sounding style became popular in the 1970s, girls and women found it increasingly difficult to participate in rock culture, particularly as performers. In addition to its phallocentrism as a musical style, blues rock's increasingly technologized production culture, via a focus on high-end instruments and spectacular stage shows, was somewhat exclusive to men and thus contributed further to female marginalization. Nevertheless, femininity was not completely removed from this genre. Indeed, several male blues rockers, especially vocalists, adopted some effeminate attributes associated with psychedelic rockers at that time, such as long hair, jewelry, and tight-fitting clothing. Moreover, the gendered coupling of these bands' feminized vocalists and masculine guitarists (e.g., Robert Plant and Jimmy Page of Led Zeppelin) worked to challenge the heteronormative patriarchy of rock through its suggestion of homoeroticism. As we will examine in Chapter 8, such gender-bending performances would have a significant impact on heavy metal, yet another rock genre to emerge in the late 1960s.

As the hippie counterculture dissipated and blues rock became more popular in the 1970s, psychedelic rock merged with blues rock to become **hard rock** (now sometimes referred to as "1970s rock"), a genre that also privileged virtuosic guitar playing and aggressive musical sounds. Hard rock had few of the exotic elements of psychedelic rock and less of the gender exclusiveness of blues rock. Indeed, several early hard rock bands, like Heart and the Runaways, were among the first groups in rock history to demonstrate that women performers could be something other than vocalists. Nevertheless, established male bands, like the Rolling Stones, the Kinks, and the Who, as well as newer male groups, such as Aerosmith, Boston, and Van Halen, ruled the scene throughout the 1970s and into the 1980s, helping to further cement the common-sense notion that rock was performed, and consumed, predominantly by males. Indeed, while some hard rock bands, like AC/DC and Queen, had names toying with homosexual connotation, the latter was one of the few rock groups of this era to have a gay performer, Freddie Mercury, although he did not publicize his sexuality.

Glam rock had strong sonic roots in the blues-inflected hard rock of the late 1960s yet developed along the experimental lines of psychedelic rock in the early 1970s, most especially in the bizarre costuming and stage performances of white British performers, like David Bowie, who flirted with androgyny and queer culture. Meanwhile, back in the United States, a new musical style was emerging from African American performers who blended rock with soul, jazz, and R&B. Called **funk**, this music privileges danceable rhythms and grooves created by deep bass lines. While Jimi Hendrix had an influence on this new style, James Brown is commonly understood as one of funk's greatest pioneers, as are Stevie Wonder and George Clinton, who performed with Parliament and Funkadelic. Sly and the Family Stone, the Isley Brothers, and the Ohio Players are important early funk groups also, and all, like Parliament, had an influence on rock music as well as disco. As with blues and hard rock, funk groups tended to be male-dominated and phallocentric in their approach to both lyrics and sound. (Funk lyrics are often sexually suggestive if not explicit.) Nevertheless, several female musicians and groups gained success in the funk genre, including Chaka Kahn of Rufus, Joyce Kennedy of Mother's Finest, and LaBelle.

As funk was taking off in the United States in the late 1960s, **reggae** was emerging in Jamaica from such forms as ska and rocksteady, both informed by rock music. Popular reggae artists of the 1970s included Peter Tosh, Bob Marley and the Wailers, and Toots and the Maytals. As with other forms of rock during this period, reggae groups commonly featured men, and female performers were often marginalized via the position of backup vocalist.

Heavy Metal

As white male rock bands with a heavier sound grew in number during the late 1960s, some eventually moved away from blues influences to form the genre of **heavy metal** (now commonly referred to simply as metal). Several American bands were influential in heavy metal's development, particularly later on, but it was British bands that led the way in the early years of this genre's formation. Deep Purple, Black Sabbath, and Led Zeppelin are typically noted as the pioneering bands of the late 1960s and early 1970s heavy metal scene. By this point in rock history, the role of musician was almost completely dominated by white males, as women and black musicians were excluded from rock and marginalized in other genres. In turn, by the late 1960s the electric guitar had achieved dominance in the soundscape of rock music.

Heavy metal music features a thick, "heavy" sound produced through considerable guitar distortion and volume as well as low bass notes, dense rhythmic patterns, and operatic-like vocals. Often this heavy sound is produced through the doubling or tripling of guitarists, bass players, or drummers on stage. "Excess" is the best adjective to describe the aesthetics of this genre. Influenced by blues rock strategies, heavy metal performances typically feature extensive guitar solos meant to highlight performers' technical virtuosity, though often metal guitarists and vocalists play off each other. As Chapter 8 will explore further, when such duos are composed of two men, they often complicate traditional notions of both gender and sexuality, particularly when one of the performers is effeminate or androgynous.

As rock music developed in the 1960s, the community increasingly privileged serious lyrics written by performers over lighter fare written by professional songwriters. As with the blues and many harder rock styles, sex is a prominent lyrical theme in heavy metal. Yet, as the genre expanded, other lyrical themes emerged, such as violence and the occult, which in turn have worked to separate metal from other rock genres. Many conservative adults have labeled these themes offensive if not immoral, and feminists have often derided metal for its masculinist lyrical content and sexist representation of women. Yet, as much as heavy metal songs have long affirmed an aggressive form of masculinity associated with heteronormative patriarchy, the genre has become home to a considerable number of women musicians, especially vocalists, as well as several all-female bands, including Vixen, Girlschool, and Kittie. The increasing presence of women in heavy metal since the 1980s signifies not only the pleasure some girls and women take in this genre but also the growth of feminist ideologies, such as gender equality and female power, in rock culture as a whole.

Over the past thirty years, heavy metal has spawned an extraordinary number of subgenres via experimentations with different sound aesthetics, lyrical themes, and performance strategies. The New Wave of British heavy metal, which emerged in the United Kingdom in the mid-1970s, helped to revive mainstream metal from its decline because of punk's popularity. Other metal subgenres include thrash metal, death metal, doom metal, black metal, and metalcore. Nu metal (also known as "rap metal") was a short-lived subgenre developed in the 1990s by such groups as Korn and Limp Bizkit, which were influenced strongly by gangsta rap and hip-hop culture. (In contrast to many other African-based popular music styles, like the blues and jazz, rap has had minimal influence on rock outside rapped lyrics. However, numerous rap DJs have sampled from rock songs.)

Much in line with working-class male values, the common attire for early heavy metal performers was typically denim jeans, T-shirts, leather jackets, and work boots, a look still popular among rockers of any genre. In the 1970s, some metal bands, particularly Alice Cooper and KISS, incorporated more spectacular costumes that were part of their elaborate stage shows. As heavy metal became more mainstream in the 1980s, largely because of exposure on MTV, some performers in Southern California adopted costuming strategies associated with glam rock to create a style known as **glam metal** or pop metal. Because many of these male musicians wore make-up, had long hair, and dressed in tight clothing and feminine accessories, they often looked feminine, which was an odd but provocative contrast to their machismo performances both on and off stage.

Heavy metal concerts have been among the most elaborate and expensive in rock culture to date. Many major-label bands have dramatic stage shows involving spectacular props and special effects as well as high-end lighting systems. Heavy metal fans—known as headbangers or metal heads—have predominantly been young, white, working-class males. Interestingly, more girls and women became interested in metal as both performers and fans during its glam period, and contemporary metal bands often have a significant female followings. Despite the influence of hip-hop since the 1980s and an increase in female metal acts since the 1990s, metal remains a predominantly white- and male-dominated rock genre whose performers and fans consistently privilege, or attempt to reaffirm, white heterosexual masculinity. In the late 1970s this phenomenon revealed itself not only through sexist representations of women but also in the "disco sucks" movement, a backlash against a form of dance music strongly associated with homosexuals, Latinos, and African Americans. Indeed, rock, and heavy metal especially, became even more dominated by white musicians and consumers in the late 1970s and 1980s because of disco's decline and hip-hop's increased popularity among young people of color. Although plenty of white youth listened to rap at that time, and a good number of black youth enjoyed rock, hip-hop's primary association with African Americans contributed further to rock's prevailing whiteness during this period and afterward.

Punk

Shortly after glam rock became popular in the early 1970s, **punk** (first known as punk rock) exploded on both the British and American rock scenes. To understand the rise of this particular music form, it is necessary to recognize how commercial and excessive rock culture had become by the mid-1970s. Many popular rock bands were playing in arena-size spaces (hence the term "arena rock"), and some, particularly those associated with **progressive (prog) rock**, were abandoning the traditional structure of rock songs and utilizing virtually all the technology at their disposal to create music that would be considered as artistically sophisticated and significant as art music. In other words, rock was no longer "small" music, and rock musicians had become increasingly isolated from their audiences because of excessive commodification, technical bravado, and performance strategies. None of that rang true for musicians who were struggling to make ends meet during the 1970s recession. Meanwhile, the hippie counterculture didn't seem to be providing answers for nonconformists any longer, and many disaffected youth were looking for cultural forms potentially expressive of their alienated identity and worldview. Angry about the world they were left in, punks rose to that challenge by revolting sonically, sartorially, and socially, collectively creating a shocking, provocative subcultural style few bystanders could ignore. Indeed, although the metal and glam genres emerged before punk rock and were similarly spectacular and geographically diffuse, punks developed the first music-oriented subculture to receive considerable attention by scholars.

The origins of punk are interestingly diverse, since the genre developed in both New York and London somewhat simultaneously. Strongly influenced by such groups as the Stooges and the New York Dolls, the first American acts to be labeled as punk were those associated with the Manhattan clubs CBGB and Max's Kansas City: Blondie, the Patti Smith Group, the Ramones, Talking Heads, Television, and Wayne County. Malcolm McLaren, then manager of the New York Dolls, saw great potential in the rebellious aesthetics of American punk culture and returned to London to open a clothing shop and manage new groups, including the Sex Pistols, perhaps the best known punk band of that era. Other bands affiliated with the early London punk scene include the Clash, the Damned, the Buzzcocks, the Slits, X-Ray Spex, and Generation X.

The sounds of these early British and American punk bands were quite different from each other. Indeed, while New York punk bands were influenced by surf rock, garage rock, and art rock, all of which emerged in the 1960s, many of the first British punk groups were influenced by ska and reggae. As punk grew in popularity and American and British bands influenced one another, certain aesthetic tendencies emerged. The aesthetics that came to be attached to the punk genre include short songs with minimal chord changes and an extremely fast tempo. Punk bands have relatively few members, musicians tend to use unsophisticated equipment, and there are few demonstrations of technical virtuosity. In privileging this "stripped down," amateurist style, punk musicians modeled themselves on garage bands and attempted to return rock to its original populist roots.

Punk lyrics, which often contain offensive language, are often shouted more than sung, making them difficult to interpret. By screaming their lyrics, female vocalists profoundly challenge hegemonic ideals of feminine appearance and performance. Avoiding the pop themes of romance and sex, punk songwriters frequently comment on political issues, thus making punk lyrics as confrontational as the sounds supporting them.

Punk performance strategies also attempt to be revolutionary. In privileging small clubs over big arenas, punk musicians are more readily capable of mingling with their audiences. In turn, many punk bands eschew the traditional proscenium stage set and play on the same level as their audiences. Those who do perform on conventional stages often encourage audience members to participate actively in the performance, either through stage diving and crowd surfing or through mosh or slam dancing (an aggressive, predominantly male form of dance performed immediately in front of a stage).

Early punk costuming for performances was quite similar to that associated with other hard rock forms—jeans, T-shirts, leather jackets, work boots, typically in black—and many punks today continue with this proletarian fashion style, often by shopping in thrift stores. Nevertheless, punk musicians and fans have developed many innovative approaches to dress, hairstyles, and make-up, some of which have been appropriated by musicians and fans associated with other rock genres, such as goth, which took punk in a darker direction. Ripped clothing held together with safety pins was fashionable among punks for awhile and, punks have made S/M bondage gear, once shocking, somewhat ubiquitous in contemporary rock culture. Meanwhile, the Mohawk—a Native American hairstyle wherein the sides of the head are shaved and the middle strip of hair is sprayed upright—became fashionable so quickly in punk culture that it now serves as a dominant signifier of punk culture, if not rock culture at large. In trying for a shocking look, punks have also gravitated toward bright hair dyes, piercings, and tattoos, all of which entered mainstream youth fashions by the late 1990s.

While many early punk bands, including the Sex Pistols, signed recording contracts with major labels, an anticorporatist spirit permeated the scene by the late 1970s, and musicians began to work with independent labels or to start their own during a phase now known as postpunk. This DIY ethos filtered out to audience members also, as numerous fans began publishing fanzines and some formed their own bands. While female musicians and fans were active members of the early U.S. and UK punk scenes from the start, the increased privileging of the DIY ethos and amateur aesthetics in punk culture since the late 1970s has encouraged many girls and women to become active cultural producers. The British punk scene was a more ethnically diverse demographic than American punk. (Nonwhite performers in bands like the Bad Brains, the Nuns, the Beatnigs, Tribe 8, and the Butchies remain anomalies and are sometimes called out as tokens of diversity to bolster arguments that American punk is neither racist nor dominated by white people.)

During the 1980s, as punk went further underground to avoid commercialization and censorship, its "hardcore" culture became male-dominated and misogynist, causing many girls and women to look elsewhere for entertainment and cultural politics. Since that time, punk has diversified greatly, helping to influence the development of numerous other rock genres, including **alternative** or **indie (independent) rock**. Some punk musicians, particularly those involved in Oi!, have continued to reaffirm the heterocentrist, white supremacist, and patriarchal traditions of rock culture and mainstream Western societies. However, other performers associated with more recent forms of punk, including **queercore** and **Riot Grrrl**, have pushed the genre's rebellious spirit in provocative new directions by actively subverting the binary sex/gender system.

Electronic Rock

Although the history of electronic music is over a century old, popular musicians have mostly used electronic technologies since the 1960s and the development of such technologies as the Mellotron, the tape playback machine, and the synthesizer, which allow for considerable more flexibility in sound frequency and pitch than conventional instruments. Nonetheless, with the broad proliferation, declining expense, and greater usability of digital technologies since the late 1990s, the use of synthesizers, samplers, mixers, drum machines, and computers has become increasingly prevalent in early-twenty-first-century popular music. In fact, professional and amateur musicians alike are actively involved in this trend. While professional performers often utilize several different interfaced digital technologies to produce music, even individuals with no training can create music today via inexpensive and user-friendly computer software packages, like Apple's GarageBand and Cakewalk's SONAR Home Studio.

Like other popular music forms, rock has been transformed by the early twenty-first century's digital wave. Contemporary performers and bands categorized as electronic rock (or one of its various subgenres) typically employ electronic and digital technologies (sometimes vintage) alongside traditional rock instruments, such as guitars. Additionally, such bands often incorporate a variety of musical genres in their sound and lyrical styles, including punk, industrial rock, hip-hop, techno, and synth-pop. Sometimes paying homage to their favorite electronic groups of previous decades, the electronic musicians performing such stylistic convergences have provocatively expanded the boundaries of what rock music can be while also helping to form new subgenres, such as indietronica, dancepunk, electroclash, new rave, post-punk revival, and post-rock. With regard to gender politics, it is worth noting that such performers have revived dance beats for rock culture, whose prevailing machismo in the late twentieth century led to the replacement of hippies' genderless freestyle grooving by male-dominated slamdancing and moshing. Such inhospitable dance styles have been especially problematic in rock culture for women and queer people who have long valued dance as a liberatory cultural practice.

Although often present, the guitar is somewhat deprivileged in electronic rock bands, and other instruments, including keyboards, synthesizers, and other electronic equipment, have a more prominent role. While many groups in this genre are influenced by punk's oppositional values, in contrast to most punk groups, electronic musicians reconfigure rock in the direction of pop and dance music, creating catchy melodic tunes and long, rhythmic runs through the practices of looping and sampling. In turn, lyrics are often minimized, and the voice is sometimes less a medium of verbal discourse than of sound exploration, particularly through the use of Auto-Tune and other electronic processors.

In the past ten years, electronic rock has become increasingly popular and thus more commodifiable. Yet many musicians affiliated with this genre are independent artists who, influenced by the DIY ethos associated with punk, self-produce and self-distribute their own music. The age-old problem of audience building for new acts continues for these performers also; however, self-distribution has been made much easier recently for musicians at large because of MP3s and the Internet. Yet for some electronic musicians, a computer laptop serves as their only equipment, as musical composition, performance, distribution, and promotion are all facilitated via one machine. In turn, for those fans of electronic rock who cannot attend live performances, the broad array of digital platforms for musical listening, blogging, and social networking allows them to participate actively in this community.

More important for the study of gender in rock culture is the significant involvement of women and queer musicians in the production of electronic rock and its various subgenres. In fact, several popular acts associated with electronic rock, including Stereolab, Le Tigre, Broadcast, Lady Tron, Peaches, and Grimes, prominently feature female and queer performers, often on vocals, keyboards, and synthesizers. While electronic music at large has been a male endeavor, the growing number of women musicians performing electronic rock can be understood in the larger context of popular music's democratization via the proliferation of inexpensive digital technologies. (Nevertheless, like most other forms of rock, electronic rock is predominantly produced and consumed by white people.) As noted, such equipment is read-ily accessible, and much of it can be learned somewhat easily even by those with minimal musical training. Moreover, unlike guitars and drums, the pri-mary instruments in traditional rock bands, keyboards are musical instru-ments to which girls and women have long had access. In turn, dance music, much of which is electronic, has a long history of female involvement and has been feminized as a result. It is important to note, however, that, in keeping with the traditions of popular music, many women performers in electronic rock bands occupy the role of vocalist, and, despite their adept use (and some-times manufacturing) of electronic instruments, their often hyperfeminine ethereal voices can work to reproduce the binary gender system that has long structured the sounds of popular music.

Perhaps because of the historic marginalization of women in rock, not to mention the long association of electronic music with men, it is no surprise that some women associated with electronic rock have voiced their femi-nist values in both lyrics and interviews, while also paying their respects to the female electronic musicians who came before them. (LeTigre is a prime example.) Yet some women musicians in this genre do not identify as femi-nist or see their art as specifically related to feminist politics. Nevertheless, as electronic musician and scholar Tara Rodgers argues, today's female elec-tronic musicians necessarily complicate the traditional gender politics of musical soundscapes as well as common notions of who has creative talent and technological savvy. Rodgers, who performs as Analog Tara, has worked with other female DJs, sound artists, and electronic musicians to form a sup-portive online community via her website pinknoises.com. While the efforts of Rodgers and other female electronic musicians have increased attention to women's talents in numerous musical genres, to a degree not seen since the heyday of Riot Grrrl and queercore, the greater involvement of female electronic musicians in contemporary rock culture has inspired a number of girl (and boy) fans to perform. With many of the tools for electronic music already at their fingertips, it is exciting to think what rock genres these young musicians will create and how their sounds and musical practices might con-tribute to the decay of rock's traditional gender politics.

Summary

Beginning with an overview of genre theory, this chapter has consid-ered the various functions genre has in music culture as well as the role gen-der plays in rock genres. Genre categories are difficult to pin down, since they are used by many different individuals and institutions and thus morph regu-larly. Nevertheless, studying such genres is important because they provide the primary frames of reference through which musicians and consumers under-stand themselves and each other. Indeed, each rock genre has developed in a sociohistorically specific music scene, and some have become so popular as to inspire subcultures stretching across the world.

Rock is typically categorized as a form of popular music. Therefore, it has been necessary to explore its difference from art music as well as its relation to other forms of popular music, especially pop, to which rock has been routinely opposed since the mid-1960s. Emerging from the convergence of both white and black American folk musics, the first rock genre—rock 'n' roll—blended country and R&B into a musical style that helped to subvert racial divisions in the United States. The lyrical, sonic, and performance styles associated with rock 'n' roll music, not to mention its fans, helped to define this genre as unique.

By paying close attention to the gender politics involved in four rock genres—rock 'n' roll, heavy metal, punk, and electronic rock—this chapter was able to explore how some musical styles affirm the traditional sex/gender system and how some challenge it. In turn, we traced the different roles females have played in rock's various musical cultures. And, to a lesser extent, we considered how whiteness has persisted in this culture, despite the significant role that African Americans had at its start. Chapter 6 begins a new part of this book that considers the creative context of rock musicianship.

Further Exploration

1. Consider your own listening preferences.

Which genre of music do you prefer? Why? How might this preference be related to your gender identity?

2. Make a visit to your favorite record store.

Make a note of the genre labels used to classify different forms of music, including different kinds of rock. Talk to the manager about her or his reasons for using these labels. (Check with your instructor first about your institution's guidelines for human subjects research.) Does the manager determine these labels, or does the store rely on an external system of classification?

3. Consider genres in your local music scene.

By perusing your local entertainment paper or talking with others in your community, determine the music genres most supported by popular bars and clubs. What might the pairing of venue and genre say about the possible clientele? If possible, talk to the venue manager about her or his reasons for supporting this particular musical genre. (Check with your instructor first about your institution's guidelines for human subjects research.)

4. Analyze a rock genre.

Moving beyond the genres discussed in this chapter, explore one rock genre by considering its particular sound, lyric, performance, and fandom. In turn, compare that genre to other genres discussed in this chapter.

Further Reading

Auslander, Philip. *Performing Glam Rock: Gender and Theatricality in Popular Music*. Ann Arbor: University of Michigan Press, 2006.

Charlton, Katherine. *Rock Music Styles: A History*. 7th ed. New York: McGraw-Hill, 2014.

Ennis, Philip H. *The Seventh Stream: The Emergence of Rocknroll in American Popular Music*. Hanover: Wesleyan University Press, 1992.

Fabbri, Franco. *Popular Music Perspectives*. David Horn and Philip Taggs, eds. Exeter: IASPM, 1982.

Frith, Simon. *Performing Rites: On the Value of Popular Music*. Cambridge: Harvard University Press, 1998.

Gottlieb, Joanne, and Gayle Wald. "Smells Like Teen Spirit: Riot Grrrls, Revolution and Women in Independent Rock." *Critical Matrix* 7.2 (1993): 11–43.

Hebdige, Dick. *Subculture: The Meaning of Style*. London: Methuen, 1979.

Holmes, Thom. *Electronic and Experimental Music: Technology, Music, and Culture*. 4th ed. New York: Routledge, 2012.

Laing, Dave. *One Chord Wonders: Power and Meaning in Punk Rock*. Milton Keynes: Open University Press, 1985.

Nault, Curran. *Queercore: Queer Punk Media Subculture*. New York: Routledge, 2017.

Negus, Keith. *Music Genres and Corporate Cultures*. New York: Routledge, 1999.

Rodgers, Tara, ed. *Pink Noises: Women on Electronic Music and Sound*. Durham: Duke University Press, 2010.

Sabin, Roger, ed. *Punk Rock: So What? The Cultural Legacy of Punk.* London: Routledge, 1999.

Stuessy, Joe, and Scott Lipscomb. *Rock and Roll: Its History and Stylistic Development.* 7th ed. Upper Saddle River: Pearson, 2012.

Vincent, Rickey. *Funk: The Music, the People, and the Rhythm of the One.* New York: Macmillan, 1996.

Walser, Robert. *Running with the Devil: Power, Gender, and Madness in Heavy Metal Music.* Hanover: Wesleyan University Press, 1993.

Weinstein, Deena. *Heavy Metal: A Cultural Sociology.* New York: Macmillan, 1991.

III

Rock's Creative Contexts

Training, Technology, Performance

6 IN THE BAND
Rock Musician Roles and Training

LISTEN: BRATMOBILE, "I'M IN the Band" (*Girls Get Busy*, Lookout, 2002). *As the musicians sweep us along with their raucous beat and put the lyrics into action, this song encourages us to value female involvement in rock bands and to reject discourse that discourages it.*

Although this book draws attention to numerous roles in rock culture, the role of **musician** (which encompasses both vocalists and instrumentalists) is key, since musicians perform the music at this culture's center. Throughout rock history, men have primarily occupied this important position and benefited the most from **cultural consecration**, or the process by which individuals achieve high public acclaim. Meanwhile, far fewer women have performed as rock musicians, and, when they do, they typically are not as celebrated as men. It is difficult to obtain objective data to substantiate these claims. Yet the historical imbalance of male and female rock musicians can be gleaned from music industry reports, such as *Billboard*'s sales and radio play charts. Another less arduous method involves examining the winners and nominees of prestigious music awards, such as the Grammys, which are presented in the United States by the National Academy of Recording Arts and Sciences. A quick glance at the list of musicians who have won or were nominated for Grammys in rock categories reveals a significantly unbalanced world with regard to rock musicians' gender.[1]

Most Grammy awards in the rock category have been won by at least one band with at least one female performer. Yet in *no* rock category have more than five acts with women won, despite some awards being over thirty years old. Moreover, no bands with female performers have won the "Best Rock Album" award since 1999, and no acts with women musicians have been nominated for it since 2004. In turn, no band with women performers was nominated for the "Best Rock Instrumental" award in its last fourteen years (1997–2011). Meanwhile, Bonnie Raitt is the only female performer to have won the "Best Solo Rock Vocal Performance" award, and she did so more than two decades ago (1992). More concerning, two rock awards—"Best Rock Performance" and "Best Heavy Metal Performance"—have had *no* women winners. And *not one* all-female band and *not one* solo woman artist has won in any of the Grammy rock categories.

When we step back and look at the larger picture, an even more troubling image of the Grammy's gender imbalance appears: Of the thousands of musicians who make up the 823 acts nominated for rock awards between 1980 and 2014, only thirteen women have won. That number represents only 0.8 percent of the total if each nominated band has on average only two members. That percentage drops to 0.5 if we consider that most rock bands have at least three members. The flip side of this picture is that of all musicians nominated for a Grammy award in a rock category, men have made up at least 99.2 percent. Yet the Grammys are not alone in this practice of gendered cultural consecration: It has happened elsewhere, including in popular reviews of rock music and histories of rock culture.

Rock has not always been dominated by male artists, including male instrumentalists. From the mid-1950s to the early 1960s, when rock 'n' roll was emerging, a considerable number of teenage girls and women musicians participated in shaping this unique style. Since the mid-1960s, however, there has been a comparative dearth of female rock musicians. Indeed, even with the broad diffusion of feminist ideologies during the late twentieth century, women still primarily occupy the role of consumer in rock culture, while the role of musician continues to be filled predominantly by men. This chapter explores the reasons behind this phenomenon by considering the gendered nature of musical roles and access to rock musicianship, as well as training for rock music performance. Chapter 7 considers these issues via a specific focus on the gendering of rock instruments.

Access to Rock Musicianship

To understand why there have been so few women rock musicians to date and why males have dominated this position for so long, we must first consider which people have the most access to this role. Economics plays a major role here, as one's socioeconomic status determines how much disposable income can be spent on rock instruments, as well as the amount of time one has to play them. Moreover, the equipment used for performing rock music—traditionally, electric guitars and basses, drum sets, and amplifiers—has historically been more expensive than that required for many other cultural activities, such as sports. While aspiring rock performers often borrow or rent instruments when they are first learning to play, as musicians' skills improve and they participate in public performances, instrument ownership is expected. In addition, rock musicians need space to practice their instruments, rehearse their performances, and store their equipment, as well as transportation to and from rehearsals and gigs.

If rock musicians want to gain legitimacy for their practices, they must record their music, and sound reproduction always requires expenditures above and beyond the equipment used in rock performances. Recording an album usually involves leasing recording space and equipment, paying sound engineers, reproducing the recording, contracting with a distributor, and packaging and promoting the final product. Thus, being a rock musician, particularly a *recording* rock musician, can be costly, and this reality has prevented many individuals from having access to this role.

Beyond these material constraints, several other factors impact an individual's access to the role of rock musician, including identity. Younger musicians are especially at a disadvantage when it comes to the skills, equipment, space, and transportation needed to perform and record rock music. Ethnicity and race also play a role. As discussed in Chapter 5, many early rock 'n' roll musicians were African American. Nevertheless, with the recording industry's interest since the late 1950s in exploiting this music as a commercial product, white performers have been consistently privileged in rock culture, just as African American performers have been marginalized in the "black genres" of R&B, blues, and jazz. Since the 1980s, the association of rock music with white culture has been further solidified by rap's association with racial minorities, particularly black people. As a result, many young people of color are disinterested in rock music. At the same time, however, it is important to note that as rock culture has spread globally, rock's traditional racial and ethnic connotations have been negotiated differently in countries where white people are not in the majority.

Age and race are not the only components of identity that impact access to the role of rock musician, however. Gender is also a primary determinant of such access. Indeed, there is no other way to explain the vast disparity between the number of males and females occupying the position of musician in rock culture, for just as the role of musical performer is not linked inherently with a particular race, nor is it tied to a specific gender. In turn, although rock instruments have long been designed with male musicians in mind, women are just as physically capable of performing (and composing) rock music as men. Nevertheless, female musicians, especially instrumentalists, have historically been few and marginalized in rock culture. Therefore, we must look elsewhere to discover why women do not gain more access and success as rock musicians.

Cultural Tastes and Practices

If there are no physical, intellectual, or creative requirements for rock musicianship that preclude women's involvement, then we need to examine how men's domination of this activity has been socially produced and perpetuated in various sites in and beyond rock culture. To start, we might consider the types of cultural practice historically linked to males and females as a result of the sex/

gender system. Because gender norms in patriarchal societies suggest that men are supposed to occupy the public sphere and to demonstrate in it such qualities as mastery, confidence, and technical skill to affirm their masculinity, their entitlement to and occupation of the role of rock musician have rarely been questioned. In contrast, prior to the late twentieth century most women, out of others' fears about their not achieving femininity, were discouraged from displaying such traits, except with regard to domestic tasks and physical beautification. Because rock has been so closely aligned with masculinity, girls' involvement in it as musicians has meant risking their gender identities and thus their sexuality identities. Enid Williams of Girlschool calls attention to how the traditional rock musician lifestyle has been off-putting to many girls who value heterosexual femininity and aspire to traditional family life: "I think if a young girl reads something [about] that she's gonna think, . . . 'I want a boyfriend and I want kids. And no man's gonna want me if I'm travelling around all the time.'"[2]

Another factor we might consider is how adolescents' cultural tastes are gendered and thus impact their different levels of access to the role of rock musician. On the one hand boys are often encouraged to seek out loud, aggressive forms of popular music, such as rap and rock, as a means of affirming their masculinity. On the other hand girls are encouraged to find pop music more suitable for displaying their feminine identity, and they typically avoid louder, harder music, especially during early adolescence, a crucial time for the formation of both cultural tastes and musical skills. As a result of boys' greater exposure to rock music as music consumers, they often feel more entitled to participate in rock culture than girls do and can be suspicious when females cross this gendered musical boundary. As Samantha Maloney recalls, "I never thought there would be a problem for a girl to play drums but when I first started in Shift, my friends overheard some kid saying we couldn't possibly be hardcore with a girl drummer."[3] Even with women's greater access to the public sphere and traditionally masculine characteristics, as well as the broad diffusion of feminist ideologies, girls are still discouraged from aspiring to be rock musicians. Thus, other factors besides the traditional gendering of cultural tastes and practices must be at play in the historical male domination of the role of rock musician.

Role Models

Another significant factor in girls' historical disinterest in performing rock music is the dearth of female **role models**. As a result of the patriarchal ideologies and sexist practices that have structured rock culture, relatively few women have had careers as rock performers, and even fewer have received enough attention from the recording and other media industries to be considered acclaimed musicians. Yet, as Mary Ann Clawson argues, the lack of female role models alone cannot explain girls' historically low involvement in rock musicianship. While listening to the music of assertive, talented women rock musicians can be inspiring, it is usually not enough to motivate a girl to learn an instrument, write music, and form a band. Nevertheless, the dearth of female role models certainly has been a factor in girls' wariness of engaging in this type of performance, particularly in public. Without knowledge that other girls have successfully transgressed the gendered barriers of rock musicianship, aspiring female rock performers likely feel isolated and unsupported in their practices, often losing interest after only a short while. Thus, Debbie Smith of Echobelly highlights the need for connection with other women who are transgressing rock's gendered musician roles when she recalls hearing female rock bands in the 1980s and thinking "there are women in those groups who can play guitar, bass, drums. Right. I can do it as well."[4] Some women rockers thus embrace the position of role model. As Nina Gordon of Veruca Salt asserts, "if we look down and see one little 16-year-old girl looking up who is totally into it, then everything else is worth it."[5]

The media have played a significant role in exacerbating female rock performers' feelings of isolation. For example, women rock musicians have had a historically difficult time getting their music played on the radio, a phenomenon that has contributed to the male dominance of MTV and other music-related television programs. The patriarchy and sexism of the airwaves has long persisted in print and other audiovisual media as well. For example, as will be discussed in Chapter 11, male rock performers have historically dominated the content of magazines produced for rock musicians, such as *Guitar Player*. Histories and encyclopedias devoted to rock—most of which have been written by men—predominantly feature male musicians also. In turn, far more fictional and documentary films have featured male rock groups than those with women.

This is not to say that girls necessarily need female role models to look up to; many women rock musicians have credited men as their mentors. (Conversely, only a few male performers, including Mick Jagger and Kurt Cobain, have credited women rockers as important role models.) Nonetheless, given the relative absence of female performers in media sites that should call attention to their presence, it is not surprising that girls have little knowledge of the history of women's involvement in rock culture and thus do not see it as a realm welcoming or supportive of their gender. Thus, while there have long been women brave enough to transgress the gendered barriers to rock musicianship, they have always been exceptions to the thousands more who do not feel confident enough, talented enough, or assertive enough to engage in this historically male-dominated arena.

Skill Acquisition

Research demonstrates that historically girls have been more active and successful than boys in most school-based music programs. Yet female youth are at a disadvantage when it comes to learning to be a rock musician. As noted, this phenomenon is not related to any lack of physical, intellectual, or creative capability on the part of girls. Therefore, as Clawson argues, we must look also to the processes of skill acquisition to understand why so many female youth are disinterested in being rock musicians as well as to comprehend the various challenges faced by girls who do want to perform this music.

A key component of Clawson's argument is that in the musical style of rock, the band, not the individual musician, is the central **performing unit**. Traditionally rock bands have been made up of one or more guitarists, a bass guitarist, and a drummer. Most rock musicians learn to play during adolescence, on their own outside traditional educational programs, and by copying the sounds of recorded rock bands. Yet, as these musicians' skills improve, they will typically become dissatisfied that they, as individual performers, are incapable of replicating all the sounds of the bands they seek to emulate. At this point, most aspiring rock musicians turn to their preexisting friendship groups to form an ensemble that can produce conventional rock band sounds.

Historically, adolescent friendship groups have been homosocial, as parents, teachers, and other adult authority figures have discouraged social events where heterosexual activity among youth might occur. Girls have been socialized to form friendship groups around traditional feminine activities, such as shopping, beauty makeovers, and pop music fandom, whereas boys have been encouraged to bond over traditionally masculine pursuits, particularly those involving technology and physical activity. Boys-only friendship groups, therefore, serve as perfect training grounds for young males interested in learning rock instruments. Since girls have traditionally had limited access to boys' friendship groups, their chances for gaining access to rock music training have been constrained also. In turn, those girls who want to perform rock music sometimes have a difficult time finding other female musicians with similar tastes who want to form a band. As Jody Bleyle of Team Dresch recalls: "I didn't think I'd ever find any girls that would want to play the way I wanted to play."[6]

Since gender politics have changed considerably since the time Clawson's survey respondents were teenagers (i.e., the late 1970s and early 1980s), her theory that the male dominance of teenage rock bands can be explained by sex segregation during adolescence is somewhat problematic when applied to contemporary youth. Today many boys and girls have coed friendship groups, and a considerable number of female youth pursue activities once deemed unfeminine, such as sports. Indeed, many girls today do not ascribe to traditional gender norms, and anecdotal evidence suggests that those girls have a somewhat easier time learning to play rock instruments and joining rock bands. A recent ad for Skyla IUDs seems created especially for young women wanting to focus on developing their musical skills rather than having a family (see Figure 6.1). Nevertheless, adolescent rock bands continue to be dominated by boys. Determining why this gendered pattern persists requires analysis of the gender dynamics that have been privileged in adolescent male friendship groups and thus rock bands.

Figure 6.1   Skyla IUD advertisement
Bayer, 2016

Clawson, having interviewed numerous male and female rock musicians, has made a convincing argument for how bands formed by adolescent males operate as cultural sites where masculinity can be easily reaffirmed. Rock bands have historically privileged the use of band names connoting power, the playing of loud, discordant music, and the perfection of aggressive, space-occupying performance styles. Hence, boys who engage in such practices are typically perceived as masculine. In turn, as Mavis Bayton observes, rock relies on the use of somewhat complicated mechanical and electrical technologies that are themselves overloaded with masculine connotation. Rock has been an excellent space, therefore, for the rehearsal of masculinity by boys who are not interested in traditionally masculine forms of recreation, like sports. Moreover, adolescent rock musicianship typically happens outside the realm of adult supervision and thus can serve as a site for rebellion against authority, another characteristic that bolsters rock's masculine connotation. Girls who are invested in affirming their femininity have a difficult time negotiating these gender dynamics and frequently have little interest in participating in adolescent rock bands.

We can add to Clawson's argument by noting that rock bands have historically developed a particular form of camaraderie associated with males and masculinity because of its privileging of technical jargon, sharing of subcultural capital, or insider knowledge, and, often, its reproduction of sexist and homophobic discourse. Since these practices are encouraged in boys from an early age so that they can display their heterosexuality and membership in the male sex category, most boys are well-trained in such masculine performances long before they learn to play rock instruments and form bands. Girls who might want to participate in such groups are at a disadvantage, however, since the practices in which female youth are encouraged to engage and the knowledge that they are urged to accumulate are primarily associated with beauty, fashion, and the domestic realm. Moreover, when girls, particularly those in their preteen to early teen years, form friendships around a common interest in music, it is typically via pop fandom, not the performance of rock music. Given its historical connections to femininity, pop helps to affirm girls' normative gender identity, whereas the adoption of rock's rebellious masculinity makes them suspect with regard to both gender and sexuality.

In addition, girls typically have less disposable income and leisure time to spend on cultural activities in comparison to boys. Indeed, as a result of their gender and training for the future roles of wife and mother, girls are more often bound to the domestic sphere and thus have fewer opportunities to engage in recreational practices outside the home, such as band practice. For poor girls, this is especially true, as, with both parents working outside the home to support a family, female youth are often called on to help with domestic tasks and have little time for leisure activities.

Another factor to consider in girls' limited presence in adolescent rock bands is the gendered process of psychological development. As many feminist researchers have demonstrated, this process affects teenage girls quite differently from their male peers, leading many female youth to lose confidence in themselves during adolescence. Struggling against low self-esteem and a lack of confidence in their skills and knowledge, girls often distance themselves from practices that they cannot perform well, particularly those traditionally associated with males, like performing rock music. It is no surprise, therefore, that many adolescent girls who play rock instruments devalue their talent and demonstrate a cavalier perspective in developing their skills. Commonly describing their musical practices as "just playing around," Clawson observes that most young women do not commit to identifying as rock musicians and joining bands until their early twenties, when the angst-ridden days of adolescence are behind them and young men of comparable age are less invested in proving their masculinity and more amenable to having female bandmates. (Many male rock musicians continue to privilege masculinist forms of camaraderie well into their adult years, however, thus unconsciously excluding women performers from their friendship networks and bands.)

Although Clawson focuses on the adolescent rock band as the central site for skill acquisition, girls are discouraged from being rock musicians in several other ways. For instance, while many parents give boys guitars and drums as gifts, a considerable number of parents are less inclined to encourage girls to play rock music, as a result of their attempts to properly socialize their daughters with regard to gender. Teachers also contribute to the gendered musical interests of youth by relying on the sex/gender system to select instruments for students and to compose the formation of school bands. Band instructors often encourage girls to play small instruments that produce soft sounds, such as flutes and violins, while boys are steered toward large and loud instruments, like drums and horns. Many young people carry the gendered connotations of classical instruments and music over to the popular music styles in which they engage outside school.

While Clawson's research focuses on the negative effects of rock's gender politics on girls' interests in learning rock instruments and forming bands, Mavis Bayton takes a more positive approach in highlighting the various factors that contribute to women seizing the role and lifestyle of rock musician. In particular, she foregrounds the important role parents, especially musician parents, play in encouraging their children's musical aspirations. For example, Jennifer Bishop of Tampasm recalls: "I used to sit there with my dad and listen to him play the guitar. . . . I think that if he hadn't encouraged me to play the guitar and said 'bands are good fun and if you want to do that you should,' then I don't think I would have been in a band."[7] Parents can be supportive of young rock musicians by renting or purchasing equipment and by providing rehearsal space and transportation. In addition to arguing for more exposure to role models, Bayton offers several other factors that can encourage aspiring female rock musicians, including a background in classical music and other arts; the freedom of college life; gender and sexual nonconformity; and feminist values. We could also add: education in the history of rock, particularly women's involvement; engagement in an entrepreneurial youth culture, like punk; interaction with professional female musicians; and support from the larger rock community, including equipment retailers, booking agents, venue owners, and disc jockeys. As discussed below, all of these factors can help to enliven and sustain girls' engagement in a cultural practice that has long been off limits to members of their gender.

Musician Roles

Once a young person becomes involved in rock culture, even if only as an amateur, other gendered constraints can appear. Two primary sites for the persistence of traditional gender norms in rock culture are the roles associated with rock musicianship: **vocalist** and **instrumentalist**. In Western music cultures, girls and women have historically been confined to the role of vocalist, while boys and men have dominated the role of instrumentalist. This phenomenon has persisted for many decades in popular music forms like rock, despite women's greater access to musical training and instruments during the last two decades. As Mary Genis of Dread Warlock observes, "I don't think enough women organize themselves beyond singing and dancing . . . because that's their role. We're all role-playing. So the women sing and dance and the men play the instruments."[8] Keyboardist Joy Askew concurs: "a female singer has a place, but if you're a female [instrumentalist] you're breaking into a special enclave."[9]

Feminist musicologist Lucy Green helps to explain the preponderance of female vocalists over female instrumentalists by noting women's problematic relationship to performance in public spaces. She explains performative forms of **display** by noting its similarity to wearing a mask: display both presents and protects the performer since it does not necessarily involve the presentation of a real person. Moreover, Green argues that performance is not an autonomous act but an exchange constructed between at least two individuals: a displayer and an onlooker. As a feminist music scholar, Green is particularly concerned with how display in musical performance is related to ideologies of gender and sexuality. As she notes, in heterosexual patriarchal societies, most forms of intentional, institutionalized displays of the body are associated with women, while most intentional, institutionalized forms of onlooking are performed by men. The gendered connotations of displayer and onlooker are further exacerbated via women being encouraged to privilege their appearance above all other components of their identity. As a result, women are understood as always already on display in our society, while men are configured primarily as onlookers. As Laura Mulvey argues, men look, and women embody "to-be-looked-at-ness." Women are encouraged to be the passive spectacles of men's active spectatorship.

A significant component of the traditional gender dynamics of intentional, institutionalized forms of display is that they are often linked to sexuality. In other words, it is commonly assumed that when women perform, it is for men's sexual arousal. This phenomenon is likely connected to the historical reality of public forms of female bodily display being related to prostitution. In traditional societies, wholesome women cover their bodies and remain indoors, preferably at home. As a result of the historical perpetuation of the sexualized connotations of women's public display, female performers of any kind (including musicians) are always at risk of being considered sexually alluring, even if they do not intend to occupy this position. In fact, they are doubly at risk because of their simultaneous occupation of the role of woman and performer. Many feminists see women's public display as potentially problematic because of its possible result in **sexual objectification**, a process that can limit their power by constructing them as objects to be used by others for sexual enjoyment rather than as subjects with thoughts, emotions, and agency.

According to Green, one of the reasons women have been allowed to occupy the role of vocalist is that it privileges the display of the body and thus affirms the woman's femininity. Moreover, the vocalist role often decreases the threat of the public female performer through its association with sexual objectification and thus reproduces patriarchal ideologies of gender and heterocentric ideologies of sexuality. In other words, by connecting female performance with heterosexual feminine gender display, the role of the vocalist allows the status quo to be maintained. Thus, women vocalists are still typically constructed as the passive, sexualized objects of men's active gaze, even though they perform in public and demonstrate skill. Perhaps because of the gendered and sexual connotation of the vocalist position, singers do not have as much respect in rock culture as instrumentalists do. As Genis argues, "no one takes a singer seriously,

. . . unless they're a big singer. As a musician [instrumentalist], you're treated a little bit more respectfully."[10]

Green delineates several other ways in which women's role as vocalist further affirms their femininity and reproduces heterocentric patriarchy. First, she reminds us that in patriarchal societies, men and masculinity have historically been associated with the mind, while women and femininity have often been connected to the body. Since female vocalists use their bodies (their voices) instead of technology as their musical instruments, they are less threatening to the status quo and male power. Indeed, a considerable number of male musicians devalue singing because they see it as a natural practice that anyone can perform rather than a skill requiring practice to perfect. Thus, as Clawson argues, women vocalists are doubly devalued in the musical world because of their simultaneous occupation of a subordinate gender and a subordinate musician role. Nevertheless, as Green reminds us, in the system of display, the displayer always has the power of the lure, controlling the viewers' gaze and pulling them into the performance. It is interesting to note, therefore, that female vocalists who are deemed physically attractive (i.e., those who have power over the heterosexual male gaze) are often deemed less skilled musically. In other words, such women's agency is confined to only one realm, that which positions them as object to the male subject and allows men to feel superior in the musical field.

Another reason Green notes for female vocalists' lack of threat to the patriarchal status quo is that, unlike instrumentalists, they do not rely on technology to produce musical sound. As noted, a singer's instrument is the voice, and technology comes into play only when amplification is necessary. Technology has long been gendered masculine because of men's development and uses of it, particularly for work and cultural practices. Therefore, men's technical competencies affirm their masculinity and power. Women, by contrast, are more commonly linked to nature and thus thought to be technophobic, despite the many tools historically used for female-dominated practices, such as housekeeping. Female vocalists are thus able to reaffirm their connection to traditional femininity through the absence of manufactured instrumentation and thus their distancing from the masculine world of technology. It should not be surprising, therefore, that the one musical style in which female performers are most present is pop, a form that, counter to rock, privileges vocalists over instrumentalists.

Women singers have not always affirmed their femininity and reproduced patriarchy through their occupation of the vocalist role, however. Twentieth-century popular music history is populated by women vocalists who have defied traditional gender norms and in so doing risked the subversion of their femininity. Some female singers have done this by exploiting their power to lure and control their audiences, thus refusing the position of sexual object and insisting on their right to sexual agency. The blues queens of the early twentieth century, like Bessie Smith, were well known for this, and more recent female singers, such as

Madonna and Beyoncé, have followed suit. In turn, some female vocalists have troubled the feminine connotation of singing by rejecting conventionally gendered singing styles. Here, we might consider the primal screams of Yoko Ono and female hard rock performers, like Kat Bjelland of Babes in Toyland, or the quavering voice of Sleater-Kinney's Corinne Tucker. Other female singers have used technology to alter their voices, Laurie Anderson being perhaps the best example in this regard. Still others have subverted the feminine connotation of their profession through their control of their images and careers. By establishing their own record labels, popular female vocalists like Queen Latifah have helped to problematize the notion of the woman singer as a passive sex object manipulated by men in the recording industry. Yet perhaps the best way that a female vocalist can distance herself from the marginalized and feminized position of vocalist is by playing an instrument (other than her voice), for, as noted, this practice has been overwhelmingly dominated by men and thus linked to masculinity throughout rock history.

This is not to say that occupying the position of instrumentalist is easy for women, for the sex/gender system has worked a long time to keep such technologies associated with men alone. For example, Tori Castellano of the Donnas reports: "we get asked all the time if we're really playing on the records."[11] In turn, Kim Shattuck of the Muffs states: "it's so typical that people think the girls write the lyrics and the boys write the music, like my little girl fingers can't press down on the guitar strings."[12] As a result of such sexist thinking, bassist Suzi Quatro, who has been performing since the mid-1960s, advises female rockers: "if you're going to play an instrument, you have to be better than the guys."[13]

For the same reasons that women's occupation of the role of vocalist typically affirms their adherence to femininity, men's avoidance of this role helps to construct them as masculine. Contemporary male artists often distance themselves from the accusations of femininity historically ascribed to musicians by investing instead, or simultaneously, in the role of instrumentalist, which historically has been linked to masculinity because of its association with agency and reliance on technology. As John Berger argues, a man's identity is specifically related to his ability to act, and, through action, his ability to display power. Rock instrumentalists typically do this by using musical technology to display their technical virtuosity. It is interesting to note, therefore, how male hard rock vocalists who have distinctly feminine performance styles—Mick Jagger, Robert Plant, and Steven Tyler, for example—often bolster their masculinity by teaming with a male guitar virtuoso, in these cases Keith Richards, Jimmy Page, and Joe Perry respectively.

Yet not all musical instruments, and thus not all instrumentalists, connote masculinity. For example, many of the instruments associated with classical music, especially woodwinds and string instruments, produce soft sounds traditionally linked with femininity. Thus, it is no surprise that girls have long had considerable access to such instruments. In contrast, boys often limit their musical interests to a different range of instruments, engaging primarily with those that produce heavy, aggressive sounds and thus can help to affirm their masculinity, such as horns and drums. As a musical style that privileges loud, discordant music made by electronic, amplified instruments, rock allows boys to display their masculinity in ways that classical music often does not. Meanwhile, female musicians' investments in rock are somewhat problematic in societies where the sex/gender system still dominates. Indeed, if a girl demonstrates an interest in learning to play a musical instrument, more often than not she is encouraged to invest in one associated with classical music rather than those that are electronic and used to produce popular music. (See Chapter 7 for more discussion of gender and rock instruments.)

Another factor to consider with regard to women's involvement in instrumentalist roles is the type of rock music they play. For instance, punk is a rock style that, despite some of masculinist elements, has rebelled against the sexually virulent and technically virtuosic form of musicianship privileged in many older forms of rock, such as heavy metal. Many females without musical training have been encouraged by punk's privileging of musical amateurism and thus have experienced punk culture as supportive of their involvement as instrumentalists. As Jennifer Lynch of L7 recalls, "when I was young I remember seeing Mick Jagger's wife. Then I got into punk music, and I started wanting to be Mick Jagger, not his girlfriend. It became an option [for women] to be Mick Jagger."[14] Since the 1970s, punk's rebellious spirit has strongly informed rock culture at large, helping to give rise to the subgenre of rock music commonly referred to as indie rock because of its anticorporatist ethos. Other forms of oppositional politics and cultural practices, such as those associated with feminism and queerness, are far more supported in indie rock's countercultural scene than in other forms of rock, thus contributing to male musicians' greater comfort with and inclusion of female instrumentalists. Indeed, over 31 percent of the acts nominated for the "Best Alternative Album" award include at least one female member, by far the best statistic for women rock musicians in the history of the Grammys, even if it demonstrates the continued male dominance of all forms of rock music.

Support Systems for Female Rock Musicians

When considered collectively, the gendered barriers discussed above help to explain the minimal number of women musicians (and thus the preponderance of male performers) over rock culture's long history. For if girls are discouraged from liking loud music, playing electronic instruments, developing friendships with boys, committing to musicianship, joining bands, and obtaining and exchanging technical knowledge and subcultural capital related to rock culture, how in the world do any of them get up the nerve to pick up an instrument or a microphone, much less perform publicly or make a record?

Unfortunately, a strong support system for aspiring girl musicians does not yet exist, and its absence has contributed also to the widespread lack of girls' interest in being rock musicians. Since the mid-1980s, however, numerous women have made concerted efforts at the local, national, and international levels to create a more solid infrastructure for galvanizing and sustaining female interest and engagement in rock musicianship. For example, more women radio disc jockeys are on the air today than ever before, and those interested in female-driven rock have insisted on including such music in their playlists. Commercial stations have been less open to this change because the work of male rock musicians typically attracts more advertiser revenue. Yet many female DJs at independent and public stations who have more control over their musical selections have launched their own women-only programs, thus helping to promote women rock musicians well outside their local scenes. In addition, several magazines and websites have been designed specifically for women performers, including *Rockrgrl Magazine*, *Women Who Rock*, *Tom Tom*, and *She Shreds* (see Figure 6.2). Such media texts are important for spreading the word about women rock performers, since, despite their genderless titles, traditional rock musician magazines, like *Guitar Player* and *Modern Drummer*, are anything but gender-neutral. Men have historically dominated such texts, even when women serve on the magazines' editorial and writing staffs.

Unfortunately, the movie business has only rarely demonstrated interest in making fictional films about women rock musicians. *The Rose* (1979), *Prey for Rock and Roll* (2003), *The Runaways* (2010), and *Ricki and the Flash* (2015) are notable exceptions, yet they all feature troubled female artists. Since the early 1980s, however, several independent documentarians have focused their lenses on women rock musicians in such films as *Girls Bite Back* (1980), *Girl Groups: The Story of a Sound* (1983), *Women in Rock* (1986), *In 1993 Bikini Kill Toured the UK. It Changed My Life.* (1993), *Girl Groups: The Story of a Sound* (1994), *Not Bad for a Girl* (1995), *The Righteous Babes* (1998), *Kiss My Grits: The Herstory of Women in Punk and Hard Rock* (2001), *Welcome to the Club: The Women of Rockabilly* (2002), *Rise Above: The Tribe 8 Documentary* (2003), and *The Punk Singer* (2013). Once difficult to find in video stores, such films are more readily accessible today via Netflix, YouTube, and other online venues.

Another significant initiative to raise people's consciousness about women rock musicians are the female-centered rock histories that have been published in recent years, including Gillian Gaar's *She's a Rebel* and Lucy O'Brien's *She Bop*, as well as *Trouble Girls: The Rolling Stone Book of Women in Rock*, edited by Barbara O'Dair. Such books have radically rebalanced male-dominated accounts of rock history, foregrounding multiple generations of women musicians who can be used as role models for aspiring performers. And, as with the radio shows, magazines, and movies mentioned above, such books' women-centered perspective demonstrates not only the diffusion of cultural feminist

Figure 6.2 *She Shreds* 11

She Shreds, 2016

ideologies but also the necessity for separatist forms of media for women in the context of rock culture's ongoing patriarchy and sexism.

Several women have created camps and workshops with the goals of instilling in girls more interest in performing rock music and providing them with the instruments, facilities, knowledge, and support they need to engage fully and often in rock performance. Largely as a result of their own experiences of patriarchy and sexism when they were aspiring musicians, June Millington (of the 1970s all-female rock band Fanny) and her partner Ann Hackler founded the Institute for the Musical Arts (IMA) in 1986 in Bodega, California, to provide women with more access to and confidence in performing music. In 2003, IMA relocated to Goshen, Massachusetts, and a year later established its Rock & Roll Camp for Girls. At these summer camps, girls have access to musical instruments, as well as performance and recording facilities, and are mentored in musical performance and recording by experienced women musicians and sound technicians. Though modeled in part on summer rock camps designed by men for teenage boys, IMA's camp has roots also in girls-only schools, which are designed with the understanding that female youth are disadvantaged as a result of their gender and thus need supportive mentors and communities that can facilitate girls' confidence in historically male-dominated practices without worrying about what boys think of them.

Rock 'n' Roll High School (RnRHS), located in Melbourne, Australia, was launched in 1990 and was in operation for eleven years. The school was the brainchild of Stephanie Bourke, a musician and musical instructor who wanted to provide girls with a supportive space for learning to be confident and accomplished rock musicians. Taking its name from a Ramones' song and run as a collective of women impassioned about rock, the school facilitated over two thousand musicians' development in performance as well as such professional practices as recording, booking tours, and signing record deals. Key to the promotion of RnRHS and its students were the school's compilation recordings, which attracted the attention of several U.S. rock acts that visited the school when touring Australia, including L7, Fugazi, Rancid, and Sonic Youth. Several of the schools' students achieved commercial success, including Brody Dalle of the Distillers and Spinnerette.

Riot Grrrl, a punk feminist community that emerged in the early 1990s, has also facilitated girls' interest and engagement with rock musicianship. Inspired by the DIY philosophy that grounds punk and other forms of countercultural production, Riot Grrrl created an informal network for young female musicians interested in independent music. In the spirit of feminist collaboration, mentoring, and training, Riot Grrrl conventions and Ladyfest festivals (a spinoff) have organized workshops for aspiring musicians on performing and purchasing musical equipment, as well as other practices related to recording and distribution.

In 2000, Misty McElroy created the Rock 'n' Roll Camp for Girls in Portland, Oregon. She was inspired to start the camp because of her experience of rock culture's patriarchy and sexism, as well as the success of other women-led grassroots initiatives, such as battered women's shelters and Ladyfest. Understanding rock as a genre of rebellion and expression, McElroy founded the Rock 'n' Roll Camp for Girls to enliven girls' interest in rock music and to facilitate collaboration between girl campers and women role models. Taking its mission one step further than IMA or RnRHS, the Portland camp also offers girls' training in self-defense so as to improve their overall confidence, assertiveness, and self-esteem, characteristics sorely lacking in female adolescents. The phenomenal success of the Rock 'n' Roll Camp for Girls over its first three years inspired the staff to launch the Girls Rock Institute, which now provides year-round classes and private lessons in rock musicianship for female youth aged ten to eighteen. Arne Johnson and Shane King's documentary *Girls Rock!* (2007), about the Portland camp, has inspired numerous parents, teachers, and activists to get involved in training girls and women in musical performance.

Since the Rock 'n' Roll Camp for Girls was introduced, several other girls-only music workshops and camps have sprung up around the United States and beyond. At the time of this writing, twenty-four rock camps for girls were operational in the United States alone. Girl-centered rock camps have been introduced also in Canada, Sweden, Germany, and the United Kingdom in recent years, thus leading to the formation of the international Girls Rock Camp Alliance, which helps to coordinate efforts among all these camps. Since 2014, funding for the Alliance and member camps has come from the Girls Rock Camp Foundation, which has such notable advisory board members as Beth Ditto, Kathleen Hanna, and Tegan and Sarah. Several camps have organized workshops for women, recognizing that many of the barriers girls face when wanting to learn to play rock do not disappear with age. Indeed, adult women often have additional challenges as a result of the prevalence of ageism and the ethos of youthfulness in rock culture, as well as the greater support shown to younger females in this realm.

Some women involved in rock culture have attempted to offer cheap, accessible guidance for girls and women interested in becoming instrumentalists, particularly for those who live outside urban areas, where more training and mentoring can be found. For example, since in the mid-1990s several zines focused on this topic have been published, including *Girls Guide to Touring* and *Girls Guide to Making a Band and a Record*. Hoping to reach a larger audience, the Portland Rock 'n' Roll Camp for Girls published the book *Rock 'n' Roll Camp for Girls: How to Start a Band, Write Songs, Record an Album, and Rock Out!!* (see Figure 6.3). Since the broad penetration of digital media technologies, several women have developed websites, like girlmusician.com and femalemusician.com, as means for supporting and disseminating more information to girls and women interested in performing rock music.

In turn, Tish Ciravolo, founder of Daisy Rock Girl Guitars, has worked with Alfred Publishing since 2002 to produce several guidebooks that teach girls basic guitar methods. Since such books are addressed to girls, they are more

Figure 6.3 *Rock 'n' Roll Camp for Girls*
Chronicle Books, 2008

inviting than traditional guitar guidebooks, which have long been written by and for males. Daisy Rock Girl Guitar's guidebooks, like the zines and websites cited above, are especially important for female youth who have no access to lessons or an informal learning community (see Figure 6.4).

Most of the initiatives noted above have been introduced only in the past decade. Therefore, we have yet to see any demonstrable effects of these endeavors on girls' music-making, particularly in terms of recordings (although some camps have released compilations from their students). Nevertheless, as this infrastructure becomes more solid and expands further, it is likely that we will witness the increased presence of numerous girls and women who feel confident and supported in their roles as rock musicians.

Figure 6.4   *Girl's Guitar Method Complete*
Alfred Music, 2007

Summary

With this chapter we began our exploration of the gender dynamics of the creative context in which rock musicians work and perform. Specifically, we have examined the different levels of access that males and females have to rock musicianship and the various reasons women have historically been marginalized or excluded from this practice while men have felt entitled to it. The processes of rock musicians' skill acquisition and band formation were also explored so as to understand better the difficulties females face in this male-dominated realm. Although women have been rock musicians since the earliest days of this musical form, they have largely been confined to the position of singer. To understand this conundrum, we have considered the primary roles that rock musicians occupy, specifically vocalist and instrumentalist, and the reasons so few women have been played instruments in rock bands.

Since the early 1990s, many women have developed support systems to encourage girls' interest and participation in rock musicianship. Through an exploration of the various components involved in this support system, we can realize better the many challenges girls face in learning rock instruments and feeling legitimate as performers in rock culture. Chapter 7 will take a closer look at the various instruments rock musicians use and the way gender politics impact male and female access to and engagement with such technology.

Further Exploration

1. Watch Time Warner's *The History of Rock 'n' Roll,* part 7, "Guitar Heroes" (1995).

Discuss the gender dynamics of rock guitar playing as represented in the film. How many male guitarists are interviewed? How many women guitarists are interviewed? Do the featured guitarists share any similarities with regard to their identity? How do the guitarists describe their relationships to their guitars? What different performance styles of guitar playing are represented in the film? Does the film affirm or refute theories of the electric guitar as a phallic device?

2. Watch the documentary film *Women in Rock* (1985).

How many musicians in the film are vocalists? How many of the musicians in the film play instruments? What problems do women discuss with regard to playing instruments? Have the gender dynamics of rock instrument playing changed since the mid-1980s, when this film was made? If so, how? If not, why not?

3. Watch the documentary film *Girls Rock!* (2008).

What are some of the issues the film raises with regard to girls' learning to perform rock music? Are any of these issues specific to vocalists? To instrumentalists? What other skills besides music are girls learning at rock camps? Why? What kinds of girls enroll in girls' rock camps? How would you describe the intergenerational relationships at the camp?

4. Analyze a youth music camp.

If a music camp for youth exists in your town, explore the gender dynamics of the staff, teachers, and students. (Be sure to check with your own instructor first about your institution's guidelines for human subjects research.) How many are female? How many are male? If the camp is centered on only one gender of students, why? What kind of musician roles do most boys take on in the camp? What kind do most girls take on? What genre of music is most privileged by the camp's teachers and students? How does the camp advertise itself, and what might that have to do with the students who enroll?

5. Learn to play a musical instrument.

Determine what instrument you would like to play and find someone who can help you to learn it. You might also use online videos to help with your instruction. Consider what draws you to this instrument (e.g., sound, size) and what you find pleasurable about playing it. Also consider what you or others might find troublesome about it. Reflect on how those qualities relate to gender politics.

6. Form a band.

Gather a group of friends who are interested in forming a band. Consider the type of music you want to perform and determine which musical role each of you will play. Reflect on how those decisions might be impacted by gender politics. Once you begin performing, switch roles so that each of you can experience the pleasures and challenges of different roles in the band, including songwriter. What did you learn from this experience?

Further Reading

Bayton, Mavis. *Frock Rock: Women Performing Popular Music.* New York: Oxford University Press, 1998.

Clawson, Mary Ann. "Masculinity and Skill Acquisition in the Adolescent Rock Band." *Popular Music* 18.1 (1999): 99–114.

Clawson, Mary Ann. "'Not Just the Girl Singer': Women and Voice in Rock Bands." *Negotiating at the Margins: The Gendered Discourses of Power and Resistance*. Eds. Sue Fisher and Kathy Davis. New Brunswick: Rutgers University Press, 1993. 235–54.

Cohen, Sara. "Men Making a Scene: Rock Music and the Production of Gender." *Sexing the Groove: Popular Music and Gender*. Ed. Sheila Whiteley. New York: Routledge, 1997. 17–36.

Cohen, Sara. *Rock Culture in Liverpool: Popular Music in the Making*. Oxford: Clarendon Press, 1991.

Gaar, Gillian G. *She's a Rebel: The History of Women in Rock & Roll*. Seattle: Seal Press, 1992.

Green, Lucy. *Music, Gender, Education*. Cambridge: Cambridge University Press, 1997.

O'Brien, Lucy. *She Bop II: The Definitive History of Women in Rock, Pop and Soul*. New York: Continuum, 2002.

O'Dair, Barbara, ed. *Trouble Girls: The Rolling Stone Book of Women in Rock*. New York: Random House, 1997.

Schippers, Mimi. *Rockin' out of the Box: Gender Maneuvering in Alternative Hard Rock*. New Brunswick: Rutgers University Press, 2002.

Whiteley, Sheila. *Women and Popular Music: Sexuality, Identity and Subjectivity*. New York: Routledge, 2000.

7 GEARING UP
Rock Technology

LISTEN: PRINCE, "GUITAR" (*PLANET EARTH*, Columbia, 2007). *At the center of this song's lyrics, sound, and music video is the instrument for which rock music and this artist are best known. Just as the song's solo reveals the musician's passion for his instrument, its lyrics play on the relational dynamics that can result from excessive involvement in gearhead culture.*

Technologies, those objects that are purposefully created and used to complete a task, are central to the performance of music. While musicians use parts of their bodies, particularly their voices and hands, to create music, few rock musicians perform without additional technologies, such as musical instruments and amplification systems. In rock culture, many musicians describe their unique sound by referencing specific musical gear. Thus, an examination of the various instruments and other equipment used to make rock music is essential for understanding this particular form of popular music. Such an analysis can also reveal the cultural values that are important in rock culture, including in terms of identity.

How rock technologies are designed, manufactured, purchased, and utilized has considerable bearing on the various meanings associated with the identities of those who play them, not to mention the music itself. Yet, despite this significant relationship, few scholars of either music or technology have studied musical equipment from the perspective of identity politics. This chapter's objective is to examine how gender politics impact the design and use of musical instruments and other technologies used to create rock music. Particular attention is given to the electric guitar, which is highly privileged in the rock sound and has become the icon for this type of music and rock culture at large. Also addressed are the gender politics of rock's "gearhead" culture, which has been developed by individuals passionate about using, buying, and collecting instruments. Key to such discussions is the possible impact of rock's gendered gear on the individuals who buy, use, and converse about it, as well as those with whom they associate within and beyond rock culture.

Given this chapter's focus on musical instruments, its content is closely related to other parts of this book, including Chapter 6, which focuses on rock musicians' training, and Chapter 9, which explores rock's musical sounds. The technologized practices of those individuals in rock culture who are not musicians are discussed elsewhere in this book. Specifically, record engineering is analyzed in Chapter 4 as part of a larger discussion about the recording industry's various practices, whereas sound engineering is examined in Chapter 8, which focuses on rock performance. Finally, phonographs, radios, MP3 files, and other technologies for listening to rock music are explored in Chapter 13, which is about rock consumers.

As is made clear by this book's breadth of discussions of gear and equipment-driven activities, rock is very much a technologized culture, born in part of transformations in musical instrumentation, amplification, recording, distribution, and consumption during the mid-twentieth century. Yet rock's technologized culture is also in constant development because of ongoing advancements in instruments and other forms of musical gear.

Gender and Gear

Musical instruments are among the broad array of technologies developed and used by humans in our everyday work and recreational practices. Although such tools are designed and manufactured for specific purposes during specific moments and in specific locations, they necessarily accrue social meanings apart from their creation and utilization for a particular practice. In turn, as technology scholars have demonstrated, tools are never neutral with regard to power, since tools require resources to produce, access, and use. Moreover, technologies are meant to increase the abilities of the person using them and thus that person's control over the environment. In particular, feminist researchers have argued that normative gender politics have been inscribed into many technologies and, as a result, have limited the types of people deemed appropriate for their use and further development.

In Western culture, men have historically been in control of the design, if not the manufacturing, of musical instruments. (Women's small and nimble fingers are commonly understood as useful for the construction of instruments.) Nevertheless, not all instruments have accrued a masculine connotation as a result of their design by men. We must also consider the intended consumers of such instruments and how ideas about those consumers may enter into their particular design. For example, as scholars of psychology and music education have discovered, many individuals, including school band directors, understand woodwind and small string instruments, like violins, to be feminine and therefore most appropriate for females. This is likely because of such instruments' high pitch, which resembles that of a woman's voice, and minimal size and weight, which ostensibly makes them easier for women to manage. In contrast, brass, percussive, and larger string instruments, like the stand-up bass, are commonly gendered masculine as a result of their low pitch and/or heavy weight and thus often deemed best for males.

Unlike instruments used in classical/art music, most rock instruments are amplified via electrical technologies to produce a loud and heavy sound that will carry over people talking and other noise. Hence, when analyzing the relation of gender and rock instruments, it is important to consider the gender connotations that have accrued to the broader realm of electrical technologies and not just instruments. As feminist technology scholars have demonstrated, electric (and mechanical) technologies have long been understood as masculine. Indeed, when the term "technology" is raised, many people think first of the electrified and mechanized equipment used by men for work, including weapons, factory machines, scientific apparatuses, and tools for building. The masculinizing of these technologies has resulted primarily from men's historical dominance of their invention, design, and use. Yet another reason for such gendering is that such tools allow human beings to manipulate and control nature to a considerable degree. As a result, such gear connotes mastery and power, characteristics historically ascribed to men.

Of course, women have invented and employed numerous technologies also. Yet for most of human history, most women's work was unpaid, confined to the domestic sphere, and thus devalued. As a result, women's tools and technical knowledge have been excluded or marginalized in discussions about technology, which have focused primarily on the electrical and mechanical gear created by men and associated with men's labor. While ignoring how gender politics have impacted technological invention and use, researchers have historically paid less attention to tools utilized by women, such as those used for cooking, cleaning, sewing, and grooming.

The masculinization of most electrical and mechanical technologies has had considerable influence on young people's gender socialization, as the use or nonuse of such gear can readily establish a child as either masculine or feminine. For example, many adults encourage boys to find mechanical and electrical gadgets exciting and to engage with them regularly in play. Learning to dismantle, repair, and reconstruct such items as radios and bicycles supposedly prepares boys for adult male work while also conferring on them a masculine identity. In contrast, girls have historically been taught to avoid electrical and mechanical technologies unless they can be employed for such "feminine" purposes as housework, beautification, and managing relationships. Moreover, girls are rarely encouraged by adults to tinker with gear or to learn to repair it, even if women are the primary users of that technology. Girls' avoidance of mechanical and electrical gear works to establish them as nonmasculine, or feminine, as well as technophobic. Socioeconomic status impinges on gender identity, however, and therefore such practices of socialization do not always ensure normative results. For example, working-class women have long used mechanical and electrical technologies because of their participation in farming and factory work. Meanwhile, upper-class men have traditionally avoided the use of heavy mechanical gear, except as it relates to leisure (e.g., boats, airplanes).

The increase in women in the paid labor force since the mid-twentieth century and thus the amount of female exposure to once masculinized technologies has somewhat subverted the historical patterns of gendering such equipment as masculine. In turn, the broad spread of digital media technologies, such as personal computers and mobile devices, since the 1990s has also complicated the traditional gendering of gear. Indeed, women have become heavy users of digital technologies, especially those involving communication and social networking.

Nevertheless, the masculinization of some electrical and mechanical technologies continues to be affirmed and reproduced in many contemporary sites of work and recreation. This includes popular music cultures, like rock, where such gear is highly valued. In rock culture, the primary technical objects inscribed with masculine connotations are the instruments used to perform music. This phenomenon has contributed not just to men's historical dominance of such technology and the musical positions it supports (e.g., guitarist) but also to women's avoidance of both. In fact, even with an increase in female rock musicians since the 1990s, most women who want to perform rock today sing rather than play an instrument. Thus, via the social meanings attached to technology, the role of rock instrumentalist remains naturalized as masculine, and the number of contemporary all-female rock bands remains quite low.

Rock Instruments

Historically, the primary instruments used by rock musicians have been electric guitars, drum kits, electric bass guitars ("basses"), and microphones. These are not all the instruments used to perform rock, of course. Many early rock 'n' roll acts included keyboards and brass instruments, and numerous rock artists today utilize digital technologies to produce their music. Nevertheless, the three-instrument grouping described above remains conventional in rock bands to this day. Despite this small number of instruments, rock bands are able to produce considerable volume as a result of the amplification of such equipment. (The number of instruments in rock bands is somewhat related to the genre of rock performed. For example, progressive rock groups privileged a broad array of instruments to produce more complex soundscapes, while punk bands have championed a "less is more" motto with regard to gear.)

Before such instruments were used to make rock music, the guitar, drum, and bass acquired gender connotations that are worthy of exploration, for they have had a direct impact on which people have interest in and feel legitimate using these technologies and which do not. Moreover, the gendered meanings associated with rock's primary instruments have contributed significantly to the genders associated with specific musician roles and to the overall gendering of rock music and its culture. In this chapter we will explore each of rock's primary instruments and the gendered associations that have accrued to these technologies. (Chapter 9 explores the sounds produced by these various instruments.)

Drums

The **drum** is part of the **percussion section** of a rock band and is classifiable as a **membranophone**, a technology that produces sound via a vibrating membrane. Although drums have been used as a form of long-distance communication, they are primarily understood as musical instruments. Indeed, they are the oldest form of musical instrument. Drums create rhythm, an essential ingredient of music.

The drum's various parts include a hollow body or "shell" (either natural, such as a gourd, or manufactured, typically from wood and as a cylindrical object), a thin membrane or "skin" stretched over one or both ends of the shell, rims (which hold the skin taut to the body), and tension rods. Drum sounds are produced by striking the skin with some type of object, usually a hand or stick. A drum's tension rods ("lugs") can be adjusted so that the skin produces different tones. The shape and size of the shell and the object used for striking also affect the tone produced by the membrane.

While orchestras typically include several drummers and **cymbal** players, rock bands rarely have more than one drummer. Therefore, most rock drummers use a **drum kit**, which includes a collection of various drums and cymbals. Because of their compact amalgamation of percussive instruments, drum kits allow a single individual to produce a great deal of sound in a small amount of space, an economic issue important to most rock musicians.

When used to perform rock music, drum kits usually include a minimum of three drums: a **bass drum**, a **snare drum**, and a **tom-tom**. The bass drum is large and two-headed; it produces a low, powerful pitch. Also called the "kick drum," the bass drum is played via a foot pedal. The snare drum is also two-headed but includes a set of wires or cables ("snares") that create a distinct, rattling sound when vibrating. Tom-toms, which produce a midrange pitch, can be stand-alone floor units or attached to the bass drum. Rock kits typically incorporate three styles of cymbals also: the **crash cymbal**, a single metal plate used for punctuating specific moments; the **ride cymbal**, a single plate used primarily for rhythm; and the **hi-hat**, which is played via a foot pedal and consists of two plates mounted on top of one another.

Drums were affiliated primarily with women in many premodern societies as a result of women's common association with nature's rhythms, particularly menstrual cycles but also those of the sun, moon, and seasons. Moreover, in the ancient civilizations of Rome, Greece, Egypt, and India, drumming was a sacred practice performed by women during healing, religious, and agricultural ceremonies.

In modern Western societies, men have been the primary professional players of drums. Perhaps a result, many people assume (incorrectly) that brute strength is required to produce sound via these instruments. Indeed, not using too much force is an early lesson for beginning drummers. Nevertheless, the drum has taken on connotations of power and masculinity in Western cultures. Important to consider here is the bodily stance and movement of drummers using kits. As someone who is required to play numerous individual instruments at one time, the drummer strikes a pose of mastery even when seated. Together with the display of sweat and arm muscles, not to mention the loud noises such instruments produce, these characteristics align drumming with machismo, a gender performance assumed to be inaccessible for women. As Janet Weiss, drummer for Sleater-Kinney and Wild Flag, notes, being loud and aggressive "are crucial in the drummer's world—they cannot and should not be avoided."[1] It is no surprise, therefore, that in most popular musical cultures, including rock, drumming is a masculinized practice associated primarily with men.

The masculinization of drums has resulted in many girls being disinterested in playing these instruments, including in rock culture. Indeed, many adults simply assume girls' disinterest. As Kate of Luscious Jackson remembers: "I took piano lessons when I was four or five years old, and I remember sitting in the waiting room and these little boys had drumsticks and were banging away on a table. I was like, 'God, no one asked me if I wanted to do that!'"[2] Moreover, as percussionist Zaneta Sykes comments, "many girls aspiring to play drums will be discouraged from playing percussion and if they do continue, will face gender discrimination."[3] Drummer Helene Stapinski of Stephonic recalls not being taken seriously early on, especially by males: "when I was in high school I would say I played the drums and the boys would laugh at me. It was sort of a joke. . . . As a female, you really undergo scrutiny when you're playing drums. . . A girly girl would not want to play the drums."[4]

Gendered ideas about drums and drummers have contributed to men's continued dominance of the drummer position in rock bands, as well as broader notions about drumming as a male activity. In addition, such ideas have contributed to women drummers' marginalization if not exclusion from rock discourse. In fact, in most lists of rock's best drummers the only artists mentioned are men (e.g., John Bonham of Led Zeppelin, Keith Moon of the Who, Stewart Copeland of the Police). In contrast, notable female rock drummers—such as Sheila E., Maureen (Moe) Tucker of the Velvet Underground, Meg White of the White Stripes, Georgia Hubley of Yo La Tengo, and Cindy Blackman, who has played with many rock musicians, including Lenny Kravitz—are typically ghettoized in lists devoted solely to women musicians, where they are compared only to members of their own gender rather than men. Recent initiatives, like the introduction of *Tom Tom Magazine*, which is devoted to women drummers, and MoMA PS1's recent exhibit on the oral history of female drummers, are drawing more public attention to women who drum in an effort to further legitimize and honor them as well as to inspire and support aspiring girl drummers.

Electric Guitars

Because of its unique tones, the **electric guitar** is the most privileged instrument in rock music, which is likely one of the reasons this instrument is the primary symbol of rock culture. In rock music, electric guitars are responsible for performing melody as well as producing rhythm. **Lead guitarists** typically play a song's melody along with the lead vocalist. Rock's lead guitarists are often more dominant on stage than **rhythm guitarists**, who help (along with the drummer and bass guitarist) to produce a song's pace. In rock bands with more than one guitarist, these roles are often interchangeable, even in the same song.

Although electric guitars are less than one hundred years old, the **acoustic guitar** has a much longer history. Strummed and plucked instruments were made and used thousands of years ago. What we know as the modern guitar is a descendant of both the Persian *chartar* and the Spanish *guitarra*. Guitars consist of several parts, including the body, the neck, and the headstock (all typically made of wood), as well as strings (nylon or steel). Acoustic guitars always have hollow bodies, while electric guitar bodies can be hollow, semihollow, or solid. Strings are attached to the guitar's headstock via tuning keys or machine heads and to the body via the bridge. The top of the guitar neck is called a **fretboard** and contains metal strips (**frets**) at specific intervals that divide the scale length of the strings. Most guitars are six-string instruments; however, some models have twelve strings.

Typically, a guitar player's dominant hand plucks or strums the strings, while the nondominant hand holds the neck and depresses strings. When a string is played, pressure from the player's fingers forces that string to come into contact with a fret. This connection produces a vibration, which travels down the string and is amplified by the body of the guitar, if acoustic, or by pickups, if electric. (**Pickups** capture the vibrations produced by fretted strings and convert them into electrical signals heard via an amplifier.) The pitch produced by such vibrations is determined by the fret played and thus the scale length of that particular string.

Acoustic guitars are able to produce sound on their own. In contrast, electric guitars are usually connected to amplifiers that enable their players to create and manage tone. (Acoustic guitars can be amplified via the addition of microphones and/or pickups.) **Amplifiers** magnify the volume of guitar sounds, and they can also change the tone of such sounds through manipulation of various signals. In addition, the tone of an amplified guitar can be altered via a **whammy bar** (or Bigsby), which produces a vibrato effect, as well as via **effects pedals**, which create fuzz, reverberation, or distortion.

Few scholars have performed a gender analysis of electric guitar design and use. However, Mavis Bayton has noted the difficulties women have in playing this instrument because of its historic design by and for men. In particular, she discusses how large-breasted females find the flat backs of most guitars uncomfortable when playing. Yet Bayton does not address the typical complaints women have about the male-oriented design of most guitars: their necks are too thick, scales too long, and bodies too large and heavy for most women to use comfortably. Since the mid-twentieth century, several guitar manufacturers have designed smaller models for young novices, but most girls have found the design of even these student guitars to be based on gendered assumptions about their users' size and strength. In addition to weight and shape being a deterrent for many potential female players, Bayton notes that regular electric guitar playing also requires women to relinquish some of the physical characteristics conventionally associated with female bodies, particularly soft hands and long fingernails.

The guitar's traditional figure-eight shape helps to produce both low- and high-end tones while also allowing the instrument to rest comfortably on the player's thigh when seated. Although neither of these functions is gendered, the guitar's figure-eight design is understood by many people to be an abstract

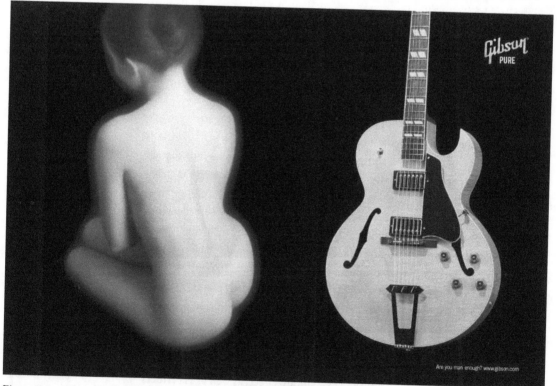

Figure 7.1 Gibson Pure advertisement
Gibson Guitar Corporation, 2001

Figure 7.2 Gibson Pure advertisement
Gibson Guitar Corporation, 2001

representation of a woman's body. This belief is evident in a broad array of images that compare women's bodies to those of guitars (for example, see Figures 7.1 and 7.2). The association of guitars and women's bodies by guitar makers (luthiers) has been noted also. As a result of this association, which can be understood as a form of women's **objectification**, some feminists feel uneasy about guitars, particularly as used by male guitarists to perform music conventionally associated with sexism and misogyny, like heavy metal.

Many male guitarists have challenged this guitar-as-woman perspective by arguing that the guitar functions as an extension of their male bodies rather than as a gynopomorphized object, as Paul Stanley of KISS and Slash from Guns 'n' Roses do in Time-Life's video series *The History of Rock 'n' Roll*. Pete Townshend of the Who has stated that during the late 1960s the electric guitar functioned for him like a weapon, a tool he could use to challenge the establishment. Other male guitarists, such as Les Paul, report that their guitars function for them like a friend or therapist.

Some music scholars have argued that the electric guitar connotes masculinity because of its common use by rock guitarists as a **phallic device**. As Bayton notes, some male rock guitarists use the electric guitar in a way that conflates their musical skills with their sexual skills, either via pseudomasturbatory behavior or stroking the guitar as if it were a woman. Although Bayton does not say so explicitly, this particular form of gendering and eroticizing the electric guitar has roots in R&B culture and is associated today primarily with hard rock, a musical style whose sonic and performative aesthetics of power were developed in the late 1960s via virtuosic male guitarists, like Jimi Hendrix and Jimmy Page of Led Zeppelin. Indeed, because of such hard rock guitarists' frequent sexualized use of their instruments—as well as their onstage accompaniment by vocalists singing sexually explicit lyrics and their offstage accompaniment by young women with whom they had primarily sexual relationships—the musical style they helped to create is often referred to as "cock rock."

Steve Waksman problematizes Bayton's theory of the electric guitar's signification of virulent masculinity by noting that phallic devices (first theorized by Sigmund Freud) are typically used when the power of their users is *not* assured and therefore needs to be produced through artificial means. By extending the male body beyond its physiological boundaries through electrical technology, and thus increasing the power (sexual and otherwise) that is symbolically affiliated with that body, the electric guitar functions as what Waksman calls a **technophallus**. (We might apply this theory to basses and drum kits also.) Masculine power is further attributed to electric guitars via the other electronic components that are commonly attached to them, particularly amplifiers, which are used in rock to increase both volume and distortion.

Thus, according to Waksman's thinking (which aligns with that of gender theorist Judith Butler), females as well as males have access to the power connoted by the electric guitar. Several female rock guitarists have discussed their instruments in just that way. As Janet Wygal, guitarist for Splendora, recalls, "I used to watch my brothers load up a van with their rock gear and just take off! I *knew* I had to get some of that for myself, and to this day I still plug in a guitar for that power and freedom they gave me a glimpse of. . . . I never thought wanting it was weird."[5] Yet as Erin Smith of Bratmobile suggests, many girls are put off of guitar playing by the virtuosic performances of male musicians regularly celebrated in rock culture: "I never thought I could play guitar because I thought you had to be perfect as well as male."[6] Other female rock guitarists have helped to demystify guitar playing as a difficult art form, thereby challenging the notion that only men can play this instrument well. For instance, Ivy Rorschach of the Cramps argues: "guitar-playing's not hard. . . . I don't know why guitar-playing is considered a masculine art, except it's just been appropriated that way. It doesn't require any great strength or male brain pattern."[7] As Andy Bennett argues, many male guitarists performing indie rock have worked against the phallic performance style of heavy metal guitar players by adopting a somewhat static pose on stage. And since the late 1970s, the masculinization of virtuosic guitar playing has been challenged by such talented female rock guitarists as Bonnie Raitt, Lita Ford, Nancy Wilson, and Carrie Brownstein. More recently, a new generation of virtuosic female **shredders**—including Orianthi

Panagaris, Marnie Stern, Marissa Paternoster of the Screaming Females, and Tara McLeod of Kittie—has been celebrated in rock culture, especially by the women-run magazine *She Shreds*.

While girls' rock camps have provided a supportive training ground for aspiring female musicians, musical instrument manufacturers have also contributed to the support system necessary for facilitating female guitar playing. For example, in 1996 Fender introduced as part of its Signature Series the first guitar line named after a woman musician, Bonnie Raitt. Four years later rock musician Tish Ciravolo founded Daisy Rock Girl Guitars so as to attract more girls to this historically masculinized instrument. The company's catalog includes acoustic, acoustic-electric, and electric guitars (as well as basses) in a variety of colors and styles that extend the company's "girly" aesthetic (see Figure 7.3).

In 2005, Yvonne de Villiers founded Luna Guitars, a manufacturer of guitars designed specifically for women's bodies and tastes. And female rock musician St. Vincent has recently teamed with manufacturer Ernie Ball to produce a signature line of guitars that are lighter and more comfortable for any player. Not to be shut out of the potential profit to be made by the increased popularity of electric guitar playing among women, several popular but historically male-oriented instrument manufacturers, including Epiphone and Gibson, have recently begun producing electric guitars for female players, often via superficial elements, like paint color. While the "pinking up" of such electric guitars may encourage more girls to purchase guitars, it remains to be seen whether

Figure 7.3   Daisy Rock Girl Guitars logo
Daisy Rock Girl Guitars

this design strategy can sustain their interest in playing this instrument and the musical genre with which it is most associated.

Electric Bass Guitars

Like the drums, the **electric bass guitar** is a key component of every rock band's rhythm section. Derived from the much larger and heavier **upright bass** used in classical/art music and other popular musics, the electric bass is similar in design to other stringed instruments, especially the electric guitar: It consists of a body, headstock, strings, neck, and fretboard, and its sound is produced by the electrical currents that are carried from fretted strings to pickups and then managed and released via amplifiers. The key differences between the designs of the electric bass and the electric guitar are: the former has only four strings, while the latter typically has six; the overall scale of the former is greater than that of the latter; and the strings of the former are usually played via plucking or tapping, whereas the strings of the latter are typically strummed with a pick. The electric bass also produces lower pitches than the electric guitar, thus rounding out the overall musical tones produced by rock bands.

The electric bass has traditionally had a masculine connotation as a result of its dominant use by men, its derivation from the upright bass (which requires strength to hold and play), its relationship to electrical technology, and its similarity to the electric guitar. In turn, many male bassists hold the instrument lower than a guitar, which may be read as phallic. Nevertheless, the masculinizing of the electric bass is not as strong as that of the electric guitar, perhaps because the former is not as privileged in rock culture.

Prior to the 1990s, it would have been difficult for most rock fans to mention any female bassist other than Tina Weymouth of Talking Heads. Yet, as a result of more women occupying the role of bassist over the last two decades, the masculinizing of the electric bass has become increasingly unstable in rock culture. Women's increased involvement in rock bands as bassists can be explained in part by the perceived ease by which this instrument is learned and played. With only four strings, the bass allows aspiring musicians to learn it more quickly than a guitar. This factor is important for girls, who tend to learn rock instrumentation on their own and join bands much later than males. As bassist Ellen Berkshire argues, "I think for women starting out, maybe they think it is going to be easier and so they can learn faster so they can be in the band quicker."[8] In turn, Sue Garner notes, that as a bassist, "you're in the back and are keeping things under control, you're not in the spotlight. It's not like you have to be the [obnoxious] lead guitar player doodling around."[9]

Moreover, because the bass requires less skill to perform adequately than the guitar or drums, it is often the least privileged component of a rock ensemble, and some rock musicians consider the bass the instrument of failed guitarists. Because the bass has been increasingly devalued among male rock musicians over the last twenty years, there has been an excess of vacant bassist positions in rock culture that many aspiring female musicians have gladly filled. Interestingly, this phenomenon has contributed to the emasculation of the bass guitar, resulting in a Catch-22 situation wherein male rock musicians invested in machismo avoid the bass, which in turn contributes to women's increased access to it and thus the instrument's further feminization. Such feminizing of the electric bass has been exacerbated somewhat by the production of short-scale and lighter basses for female performers by instrument manufacturers, like Luna and Daisy Rock Girl Guitars.

Although many feminists have celebrated women's greater presence as bass players, it is important to consider how the current feminization of the bass guitarist position might work to ghettoize female rock musicians by simultaneously encouraging their disinterest in the traditionally masculinized roles of guitarist and drummer. Indeed, rather than concluding that female rock bassists challenge traditional gender norms, researcher Mary Ann Clawson discovered that many of these musicians see the bass as an instrument especially well suited for women because of its function as timekeeper and the necessarily collaborative role it plays in rock bands. While this rationale might serve a strategic function in terms of claiming more space for women instrumentalists in rock's historically male-dominated creative culture, it may nevertheless reproduce the sex/gender system that restricts males to masculine traits and practices and females to those that are feminine.

Microphones

Most people consider vocalists to be musicians but not instrumentalists, because the tool they use to perform, their voice, is embodied and therefore unlike musical instruments. Nevertheless, the voice can be considered an instrument or form of technology, because singers purposefully manipulate its sounds to create music. Yet rock, as an amplified and recorded form of music, requires its singers to be dependent also on nonbodily technologies, specifically amplifiers and **microphones**. The common but often unacknowledged practice in rock culture of not discussing the technologies used by vocalists might be attributed to singing's important function of communicating lyrics, which in rock culture are meant to be authentic expressions of sentiment and thought. According to this logic, the less technologized the communicator, the more authentic the message and form of communication. (This may be why rock vocalists rarely use audio processing devices, like Auto-Tune.) Nevertheless, to be heard over the din of the audience and at the same volume as the instruments being played, rock vocalists must be mic'ed during both live performances and recording sessions.

Microphones capture acoustic sounds (either natural or humanmade) and convert them into electrical signals. Such signals are transmitted to an amplifier, soundboard, and loudspeakers during live performances, or to a mixing console for recording purposes. Microphones come in many shapes and sizes due to their use in amplifying different sounds. Contemporary vocal microphones are designed to fit in and be easily manipulated by an adult hand. Thus, most are relatively short (six to eight inches) and thin (one to one and a half inches in diameter) and have a cylindrical shape similar to a cigar or phallus. This phallic design is interesting to consider alongside the conventionally feminized construction of the vocalist role and the masculinization of rock culture at large. Yet, as with all musical gear, the gendered meaning of the microphone is not predetermined by design but rather produced in the act of interpreting musical performances. For example, Angela McRobbie and Simon Frith have argued that the microphone becomes phallic when used by hard rock singers, like Robert Plant of Led Zeppelin, to create a sexualized aura around themselves and their music. Other rock vocalists, especially punks, like Lux Interior of the Cramps and Wendy O. Williams of the Plasmatics, have used mics in sexually suggestive ways meant to shock the audience. Still other rock singers, especially those in parody bands, have exploited the stereotypical presentation of the mic as phallus to poke fun at or undermine rock's sexualized machismo.

Electronic Instruments

As discussed in Chapter 4, digital technologies have radically changed music culture since the 1990s. That chapter explores such technologies' impact on record production, distribution, and promotion. Yet it is also important to consider how computers and electronic technologies have altered the performance of music. Electrical instruments, like electric guitars, use electricity as power, whereas electronic instruments, like synthesizers, utilize electricity as the medium to manipulate information.

The first electronic musical instruments were introduced in the early twentieth century. However, rock musicians did not embrace such instruments until the 1960s arrival of the theremin, which produces oscillating tones, the Mellotron, a tape replay keyboard, and the Moog **synthesizer**, a machine capable of producing and imitating a broad array of sounds. Many rock bands of the late 1960s and early 1970s were strongly influenced by these electronic technologies, and their popularity eventually resulted in the development of the progressive rock ("prog rock") genre. While punk musicians of the late 1970s called for a return to more basic forms of rock that avoid such high-tech gear, new wave groups of the 1980s commonly embraced electronic technologies as modern rock instruments.

Electronic music has become increasingly popular in the early twenty-first century, including in rock culture, likely due to people's greater access to and use of digital technologies in their everyday lives, from laptops and tablets to MP3 players and smartphones. Also key to consider in relation to the rise of electronic music is the wide availability of inexpensive composition software packages for personal computers. The most popular of these "soft-synth" programs is Apple's **GarageBand**, introduced in 2004. Less costly software applications, like GarageBand, allow those without access to or capital for traditional instruments to develop musical skills via just a computer. Such soft-synth programs are likely especially appealing to girls who might feel uncomfortable with the male-dominated spaces typically affiliated with rock music production.

Due to stereotypical assumptions about the relationship of gender and technology, the history of electronic instruments in rock culture has long highlighted male groups, like Kraftwerk, Pink Floyd, and Emerson, Lake & Palmer. Nevertheless, as Tara Rodgers's book and website *Pink Noises* demonstrates, many women have used electronic instruments to perform rock music. Laurie Anderson is commonly understood as a key pioneer, and contemporary female electronic artists, like Grimes and those in Le Tigre, Uh Huh Her, and Chicks on Speed, continue to push technological innovation within and outside rock culture while also challenging the historical masculinization of electronic technologies.

As long as rock continues to privilege authenticity and emphasize live performance as a signifier of musical legitimacy and quality, playing traditional instruments, like guitars and drums, will likely win out over playing those that are electronic. Yet we might consider how computers produce different forms of music and musicians and thus how young people raised with digital technologies are reimaging rock instruments, music, and culture.

Rock's Gearhead Culture

Because rock culture involves a form of musical production that relies on electrical equipment, it is one in which technical savvy dominates, particularly among musicians. As suggested by Prince's song "Guitar," many rock performers are passionate aficionados of the technologies used to create this music and spend a great deal of time becoming knowledgeable about and purchasing such instruments. If money allows, a smaller group collects such gear. These connoisseurs are often referred to collectively as **gearheads** and have developed a unique subculture within and beyond rock culture.

A good number of individuals learn to play rock music on borrowed or inexpensive instruments. As a rock musician's talent increases, their listening skills and thus sonic tastes often become further refined. As a result, low-end instruments, which usually have poor sound quality, are typically exchanged for more sophisticated and thus more expensive models. This is not to say that those people who own the most expensive and sophisticated instruments are necessarily great performers or that those who own the least expensive and unsophisticated are necessarily the worst. Access to considerable economic resources allows many poor players to have expensive gear, and plenty of talented musicians privilege "stripped down" instruments that they feel contribute to their authenticity as performers.

As with many other cultures centered on technology, rock's gearhead culture has a subgroup that is devoted to vintage instruments, amplifiers, and other musical gadgetry. As Trevor Pinch and David Reinecke argue, these gearheads participate in a particular form of "technonostalgia." Instrument manufacturers are aware of this group and have capitalized on its tastes through the creation and sale of **relic** instruments that are new but made to look old. The **lo-fi subculture** is also interesting with regard to vintage equipment, since its members value economy of scale in terms of musical performance and recording yet also privilege old equipment that is rarified and thus expensive. In contrast to gear-heavy major-label bands that play in large arenas, such as U2, lo-fi performers have few instruments, play small venues, often record at home, and oppose the "perfect" sounds produced by the latest digital technologies.

Because of the expense of collecting musical equipment, socioeconomic status impacts one's involvement in gearhead culture. Gender seems to be a dominant determinant also, although one infrequently noted in the culture itself. Like the gear-based cultures developed by fans of automobiles, motorcycles, computers, and home entertainment technologies, rock's gearhead culture is dominated by heterosexual men. Evidence of this common identity can be seen in gear-oriented discourse online. For example, Shark Inlay's "R U a Gearhead?" webpage includes several gender references revealing the presumption that gearheads are straight males: "if your wife refuses to have sex with you until you clear your guitars off the bed . . . and you have to stop and think about it—you might be a gearhead." (Most rock gearheads are also white, which is not surprising, given the historical dominance of rock culture by white people.)

The masculinization of rock's gearhead community can be attributed to technology's role in gender socialization. In addition to being encouraged by adults to play and tinker with electrical and mechanical gadgets, boys are urged from a young age to be conversant in technical jargon related to various sorts of gear and to utilize such discourse when socializing with other males. As Mavis Bayton and Sara Cohen have noted, male rock musicians often use gear jargon not only to assert their musical skills and knowledge but also to form their identities and to bond with each other. In the world of rock music production, men often employ such discourse—consciously and not—to marginalize or exclude women and to maintain male homosociality. Since most girls are not socialized to be interested in technical gear or jargon, those interested in playing rock are at a disadvantage in rock culture.

Rock gearheads primarily congregate to obtain information and exchange knowledge about gear in music stores, musician magazines, and, increasingly, online forums related to rock instruments, such as FenderForum.com and TheGearPage.net. As Paul Théberge argues, these various sites are dominated by males and historically masculine forms of camaraderie, creating environments that further perpetuate female disinterest and women's marginalization in rock culture. Despite the increase in women rock musicians in recent years, music shops and musician magazines rarely hire female employees, and women are often marginalized in online groups organized around discussions of rock gear. As Bayton's research demonstrates, instead of finding assistance and support in such spaces, girls and women often report being ignored, intimidated, and, sometimes, sexually harassed. For example, Melissa Bobbitt comments: "it drives me nuts that so many people *still* consider strong female musicians a novelty. It's especially bad in the retail sector, where buying a pedal can be as intimidating as getting a major overhaul on your car. If you can't talk the talk, you'll get walked on."[10]

Musician magazines also tend to perpetuate stereotypical assumptions about men's and women's technical knowledge via editorial content and advertisements. Journalists routinely ask male rock musicians to comment on their instruments and other musical equipment. For example, guitarist Steve Hillage of Gong was asked by Anil Prasad of *Guitar Player* the following questions: "Why is the Steinberger GL2T ideal for all your projects?" "What are your other guitars?" "How do you create your classic glissando sound today?" "What amp modeling settings are you using?"[11] Male-oriented musician magazines further promote the idea of male musicians' interest in and familiarity with instruments and other musical equipment via advertisements and editorial photographs that feature such gear or depict performers actively engaging with it.

With few female artists included in musician magazines, little opportunity exists for them to discuss their use and interest in musical equipment. When women rock musicians are featured in magazines, many journalists seem to assume that they have no interest in gear and therefore rarely ask them about it. Even female-oriented musician magazines, which regularly feature women with musical instruments, often do not show such performers playing such gear. For example, of the first eighteen covers of *Tom Tom Magazine*, only three show women drumming. Of the first six covers of *She Shreds*, just two depict women with guitars, only one of whom is playing her instrument. Instrument manufacturers often perpetuate this trend via their advertisements. For instance, a 2004 advertisement for Daisy Rock Girl Guitars features Ann and Nancy Wilson of Heart holding rather than playing guitars. An ad from the same company, featured in *Guitar Players'* 2011 women-centered publication "Guts and Glitter" shows Vicki Peterson of the Bangles passively holding a guitar.

As Chapters 11 and 12 will discuss, when women are depicted in male-oriented magazines and other promotional material focused on rock instruments, they are more often represented as the sexually objectified "bonus" items that men ostensibly acquire along with their purchase of such equipment rather than as musicians. Nowhere is this more evident perhaps than in *Guitar World*'s annual "Buyer's Guide" (see Figure 7.4). Such sexually objectified portrayals serve to downplay, marginalize, and delegitimize women's presence as rock instrumentalists while also bolstering the sense that gearhead culture is a boys-only club. Although plenty of women rock musicians are interested in musical equipment, just like their male peers, and some instrument manufacturers, like Daisy Rock Girl Guitars, are helping to facilitate female access to gear, female rockers have not yet developed a broad gearhead subculture of their own around rock technologies.

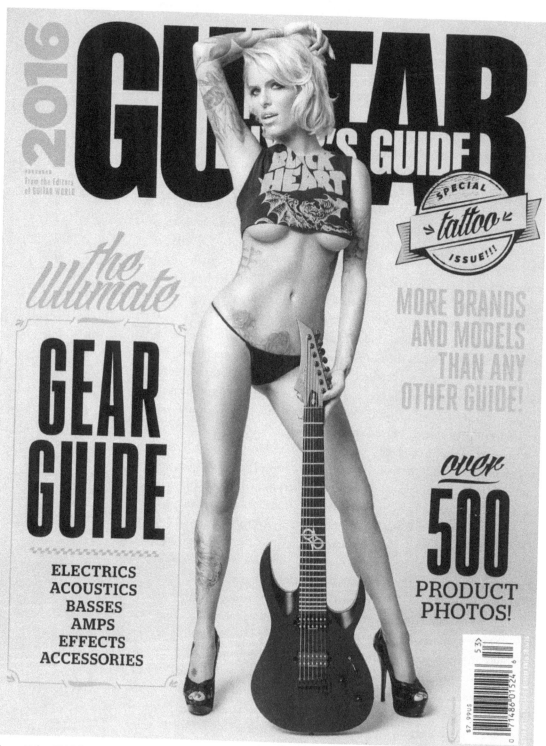

Figure 7.4 *2016 Guitar Buyer's Guide*
Harris Publications, 2016

Summary

Focusing on rock instruments, this chapter has begun a critical discussion that will be taken up further in Chapter 9 on rock sounds, the end product of such technologies. With a particular concern for how social norms influence the use and understanding of musical technologies, we examined the gendered connotations of rock's primary instruments—drums, the electric bass, and the electric guitar, which is essential to the rock sound. Furthering the discussion in Chapter 6 of gender socialization and engagement with musical instruments, this chapter examined the different ways male and female children are encouraged to interact with mechanical and electrical technologies. Since males have long dominated the world of gear and gadgets, we explored why so many girls are disinterested in engaging with them. In turn, the historical masculinizing of rock instruments has proven off-putting for many girls, thus contributing to far fewer female than male guitarists, bassists, and drummers over the course of rock's history. In fact, women interested in performing rock music regularly opt out of being instrumentalists, choosing instead to occupy the role of vocalist, which neither compromises their femininity nor requires much in the way of technical savvy and interaction with gearhead culture.

This chapter's survey of rock's gearhead subculture revealed how male involvement in it works to affirm masculinity. Also discussed were the ways females are discouraged from participating. Nevertheless, the number of women rock instrumentalists has risen dramatically since the early 1990s as a result of greater support from older women, including the design of instruments for girls. What remains to be seen is whether that phenomenon will be enough to destabilize the masculine gendering of rock equipment and the patriarchy historically maintained in gearhead culture. In Chapter 8 we will consider rock musicians' creative work, particularly local performances and touring shows, both of which rely on the technologies discussed here.

Further Exploration

1. Consider your own training with musical instruments.

Recall your training as a young musician. Which instrument did your parents encourage you to play? Did that differ from the instrument you wanted to play? Did that differ from the instrument your sibling(s) of the opposite sex played? If so, how? If not, why not?

2. Compare popular imagery related to guitars and drums.

Via your web browser's search page, look for images via the terms "man guitar" and "woman guitar," and then "man drums" and "woman drums." What similarities do you see among the images related to each search term? What differences do you see? How might you explain the differences among these images?

3. Compare guitar manufacturers' websites.

Visit the websites for Fender Guitars (http://www.fender.com) and Daisy Rock Girl Guitars (http://www.daisyrock.com). Discuss the gender dynamics suggested by each manufacturer's guitar designs. How are these instruments similar? How are they different? Is the feminizing of guitar technology by Daisy Rock Girl Guitars politically progressive or regressive? Is this design strategy necessary to get girls interested in playing guitars?

4. Study a musical instrument store.

Visit a musical instrument store in your local area with a group of friends that contains at least one female. (Be sure to check with your instructor first about your institution's guidelines for human subjects research.) Observe the gender of the salespeople and their interactions with customers. Note the gender of the customers and their interactions with each other and the salespeople. Do the employees treat male customers differently from female customers? How do female customers interact with male employees? How do male customers interact with female employees?

5. Analyze a gearhead forum.

Subscribe to an online forum for music gearheads, such as the Fender Forum. What is the gender make-up of the subscribers? Peruse recent topics, threads, and posts in the forum. Is gender raised in any of these posts? If so, how? If any particular gender appears dominant, discuss how such dominance is achieved. If any particular gender is marginalized or excluded, discuss how that is achieved.

Further Reading

Bayton, Mavis. "Women and the Electric Guitar." *Sexing the Groove: Popular Music and Gender.* Ed. Sheila Whiteley. New York: Routledge, 1997. 37–49.

Bennett, Andy, and Kevin Dawe, eds. *Guitar Cultures.* New York: Berg, 2001.

Clawson, Mary Ann. "When Women Play the Bass: Instrument Specialization and Gender Interpretation in Alternative Rock Music." *Gender & Society* 13.2 (April 1999): 193–210.

Gay, Leslie C., Jr. "Acting Up, Talking Tech: New York Rock Musicians and Their Metaphors of Technology." *Ethnomusicology* 42.1 (1998): 81–98.

Grajeda, Tony. "The 'Feminization' of Rock." *Rock over the Edge: Transformations in Popular Music Culture*. Eds. Roger Beebe, Denise Fulbrook, and Ben Saunders. Durham: Duke University Press, 2002. 233–54.

Kearney, Mary Celeste. "Pink Technology: Mediamaking Gear for Girls." *Camera Obscura* 25.2 (2010): 1–39.

Rodgers, Tara. *Pink Noises: Women on Electronic Music and Sound*. Durham: Duke University Press, 2010.

Théberge, Paul. *Any Sound You Can Imagine: Making Music/Consuming Technology*. Hanover: Wesleyan University Press, 1997.

Waksman, Steve. *Instruments of Desire: The Electric Guitar and the Shaping of Musical Experience*. Cambridge: Harvard University Press, 1999.

8 UNDER THE LIGHTS AND ON THE ROAD
Rock Performance

LISTEN: JON LANGFORD AND His Sadies, "Are You an Entertainer?" (*Mayor of the Moon*, Bloodshot, 2003). *This melancholic song focuses on the sublime power of musical performance and the heartache of musicians' typically impoverished on-the-road existence.*

Live musical performances are forms of entertainment, and several rock musicians have been among the best entertainers of modern times. Indeed, rock history has been punctuated regularly with brilliant shows that awe and delight audiences. Yet rock's most entertaining moments have entailed far more than evocative singing and virtuosic instrument playing, seemingly the central focus of such performances. Those moments are memorable also because they have been theatrical, employing striking clothing and make-up, spectacular stage designs, and creative body movements.

Rock's most memorable performances include Chuck Berry's duck walk, Little Richard's piano straddling, Elvis Presley's hip gyrations, Tina Turner's energetic kicks, Jimi Hendrix's guitar burning, Alice Cooper's macabre stage props, David Bowie's gender-bending outfits, Iggy Pop's stage dives, Linder's meat dress, Prince's gymnastics, Wendy O. Williams's chainsaws, Kurt Cobain's dress, and Lynne Breedlove's dildo castrations. Yet each of these elements is just part of the performer's more complex signature act. To appreciate fully any rock performance, we must attend to all the practices, objects, and spaces each member of a band uses, and consider how those work together in a band as well as with the music to create an entertaining experience.

Although rock music is most often consumed via recordings, live shows are essential to rock culture. Such performances offer rock musicians opportunities to practice their art, develop their image, build audiences, and, sometimes, attract the attention of critics and talent scouts. As a result, rockers work strenuously before and during such shows to create not only great music but also entertaining, memorable events. Indeed, many rock aficionados value audio and video recordings of live shows over studio recordings because they capture the spontaneity and vitality of the music and help the listener to remember (or imagine) "being there" in the moment of creative expression and theatrical entertainment. Such recordings are also invaluable to scholars interested in analyzing the finer details of rock performances.

In this chapter we will explore the activities, spaces, and objects associated with live rock performances, with a special focus on how they are impacted by gender politics. The chapter will begin with an examination of music-making as a form of creative labor with particular values in rock culture. **Gigging** (performing locally) and **touring** (performing in several towns) are explored also, especially since these activities have posed problems for women musicians. In turn, we will examine how gender politics affect the various elements of live performance, including costuming, stage design, and physical movement.

Music Performance as Work

The reconfiguration of labor by bohemian subcultures, such as the Beats and hippies, has directly influenced how creative work is practiced in rock culture. Inspired in part by Marxism, those communities repudiated capitalism because they understood it as exploiting laborers and leaving little time for meaningful reflection and art. As a result, rock culture inherited an alternative approach to creative labor that often privileges expressive authenticity and creative innovation over popular taste and commercial potential. In turn, rock culture has inherited a focus on collective rather than individual creative practice, which is perhaps best exemplified by rock's privileging of bands over solo artists.

Rock musicians' privileging of such alternative labor values does not mean they avoid perfecting their music and performance strategies. Even the most authentic-seeming live performances are carefully crafted, and rock musicians work rigorously on developing their skills, sometimes to the detriment of their health, relationships, and income. Because rockers place high value on artistic spontaneity and a bohemian lifestyle, many eschew the traditional 9-to-5 middle-class worklife. Yet, because wages from gigs are typically meager, musicians often supplement whatever pay they receive from performances with income from jobs that can accommodate the irregular schedules of rehearsals, gigs, and touring. Even bands signed to major labels must shoulder a considerable amount of the expenses related to promoting their music, which leaves little income after everything else has been paid for.

Making music is central to the work of a professional rock musician, yet performing entails far more than composing and playing music. It involves many other nonmusical practices, such as pursuing gigs, transporting equipment, and selecting clothes. As a result, rock musicians necessarily interact with many other types of cultural worker, even when they have no intention of recording music. Such networked communities form the backbone of rock's larger culture, for without them, music would not circulate beyond musicians and their friends.

The Social World of Rock's Creative Labor

Most rock musicians are affiliated with a local musical community before they achieve fame on a larger scale. Originally used to describe jazz culture, a **music scene** includes a group of musicians and fans as well as a cluster of musical venues organized around a particular genre. Those music scenes that expand beyond their original geographical boundaries, gain visibility through mainstream media, and are exploited by commercial entities are sometimes referred to as **subcultures**.

As Howard Becker's theory of **art worlds** makes clear, art—including music—is not created, circulated, and commodified by artists alone. It takes a much larger, networked group of people to record, distribute, publicize, and evaluate such work. Clearly, record label employees and radio DJs are essential to rock's various scenes, given their roles in recording, distributing, and promoting rock music. Yet others who work at the local level, including band managers, booking agents, and sound technicians, are important to such art worlds also. Together these workers participate in what Paul du Gay would call rock's **culture of production**. (Although fans are most often considered part of the consumption side of rock's circuit of cultural production, they, too, are essential to rock scenes.)

Music scenes consist of more than just people, however. As Donna Gaines argues, they also involve particular types of communication practices and social networks, as well as specific spaces, like clubs, rehearsal rooms, and music stores. While local publications and radio stations are central to the development and maintenance of scenes, touring musicians and other mass media—especially magazines, television, and the Internet—help music scenes to grow and spread beyond their original boundaries by informing a larger public and encouraging commitment from new fans.

Despite the alternative views most rockers have of work, traditional gender ideologies still influence how labor is viewed in rock culture. Productive practices, particularly those involving payment, have been affiliated with men for millennia. Thus, the jobs associated with rock performance, especially those that are most lucrative, have long been understood as masculine and available primarily for men. For example, most rock musician roles are occupied by men. Males have also dominated the paid roles associated with rock's commercialization, as well as live performance. In contrast, women in rock scenes have usually occupied unpaid or minimum-wage supporting roles, such as administrative assistant. Such conventions have had significant consequences for female rock musicians who are gigging or touring, since there are typically fewer women than men involved behind the scenes.

Rock's Gig Culture

The absence of scholarly attention to the labor required in securing gigs and promoting bands has contributed to the common idea that performing rock does not entail effort but rather comes naturally and easily. In addition, such lack of attention helps to reproduce the notion of rock culture as focused on art more than commerce. Yet musicians, to promote their art, must perform for people other than their bandmates. Opportunities for unpaid gigs abound, but paid, professional performances are what many amateur musicians aspire to. Getting a chance to perform in a bar or club, however, can be difficult, particularly in towns with active music scenes and many competing musicians. Yet the rewards can be enormous in terms of creative expression with others, broadening a fan base, being appreciated by critics, and attracting record label representatives.

Given the amount of work required to promote a band, musicians with professional aspirations typically hire **band managers** to be responsible for the business-related tasks that musicians do not want to perform or feel incapable of completing successfully. Often friends volunteer such labor for bands just starting out, and many times the manager's duties fall to female partners of male musicians. Chief among the manager's tasks is securing paid performance opportunities. To do so, musicians must produce a **demo** (demonstration) recording that reveals their talents and can be used to garner attention from bar and club owners (as well as radio DJs and talent scouts). Demo recordings are sent to **venue buyers** and managers to secure gigs. The band manager is often also responsible for publicity, including producing and circulating show flyers and press kits. As a musical group becomes more successful, its manager or record label typically works with **booking agents** to negotiate contracts with venue buyers, including band payment and sound system requirements.

Since competition can often be stiff, securing a gig is difficult for all-male and coed bands. Yet such opportunities have been far fewer for female-only bands, since many venue owners have assumed women cannot play rock instruments and are incapable of drawing a crowd. Recalling the days before punk, Alison Raynor of Jam Today and Guest Stars notes: "promoters . . . didn't use [sic] to believe that a women's band could play. So they wouldn't want to take a women's band."[1] Even as rock culture opened to more women musicians, securing gigs was difficult since all-female or mostly female bands were placed in competition with each other. As Delia from Mambo Taxi remembers: "there was the obstacle of being a girl-band, turning up at venues and [promoters] saying, 'we've already had one girl band this week and we didn't think it was a good idea having another one in such a short period.'"[2] At the same time, some all-female and mixed-gender groups have reported getting attention from club owners who see all-female bands as lucrative novelties able to attract customers. Rosie Flores, who has been performing since the late 1960s, recalls: "back in my day, it wasn't very popular for a girl to be playing lead guitar so I had a lot of calls for my band because we were so different."[3] Although progress has been made on some fronts, some women rockers still experience sexism when attempting to secure bookings. As Jenni Black from Free Verse relates: "we've had . . . booking agents move us to the opening slot on the bill once they found out we were all women."[4]

Once a gig has been scheduled, musicians must arrange for time off from other conflicting responsibilities, such as work and family. In addition, they (or their manager) must secure equipment if they do not own it themselves, inspect the venue's sound and lighting systems, get transportation that can carry both equipment and musicians, and promote themselves via fliers, the Internet, and local radio. Once the band has arrived at their gig venue, other tasks await them before they perform, including loading equipment into the club, developing a set list, tuning instruments, setting sound levels, and performing sound checks.

Mavis Bayton has spent numerous years both performing rock music and interviewing women musicians about their experiences in rock culture. As a result, she has discovered the numerous difficulties females have faced when gigging, difficulties many female performers have shared with other scholars and journalists as well. For example, once women musicians have conquered the difficulties of securing performance opportunities, they often have to deal with sexist male venue staff and management. Because of the prevalent notion that women cannot play rock, venue staff sometimes mistake female rockers for girlfriends or fans of male musicians rather than musicians themselves. For instance, Cinder from Tilt reports: "I have problems with security guys because they think I'm someone's girlfriend or a groupie and they try to bar me from going backstage."[5]

Women musicians often have particular difficulties with male sound technicians who presume women know nothing about sound technology. For example, Tara Key of Antietam reports: "soundmen are pretty bad. . . . They always pull my mike down for me. It's like they want control of my sound, and I have to assert myself to get control. I don't think they do that to guys."[6] Oddly, women musicians' technical knowledge does not always ensure respect or consideration, since some male sound technicians refuse to listen or agree to female performers' requests. Other reports have surfaced of male technicians sabotaging women's performances by producing poor sound quality on purpose. Female sound technicians have experienced similar forms of sexism at gigs. Steph Hiller recalls: "the amount of times I've turned up at gigs and people have assumed I'm the girlfriend of somebody in the band or that I'm an accessory. And when you go up to the mixing desk they look at you like 'No way!' It's a look of complete disbelief most of the time."[7]

Female musicians have also reported that performance venues do little to make their **green rooms** (performers' backstage waiting rooms) hospitable to women. Since all-male rock groups are the norm, women's privacy is often not available. And since rebellion is highly valued in rock culture, such spaces are often dirty or in a state of disarray because of male performers' mistreatment or vandalism. Raucous behavior and disregard of cleanliness distances male rockers from both the wholesomeness and domesticity associated with the middle-class lifestyle while also affirming such musicians' masculinity by suggesting their ability to endure harsh environments. In contrast, most women are socialized to find dirt and mess unacceptable and to understand cleaning as part of performing femininity. Such conflicting gender dynamics can cause discomfort for women rockers, who must acclimate to unhygienic working conditions if they want to be successful. Musician parents also find such negotiations of unkempt greenrooms difficult, for rock clubs are rarely accommodating of children. Not only are such spaces typically unhygienic and filled with rebellious individuals consuming alcohol and drugs, floors are usually covered in electrical cords and other technology that can make a child's crawling or walking across them risky if not dangerous.

Once women performers are onstage, the sexism they sometimes face backstage is often exacerbated. Many female rockers have reported being sexually harassed or treated as incompetent by male audience members. As Terry Hunt of Jam Today reports: "there's always either a comment or some uneasy atmosphere or something. Every gig there'll be some little something that has to be dealt with. . . . We're so used to being harassed."[8] In a musical culture that privileges male sexuality and undervalues female musicianship, the catcall of "Show us your tits!" by men in the audience has become so prevalent as to be naturalized now in rock.

Such gendered harassment likely emerged as a result of the dearth of women musicians in rock culture historically as well as some men's desire to keep this culture, or at least its musicians, predominantly male. Thus, this harassment serves to construct and constrain women as outsiders infiltrating a male homosocial space. Moreover, by drawing attention to women's bodies, men's catcalls send a message to women musicians that they are thought of as women first and only secondarily as musicians. Bayton found that female vocalists are more susceptible to such harassment than instrumentalists, likely because singers are meant to be visible and to draw crowd attention. Dave Laing also raised this point by associating the fetishistic gaze of male rock fans with that of male film spectators (as theorized by Laura Mulvey). Skin of Skunk Anansie comments: "the minute that you are a female fronting a rock band, everybody looks at you sexually. Everybody takes a sexual perspective: do you fancy her, or do you not?"[9] Typically, younger women are assumed to be more sexually alluring than older women, who, like female instrumentalists, tend to get more respect from men in rock clubs. As Mary Genis of Dread Warlock comments: "one of the reasons I decided to be a musician in a band, as opposed to a singer, was because you get taken a bit more seriously. No one takes singers seriously, even now, unless they're a big singer."[10]

Bayton found male musicians who share concert venues with female rockers frequently demonstrate sexism also by flirting or making harassing comments, as well as by overemphasizing their own musical knowledge and virtuosity and by not taking the women's musical talents seriously. Drawing attention to differences between male bands in this regard, Shira reports: "there's always going to be those bands that are sexist, and you actually get more sexism from the baby bands than you do the bigger artists. . . . And maybe it is just a question of them being younger and more ignorant, but the younger guys will make comments."[11] Some venue owners unconsciously legitimate such behavior by placing female bands as opening acts for male groups, thus suggesting that women cannot perform as well as men and assuming that audiences aren't as interested in hearing them.

Despite her findings of male privilege and female subordination in gigging culture, Bayton also noted that some women rockers actually employ their gender to their advantage. For example, some female performers have emphasized their femininity to avoid the heavy lifting, technical expertise, or business acumen that is required of professional musicians. By encouraging men to help them, such women musicians perform the passivity and dependency associated with emphasized femininity. Such complicity with traditional gender norms (not to mention postfeminism) may work as a survival tactic in a male-dominated community. But it must be understood also as reproducing patriarchy and women's subordination.

Since Bayton's study focuses on women musicians, she does not address how male musicians who resist or do not conform to hegemonic masculinity navigate the machismo climate of gigging culture. Yet it is important to reflect on how such men negotiate the gender politics associated with live rock performance, where technical knowledge, brute strength, rebellion, sexism, and homophobia are deemed signifiers of masculinity just as much as musical skill is. At the same time, individual musicians in all-male bands may be less obliged for upholding these traits, since other men can share that responsibility. Moreover, male privilege affords even nonmacho males entitlement to rock culture in a way that being a woman does not. Intersex and transgender identities complicate these matters further. Therefore, we should also be mindful of how the gender binary impacts genderqueer musicians' gigging experiences.

Rock's Touring Culture

If rock musicians want to gain a larger audience for their music and make more money, **touring**—performing in places beyond one's hometown—is necessary. Typically, a rock tour involves performing only one night in each town, as musicians attempt to reach as many audience members as possible. The scheduling of performances is dependent, however, on the distance between towns on the tour. Often rock bands will perform four to five shows in one week, which, depending on traveling distance and mode of transportation, can be a grueling schedule.

Bands without managers face the difficulty of coordinating multicity tours on their own, as tours require working with several booking agents, venue owners, and promotional people, as well as arranging transportation, food, and overnight accommodations in multiple locations. Lesser-known bands typically travel by van, often filling such vehicles to capacity with musicians and equipment to lower transportation costs. More popular groups tour via buses outfitted with sleeping accommodations and have **road crews** or **roadies** who help with logistics and equipment. Successful musicians may tour by airplane, which helps to minimize the time spent traveling and maximize the potential for concerts and thus further commodification. The more successful a band is, the more comfortable its sleeping accommodations. Many bands without recording contracts stay overnight at friends' homes rather than pay for hotel rooms.

Because of rock culture's historic association with independence, nomadic bohemianism, and Beat culture, rock musicians are encouraged to embrace life "on the road" as an experience that will enrich their creativity and worldview. Many younger musicians surrender themselves to such travel, welcoming the opportunity to escape from their everyday roles and responsibilities while opening themselves to meeting new people, experiencing new places, and having new adventures. A typical part of the rock tour experience, therefore, is play, often heightened through the use of alcohol and drugs.

Despite the various pleasures of traveling, many rock musicians have discussed the challenges posed by concert tours. For instance, a performer's health can be compromised by the lack of privacy, as well as minimal sleep, poor nutrition, and substance abuse. In turn, both band and family relationships can be strained by a lengthy tour schedule that demands moving from town to town each night. If a tour interferes with the schedule for another job, a musician's livelihood can be affected also.

Many women musicians have reported experiencing the same gendered problems associated with gigging when they are touring, from securing shows to performing to a mostly male audience. Others female performers have discussed the unique difficulties that come with touring as a result of their gender. For instance, because of traditional gender norms that label females the "fairer sex," many people do not believe life on the road is acceptable for women. As Terry Hunt of Jam Today comments, journalists have repeatedly asked her, "'Do you go on tour? Oh. How does your boyfriend feel about that?'" She questions the sexism of such remarks: "I've never [heard] them ask that question of male musicians. It's accepted. But they find it really freaky, the idea of women going off and touring on their own."[12] It is likely this idea has lead to the difficulty of female-centered rock bands getting booked for large annual tours like Vans Warped Tour. As Megan Seling reports, of the 120-some acts in the 2014 Warped Tour, less than 20 percent included women. Meanwhile,

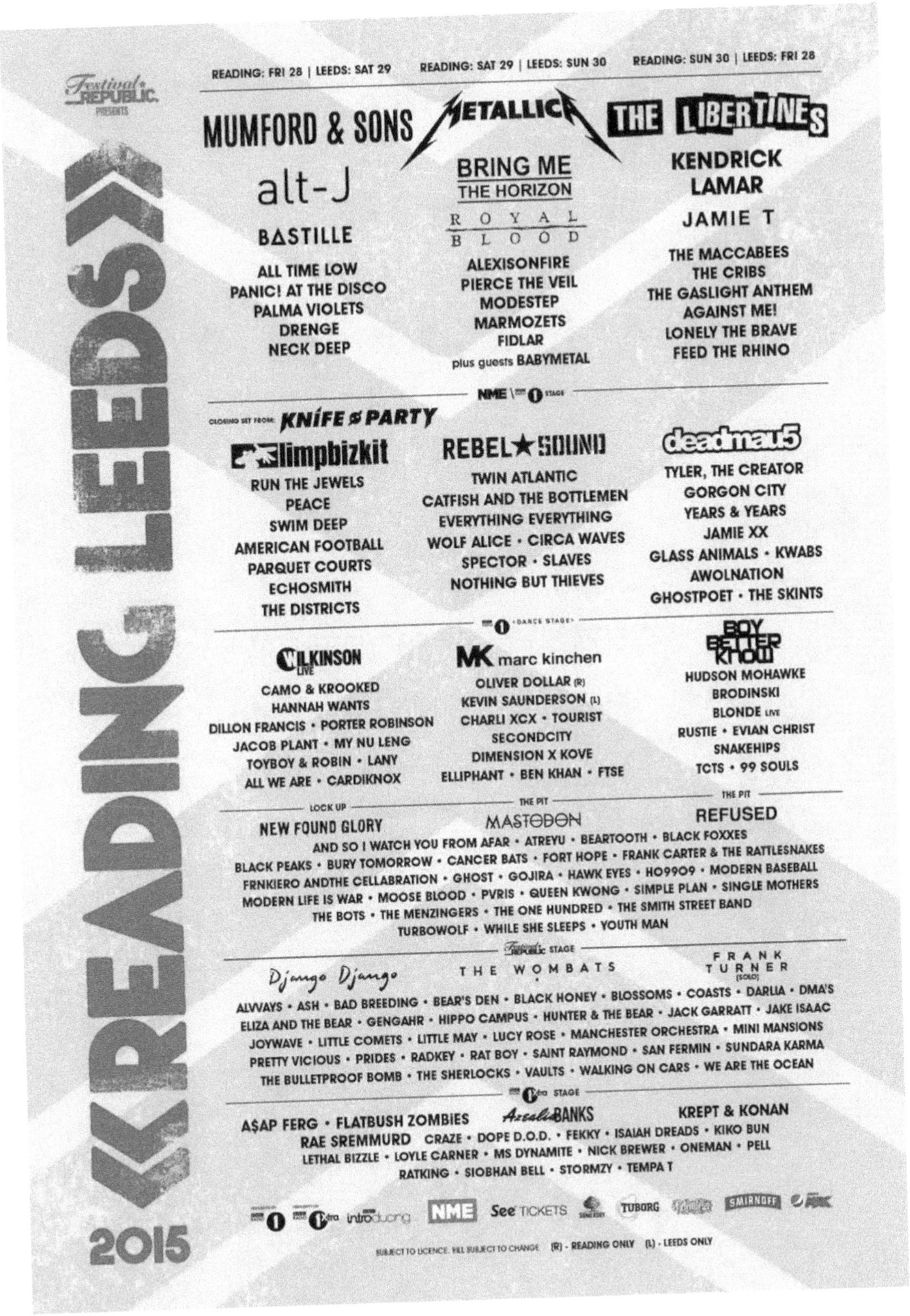

Figure 8.1 Reading Leeds concert poster (original)

Festival Republic, 2015

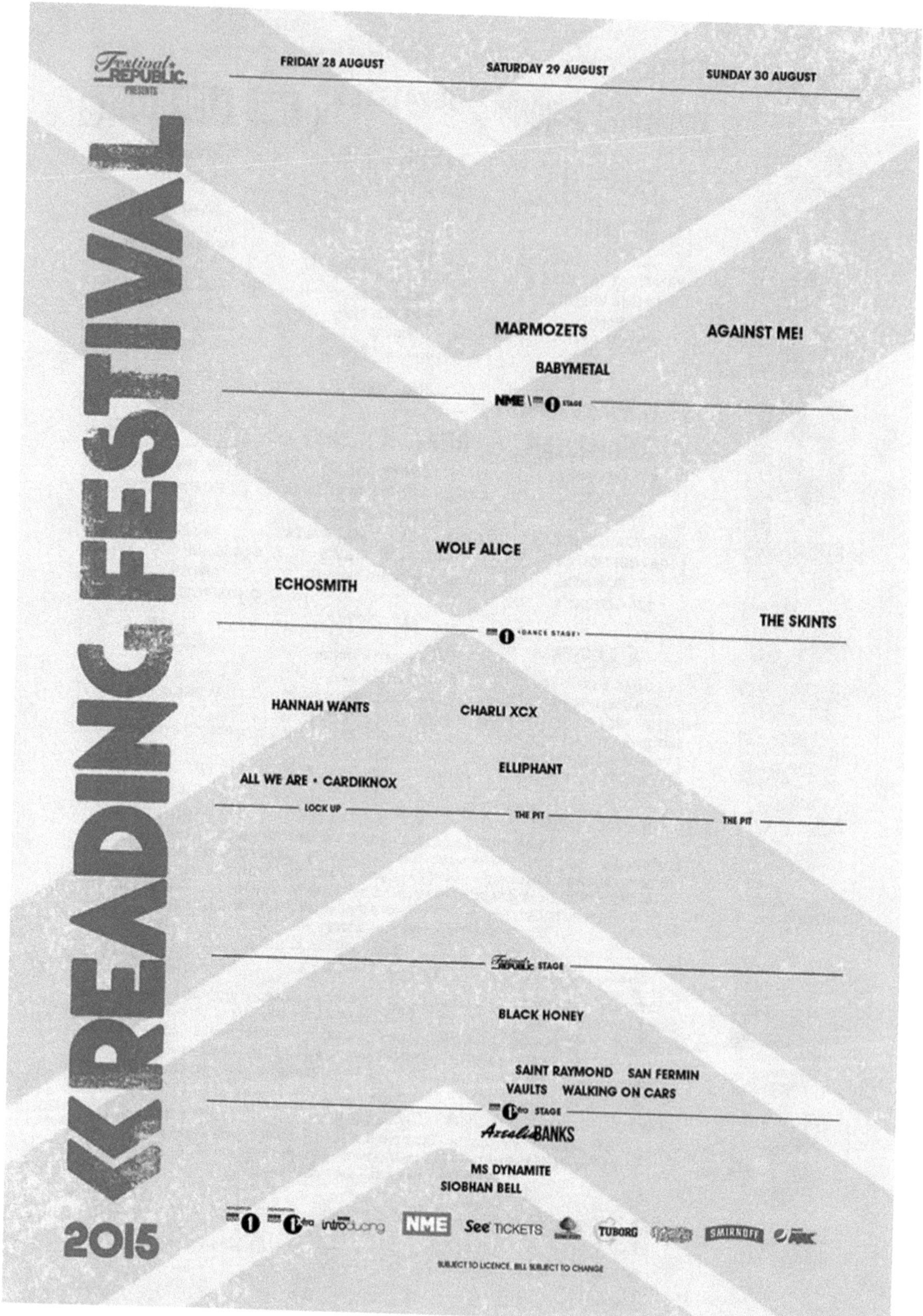

Figure 8.2 Reading Leeds concert poster (revised)
Crack in the Road, 2015

only 15 percent of bands playing at other summer rock festivals in 2014 had at least one female member. To draw attention to this problem, Crack in the Road redesigned several tour posters in 2015 to reveal the marginalization of bands with female performers (see Figures 8.1 and 8.2).

In addition, because women are often thought of as family managers and typically have primary childcare responsibilities, female musicians who live with partners and those who are mothers have expressed frustration with attempting to balance their domestic roles with their professional need to tour. Since many female rockers are vocalists in bands with only male instrumentalists and road-ies, those women have the additional challenge of living with a predominantly male homosocial group that may not respect their personal needs or accommo-date their off-road lifestyle. Several women musicians have commented on their male bandmates' or roadies' sexual advances.

But male musicians are not the only men with whom women musicians must interact while on tour. Often they find themselves in an overwhelmingly male-dominated community. Fiona Sturges has reported that only ten of the tour managers currently working in the United Kingdom are female, while tour manager Storme Whitby-Grubb has noted that barely 7 percent of the back-stage crew members with whom she has worked over the course of her career have been female.[13] While there is no guarantee that women musicians will have an easier time working with female managers or roadies while on tour, a con-siderable amount of anecdotal evidence suggests that plenty have had a difficult time working with males in these positions.

These challenges only exacerbate the problems women musicians face dur-ing gigs and often lead female performers to avoid touring, despite the potentially negative effects of that decision on their musical careers. Meanwhile, such difficul-ties have encouraged some women to adopt what Theodore Gracyk calls a philoso-phy of **gender solidarity** by starting their own female-centered rock tours, such as the Lilith Fair festival introduced by Sarah McLachlan in 1997 and revived in 2010 (see Figure 8.3) and Warped Tour's Shiragirl Stage, which Shira launched in 2005. Although the Michigan Women's Music Festival was originally opposed to booking rock bands, since the mid-1990s more all-female rock groups have been welcomed there. While such separatist ventures have helped some women musi-cians to expand their audiences, other female performers object to being segre-gated by their gender when touring since it implies: they are women more than musicians; they are inferior to their male peers; and their performances should be judged based on different criteria from those used for male musicians.

Performance Practices

Despite the primacy of musical recordings in rock culture, live performance remains its most privileged type of musical experience. As Ian Inglis argues, musicians value live performance as a means of demonstrating skill, expressing

Figure 8.3 Lilith Fair poster
Lilith Fair, 2010

themselves authentically, experimenting creatively, and connecting with audience members and other performers. Rock consumers use such experiences to explore their identities, form communities, and transcend their everyday lives. And both consumers and critics commonly use live performance as a standard by which to evaluate rock musicians' recorded material. Thus, learning the practices that compose live rock performance can help us also to comprehend the production and consumption of studio recordings. Yet Inglis notes that another primary reason to study musical performances is that they often function as sites of musical transformation, as musicians' emergent practices can challenge convention and redirect a genre or scene in new directions.

Live rock performances come in every shape and size. Some are expensive spectacles that take place in front of thousands of people or are taken on the road and performed in multiple cities across the nation or world. The most conventional rock performances, however, are short, one-hour or less sets played in front of a few dozen people at a local bar. Nevertheless, all good rock performances rely on musicians' successful engagement in the numerous music-related practices discussed in previous chapters, including learning instruments, forming bands, writing lyrics, and composing songs. In addition, live performances involve theatrical activities associated not only or primarily with music, including stage design, characterization, costuming, and movement. These elements are important to consider when analyzing rock culture, for they tell us much about both the multiple forms of work involved in being a rock musician and, more specific to the focus of this book, how gender ideologies impact rock performance.

Venues

Rock musicians play in many different **venues**, typically bars and clubs designed for live music shows, yet also spaces constructed for different forms of live performance, such as sports arenas and theaters for drama. Most of these venues have performance areas built with traditional dramatic performances in mind. That is, the stage is raised, and a **proscenium arch** frames the performance area so audience members can focus on musicians rather than the crowd. When rock musicians play outdoor concerts, similar stages are often constructed. Raised stages physically separate performers from the audience.

Some rock musicians have eschewed traditional stage conventions to subvert the imbalance of power suggested by having musicians appear above audience members. For instance, many punk bands have performed without raised stages to encourage musician interaction with the audience and to allow the crowd to become part of the performance. In turn, many rock groups encourage **stage diving** and **crowd surfing** for similar reasons.

While dancing, both solo and in couples, often occurs in the area just in front of a rock stage, **moshing**, a fast and aggressive style of dance associated with punk, can often produce a male homosocial atmosphere that is off-putting to women. To create a more equitable gender balance at their shows, many female rock bands, especially those associated with Riot Grrrl, encourage women to come to the area in front of the stage and have policies against moshing, stage diving, and crowd surfing.

In addition to having to negotiate the established design of the physical space where they are performing, rock musicians must attend to its *mise-en-scène*—the control of everything seen within the proscenium arch—by determining how their bodies, instruments, and other objects will appear within it. Such decisions involve set design, characterization, costuming, and physical movement, all major practices in theatrical performance.

Set Design

For most rock performances, **set design**—the aesthetic decoration of a stage—is kept to a minimum because of concerns about cost and efficiency. Typically only those bands that have considerable financial and labor support from their record labels are able to use sophisticated lighting, artwork, visual media, **props**, and **special effects**, since all of these materials can be expensive to purchase and difficult to install and disassemble. Moreover, because most rock gigs involve several bands performing in the same venue on the same night, performers have little time to construct and deconstruct elaborate sets between performances. Thus, while some lesser-known groups create their own backdrops and video projections to lend further ambience to their music, most rock bands rely on the lighting system and scenery already in place at their performance venues.

As Philip Auslander argues, the degree to which a rock band delves into theatricality, and thus elaborate set designs, is dependent on the type of music its members perform. For example, largely as a result of rock 'n' roll's roots in the blues, hillbilly, and R&B—musical genres that privilege authenticity—early rock shows tended to focus primarily on the performers and their music. Thus, the most spectacular elements of such performances were the musicians themselves. This tradition has continued to this day among many rock musicians.

Nonetheless, as rock music developed into a highly lucrative and global commodity by the early 1970s, record labels invested heavily in elaborate stage shows for their most successful artists, particularly those associated with hard rock and heavy metal. Such bands quickly became well known for having spectacular stage shows that expressed more fully the characters the musicians played in song and on stage. For example, Alice Cooper gained attention during this period for developing an excessively theatrical live show that privileged horror aesthetics. Other bands, such as Pink Floyd and KISS, took Cooper's theatricality to new levels in the late 1970s and 1980s with bizarre props, fantastic

Figure 8.4 *KISS Rocks Vegas Nevada*
Eagle Rock Entertainment, 2016

light shows, intriguing visual media, and spectacular pyrotechnics, all of which suggested power and thus helped to affirm the musicians' masculinity. Such excessive and expensive shows often live on via documentaries, such as *KISS Rocks Vegas Nevada*, which are then sold to fans via DVDs and subscription television (see Figure 8.4). Given punk's emphasis on amateurism, most bands performing this style of music have rejected elaborate stage designs, since they are seen as exemplifying corporate culture's superficiality and spectacularity.

Influenced by earlier music traditions, many rock performers have used their instruments as their primary theatrical props. Indeed, the heavy use of the guitar as a prop has contributed to its heightened significance in rock culture. While a good number of guitarists have developed signature onstage moves that highlight their guitars' sounds, others manipulate their guitars in ways that are not necessarily musically oriented but instead foreground the musicians' flare for spectacle. For example, Prince performed with many custom-made guitars in creative shapes, including one that represents the symbol he once used as his name. Another of his guitars "ejaculated" water onto the audience when played, emphasizing the common phallic connotation of this instrument. Meanwhile, Tommy Lee's drum set has been made into a stage prop for Mötley Crüe concerts by being rotated like a ball on stage or being "floated" over the audience. As with Prince, Lee's mastery of his instrument-as-prop, particularly as used in relation to audience members, communicates his power and masculinity.

Many rock musicians, particularly those associated with hard rock and heavy metal, have employed nonmusical props to heighten their performances' theatricality. For example, Rolling Stones concerts have included inflatable phalluses and blow-up dolls, thus affirming the heteromasculinity of the band members. Other groups, like Judas Priest, have used motorcycles and other motorized vehicles during their performances. Alice Cooper became infamous in rock culture for creating over-the-top spectacles during concerts via numerous macabre stage props, including live snakes, guillotines, and electric chairs. The performance of bizarre, clownish, grotesque, or violent **stage antics** during rock shows works not only to garner the audience's attention but also to reaffirm the musician's characterization (discussed below) and power over the crowd. Therefore, such performances are commonly read as masculine.

Some female-centered rock bands, like Hole and those associated with Riot Grrrl, have been known to adorn their sets with feminine scenery and objects, such as dolls and flowers. Yet historically most women rockers have eschewed props that might foreground their gender identity over their music and thus potentially delegitimize them as musicians. In keeping with rock's masculinized connotation, several women rockers have developed shocking stage antics that preclude any labeling of them or their music as "feminine." For example, Wendy O. Williams of the Plasmatics often chainsawed guitars and blew up cars during the band's performances. As captured in Tracy Flannigan's documentary *Rise Above*, Lynne Breedlove of Tribe 8 often wore a strap-on dildo during performances, which she would unveil late in the band's set, ask audience members to fellate, and then "castrate." The meaning of such interchanges varied based on the gender and sexual identity of the fellators. By embracing and reconfiguring masculinity, such female-embodied performances offer musicians and audiences alike an opportunity to experience a form of gender politics not available in their everyday lives.

Characterization and Costuming

As entertainers, rock musicians must necessarily negotiate how audiences perceive their personal identities. As noted, acting naturally and expressing oneself authentically has been privileged in rock culture for some time. Yet several scholars, including Auslander, Simon Frith, and Susan Fast have drawn attention to rock musicians' use of theatrical **characterization** and the multiple identities they construct during live performances. More specifically, in addition to performing their real selves, they also perform public **personas** as well as the characters they conjure in songs. With rock music, negotiations of these multiple forms of characterization are most often taken up by vocalists, although instrumentalists may engage in dramatic characterizations also. As Dave Laing suggests, few rock performers call attention to public personas as constructed or of their own making, which might encourage audiences to reconsider the ethos of authenticity undergirding rock culture. However, some punk bands, like the Mekons, have been known to swap instruments and to ask audience members to perform, thereby deconstructing rock's privileging of specialized instrumentalist and star personas.

While the personas that rock musicians create have varied widely over this culture's history, performers have been somewhat confined not only by the genre of rock they are performing but also by social norms related to their own identities, including gender, sexuality, age, race, and class. As much as rock culture has repeatedly reaffirmed the hegemony of white heterosexual masculinity, many rock musicians have used their performance personas as sites for challenging identity norms, a practice that has made them appealing to audience members exploring nonconformist ways of being. At the same time, women rock performers have adopted far fewer public personas than their male peers have, since foregrounding such performative identities might further compromise women's authenticity and legitimacy as musicians.

Costuming—clothing, make-up, and hairstyles—is key to the successful communication of both public persona and song character during rock performances. As discussed in Chapter 5, the style of rock musicians' costuming has long been tied to the specific musical genre they play, thus helping to create a **homology** or correspondence with the values associated with a particular type of music. Nevertheless, rock fashions have changed considerably over the past fifty-some years since rock music emerged.

Early rock 'n' roll musicians often wore stylish, and sometimes spectacular, outfits that signified their entertainer status as well as their public personas as modern and youthful. "Dressing up" was the norm for all professional performers at that time, which meant males wore suits and ties and females wore dresses. Rock performers whose music was more closely aligned with R&B and doo-wop, such as Little Richard, sometimes wore clothing associated with African American subcultures, such as zoot suits. Early white rockers whose music developed from hillbilly, like Bill Haley and Wanda Jackson, usually wore attire similar to that of country music stars, including cowboy shirts and fringed jackets.

As Elvis Presley became successful in the late 1950s, he increasingly "dressed down" for performances, often appearing in slacks and a shirt without a jacket or tie, thus participating in the informalization of attire for white musicians. (At that time, black performers could not risk their careers by dressing informally and being seen as unrespectable.) Meanwhile, many young female rock artists, like Brenda Lee, were clothed in trendy feminine fashions, such as full skirts and sweater sets. Janis Martin, billed by RCA as "The Female Elvis,"

Figure 8.5   The Shangri-Las, *Leader of the Pack*
(Red Bird, 1965)

was one of the first female rock performers to appear in pants in promotional materials. However, the Shangri-Las, a 1960s girl group, were more famous for adopting a masculine fashion style (see Figure 8.5). Along with Presley, Little Richard popularized a pompadour hairstyle that became fashionable among early rock 'n' roll musicians as well as fans. Meanwhile, teased bouffant hairdos were popular among early women rockers. (This style, like the pompadour, required hair straightening for those with coarse or curly hair.)

By the mid-1960s, many rock performers were known to privilege mod clothing, which was influenced by Italian fashions and popularized in Great Britain, especially by members of the Beatles and the Who. Helping to signify youthful "hipness," mod attire included men's suits with narrow collars and slim-fit pants and tight tops and pencil skirts for women. Best exemplified by the Beatles, male musicians' hair was worn a bit longer than in the previous decade. Female artists continued to wear bouffant styles, although their hair, too, was typically worn a bit longer, as could be seen among the Ronettes.

During the late 1960s, costuming for rock performances became more creative and expressive. Costume designers typically followed the feminine and psychedelic aesthetics of the hippie counterculture, including colorful patterns, like paisley, tactile fabrics, like velvet, and exotic, indigenous accessories, such as beads, feathers, and fringe. Janis Joplin and Jimi Hendrix were well known for such fashions, yet their flamboyant style can be attributed also to the blues musicians whose work informed their musical styles.

This period of rock was influenced also by the privileging of an informal and androgynous look among many progressive young people, and thus the increasing presence of male performers with long hair alongside female musicians wearing pants. Some male musicians wore beards that accentuated their masculinity as well as their nonmainstream status. Other male musicians exaggerated their femininity for shows, including Mick Jagger of the Rolling Stones, who became somewhat infamous for his seductively androgynous performance attire, including make-up, flowing scarves, and skin-tight clothing. The eroticism afforded to male musicians who drew attention to their bodies via feminine attire during this period (and after) is interesting to consider in the context of this culture's insistent heterosexuality and the dramatic decrease in female performers.

With the rise of folk rock and a growing rejection of commercial culture in the mid- to late 1960s, many rock musicians moved further away from the expensive, spectacular fashions associated with pop music and embraced everyday working-class attire, such as denim jeans and jackets, which signaled their political ideology as well as their authenticity. Hard rock and heavy metal musicians, like the members of Judas Priest, developed this proletarian fashion further in the late 1970s by adding leather clothing and boots, signifiers of rebellion long associated with the motorcycle biker subculture. Several female musicians of that era, including Joan Jett, adopted this style also to signify their assertive personas and harder approach to rock music.

Yet 1970s rock fashion wasn't solely about dressing down and privileging the authenticity of working-class culture. Glam rock musicians of this period developed fashion styles that are among the most extravagant and gender transgressive in rock history. Indeed, as a result of the genre's performative aesthetic, some glam rockers repudiated the romantic lure of authenticity privileged by folk musicians and instead constructed alternate personas for themselves via **stage names** and spectacular costumes. David Bowie—whose onstage identities included Ziggy Stardust and Alladin Sane—is best known for bringing drag's excessive, gender-bending theatrical spectacle to rock culture via glam. Yet Marc Bolan of T. Rex contributed greatly to this style also. Glam rockers' gender-bending fashions and spectacular aesthetics influenced many rock musicians during the early 1970s, including LaBelle, Elton John, and those artists who would turn rock culture on its head via their development of proto-punk: Lou Reed, Iggy Pop, and the New York Dolls.

The fashions of many early punk rockers were similar to that of 1970s metal performers (minus the long hair). However, some early punk musicians, in their attempt to shock and offend, took a more performative approach to their appearance, creating a rebellious fashion style with torn clothing, safety pins, and bizarre make-up, as well as bondage gear associated with the S/M subculture. Transgender performer Wayne (now Jayne) County took punk's antifashion ethos further than most, sometimes creating a dress out of trash to complete her ensemble, as can be seen in *The Blank Generation,* a documentary of the CBGB punk scene (Figure 8.6).

Figure 8.6   Wayne County in *The Blank Generation*
The Blank Generation, 1976

Meanwhile, members of bands like the Ramones and Blondie reenergized elements of early 1950s fashion via such items as leather jackets, stiletto heels, and bleached hair. The creative eccentricity of early punk bands influenced by glam rock, like X-Ray Spex, eventually developed into the colorful and spectacular fashions associated with new wave and synth-pop acts of the 1980s, like the Eurythmics, Culture Club, and Devo.

Ironically, despite punks' rejection of social norms and corporatism, their fashion style has been the most broadly influential in rock culture and has impacted mainstream fashions considerably as well. Black clothing, work boots, body piercings, tattoos, bizarre hair styles, and unnatural hair colors and make-up—all of which were embraced by punks in the mid-1970s to signify their oppositionality—have become naturalized components of contemporary rock fashion, as well as heavily commodified elements in youth fashion more broadly.

While the goth subculture further accentuated punk's dark aesthetics in the 1980s, alternative and indie rock bands, like Beat Happening, Nirvana, and Yo La Tengo, have broadened punk's fashion style over the past two decades, adding thrift store clothing as yet an additional signifier of such musicians' unconventionality and resistance to corporate culture. Indeed, inexpensive, everyday clothing has predominated in rock fashion since the late 1980s, as most rock musicians have eschewed costuming and stage personas in favor of expressive authenticity.

Costuming has been a difficult site of negotiation for female musicians because of the long history of women's assumed sexualization in public arenas. The tradition of associating women with the body rather than the mind results in many audience members expecting female performers to wear tight, revealing clothing to accentuate their physical features, especially breasts, hips, and legs. This common expectation of the sexualized female performer is a burden most endured by women of color, who have been constructed as more licentious than white women. Thus, the Motown label, which produced many acts associated with the girl group sound, was adamant about adorning African American musicians in clothes that produced a wholesome yet fashionable look easily read as respectable by the middle class.

In contrast, the all-white Shangri-Las shocked mainstream society in the early 1960s with their rebellious image, which included wearing pants. By the late 1960s, more female rock musicians, such as Janis Joplin, Grace Slick, and Patti Smith, were inspired by the androgyny of hippie and feminist fashions and began to wear pants during performances for comfort as well as to prevent sexual objectification. As roles for women musicians expanded beyond vocalist over the course of the late twentieth century, many women performers—especially those who played harder styles, such as punk and heavy metal—continued to choose jeans, T-shirts, and comfortable shoes for live performances over the more revealing feminine attire commonly worn by women pop artists. (By comparison, few male rock musicians have regularly worn entire outfits of women's clothing for live performances. Yet several all-male "hair bands" of 1980s, such as Poison, became infamous for accentuating their femininity with long hair, make-up, scarves, jewelry, tight clothing, and high-heeled boots.)

In addition, many female rockers have eschewed traditional beauty regimes used to affirm femininity, such as make-up, long nails, and elaborate hairdos. Punk culture in particular gave women rock musicians license to offend by subverting feminine beauty standards. While the braces worn by Poly Styrene of X-ray Spex challenged audience's expectations for conventional beauty in the late 1970s, the graying of L7's members' hair in the 1990s called attention to our society's repudiation of old age and rock culture's naturalization of youthfulness. Meanwhile, several black female rockers, like Cindy Blackman Santana, Alison Martlew, and Skin of Skunk Anansie, have signified racial pride while resisting tropes of white feminine beauty by shaving their heads or wearing their hair in Afros.

Despite the continued prevalence of masculine appearance among women rock musicians, since the early 1990s, female costuming choices have become more varied. In part this is because third wave feminism reclaimed femininity, including feminine apparel, like dresses. Another crucial factor during this period was the rise in self-consciously performative feminine practices meant to call attention to gender as a construction (a strategy for which Madonna is most commonly credited). For example, Kat Bjelland of Babes in Toyland and Courtney Love of Hole developed a costuming style in the early 1990s that came to be known as **kinderwhore**. Composed of baby-doll dresses and accessories associated with girls, such as barrettes and knee socks, along with poorly managed red lipstick and bleached-blonde hair, the kinderwhore style could be read as a critique of society's hypersexualization of girls and infantilization of adult women as well as a subversion of the female body politics promoted by the beauty and fashion industries.

Meanwhile, other women rockers have expanded costuming choices into new realms of bodily display. For example, some female performers, like Peaches, have heightened public attention to female masculinity via the camp techniques of **drag**. In turn, several female punk performers have been known to perform topless, thus calling attention to the double standard that allows for male nudity while labeling female nakedness "offensive." (Men's disrobing is more common and reaffirming of hegemony in rock culture, despite its playful irony.) Lynne Breedlove of Tribe 8 further complicated the gendered meaning of her toplessness by wearing boxers and a strap-on dildo as part of her stage act.

Likely a result of the spread of postfeminism and an increase in discourse about women's sexual agency, more women rockers today are drawing attention to their bodies during performances via revealing outfits. As Amanda Rootes of Fluffy argues, "I feel much more powerful if I'm in a sexy outfit."[14] Because of the persistence of sexism and the multiple forms of feminist ideology currently in circulation, debate continues over whether this costuming choice is oppressive or liberating for women performers. Many female rockers continue to feel uncomfortable in having to negotiate this physical aspect of performance when their male peers do not. Moreover, with success comes even greater public attention to women's bodies, not to mention evaluation based on cultural norms. As Allison Robertson of the Donna notes, "the bigger you get, the more you get compared to pop stars and people with perfect bodies."[15]

Blocking

In addition to deciding what they should wear and what objects they might interact with during performance, rock musicians must determine how their bodies will be move, a practice known as **blocking**. As Frith argues, the body is yet another instrument of expression in live music performances. Therefore, the body's movements can be understood as part of the larger communicative act that is a musician's performance. Position, posture, and movement are all important to this process. Unlike pop shows, rock gigs infrequently involve formalized dance **choreography**, as the experience is meant to be authentic and spontaneous. This does not mean, however, that there are no ritualized movements of rock musicians' bodies on stage or that musicians do not develop particular moves that become part of their standard acts.

The typical position of rock musicians on stage is the vocalist center stage front, the drummer center stage back, and the guitarist, bass player, other instrumentalists, and backup positioned either stage left or right. These places are taken up at the start of the performance and help to guide the audience's focus. Yet, despite this norm, rock musicians rarely stay in one spot when performing. Rock music is meant to move people, and movement is key to the blocking of rock musicians.

Most rock vocalists, guitarists, and bassists stand upright when performing. This **posture** draws attention to their bodies and music while also allowing for greater flexibility with technology and movement. In addition, such a posture has meanings connected to gender politics, especially when combined with other elements of performance. For example, a standing posture is visually large and suggestive of action, power, and thus masculinity, particularly if performers stand on a stage above the audience. Keyboardists and percussionists can either stand or sit, although their posture, and thus its gendered meaning, is often dependent on their instrument.

Bodily movements, including gestures and facial expressions, are essential to blocking also, since musicians express through them not only the song being performed but also their own identities and public personas. For instance, face muscle movements express emotional states, including happiness, excitement, and anger. In rock, vocalists' facial expressions are perhaps most significant because of such musicians' important role in conveying the meaning of a song. Paul Eckman also discusses "illustrative" gestures that are used like speech, such as nodding or shaking the head. In rock music, thrusting one arm in the air to emphasize lyrics has become conventional. "Emblems" are another important form of bodily movement and are typically understood only by those "in the know." Perhaps the most emblematic movement in rock is the "sign of the horns," wherein the index and pinky fingers are extended and the thumb holds the other two fingers to the palm. This emblem is commonly used by rock fans to signify pleasure in a song or band; yet it is also commonly misunderstood as satanic and evil by those who are religiously conservative.

Because vocalists are commonly understood as being the "front persons" of their bands and thus those most responsible for entertaining the audience, numerous rock singers have developed particular bodily movements to express a song's meaning and/or to communicate a specific stage persona. Since rock music is typically up-tempo, it is not surprising that during most rock performances, singers move frequently and quickly, walking or running back and forth across the stage or into the audience, often with their microphones in hand. For example, during Freddie Mercury's performance of "Radio Ga Ga" with Queen at the 1985 Live Aid concert (broadcast internationally by the BBC), he carried a shortened microphone stand in one hand as he strutted and ran across the stage, fist raised. His quick movements and forceful performance could easily be read as masculine, which is in keeping with male rock stardom. But knowledge of Mercury's gay identity and the gay subcultural elements of his attire complicate such a reading (see Figure 8.7).

As with those of rock instrumentalists, rock vocalists' onstage movements can be understood via attention to their particular historical context as well as to the genre of rock music being performed. For example, Elvis Presley wowed rock 'n' roll

Figure 8.7   Freddie Mercury in *Live AID*
BBC, 1985

audiences with his lively arm movements and pelvic thrusts in the otherwise staid 1950s by borrowing from the energetic performance styles associated with African American boogie woogie and R&B musicians, like Louis Jordan. Although Presley set the bar for other rock vocalists' performances for many years, at the time some conservatives considered such dancing as overtly sexual and thus immoral. Moreover, it was commonly understood as troubling gender norms, as few men, including actors, put their bodies on display in such a fashion in the 1950s.

The conservative values that ultimately led to photographing Presley only from the waist up had a broader impact on other rock 'n' roll performers and were echoed in the limited movement of female singers' bodies during the girl group era. Since black women were commonly stereotyped by white people as hypersexualized, some managers and producers discouraged members of girl groups from moving their bodies, especially when being photographed, to make their performances less threatening and more respectable to white, middle-class consumers.

As sexual standards loosened over the course of the 1960s, an increasing number of rock vocalists, particularly those influenced by R&B, used lively dance moves to express themselves and garner audience attention. Commonly associated with soul and R&B more than rock, James Brown's highly energetic dance moves, which included show-stopping splits, slides, and leaps, became a huge influence on rock vocalists' movements. Much like Brown, Tina Turner threw herself physically into her performances by moving her feet quickly, kicking her legs, thrusting her arms, shaking her head, and whirling her hair, a style perhaps best on display during her performance of "Proud Mary" (see Figures 8.8–8.11). Via extensive touring and nationwide broadcasts on shows like *Midnight Special*, Turner didn't influence only women or other black performers. Mick Jagger's flamboyant strutting, which became a major part of the Rolling Stones' stage act by the late 1960s, was indebted to Turner's, although his performance moves were read differently as a result of their gender and racial identities.

In the latter part of the twentieth century, other rock vocalists, particularly those associated with punk and alternative rock, developed stage moves that were not erotic, perhaps because such genres do not privilege sexuality. For example, Ian Curtis, Joy Division's vocalist, was known for his epileptic-like dancing when performing songs like "She's Lost Control." In turn, many female punk singers, including Siouxie Sioux, Patti Smith, and Kathleen Hanna, have developed assertive stage moves meant to signify power and thus to subvert the conventional eroticization of women vocalists.

Numerous punk and alternative rock performances have also involved vocalists' stage diving and crowd surfing, bold movements meant to bring band members closer to audiences and to lessen the power balance between them. Indeed, the vocalist surrenders their body to the audience members, who struggle to keep them "afloat." Yet, as demonstrated by incidents of male audience

Figure 8.8   Tina Turner on *The Midnight Special*
NBC, 1974

Figure 8.9   Tina Turner on *The Midnight Special*
NBC, 1974

Figure 8.10   Tina Turner on *The Midnight Special*
NBC, 1974

Figure 8.11   Tina Turner on *The Midnight Special*
NBC, 1974

members groping women performers' bodies during such occasions, the gender politics of such moves should be considered.

While rock vocalists typically command the most attention during live shows, plenty of rock instrumentalists have also created signature moves to attract the audience's gaze. Indeed, despite keyboardists and drummers' traditional pose of sitting, many who play rock music have been known to move extensively if not spectacularly while performing. For example, Little Richard and Jerry Lee Lewis became popular in part because of their lively piano performances, which often included standing and dancing while playing.

Yet far more attention has been paid historically to guitarists than other rock instrumentalists in discussions of blocking. Jimi Hendrix, considered by many to be one of the best rock guitarists and thus a major influence on other guitarists, developed some of the most creative and outrageous guitarist movements in rock history. His performance of "Wild Thing" at the 1967 Monterey Pop Festival—which was accompanied by "humping" the amplifier stack, "picking" his guitar with his teeth, lighting it on fire, and smashing it to pieces (all captured in the documentary *Monterey Pop*)—demonstrated his understanding of rock performance as theatrical, not to mention his innovative experiments with sound creation (see Figure 8.12). Indeed, Hendrix was trying to upstage Pete Townshend, who had smashed his guitar earlier in that concert.

As much as guitar smashing has become somewhat normalized in hard rock performance (at least for those who can afford it), it has also contributed to the connotation of rock guitarists as strong, aggressive, and thus phallic, a

Figure 8.12 Jimi Hendrix in *Monterey Pop*
Leacock Pennebaker, 1968

meaning that is furthered when male performers hold their instruments low in the groin area. Nevertheless, some male guitarists who perform punk and alternative rock have been known to avoid phallic uses of their instrument by playing their instruments higher on their bodies in the way women commonly do.

Also important to consider when analyzing rock performers' blocking is that two or more band members often move together as a performing unit as they collectively take pleasure in their joint music-making. This is perhaps most notable in interactions between the vocalist and the lead guitarist, the two most privileged positions in rock bands. When male and female performers, like Fleetwood Mac's Lindsey Buckingham and Stevie Nicks, interact as a unit, heterosexual relations are often suggested as a result of the "coupling" of the two differently gendered bodies involved. Few female rock musicians move in sexualized ways among male band members with whom they are not already intimate, likely because they risk developing a reputation as "slutty," which might disrupt their status as musicians and relationships with male bandmates. In contrast, numerous male rock acts have employed sexualized female backup dancers who contribute to the eroticism of performances yet do not compromise the musicians' dominance on stage (a strategy found in music videos also). Few female-centered rock bands have employed male backup dancers, although this practice appears in contemporary pop somewhat regularly. Meanwhile, several queercore bands, such as Black Fag and Girl in the Nose, have utilized backup dancers of the same gender as the musicians, thus heightening the homoerotic dimension of their music.

Male guitarists and vocalists of hard rock and heavy metal bands often perform with and against each other when playing, as can be seen between Robert Plant and Jimmy Page in *The Song Remains the Same*, the documentary of Led Zeppelin's 1973 U.S. tour (see Figure 8.13). As Steve Waksman and Susan Fast argue, such intimate onstage interactions, which often involve a feminized male vocalist and a masculine male guitarist, complicate norms of both gender and sexuality through suggestions of genderqueerness and homoeroticism. Straight audience members may see sexual displays between same-sex heterosexual musicians as simply risqué and rebellious. Such dynamics are read differently, however, when performed by same-sex members of queercore bands, such as Tribe 8 and Pansy Division.

Although this chapter has teased apart the different theatrical aspects of live rock performances, from stage design to blocking, the meaning of each performance of each song is far more than the sum of these individual parts. Thus, any analysis of rock performance must consider these components collectively while also discerning their individual significance. Yet these theatrical practices, even when analyzed in aggregate, do not alone make up or determine the meanings of rock performances. Music and lyrics, the subjects of the chapters that follow, are also central to the formation, as well as the interpretation, of live rock performances.

Figure 8.13 Robert Plant and Jimmy Page in *The Song Remains the Same*
Warner Bros., 1976

Summary

In this chapter we have explored the world of live rock performance. Many people believe that there is little to public performance other than playing music, but this chapter's survey of rock's culture of production has described the many activities involved in this form of labor, from rehearsing music to securing gigs to preparing costumes to developing stage moves. Such practices are thus part of the complex labor activities in which musicians participate.

Looking at this sphere of cultural production from a gender-based perspective, this chapter discussed the challenges female musicians face given the historical male domination of rock scenes, technologies, and performance practices. By exploring research in this area, we can come to understand the difficulties female performers have in obtaining and successfully managing gigs, not least of which are their common sexual objectification and the denial of their talent by male club owners, clientele, sound engineers, and fellow musicians. Touring is hard for many females also, especially since that culture has long facilitated male camaraderie through women's exclusion.

As this chapter makes clear, not all rock musicians are able to comfortably negotiate or manage the various practices of performance, gigging and touring, as a result of the traditional gender politics that continue to inform rock culture. At the same time, however, the theatrical nature and rebellious spirit of rock culture provides a means by which musicians can experiment with alternate identities that complicate and subvert traditional gender norms. Theatrical practices are only part of any live rock performance, however. Someone needs to be listening to and watching such performances for a cultural exchange to take place and for musicians to benefit financially from their craft. Thus, rock performers must create musical texts that connect with audiences. Part IV concerns the shifting gender politics of the musical texts created and consumed in rock culture, beginning with lyrics, the focus of Chapter 9.

Further Exploration

1. Watch the film *Hype!* (1997).

Describe the music scene documented in this movie. What kind of roles, practices, spaces, and institutions are associated with this music scene? How involved have women been in this scene? How did the mass media help to expand this scene beyond its geographical borders in the late 1980s and early 1990s?

2. Map your local rock scene.

Obtain a map of your hometown and map the most popular venues for rock shows. Also mark where record stores and music stores are located. Do these businesses converge around a particular area, or are they dispersed? How does the location of these various businesses affect the scene?

3. Watch *Women in Rock* (1985), *Righteous Babes* (1998), and *Lilith on Top* (2001).

What comments do the musicians in these films make about the gender politics of gigging, touring, and performance? Have these politics changed since the mid-1980s? If so, how? If not, why not?

4. Watch *Riding in Vans with Boys* (2003).

Place this film in its sociohistorical context. What activities do the Kut U Up bandmates engage in other than performing music? How are those practices affected by gender ideologies? How do the activities of Kut U Up band members compare to those of blink-182 and Green Day? Do we see any instances in the film where rock culture's historical patriarchal heteronormativity is subverted? If so, to what effect? Compare the touring experiences of the male musicians in this film with those of female musicians offered in such films as *Women in Rock* (1985) and *Lilith on Top* (2001). Compare the male performances in this documentary to those in the fictional film *Roadie* (1980).

5. Visit a local music club featuring both a male musician or all-male band and a female musician or all-female band.

Observe the dynamics of the male and female musicians relating to the club owner, sound engineers, and audience. (Be sure to check with your instructor first about your institution's guidelines for human subjects research.) What similarities did you see between male and female experiences with these various individuals? What differences did you see?

6. Interview musicians about gigging and touring.

Discuss with both male and female musicians their experiences of performing at local gigs and being on the road touring. (Be sure to check with your instructor first about your institution's guidelines for human subjects research.) What gender specific incidents or practices do these musicians relate? How are those incidents or practices related to dominant gender politics? Do any of those experiences subvert gender norms?

7. Create gigs and tours for your own band.

If you have a band but are not yet performing publicly, pursue local shows and consider tours. As you prepare for your gigs, think about the work involved, which of your band members volunteer to do which tasks, and how those decisions may be related to gender. Also consider what form of dress, make-up, props, and movements members of your band might use during performance, and how those relate to rock's traditional gender politics.

Further Reading

Auslander, Philip. *Performing Glam Rock: Gender and Theatricality in Popular Music*. Ann Arbor: University of Michigan Press, 2006.

Bannister, Matthew. *White Boys, White Noise: Masculinities and 1980s Indie Guitar Rock*. Burlington: Ashgate, 2006.

Bayton, Mavis. *Frock Rock: Women Performing Popular Music*. Oxford: Oxford University Press, 1998.

Eckman, Paul. "Biological and Cultural Contributions to Body and Facial Movement." 1977. *The Body: Critical Concepts in Sociology*. Eds. Andrew Blaikie, Mike Hepworth, Mary Holmes, Alexandra Howson, David Inglis, and Sheree Sartain. New York: Routledge, 2003. 34–84.

Fast, Susan. *In the Houses of the Holy: Led Zeppelin and the Power of Rock Music*. New York: Oxford University Press, 2001.

Frith, Simon. *Performing Rites: On the Value of Popular Music*. Cambridge: Harvard University Press, 1998.

Gaines, Donna. "The Local Economy of Suburban Scenes." *Adolescents and Their Music: If It's Too Loud, You're Too Old*. Ed. Jonathon S. Epstein. New York: Garland, 1994. 47–65.

Inglis, Ian. *Performance and Popular Music: History, Place and Time*. Burlington: Ashgate, 2006.

Pattie, David. *Rock Music in Performance*. Basingstoke: Palgrave Macmillan, 2007.

Schippers, Mimi. *Rockin' out of the Box: Gender Maneuvering in Alternative Hard Rock*. New Brunswick: Rutgers University Press, 2002.

Whiteley, Sheila. *Women and Popular Music: Sexuality, Identity and Subjectivity*. New York: Routledge, 2000.

IV

Rock's Texts

Music and Images

9 UP TO ELEVEN
Rock Sounds

LISTEN: SLEATER-KINNEY, "WORDS + GUITAR" (*Dig Me Out*, Kill Rock Stars, 1997). *This song captures rock musicians' love of noise. Yet the lyrics and music also touch on the variance of sounds in rock culture, which has long made room for quiet feminine songs as much as the raucous masculine songs for which the genre is better known.*

Rock music is the heart of rock culture. Without this particular musical style, rock culture simply would not exist. The sound of rock music—its aural dimension—is one of its most defining features and contributes significantly to how rock culture is practiced, understood, represented, and enjoyed globally. In fact, a considerable number of rock songs are about the sonic power of this musical style, from Chuck Berry's "Rock and Roll Music" (1957) to the Velvet Underground's "Rock and Roll" (1970) to Wild Flag's "Romance" (2011). Therefore, when analyzing rock culture, it is essential to explore the music that is at the center of it.

Rock songs, like those associated with other popular music styles, typically consist of both sounds and lyrics, each informing the other and contributing to listeners' reception of the music. Popular music scholars generally agree that a song's lyrics and musical sounds should not be analyzed independently from each other, since they work together to produce meaning and affect, the listener's reception of the song. Nevertheless, for those individuals inexperienced in song analysis, it is useful to explore lyrics and musical sounds independently before engaging in studies that explore both simultaneously. With that objective in mind, this chapter focuses on rock sounds, and Chapter 10 explores rock lyrics.

Analyzing and writing about rock music can be difficult. Few rock musicians notate songs when they are composing them, so there is typically no score that can serve as the site of musical analysis. This leaves scholars interested in rock music only recordings and live performances to study. Moreover, although some musical notations are created for popular rock songs, wide variety exists in how popular music is notated, which makes broad consensus on such notations difficult. In turn, many scholars of popular music (rock included) avoid writing about the sonic qualities and structures of songs because they simply lack the tools to do so, tools typically acquired through either experience in musical performance or training in music theory. Without such knowledge, rock scholars are forced to describe musical sounds in everyday language or to focus on other phenomena associated with songs, such as lyrics.

But understanding the lyrics, or performance style, or video images associated with a particular song cannot help us in understanding its full meaning for the musicians who play it and for the audience members who listen to it. The *sound* of the song is crucial to both its performance and reception. As Simon Frith argues, rock music usually affects its consumers on the sonic rather than lyrical level, with listeners typically privileging sounds over words. Indeed, rock lyrics are often expressed in such a loud, fast, or distorted way that listeners find it difficult to capture the exact words being sung. In those moments, listeners focus on sound over meaning.

Given the centrality of sound to this particular form of popular music, it is necessary to consider closely the ways rock music signifies sonically. The first half of this chapter considers different types of musical compositions in rock culture and offers an overview of the temporal and spatial dimensions of this music, as well as its various sonic qualities. The second half explores the historical development of rock as a particular style of popular music while also examining its distinctive sonic structures and characteristics, especially volume and distortion. The gendering of rock's musical sounds and sonic structures are given special consideration, for such gendered connotations contribute to how individuals perform and consume this form of music.

Musical Compositions and Recordings

Musical compositions are individual creations of purposefully organized sounds. Musical compositions range widely in terms of their sonic qualities, structures, and length. In rock music, the typical musical composition is the **song**, which contains both sonic and lyric elements and privileges the voice. In comparison to most classical compositions, the length of a typical rock song is relatively short, anywhere between one and four minutes. This short duration is characteristic of all popular music styles, as a result of the development of the 45 rpm or **single** record, which typically can hold only one track and five minutes of sound. Such singles have been crucial to music-oriented radio programming.

The development of the 33 1/3 rpm **LP (long-play) record**, which can hold up to thirty minutes of music and thus several songs per side, allowed musicians to create longer individual compositions. An LP record featuring a collection of related songs is referred to as a **concept album**. In the late 1960s such albums became a primary means of demonstrating a rock band's creative talents, expertise, and "seriousness." Despite the development of digital recordings and the freedom musicians now have from the constraints of vinyl, the LP album continues to be the most privileged compositional form for rock bands.

Music as Aestheticized Sound

Music is an aestheticized type of sound, meaning that it is crafted to have a particular effect on its performer and listener. Therefore, the role of a musician—whether amateur or professional—is to produce and structure vocal and/or instrumental sounds as a means of creative expression. One of the primary methods used to understand how musical sound differs from natural or nonaestheticized sound is to attend to music's particular components and characteristics. These are typically divided via their relationship to music's temporal and spatial dimensions. Yet there are some musical components, such as timbre and form, that complicate this division and hence are best addressed on their own.

The Temporal Dimension

A key component of all musical expression is time. Many elements of musical performance are produced through musicians' creative manipulation of sound's temporal dimension. Perhaps the most basic temporal quality of music is **sustain**, the duration of an individual sound's audibility. Percussion instruments, such as drums, have the shortest sustain; their sounds are produced through quick **attack** movements and have a rapid **decay**. Instruments that involve air movement, such as brass horns, woodwinds, and the human voice, produce musical sounds with the longest sustain. Sustain can be prolonged through artificial mechanisms. A common practice in rock performance, particularly during solo portions of a song, is the artificial sustain of the lead electrical guitar's sounds through the use of effects pedals. Although it is difficult to know how individual listeners might interpret a sound's sustain with regard to gender, we might connect moments of intentional extended sustain with masculinity, given that such sounds require that one use technology while demonstrating mastery and control over both one's equipment and the sounds it produces. Yet, in contrast, the short sustain of drums and other percussive instruments might connote masculinity as well because of their assertiveness and sharpness. As with all musical sounds, however, it is best to consider the overall context of compositions before ascribing particular gender connotations to them.

A **beat** is a measured pulse and the most basic temporal unit in music. In turn, **rhythm**, the pattern that is produced through the arrangement of beats, is one of the most essential temporal characteristics of a musical composition. Rhythm is what makes music move us . . . literally. It is what we clap our hands to, nod our heads to, and dance our bodies to. In collaborative performances, it is the job of particular instrumentalists to provide the basic rhythmic foundation for a song's overall sound and feel. In rock bands, the **rhythm section** is usually made up of a bass guitarist and a drummer. The vocal delivery of lyrics also participates in creating a song's rhythm.

To understand how rhythm is created in rock music, we must first understand other temporal characteristics of musical sounds. For example, songs and other musical compositions are commonly divided into multiple segments of equal duration called **bars** or **measures**. As discussed below, many rock songs are composed of twelve bars that are repeated several times. Indeed, bar repetition is an essential component of popular music form and adds another rhythmic element to rock songs beyond their notes and beats.

The timing of beats in bars or measures is called **meter**. On sheet music, a composition's meter is indicated by the **time signature**, which looks like a mathematic formula for division (e.g., 4/4). The top or first number refers to how many beats occur in each bar, while the bottom or second number indicates the value or duration of those beats as expressed by a particular type of **note** (i.e., whole, half, quarter, eighth, or sixteenth). Most popular songs, including those in the rock genre, are in 4/4 time (also known as "common time" or "simple meter"). In a musical composition with 4/4 time, each bar will have four beats, and each beat will be a quarter of a whole note.

While many rock songs have the same meter, not all rhythms are produced in the same way. **Tempo** refers to the speed at which music is performed or the pace of beats. In popular music, tempo is often expressed as "beats per minute" (**bpm**). The faster the tempo, the more beats per minute. (Note the difference in tempos when reading the following out loud: 1234, 1234, and 1 2 3 4, 1 2 3 4.) Tempos can change over the course of a piece of music, but a song's general tempo is often dictated by its musical style or genre. For example, rock music inherited a fast tempo from boogie-woogie, R&B, and western swing, and some rock forms, especially punk, speed up that tempo even further. Nevertheless, plenty of rock songs, especially ballads, are slow.

The tempo at which a song's beats are played suggests particular qualities or feelings that the musician wants to express, such as happiness or sadness. Yet tempo can connote gender also. For example, songs with fast tempos are often understood as masculine as a result of their aggressive drive and lively, energetic nature. By comparison, slow songs have commonly been considered feminine since they sound passive, unassertive, and/or sentimental. For example, consider the difference in tempo between the Pretenders' "The Wait" (1980) and Coldplay's "Fix You" (2005). Yet many rock songs incorporate different tempos, often building from a slower to a faster pace. A good example of this is Ike and Tina Turner's version of Creedence Clearwater Revival's "Proud Mary" (1969).

In addition to tempo, a song's rhythm is produced by the **accent** or emphasis of particular beats. Most musical compositions involve both stressed and unstressed beats. The most common accent structure in popular music is a two-beat pattern wherein the odd beats are stressed. In other words, the first beat in a bar is accented, the third beat is less accented than the first, and the second and fourth beats are unaccented. To hear the pattern, read the following out loud: **1 2 3 4, 1 2 3 4, 1 2 3 4.** (Compare this to an unaccented pattern, where all the beats are equally stressed: 1 2 3 4, 1 2 3 4, 1 2 3 4.) This accented pattern is common in music because it follows our expectations for musical structure, which are derived less from our experiences of rhythm in nature, for example heartbeats, than from cultural conditioning.

Rock bands' rhythm sections typically vary this rhythmic structure through their use of **syncopation**, which involves accenting traditionally unstressed beats. From rhythm and blues, rock inherited the syncopated **backbeat**, which accents even ("off") instead of odd ("on") beats: 1 **2** 3 **4**, 1 **2** 3 **4**, 1 **2** 3 **4**. In rock, the backbeat is commonly performed by the snare drum. An excellent example of how different instruments can be used to fix the beat is the Rolling Stone's "Gimme Shelter" (1969). The song begins with a rhythmic pattern laid out by the rhythm guitar. Only after several other instruments and the vocals have joined in do the drums become more dominant and take control of the song's overall rhythm.

Some people see the backbeat as the most definitive feature of rock music, since it appears so often. But it has additional cultural significance. As John Shepherd and Timothy Taylor have theorized, because syncopated rhythms are made up of unexpected accents on off beats, they work well to symbolize marginalized musicians' attempts to construct sonic structures that differ from common expectations. It is interesting to consider, therefore, how the backbeat has aurally signified rock culture's larger ethos of rebellion and rock musicians' and fans' alienation from mainstream culture.

A song's tempo is largely determined by how fast or slow musicians play their instruments. Yet, as Richard Middleton argues, it is also important to pay attention to lyrics when considering the temporal structure of a song. Carefully chosen and structured by songwriters, the words of musical compositions contribute to their rhythmic patterns. The construction of tempo through lyrical delivery is perhaps most noticeable in songs that are **a cappella** (without instrumental accompaniment). Consider, for example, Ani DiFranco's "Tiptoe" (1995) and Tori Amos's "Me and a Gun" (1991). In each of these songs the vocalist's physical body is in sole control of the musical sounds, which may be on purpose, given that both songs communicate disturbing experiences about women's compromised control of their bodies.

The Spatial Dimension

Another important aesthetic component of musical compositions is their spatial dimension—the organization and structuring of sounds. The basic unit of music is a **pitch**, which is the perceived frequency of a particular sound. Such frequencies are measured via a scale called Hertz. In many cultures, musical pitch is gendered: low sounds are associated with the male voice and thus masculinity, while high sounds are affiliated with the female voice and femininity. In Western musics, a **scale** is made up of seven pitches—commonly referred to as **notes**—that are arranged from low to high frequencies: C-D-E-F-G-A-B. This type of scale is known as **diatonic**. With frequencies from 264 to 568 Hertz, the notes in the diatonic scale have also been represented by names: do-re-mi-fa-so-la-ti.

A **melody** is a coherent series of successive notes that varies over time as a result of differences in each note's duration and pitch. In most classical compositions, a primary melody is followed by variations on that theme or motif. In contrast, rock songs typically have two melodies—a **verse** and a **chorus** (or refrain)—that are repeated several times. In rock, melody is typically performed by the vocalist or lead guitarist. Consider Queen's "We Will Rock You" (1977), which has three verses and an anthem-like chorus, as well as a melody produced almost entirely via vocals. In addition to verses and a chorus, many rock songs have **bridges**, short transitional sections that are often in a contrasting key and allow for a pause in the song's main melody. The guitar solo at the end of "We Will Rock You" might be considered a bridge, although it ends the song rather than returning to the original melody. A more typical bridge can be heard in James Brown's "Get Up (I Feel Like being a) Sex Machine" (1970).

The individual notes composing a song's melody are not the only sounds we hear. Popular forms of music, including rock, are commonly structured by **chords**—a grouping of three or more pitches or notes played at the same time. (Think here of the complex sounds produced by playing several piano keys or guitar strings simultaneously.) **Harmony**, the relationship of notes played together, is produced through chords, and the movement from one chord to another is called a **chord** or **harmonic progression**. Harmony can be created by individual instrumentalists or vocalists performing more than one note at a time or by multiple people performing different notes and chords. In rock music, harmonies can be simple—involving only three chords—or complex—involving numerous chords. Punk is well known for its three-chords-or-less style, but many earlier rock songs have a minimal number of chords as well, including Buddy Holly's "Not Fade Away" (1957) and Van Morrison's "Gloria" (1964).

Many rock songs rely on what is known as a **twelve-bar blues structure**, which, as its name suggests, has its roots in the blues tradition. Songs with this progression pattern are made up of twelve bars or measures, whose harmonies alternate between three chords: the tonic (signified by a T, 1, or I), the subdominant (signified by a S, 4, or IV), and the dominant (signified by a D, 5, or V). The **tonic** is the first and primary note of a musical **key**, as in "a song played in the key of A." The **subdominant** is the fourth scale degree in a seven-note scale, and the **dominant** is the fifth scale degree and the one that most harmonizes with the tonic. Utilizing Roman numerals, the twelve-bar blues structure looks like this:

```
I    I    I    I
IV   IV   I    I
V    IV   I    I
```

Many variations on this blues pattern occur in other forms of popular music, including rock. For example, if a song has a tonic in the key of C, a twelve-bar chord progression might look like this:

```
C    C    C    C
F    F    C    C
G    F    C    C
```

Twelve-bar songs are divided into three **phrases**, each of which is four bars in length (noted above by three lines subdivided into four chords apiece). The first phrase is typically related solely to the tonic (I I I I above), while the second reveals the subdominant only to return to the tonic (IV IV I I), a pattern that allows for both similarity and contrast with the first phrase. The third phrase progresses from the dominant harmony through the subdominant and ends by reinforcing the tonic (V IV I I). John Covach notes that the three phrasings structure in a twelve-bar progression is similar to asking a question, asking it again, and then providing an answer. As a result of rock music's strong roots in the blues, thousands of rock songs use the twelve-bar blues structure, including rock 'n' roll oldies, like Little Richard's "Lucille" (1957) and Chuck Berry's "Johnny B. Goode" (1958), hard rock classics, like Cream's "Sunshine of Your Love" (1967) and Led Zeppelin's "Rock and Roll" (1971), as well as more recent songs, like Tracy Chapman's "Give Me One Reason" (1995) and the White Stripes' "Ball and Biscuit" (2002).

The twelve-bar blues structure has not received much attention with regard to its communication of social identities, such as gender or race. However, it is crucial to note the historical association of the blues with African Americans. Recalling Eric Lott's theory of white minstrelsy (discussed in Chapter 3), we might consider how playing the blues—or blues-influenced music, like rock—has functioned as a means by which white musicians can authenticate themselves as virile and powerful while also projecting an image of rebellion. Susan McClary has also complicated our understanding of harmonic relationships in music, and thus twelve-bar blues songs, by arguing that a phallocentric narrative is embedded in musical structures that subsume the subdominant in the tonic. In other words, according to McClary, the tonic, as the controlling sound in the composition, acts as the masculine hero or Self that contains and incorporates the subdominant or feminine Other. Nevertheless, some popular music scholars, such as Theodore Gracyk, have challenged McClary's theory that similar types of music, such as rock songs, have similar gendered meanings simply because of a shared musical structure.

Sound Quality

Another important essential component of rock music is **timbre**, the characteristic quality of a particular sound (the "sound" of a sound). While sounds may be distorted, amplified, and layered in numerous ways, timbre is a sound's most inherent feature. Timbre is probably the most difficult element of sound to describe, since it is produced through a convergence of pitch (the perceived frequency of a note) and **tone** (the difference between two notes or pitches).

Like human voices, each musical instrument has a unique timbre. For example, consider the difference between the plunky sounds of an acoustic guitar with the bright jangle of a tambourine. Unfortunately, the lack of a common language to describe the timbres of musical instruments has posed a challenge to scholars wanting to write about rock sound. Thus, popular music scholars often rely on adjectives used by musicians to describe the timbre of their musical sounds. An electric guitar's timbre, for example, can be labeled "heavy," "twangy," "thick," "clear," "muddy," "chunky," "woody," or "crunchy," among many other descriptive terms.

A key component to musical composition is the creative use of different timbres. The first fifteen seconds of the Beatles' "Hey Bulldog" (1969) makes interesting use of such timbral differences, for example. The song begins with just a piano. Next, guitar and drum sounds are added in, followed by bass and tambourine, and finally human voices. Moving from one instrument to many, the song's timbre becomes increasingly more complex and creative (including the addition of dog barks toward the end).

While vocalists manipulate the timbre of their voice while singing, instrumentalists do so through the instruments they play as well as effects pedals, amplifiers, and other equipment. For some, this search for the best timbre (or what some call the "Holy Grail of Tone") can become an obsession, for well-known musicians are often idolized for their unique timbre or tone. A musician's pursuit of the right tone is often about finding an instrument whose timbre seems most suggestive of their identity. Thus, many rock guitarists spend considerable time and money playing different technologies to achieve this personal timbre. While female guitarists are not necessarily excluded from such practices, male peers, like Tom Petty, have received considerably more attention for it.

Every musical genre (e.g., jazz, country, rap) has a particular timbre associated with it because of the instruments commonly used to perform it. Chuck Berry draws attention to this at the end of his "Rock and Roll Music" (1957), where the instruments of the tango, mambo, and conga are played and differentiated from those that produce rock music. Thus, as with its temporal and spatial dimensions, rock music's signature timbre is rooted in the musical styles from which it emerged, especially the blues, and its privileging of the electric guitar, bass, drums, and voice.

Form

Form is another component of musical compositions. In musicology, form refers to the overall shape or architecture of a composition as created via its most basic elements: pitch, rhythm, harmony, timbre, and dynamics. Key to a song's form is its unique interplay of these components via repetition and variation. Thus, form involves playing with expectation and memory, as listeners attend to both similarity and opposition to make sense of and appreciate the song.

As Richard Middleton argues, repeated patterns punctuated by difference are typical in all sorts of music, including rock. Repetition can appear on a large scale, such as the twelve-bar chord structure, which shapes the overall form of a song. Repetition can appear also on a small scale, such as an instrumental **riff** or short motif that is repeated from time to time (e.g., Heart's "Barracuda" [1977], Nirvana's "Smells Like Teen Spirit" [1991]). The vast majority of riffs in rock music are performed by guitarists. Female instrumentalists rarely show up on critic or fan lists of the greatest rock riffs, another indication of how the sounds associated with this style have been masculinized.

In musicology, form can refer also to particular song structures established over the years by their use in different compositions. For example, Covach highlights the thirty-two-bar **AABA form**, which was common in American popular music during the first half of the twentieth century. The overall pattern of such songs is four eight-bar phrases made up of two similar verses (A A), a bridge (B), and a third verse similar to the first two (A). The AABA form was commonly used in Tin Pan Alley songs and thus influenced many rock 'n' roll songs from the 1950s and early 1960s, including the Shirelles' "Will You Love Me Tomorrow" (1960) and the Beatles' "From Me to You" (1963).

In contrast to songs in the AABA form, **verse-chorus songs** emphasize the chorus of the song. As the **hook** used to grab listeners' attention, the chorus differs significantly from the verses in terms of melody, harmony, and rhythm. The Ronettes' "Be My Baby" (1963) is a good example of this song structure, as almost half of the lyrics consist of the three-word chorus (also the song's title). Songs without contrast between the verse and chorus harmonics are in the **simple verse-chorus form** (e.g., Ritchie Valens's "La Bamba" [1958]). Songs using different harmonics for verses and choruses have **contrasting verse-chorus form** (e.g., the Beach Boys' "California Girls" [1965]). Songs that have no chorus have **simple verse form** (e.g., Santana's "Evil Ways" [1969]).

Many rock musicians have creatively combined the various song structures described above to produce **hybrid** or **compound forms**. More complicated than the simple forms, compound structures allow for musical creativity and sonic diversity, including the addition of instrumental **solos** (when a single performer plays alone). Psychedelic rock, heavy metal, progressive rock, and electronic rock have privileged songs with compound forms. Consider, for example, Queen's "Bohemian Rhapsody" (1975) or songs by Frank Zappa or Emerson, Lake, and Palmer.

Gender is not commonly attributed to song form or structure. Yet we might understand compound forms to align with masculinity because of their privileging of complexity as well as the considerable knowledge and skill assumed to be necessary to compose, perform, and appreciate them. In contrast, McClary argues that songs with simple structures are often feminized and deemed unsophisticated because they are assumed to be easier to write and play and thus are understood as the creations of musicians without much knowledge or skill. Despite these gendered patterns in music history, rock music—a genre predominantly made up of short, simple songs written by men—has upset this conventional gendering of song structure.

Whereas some musical compositions are constructed with a goal-driven narrative, what literary theorists call a **closed form**, other songs, particularly those relying on repetition, are more cyclical and open-ended. McClary argues that because goal-oriented stories in Western literature have long been about the great achievements of male heroes and instill in readers a desire for climax, musical compositions with a similar closed form are associated with masculinity. (Consider Led Zeppelin's "Stairway to Heaven" or the Rolling Stones' "Going Home.") In contrast, since women have historically been associated with the cyclical patterns of nature (especially the moon), circular, **open forms** with no clear climax are more often identified as feminine. Most rock songs have a repetitive, open structure as a result of their historical affiliation with the blues and other African-based musics, as well as the improvisational moments that often occur in live performance. This tendency is yet another way in which rock music deviates from Western musical tradition and complicates the traditional gendering of musical structure.

Rock's Primary Musical Roots

To understand the sonic qualities commonly associated with rock music, two particular popular musical styles are worthy of further consideration: the blues and country music. Many individuals agree that country music is best described as a U.S. popular form deriving from a variety of folk musics and originally featuring acoustic, especially string, instruments. Yet this description fits the blues as well. One of the key differences between the two styles is the race of their early performers: The original blues artists were primarily African Americans, while most of the original country performers were white Americans of either Anglo or European descent. As a result of the racial and class politics prevalent during the early twentieth century when these styles were first recorded, blues music was segregated under the label "race music," while country music was labeled "hillbilly" or "old-time."

Blues

The popular music style most influential on rock music is the **blues**, a vocal and instrumental form developed in southern black communities during the nineteenth century. Blues music derives primarily from Sub-Saharan African music yet has incorporated sound and lyrical components from spirituals, field hollers, Celtic music, and other styles. Blues music is thought to have emerged in the late 1800s alongside the increased enfranchisement of black slaves.

Aesthetically individual blues songs are often idiosyncratic; yet commonalities can be found across the form. For example, most blues songs employ a twelve-bar song structure, as well as a **call-and-response** pattern, wherein two distinct musical phrases are sung or played by different performers, thus creating the sense that the second phrase is responding to the first. In turn, blues songs typically rely on **blue notes**, which are flattened or played at a lower pitch than those of the major scale. Such notes create a somber mood that is typically exacerbated by lyrics that connote melancholy or depression.

The most common instrument among blues performers besides the voice is the guitar, although banjos and piano have been used for blues music also. Several blues subgenres have developed since the original style's emergence; however, country blues and urban blues are most significant to rock music. **Country or delta blues** was originally an improvised, nonelectronic folk style developed in the Mississippi Delta region by such musicians as Robert Johnson and Memphis Minnie. A signature component of country blues is **slide guitar**, a sound produced by moving a solid object, such as a bottleneck or knife blade, along guitar strings to vary their pitch. **Urban blues**, an umbrella term encompassing Memphis blues and Chicago blues, describes an energetic and typically electrified version of the blues developed during the early twentieth century by such musicians as Willie Dixon, Muddy Waters, and Howlin' Wolf. Urban blues songs often have more complex vocal and instrumental parts than those in the country style.

Blues recordings were first marketed in the 1920s. Originally sold as "race music" and consumed primarily by African Americans, blues music began to penetrate white popular culture as more blues performers toured beyond their local communities and the mass media drew more attention to such musicians. The energetic **boogie-woogie** style, developed by such musicians as Pinetop Smith and Big Joe Turner and popular in the 1930s, reconfigured the traditionally somber blues sound via an upbeat version that featured piano and inspired dancing. In the 1940s, a new form of urban blues known as **jump blues** emerged from the influences of big band music on such musicians as Louis Jordan and Roy Brown. Jump blues bands, incorporating more instruments than traditional blues, including the trumpet and saxophone, created a lively form of music that had a major impact on the development of rock 'n' roll.

Following World War II and the increased migration of African Americans to northern U.S. cities, the blues developed further. Influenced considerably by Mississippi performers who had moved north, urban blues developed by foregrounding amplified instruments, especially the electric guitar. This form of blues contributed significantly to R&B in the late 1940s and early 1950s, one of the primary roots or streams informing rock music. As much as rock musicians have historically revered country blues, urban blues has had a significant influence on many rock guitarists, including Jimi Hendrix, Eric Clapton, Jimmy Page, Keith Richards, and Jack White.

Given the historical periods in which blues music developed, it is not surprising that the musicians most commonly referenced in its history are men. Nevertheless, a considerable number of women have performed the blues, especially in the early twentieth century. Women in the urban blues scene were largely excluded from instrumentalist roles during that period. Yet early **blues queen** vocalists, like Gertrude "Ma" Rainey, Bessie Smith, Ethel Waters, Sippie Wallace, Alberta Hunter, and Mamie Smith, fronted bands with male instrumentalists. The blues queens are crucial to the history of not only blues music but also recorded music at large, since they were among the first popular musicians to be recorded, many long before early male blues greats like Robert Johnson. Moreover, the blues queens became role models for many girls and women around the world as a result of their appearance and performance style. In rock culture, Janis Joplin is best known for performing in the blues queen style, a powerful and highly evocative vocal approach. The Delta blues scene included both women vocalists and guitarists, such as Geeshie Wiley and Memphis Minnie, one of the most influential blues musicians of all time. Bonnie Raitt is the female rock musician most cited for continuing the legacy of the Delta blues queens, although male blues artists' influence on her music has been noted more often.

Country

Rockabilly, bluegrass, and western swing are also primary predecessors to rock 'n' roll. To understand the musical contributions of those styles, it is necessary to consider the broader genre with which they are associated. **Country music** is an amalgam of so many musical styles that, in contrast to the blues, it is difficult to parcel out the particular sonic components originally associated with it. Developed by white southerners, it has been influenced by traditional European folk music, Celtic music, and African music. During the late nineteenth century, a variety of other popular forms impacted the development of country music, including spirituals, minstrels, and Tin Pan Alley.

Country music developed in two primary locations of the United States: the Appalachian region of the eastern United States, which became home to many Irish, English, and European immigrants as well as a considerable number of Africans; and Texas, where German and Czechoslovakian immigrants lived alongside Mexicans. **Old-time country music** from Appalachia predominantly featured plucked acoustic string instruments commonly used in Celtic forms, especially the fiddle, while also including the African banjo and Spanish guitar. Early country musicians in Texas added other instruments to this mix, including the dulcimer and accordion.

Country music began to be recorded in the early 1920s by many of the same record companies that were marketing "race music." Commonly referred to as

hillbilly during its early history, the style came to be known as "country" in the 1940s, when the hillbilly label was deemed derogatory. The first country musicians to have a broad impact on the genre were Jimmie Rodgers and the Carter Family. Basing his tunes on those from folk music and traditional ballads, Rodgers is perhaps best known for creating lyrics based on his everyday experiences. Commonly referred to today as the "father of country music," Rodgers was the first recording star associated with this musical style.

The Carter Family recorded numerous traditional folk songs in the first half of the twentieth century, many of which have become standards for other country musicians. The group was made up of Alvin Pleasant "A.P." Carter, his wife, Sara Dougherty Carter, and their sister-in-law Maybelle Addington Carter. A.P. collected most of the group's songs during travels in the rural South with Lesley "Esley" Riddle, an African American guitarist who memorized how the songs were performed instrumentally while A.P. wrote down their lyrics. Maybelle was a guitarist, and her friendship with Riddle influenced her unique form of playing, which came to be known as the "Carter scratch."

Bluegrass music, whose name comes from Bill Monroe's group, the Blue Grass Boys, is a lively form of Appalachian country featuring acoustic stringed instruments, such as the fiddle, banjo, mandolin, and upright bass. Although often misunderstood as a type of folk music, bluegrass emerged as a popular recorded music in the 1940s and has been influenced by various African American musical styles, including jazz and ragtime. It is common in bluegrass for each band member to take a turn performing improvisationally, a characteristic shared with jazz ensembles. The "high lonesome" sound of vocals, wherein a high-pitched harmony is sung over the melody, is somewhat unique to bluegrass.

Western swing is a type of country dance music developed in Texas and Oklahoma during the early twentieth century. Merging country styles with the blues, jazz, polka, and Mexican musics, Western swing was made popular by Bob Wills and Milton Brown via their respective groups, the Light Crust Doughboys and the Texas Playboys. Originally performed by fiddlers and guitarists, Western swing groups of the 1930s and 1940s added other instruments, such as pianos, drums, brass instruments, and steel guitars, to produce a lively mix much like the boogie-woogie sound. **Cowboy** music is primarily associated with various country musicians who adopted cowboy personas, such as Gene Autry, Roy Rogers, and the Sons of the Pioneers. The music of these "singing cowboys" was made popular nationwide during the 1930s and 1940s via their film appearances.

The term **honky-tonk** was originally associated with ragtime, boogie-woogie, and other piano-based dance musics. During the 1940s, honky-tonk referred to a form of country music employing the guitar, fiddle, upright bass, and steel guitar. Emerging first in Texas and Oklahoma, the style is now primarily affiliated with Nashville, Tennessee, where it was produced and promoted during the 1950s via such musicians as Ernest Tubb, George Jones,

Hank Williams, and Lefty Frizzell. Honky-tonk brought the electric guitar to country music.

The early history of country music is primarily associated with the various men noted above, with Charline Arthur and the Carter women being significant exceptions. Nevertheless, as this form of popular music became more popular over the latter half of the twentieth century, a number of female country stars emerged, including June Carter Cash (daughter of Maybelle), Patsy Cline, Wanda Jackson, Loretta Lynn, Dolly Parton, Tonya Tucker, Kitty Wells, and Tammy Wynette. Like the blues queens, most early female country performers were vocalists backed by male instrumentalists, although a few played guitar. The Dixie Chicks are perhaps the best-known all-female band whose music privileges both a country and rock sound.

The Rock Sound

The first decade of rock music (mid-1950s to mid-1960s) was one of tremendous sonic experimentation and thus heterogeneity. This phenomenon resulted from the postwar integration of musical styles once segregated by race. While R&B and up-tempo country music played by young musicians were increasingly labeled "rock 'n' roll" during this period, other styles were eventually included under that term as well, including doo-wop, girl groups, and teenybop.

With the "British Invasion" of U.S. rock culture during the mid-1960s, rock music became more sonically homogeneous, particularly as groups like the Beatles and the Rolling Stones privileged guitar-based genres over voice-centered pop styles. Indeed, the most significant timbral component of such bands' music was that of the electric guitar. The privileging of this one instrument had a significant impact on what we might call the "rock sound." The remainder of this chapter examines that particular sound.

The Electric Guitar Sound

The electric guitar is the central instrument in rock music, and its sound remains predominant in songs of this style. To create music, a guitarist holds strings against **frets** while strumming or plucking a guitar, which in turn creates sonic vibrations. For acoustic guitars, the amplification of those vibrations happens via the instrument's hollow body, and performers typically avoid **overtones**, high-frequency tones that accompany the fundamental pitch of a musical note. For electric guitars, pickups located on the body convert the vibrations of played strings into electrical signals, which are then transmitted to an **amplifier**. The timbre of an electric guitar is often fuller than that of an acoustic guitar because pickups amplify overtones. In turn, by exaggerating these overtones, amplifiers produce **resultant tones**, which are at a pitch or frequency far lower or higher than what an instrument can produce on its own. The effect of such tonal exaggeration is a more complex, "heavier" sound. To understand this difference, compare the guitar timbres in the Beatles' "She Loves You" (1963) and "Helter Skelter" (1969). Same guitarists, two different sounds.

The unmanipulated sound of an amplified electric guitar is often described as "dry" or "clean." Yet a guitar's timbre can be altered through the manipulation of the amplifier's various features or effects, including **reverb** (reverberation), which prolongs the amplification of a particular sound and produces longer sustain. Many amplifiers also have a **vibrato** feature, which creates an undulating tone. This vibrato effect can be produced also via a **tremolo arm** or **whammy bar**, a device on guitar bodies that slackens or tightens strings temporarily. A good example of vibrato is Tommy James and the Shondells' "Crimson and Clover" (1968), which foregrounds the guitar's undulating tones.

Distortion

One of the key elements of rock music timbre is **distortion**, which is created when sounds exceed the natural limits of a musical instrument. The musical potential of distortion was discovered through damaged amplifiers. However, guitar technology is now manufactured to facilitate this sound. An early example of deliberate distortion in rock culture can be heard on Chuck Berry's "Maybellene" (1955).

A common form of such overtone manipulation in rock music is known as **clipping**, a type of sound wave distortion that occurs when an amplifier is **overdriven**, or pushed beyond its voltage capacity by increasing volume. When an amplifier is unable to produce signals above a certain frequency, it will cut or "clip" off the signal, thus producing distortion in the form of high-frequency harmonics. Depending on the guitar and amplifier involved, the distortion created in such instances can be either a thick, fuzzy sound or an edgy growl. Electric guitarists can produce distortion also via the addition of **effects pedals**, which alter the timbre and sustain of amplified sounds. Now commonly used by all rock guitarists, the creative potential of such pedals was first used extensively by Jimi Hendrix in songs like "Voodoo Chile" (1968). Other songs featuring this type of pedal include the Doobie Brothers' "China Grove" (1973), Guns N' Roses' "Sweet Child of Mine" (1988), and Jeff Beck's "Dirty Mind" (2001). Screaming Females is also well known for its guitarists' use of effects pedals.

As discussed previously, masculinity has been excessively linked to mechanical and electrical technologies. Therefore, it is not surprising that journalists regularly question male guitarists about their effects pedals. Meanwhile female musicians are rarely asked because it is presumed that they do not care. While such gendered assumptions reaffirm male musicians' masculinity, they pose a challenge for women musicians, who struggle with such false assumptions also at shops that sell or repair musical equipment.

Because of the odd sounds that can result from excessive distortion, many rock guitarists play **power chords** to create a heavy sound yet avoid unpleasant or unwanted harmonics. For some musicologists, the name of this musical phenomenon is inaccurate, since power chords are not actually chords, which are composed of at least three notes. Power chords rely on just one **interval** or the relationship of two notes—in this case, a note and another note a fifth above it. Power chords are thought to have originated in the late 1950s with pioneering guitarist Link Wray. While the Who's Pete Townshend was the first rock guitarist to use them extensively and is thought to have coined the term, the Kinks were the first rock band to use them in a hit song, "You Really Got Me" (1964). Power chords have since become the primary sonic signifier of hard rock styles, particularly heavy metal. As their name suggests, power chords produce sounds primarily associated with masculinity, an affiliation that, as Robert Walser suggests, is further solidified via their common performance by highly skilled male guitarists.

Like manufactured musical instruments, voices can be distorted. This phenomenon can happen either naturally when the capacity of the vocal cords is exceeded, as with screaming or shouting, or via various electronic technologies. **Microphones** are typically used (alongside amplifiers and speakers) during live performances to amplify or increase the volume of the voice. Microphones are utilized also during recordings to capture the sound of the voice, which can then be distorted via amplifiers and other audio equipment.

The gendered politics of vocal distortion are interesting to consider. Because most women are assumed to have high, soft voices, such vocal sounds are commonly affiliated with femininity. Female rock vocalists sometimes distort their voices, either through screaming or technology. By aligning the timbre of their voices with the low, heavy sound of other amplified instruments, such musicians signify the power, excess, and rebellion that has become associated with rock's traditionally masculine performance style. Yoko Ono is somewhat infamous for her screeching vocals. Kat Bjelland of Babes in Toyland, Poly Styrene of X-Ray Spex, Corinne Tucker of Sleater-Kinney, and many other female punk and metal vocalists have similarly utilized distorted voices and thus disrupted the traditional gender politics of vocal performance.

In contrast to the aggressive vocal style adopted by many male singers, rock culture has at times made space for high-pitched, near **falsetto** male voices. Prince, Robert Plant of Led Zeppelin, and Chris Martin of Coldplay have all used it. This vocal style contrasts considerably with the phallic connotations of the hard rock genres with which it is typically associated, especially heavy metal. Thus, just like the screaming female voice, the male falsetto is suggestive of a form of gender trouble in rock culture.

Volume

An increase or push in **volume** is key to the production of sound distortion. Yet volume is privileged in general in rock culture, not just in relation to distortion. Indeed, volume or loudness is one of the defining features of the rock sound,

Figure 9.1 "Up to eleven" from *This Is Spinal Tap*
Embassy Pictures, 1984

as suggested in the mockumentary *This Is Spinal Tap*, when one of the band's guitarists comments proudly that he owns an amplifier with a volume knob that can be turned up to "eleven" (see Figure 9.1). (Amplifier volume dials usually range from zero to ten.) Volume has been a privileged component in rock music for many reasons, including its bridging of the distance between the performers and the audience. Listeners of loud live music feel immersed in the sound and thus in community with the performers and other listeners. Many rock recordings attempt to recreate this sense of unity by including instructions to "play it loud" or "turn it up."

Yet a connotation of opposition and exclusion exists in rock's loudness also, for by increasing volume, rock performers and listeners ostensibly create a sonic barrier between themselves and individuals not engaged in the music. For decades now, younger rock consumers have used volume to push or keep people away. Think here of teenagers in their bedrooms with their music cranked up. Such loudness isolates rock fans from others while also acting as a symbol of alienation from those around them. While media have mostly represented male youth doing this, likely because loudness is often associated with masculinity, plenty of girls have used rock music in similar ways.

Noise

When occurring simultaneously, musical volume and distortion create **noise**. Most rock musicians privilege this type of sound; however, musicians performing other musical styles have often avoided the production of noise. Theodore Gracyk helps us to understand these different values. As he argues, noise has been defined in four primary ways, each of which reveals particular ideological biases regarding sound. First, noise is defined as a *nuisance*. This criticism typically results from a bias toward a particular sound as a result of one's cultural tastes, which are shaped by one's background and identity, including gender. For example, in classical music, noise is seen as a nuisance because sounds in that style are meant to be pleasant, a value the upper class associates with beauty and fine art. In contrast, poor people, along with youth and people of color, are often understood as tolerating noise because of their supposedly less sophisticated cultural values and tastes. As another example of how noise can be socially defined as a nuisance, consider noise ordinances for different parts of a city, such as residential neighborhoods versus areas with music clubs or sports fields.

The second definition of noise is a sound that *interferes with communication* and thus may cause confusion, such as static on the radio. Third, noise is defined as a sound that *disturbs or distracts*. Think here of alarms or ringing telephones. The final definition of noise is a sound that causes *physical harm*—for example, a sound whose excessive volume damages people's hearing. Although not always considered damaging, rock music is often performed at live events at decibels harmful to the human ear because of the privileging of volume in rock culture.

According to Gracyk, the rock community has several reasons for valuing noise. First, the loudness and noisiness of rock music can be a response to performance conditions. Indeed, the invention of amplified instruments happened precisely because of musicians' desire to be heard above the din of the performance venue. Second, noise is economical for smaller bands since they have fewer musicians to create volume. A third reason is that noise intrudes; it aggressively forces itself on us. Since adult middle-class culture has traditionally valued restraint and quietness, noisy music functions as a means of opposition and resistance. Finally, noise can be used to produce new forms of creative expression.

Once considered an undesirable component of musical sound, **feedback** is a type of noise privileged by some rock musicians and fans. Feedback is produced when a sound signal that has been received by a microphone, amplified, and distributed through a loudspeaker is subsequently received by the mic again, causing a sonic loop. Rock guitarists create feedback by holding their guitars (specifically their pickups) close to the loudspeaker delivering their guitar sound. The Beatles' "I Feel Fine" (1964) was the first rock song to explicitly use feedback; however, other rock guitarists, including Jimi Hendrix, have made extensive use of feedback, creatively exploring its sonic possibilities.

Although Gracyk encourages consideration of the different ideological values related to noise, he pays little attention to how gender functions in this aspect of rock's sonic landscape. Loudness, distortion, and noise have long connoted masculinity through their suggestion of power, control, mastery, and aggressiveness. In contrast, quietness and softness have long been figured as feminine because of their suggestions of passivity and comfort. Thus, while male musicians automatically affirm their masculinity by playing rock, girls and women who become involved in rock music, either as performers or consumers, necessarily transgress age-old gender norms associated with sound and music. Some women-centered rock bands have used their ability to create noise as a feminist gesture, foregrounding their opposition to patriarchy and misogyny through their performance of loud, distorted music. As heard in Girlschool's "Not for Sale" (1980), L7's "Shitlist" (1992), Bikini Kill's "Suck My Left One" (1992), Tribe 8's "Frat Pig" (1995), and Kittie's "Daughters Down" (2004), rock noise accompanied by feminist lyrics challenge traditional femininity and trouble gender politics.

Women rockers aren't alone, however, in troubling the gender norms traditionally associated with musical sound. While less attention has been paid to it, many male rock musicians regularly trouble gender norms via their engagement with more feminine sonic styles, as mentioned above with regard to falsetto voices. In addition, we might think of the many love ballads that have been written and sung by male rockers over the decades. Eschewing the noisy, loud distortion that has become rock's sonic signature, love songs communicate in a soft, mellow, sentimental way via the use of acoustic or classical instruments or simply the voice. Distortion, loudness, and noise are not employed. Although such songs are not often considered the most representative of a male rock band's oeuvre, rock ballads, like the Beatles' "Hey Jude" (1968), Jethro Tull's "Skating Away" (1974), U2's "With or Without You" (1987), and Coldplay's "The Scientist" (2005), are often among the songs most cherished by a group's fans.

Interestingly, the use of the **power ballad** by male rock bands has worked to reclaim romantic songs from any suggestion of softness and femininity. Heightening rock's traditional sonic dimensions for cathartic affect, power ballads, like Guns 'N Roses' "November Rain" (1992) and Aerosmith's "I Don't Want to Miss a Thing" (1998), use distortion, volume, and noise to reemphasize the phallic power of their performers, many of whom nevertheless trouble gender norms with their feminized clothing and performance styles, not to mention suggestive interplay between vocalist and guitarist.

Summary

This chapter has investigated the heart and soul of rock culture: its musical sounds. By familiarizing ourselves with the basic components of musical composition and examining the development of rock as a sonic style, we can understand better the unique qualities of this musical genre and thus its attraction for performers and listeners alike. Through an analysis of such qualities as sustain, tempo, and pitch, we have explored how the performance and structure of musical sounds can affirm or subvert gender norms and considered examples of those practices through specific rock songs.

Rock music emerged in the United States from the convergence and development of white and black folk musics, specifically country and the blues, and borrowed from these two styles many of their temporal and spatial qualities as well as their aural stylings. Key to a great number of rock songs is their reliance on the twelve-bar blues structure, as well as their use of the electric guitar. Made to be played loud, the electric guitar produces sounds that can be manipulated through both effects pedals and amplifiers. Rock musicians looking for a sonic means of expressing themselves have utilized the amplified electric guitar to create the loud, distorted noise that marks rock music as distinct from other popular music forms. In some rock styles, such as heavy metal, the human voice is similarly manipulated in a manner that signifies rebellion, power, or angst.

This chapter also addressed the gendered connotations of rock music via attention to the traditional gendering of the electric guitar's fast, loud, and distorted sounds as masculine. Although electric guitars have been played most often by men, its connotation of masculinity has offered both male and female rockers alike a means for asserting a powerful image during performance and on recordings. Because of rock music's privileging of loud sounds, women's performances of this music often work to subvert the naturalized connection of masculinity and volume, as well as those of femininity and quietness. In addition, we considered the gender politics of rock's vocal sounds, noting that both female screams and male falsetto voices have been used to signify rebellion, given their challenge to gender norms. Thus, while many rock sounds reinscribe hegemonic masculinity, others subvert that gender connotation, suggesting alternate forms of expression, identity, and relationships.

Further Exploration

1. Explore song rhythm.

Listen to a favorite song and attempt to map out its rhythmic structure. Which instruments are constructing the song's primary rhythm? Does this song make you move? If so, how—finger tapping, foot tapping, head nodding, clapping, swaying, or dancing?

2. Analyze song structure.

Listen to a favorite song. Identify the verse, chorus, and bridge (if appropriate). What structure was used to organize the sounds in this piece? Is the song structure closed or open?

3. Explore sound qualities.

Listen to a favorite song. What instruments are used in this musical composition? What types of timbres do those instruments produce, and how do they make you feel?

4. Experience distortion.

Listen to a favorite song at a comfortable volume. Play the song again and turn it up the second time by two or three degrees. Describe the change in sound quality. Is it more or less pleasant to listen to at this volume? Why? Play the song again and turn it up as loud as your amplifier will allow. Describe the change in sound quality. Is it more or less pleasant to listen to at this volume? Why?

5. Determine the gender politics of musical sound.

Listen to a favorite song. Excluding the lyrical content and paying attention only to the sounds, would you describe this song as masculine, feminine, or a mixture of both? Why? What instruments contribute to this gendered association? What other sonic elements contribute to it (e.g., timbre, tempo, structure, distortion, volume)?

6. Explore your favorite band's or musician's music.

Listen to several of your favorite songs by your favorite band or musician. How would you describe the quality of their music overall? How is this sound produced (e.g., instruments, volume, distortion)? Would you label the musical sound of this group or performer as masculine, feminine, or both? Why? What elements of the band's or performer's music contribute to this gendered association?

7. Compose the music for a rock song.

Consider the different ways you can work with the song's form, rhythm, timbre, and distortion to align it with rock's sonic traditions, as well as how those relate to gender politics. Also consider ways that you might manipulate these song components to challenge rock conventions.

Further Reading

Bacon, Tony. *Rock Hardware: The Instruments, Equipment, and Technology of Rock*. San Francisco: Miller Freedman, 1996.

Burns, Lori, and Mélisse Lafrance. *Disruptive Divas: Feminism, Identity and Popular Music*. New York: Routledge, 2001.

Covach, John. "Form in Rock Music: A Primer." *Engaging Music: Essays in Music Analysis*. Ed. Deborah Stein. New York: Oxford University Press, 2005. 65–76.

Frith, Simon. *Music for Pleasure: Essays in the Sociology of Pop*. New York: Routledge, 1988.

Gracyk, Theodor. *Rhythm and Noise: An Aesthetics of Rock*. Durham: Duke University Press, 1996.

McClary, Susan. *Feminine Endings: Music, Gender, and Sexuality.* Minneapolis: University of Minnesota Press, 1991.

Middleton, Richard. *Studying Popular Music.* Philadelphia: Open University Press, 2002.

Moore, Allan F. Rock, *The Primary Text: Developing a Musicology of Rock.* Burlington: Ashgate, 2001.

Shepherd, John. "Music and Male Hegemony." *Music and Society: The Politics of Composition, Performance and Reception.* Eds. Richard Leppert and Susan McClary. New York: Cambridge University Press, 1987. 151–72.

Taylor, Timothy D. "His Name Was in the Lights: Chuck Berry's 'Johnny B. Goode.'" *Reading Pop: Approaches to Textual Analysis in Popular Music.* Ed. Richard Middleton. New York: Oxford University Press, 2000. 165–82.

Théberge, Paul. *Any Sound You Can Imagine: Making Music/Consuming Technology.* Hanover: Wesleyan University Press, 1997.

Walser, Robert. *Running with the Devil: Power, Gender, and Madness in Heavy Metal Music.* Hanover: Wesleyan University Press, 1993.

10 WORDCRAFT
Rock Lyrics

LISTEN: NICK CAVE AND the Bad Seeds, "There She Goes, My Beautiful World" (*Abattoir Blues/The Lyre of Orpheus*, Mute, 2004). *Longing for inspiration and experiencing writer's block, the writer/narrator in this song is compared to famous writers who suffered for their art. Consider how the lyrics gender the writer and the muse, and the possible impact of such connotations on rock culture.*

Just as the loud and distorted sounds of the electric guitar have been central to rock music, so have lyrics that foreground the primary values of rock culture, particularly youthfulness, rebellion, and freedom. Yet rock has also privileged lyrical themes of interpersonal relationships, especially sexuality and love. Many songs considered by fans and critics to be the greatest in rock history include several of these themes: from Little Richard's "Good Golly Miss Molly" (1958) to the Rolling Stones' "(I Can't Get No) Satisfaction" (1965) to Heart's "Crazy on You" (1977) to U2's "With or Without You (1987) to Tracy Chapman's "Give Me One Reason" (1995) to Coldplay's "Yellow" (2000) and to Arcade Fire's "Reflektor" (2013). Nevertheless, just as rock music has expanded over the last six decades, so have the lyrical themes of its songs diversified, covering a broad array of topics few would have imagined when rock 'n' roll emerged.

Rock lyrics are significant to rock musicians because, like musical sounds, they are used to communicate emotions, values, and experiences. Yet lyrics can also provide a place for musicians to transcend themselves and explore other experiences and forms of identity. Rock fans often do these things via rock lyrics also, not just by listening to songs but also by singing them. Lyrics, then, are a primary point of connection between musicians and fans.

As discussed previously, popular music scholars often avoid studying lyrics and musical sounds independently since they inform one another. But for those inexperienced in studying music, it is helpful to examine each separately before attempting simultaneous analyses. To facilitate a basic understanding of rock lyric analysis, this chapter addresses the primary methodologies used by scholars to study written works. Special attention is paid here to gender politics. Rock lyrics have been written, performed, and consumed primarily by men. Yet to understand these songwords as intrinsically patriarchal and misogynist as a result of rock culture's historical male dominance is to underestimate the fluidity of gender performance through lyric, as well as the contributions of feminist and queer songwriters. Therefore, while this chapter will consider the conservative gender politics of some rock lyrics, it will also focus on progressive lyrics that challenge traditional gender norms and provide new avenues for communicating about identity.

This chapter focuses on the critical interpretation of rock lyrics. Determining the actual impact of a song's lyrics on consumers and society is another matter. While many rock fans comment that lyrics help them to understand themselves, to connect with others, and to explore the world and alternate ways of being, a significant number indicate that they do not pay attention to song lyrics, either because they find some words unclear or because they take more pleasure in musical sounds. Nonetheless, gendered representations in rock lyrics definitely contribute to the gender politics of rock culture, and thus likely affect the ways consumers negotiate gender both within and beyond this culture. Chapter 13 is devoted to the study of rock consumers.

Song Lyrics

Songs are musical compositions containing sounds produced by the voice (typically lyrics) as well as by musical instruments. **Lyrics** are words accompanying a song's music. Yet, as Simon Frith argues, lyrics are more than words. They are **rhetoric**, language that is used in a special way. In particular, lyrics are performed stories shared between the songwriter, performer, and audience. Lyrics are meant to express and move more than to inform and educate. As a result lyricists pay close attention not just to word choices but also to the relationships created through the position and juxtaposition of specific words, as well as to the sounds and rhythms of such words when sung. Thus, how lyrics are performed is just as important as what specific thoughts or feelings they communicate.

As a musical style, rock owes its **lyrical structure** to earlier popular forms, including the blues, country, and Tin Pan Alley. Most popular songs are **sectional** in structure (i.e., each part is complete unto itself, though not independent from others), and the most typical sections are the verse and the chorus. A song's **verses** are similar to a poem's stanzas, in that they all have similar structure but different words. In contrast, a song's **chorus** (or refrain) contains the same structure and virtually all of the same words. The chorus is repeated off and on throughout a song, while verses are usually sung only once. The verses contain the song's primary narrative, while the chorus punctuates and structures that story. Many rock song titles come from a line in the chorus, which in turn is considered the **hook** that garners listeners' attention (e.g., Lucinda Williams's "Car Wheels on a Gravel Road" [2001]).

Musical genres develop around a group of songs' similar lyrical structures and themes. For example, many punk songs tend to be structurally simple, harkening back to the earliest rock 'n' roll hits, while other hard rock songs have elaborate lyrical architectures that do not follow traditional structures. The theme of rebellion, which is commonly linked to masculinity, appears across the larger genre of rock music. Yet many women-centered rock bands have used this theme to express feminist opposition to patriarchy. Meanwhile, plenty of male rockers have penned love songs, which are typically seen as feminine.

Song lyrics can be written before, during, or after the composition of a song's music. In rock culture, lyrics composed by the vocalist who sings them are typically given the most value, since they suggest authentic, personal expression. Nevertheless, lyrics should not necessarily be understood as pure reflections of the songwriter's intentions or actions or as advocating the actions discussed. As with other art forms, lyrics are often about exploring alternate ways of being more than documenting experience. Moreover, many bands, especially those that have just formed, **cover** songs written by other lyricists. Indeed, as much as originality is privileged in rock music, the ubiquity of covers suggests that both appropriation and tradition are valued in this culture also.

The vast majority of rock lyrics have been composed by men. Yet many women have achieved acclaim in rock culture for their songwriting abilities. Even before the rise of female rockers in the 1990s, such songwriters as Kate Bush, Aretha Franklin, Carole King, Ellie Greenwich, Joni Mitchell, Patti Smith, and Tracy Chapman were widely respected for their rock lyrics. Nevertheless, almost all published lists of the best rock songs typically marginalize female-written songs and their songwriters. Similarly, the Grammy Awards have marginalized women rock lyricists. Since the "Best Rock Song" category was established in 1992, women have written only 11 percent of the songs nominated. No song written by a woman won this award between 1999 and 2015, and only two won before that period.

Analyzing Song Lyrics

Song lyric analysis owes much to **literary studies**, a type of scholarship that includes the analysis of poetry, short stories, novels, plays, and other written **texts**. Since literary studies is quite old, many different methodologies have been developed to understand the meaning of texts, a process commonly referred to as **textual analysis**. This section will consider the primary methods scholars have employed to study rock lyrics.

New Criticism

New Criticism is a method of literary studies that is no longer used by most contemporary academics because of what many see as its narrow-minded approach to literature, authorship, and readers. Yet New Criticism has had an enormous impact on how most people interpret written works. Indeed, one of its basic tenets—that the foundation of literary interpretations are **close readings** supported by textual evidence—is at the heart of virtually all forms of humanities scholarship today. New Criticism's basic process is to choose a written text and to read it closely to interpret its meaning. For New Critics what matters is the text; all evidence necessary for interpreting it is supposedly contained in it. Thus, New Criticism involves **formal analysis** of the various elements used to structure written texts (i.e., word choice, syntax, point of view, narration, plot, characterization).

New Critics strived to produce the definitive analysis of individual works and believed that their interpretations were objective. However, many scholars studying written texts since New Criticism was in vogue have demonstrated that most literary works—and their interpretations—are influenced by socio-historical context, including dominant ideologies. Moreover, many contemporary scholars have shown that literature is often **polysemous** (having multiple meanings) and that readers bring their own meanings to such texts based on their background and education. As a result of scholars' greater attention to these aspects of literary production and reception, New Criticism's text-centric approach died out by the 1970s.

Content Analysis

A primary method for studying media texts is **content analysis**, a form of analysis meant to facilitate a general and objective understanding by describing a text's most superficial elements (e.g., words, sounds, images). All forms of textual analysis begin with content analysis, even if scholars are not explicit about that step. Several forms of content analysis exist; however, such studies are typically **quantitative** in approach, in that they utilize systematic methods to count particular textual characteristics. The process of conducting quantitative content analyses includes choosing a particular text; determining which characteristics, or units of analysis, will be studied; and counting the frequency of such units in the text. The data produced from content analyses can then be used to establish a general impression of a text, to compare texts to each other, to compare a text to the real object or person it represents, and to advocate for policy change.

Scholars using content analysis to study song lyrics have typically paid attention only to the superficial linguistic elements of such texts, such as the prevalence of particular words and themes. For example, in the 1980s the Parents' Music Resource Center studied song lyrics to find those that were "explicit" and to provide consumers with warnings of potentially offensive material. Some music scholars using this approach have created interpretations of songwriting practices by theorizing that lyrics of popular songs represent trends in society, such as the dominant mood of a particular demographic group or historical era.

Although popular in the mid-twentieth century, the content analysis approach has been critiqued by contemporary music scholars for its assumptions that authors alone create lyrical meaning (rather than listeners also), that the meaning of lyrics is always transparent (rather than being ambiguous and produced by listeners), that lyrics express authentic experiences (rather than those conjured in fantasy), and that a song's meaning can be found in lyrics alone (rather than in their conjunction with sounds and performance). Moreover, arguments that popular song lyrics reflect a general mood have been critiqued for their failure to consider the heterogeneity of human expression, interpretation, and values.

Psychoanalytic Criticism

Literary scholars who engage in **psychoanalytic criticism** understand written works as multilayered texts produced through both conscious and unconscious thoughts and desires. As such, all literature contains latent meanings in addition to manifest content. To discern such secondary meanings, scholars use psychoanalytic theories to analyze literature much as psychoanalysts study patients' dreams. Typically the object of such literary analysis is the protagonist, although the story's symbols and structure are often analyzed as well. Many feminist scholars have used psychoanalytic theories because of their interest in the persistence of certain patterns of gendered representation in literature. For feminist scholars, the gendered identity and actions of the protagonist are key, as are the protagonist's relations with other characters.

Central to psychoanalytic literary scholarship is Sigmund Freud's theory of **psychosexual development**. According to Freud, children must progress through a variety of stages to develop into mature adults. For Freud a significant phase is the **Oedipus complex,** wherein children learn to separate from their mothers and identify with their fathers. According to Freud, although the child is quite attached to the mother in infancy, during the Oedipal stage the child learns to dissociate from the mother. For boys, this happens through the castration complex, wherein they come to understand their mother as castrated (because she has no penis). Boys also see their father as their mother's castrator and therefore the more powerful figure after which they should model themselves. It is during this stage that boys learn to repress their love for the mother, holding it at bay until they are mature enough to enter into a relationship with a woman. For girls, dissociation from the mother occurs because they see her as disempowered yet also as a competitor for the father's attention. In sensing their lack of power as a result of castration, girls develop penis envy and yearn to find a husband like their father.

Feminist literary scholars have noted that the Oedipal complex structures much literature written by Western men, as such stories typically contain a male protagonist who struggles in his relations with both his father and, via other women, his mother. (Simon Reynolds and Joy Press privilege this interpretation of rock's machismo and misogyny.) In searching for alternate interpretations of literature that do not privilege such patriarchal narratives, feminist literary critics have turned to explanations of psychosexual development formulated by female theorists, such as Melanie Klein and Nancy Chodorow, both of whom reconfigured Freud's theories to focus on pre-Oedipal relations between children and their mothers. While some feminist scholars, like Elizabeth Grosz, have found Jacques Lacan's psychoanalytic theories to be a useful alternative to Freud's, others have accused Lacan of a similarly sexist approach.

Despite the prevalence of psychoanalytic scholarship in late-twentieth-century textual analysis, literary scholars have not been unified in their interpretations or uses of psychoanalytic theories. Because psychoanalytic criticism is concerned with only the inner workings of literary texts, it has been critiqued for not attending to the specificities of a text's sociohistorical context, and for not considering readers' differing interpretations. Many feminist and queer scholars have rejected psychoanalytic criticism also because of its reliance on a binary, heterocentric perspective of gender.

Semiotics

Semiotics is a form of textual analysis that involves the study of signs and their function in communication and meaning making. Rather than focusing on only superficial textual content, semiotics allows scholars to develop complex interpretations of texts and their relation to society.

The theorist most prominently associated with semiotics is Ferdinand de Saussure, who believed that language is structured via particular codes and conventions, which its speakers and writers must learn to communicate. For Saussure, each communicative act or **sign** involves both a **signified**—a concept or object—and a **signifier**—the sound, printed word, or image that is used to represent it. For example, when we read the letters G-U-I-T-A-R (the signifier), we understand them to mean a midsized, nonbowed string instrument (the signified). A sign's meaning is formed through convention, and it is the sharing and interpretation of signs that drives human communication.

Key to Saussure's theory is the arbitrary relationship between a signified and signifier. The arbitrariness of signs is most clear when we consider the different words (signifiers) that have been developed in different languages to express the same object or concept (signifieds). For example, the English word used to signify an instrument that makes sound when its membrane is struck is "drum." In Italian, this instrument is referred to as *batteria*. In Japanese, it is *taiko*. Although each of these words means the same thing, they are different signifiers of that thing. As Saussure theorized, a sign's meaning also comes from its relationship to other signifiers within a particular language system. For example, we understand the meaning of the word "drum" because of its difference from other similar sounding words, such as "come" and "droop," as well as its difference from other words written similarly, such as "rum" and "brim."

Roland Barthes contributed to semiotics by demonstrating a further level of complexity in signification. For Barthes, each sign has a first-order **denotative** meaning, which is its literal, "dictionary" meaning. For example, the denotative meaning of the verb "rock" is to move an object gently back and forth, as in lulling a baby to sleep. Yet, because of the arbitrary relationship between signifiers and signifieds, signs are readily adaptable to different historical and social contexts and thus often have secondary, **connotative** meanings also. For example, "to rock" a garment or outfit means to wear clothing well and confidently. This expression likely came from an earlier use of the verb "rock" to suggest that someone is superlative in what they do (as in "You rock!"), which perhaps resulted from the concept of the rock star.

Metaphor—a figure of speech that relates one concept to another unrelated concept—operates at the level of connotation. Common in rock lyrics, metaphor allows for the presence of potentially controversial meaning while cleverly avoiding censorship. Think here of how "rock and roll" was once used as a euphemism for sexual intercourse. Or consider such rock lyrics as "I am a rock / I am an island," from a song that deals with detachment and social isolation ("I Am a Rock," by Paul Simon), or "Like a windup toy, you stutter at my feet," from a song about male impotence ("Stutter" by Justine Frischmann of Elastica). While most textual analyses begin with the primary level of denotation, semioticians are often more interested in connotation because language at that level is more complex and the reasons for the use of particular signs become clearer.

Ideological Analysis

Barthes's semiotic approach also includes a third level of significatory meaning, which is **ideology**. As he argued, as much as each sign has connotative meanings that are culturally constructed, those meanings are necessarily inflected by a particular belief or value system. Thus, the job of the semiotician is to uncover not only meaning but also the ideologies that inflect that meaning in a particular direction. For example, the euphemism "rock and roll" grew out of the bawdy music cultures of swing, blues, and R&B, where sexual freedom was valued over chastity.

In the field of music criticism, ideological analyses of song lyrics were first aligned with critiques of mass culture. Marxist theorists, such as Theodor Adorno and J. G. Peatman, understood popular music as problematic since it is produced primarily for profit rather than for artistic reasons. Such scholars hoped to demonstrate how the banal themes in pop lyrics contributed to the reproduction of capitalist ideologies and unequal social relations. Not surprisingly, these researchers valued other forms of popular music, such as folk and the blues, for their authenticity and independence from commodified culture.

Since the 1980s, ideological textual analysis is no longer aligned just with Marxist perspectives and critiques of mass culture. It has become a primary methodology for feminist, queer, and other marginalized scholars who hope to expose the processes of ideological hegemony at work in written texts so that they can be overturned. Feminist scholars using this approach have been interested in determining how particular words communicate and reproduce patriarchal values. Feminists use the term **phallocentric** to describe a perspective that is patriarchal (focused on the phallus/power) and thus dismissive of women's issues and interests. **Phallogocentrism** is an author's privileging of a male-centered perspective in writing via choice of words, themes, and structure.

To reclaim and value femininity in literature, some feminist scholars have focused on literary works that privilege a woman-centered outlook, what Hélène Cixous calls *écriture féminine*. According to Cixous, *écriture féminine* works to disrupt phallogocentric writing by privileging not only women and femininity but also nonlinear, cyclical discourse. Yet, like cultural feminism, this approach has been critiqued by some for its gender essentialism, denial of women's diversity, and reliance on binary thinking.

For queer scholars, demonstrating the heterocentric ideology of authors and the written works they produce has been an important intervention in the larger process of eliminating homophobia. In turn, such researchers have analyzed writing that privileges a queer perspective to better understand how such an identity is communicated, particularly in the face of homophobic oppression. Similar processes of examining dominant ideology and reclaiming marginal perspectives in literary works have happened among scholars of color, non-Western scholars, poor scholars, and disabled scholars.

Discourse Analysis

Another approach commonly used in literary studies is **discourse analysis**. **Discourses** are the conceptual frameworks that human beings use to organize experience and to construct meanings. The term discourse is commonly used with regard to spoken or written language. However, in discourse analysis, scholars also study other communicative forms, such as images and sounds. Michel Foucault linked discourse to systems of power and knowledge developed in particular social institutions. Therefore, scholars who use discourse analysis are concerned with the assumptions behind the particular construction and uses of discourse, as well as how those assumptions contribute to people's meaning-making processes, understandings of reality, and thus engagement with other people.

Many contemporary feminist literary scholars see discourse analysis as a useful way to uncover how particular concepts related to gender have developed and been circulated in written works, such as song lyrics. Some of these researchers have explored the way discourses of gender can reproduce social inequality and disenfranchisement and have given considerable attention to those discourses influenced by patriarchy, such as the sex/gender system. Their findings reveal that the discursive construction of men in popular culture has consistently suggested their physical, intellectual, spiritual, and emotional superiority.

In contrast, patriarchal discourses have historically constructed women and femininity as inferior. In attempting to subvert the negative effects of patriarchal discourses, cultural feminists have put a positive spin on such feminine traits as relationality and nurturance.

More recently, feminist and queer researchers have been interested in the fluidity of gender discourse and thus the instability of patriarchy as an ideological institution. Judith Butler's work has been quite significant in this regard since, by highlighting the discursive construction of both gender and sex, she has pointed to ways the sex/gender system can be deconstructed. Butler's theories have been readily taken up by popular music scholars interested in how gender is represented in rock lyrics.

Studying Gender in Rock Lyrics

Although some rock lyrics do not deal with gendered themes, many reveal considerable engagement with discourses of gender, particularly in their representations of men and women. The following sections explore some of the ways rock songwriters have formulated gendered discourse, and how such language affirms, complicates, or challenges dominant gender politics. It is important to remember, however, that the meaning of lyrics is never established by the songwriter alone. Listeners always bring their own interpretations to songs and decode them according to their own experiences and values.

Phallogocentric Lyrics

Men and masculinity figure strongly in many rock lyrics for the simple reason that many writers of rock songs self-identify as men and write from their own perspective or that of other male figures, often with a male audience in mind. Yet not all rock lyrics by men and about men contain the same representation of manhood. Because of rock culture's rebellious spirit and cultural lineage, rock lyrics have long presented portrayals of male subjectivity that do not adhere to the middle-class ideal of the responsible, career-minded, family-loving father. Nevertheless, many rock lyrics construct alternate versions of masculinity that are problematic in their affirmations of heterosexuality and power, particularly in relation to women, and thus are in alignment with both patriarchy and hegemonic masculinity. (Feminist songwriters have written about such constructions of masculinity also, but primarily from a woman's perspective.)

Some feminist scholars have theorized that the prevalence of patriarchal machismo in rock lyrics is the result of male songwriters' expression of their personal experiences as well as the dominance of patriarchal ideology. Yet other scholars have argued that phallogocentric lyrics are less expressions of men's actual experiences than forms of gender performance. Robert Walser, for example, encourages us to think of such lyrics as negotiating manhood in a patriarchal heterocentric society that offers little room for alternative masculinities. Moreover, he argues that we might see phallogocentric lyrics as a form of a male writer's self-defense against a threatened masculinity. In other words, by writing (and singing) about men's power, male rockers can perform control and superiority that they (and their fans) may not actually experience in everyday life. Such feelings of masculinity in crisis are interesting to consider in relation to the broader sociocultural context, where feminist ideologies have become increasingly popular and women have become more publicly visible and achieved more power than previously.

Interestingly, paternity—a dominant method for constructing male power in everyday life as well as creative texts—is strikingly absent from most male-authored rock lyrics, likely because many male rock musicians are young and reject domesticity and the roles associated with it. Indeed, plenty of rock lyrics written by men, including Nirvana's "Breed" (1992), have suggested an anti-paternalist stance by rebelling against the romantic notion of love as well as middle-class adulthood.

Men's Sexual Power

One of the primary ways in which male songwriters construct men's superiority in rock lyrics is through references to men's sexual power, especially over women. (In contrast, women lyricists have more often constructed men's subjectivity via romance.) The history of rock is filled with assertions of men's sexual virility, particularly those referencing phallic power. This musical trend has roots in the blues, a form of popular music historically used to express sexual feelings and fantasies, particularly through connotation and metaphor. Bo Diddley's "I'm a Man" (1955), an R&B precursor to this lyrical trend in rock, explicitly associates the male narrator's manhood and power with his sexual organ: "Now when I was a little boy / At the age of five / I had something in my pocket / Keep a lot of folks alive / Now I'm a man / Made twenty-one / You know baby/ We can have a lot of fun." As Jason Lee Oakes notes, this song's essentialized, authentic construction of heterosexual masculinity is linked to blackness, a trope that can be found across many rock styles, particularly those that privilege a blues sound.

One of the first male-authored rock songs to receive critical attention for its construction of men's power as sexual is Led Zeppelin's "Whole Lotta Love" (1969), which is based on Willie Dixon's "You Need Love" (1962). In the Zeppelin version, the line "I'm gonna give ya every inch of my love" denotatively signifies the length of the narrator's penis while also connotatively suggesting his sexual virility. Moreover, through the rhetorical strategy of **metonymy**, wherein a part comes to stand for the whole, the narrator's "whole lotta love" is meant to suggest his power in general.

Men's Technical Power

Another prevalent way in which men's power has been constructed in male-authored rock lyrics is through the metaphoric connection of men with technology. In such lyrics technology is rendered masculine and thus helps to construct the men in the song's narrative as manly. For example, in Bruce Springsteen's "Born to Run" (1975)—an homage to downtrodden, working-class youth—young men are represented as empowered through their connection with automobiles: "Sprung from cages out on Highway 9 / Chrome-wheeled, fuel-injected and stepping out over the line." The lines "just wrap your legs round these velvet rims / and strap your hands cross my engines," which the narrator addresses to his girlfriend, take the metaphoric connection of men's power and machine power one step further through sexual innuendo.

Springsteen's technology-laden lyrical themes borrow much from Steppenwolf's heavy metal anthem "Born to be Wild" (1968): "Get your motor runnin' / Head out on the highway / Lookin' for adventure / And whatever comes our way." By associating men's technological power with mobility, such lyrics also project an antidomestic perspective that is in keeping with rock's privileged ideologies. Much like AC/DC's "Heatseeker" (1988), the Jesus and Mary Chain's "The Living End" (1985) heightens the narcissism of this technomobile masculinity: "I get ahead on my motorbike / I feel so quick in my leather boots / My mood is black when my jacket's on / And I'm in love with myself."

Men's Opposition to Women

Many feminist critics have drawn attention to male rock songwriters' negative portrayals of women as a means of affirming men's superiority. Such lyrics are in keeping with patriarchal ideology's dualistic perspective, since they present the two genders via opposition, with femininity subordinate to masculinity. While songs of this type reaffirm hegemonic masculinity, of particular concern to feminists have been male-authored lyrics that are **misogynist**, revealing a hatred of women through their representation as dangerous, objectified, or abused.

The one rock song to have received the greatest amount of attention from feminists as a result of its misogyny is the Rolling Stones' "Under My Thumb" (1966). Here the narrator comments on his new-found control over his girlfriend, who has strayed and hurt him. The lyrics repeatedly note his control ("it's down to me / ... she's under my thumb") and her passive objectification as a result ("the way she does what she's told / ... she's the sweetest pet in the world"). Other rock performers and bands of the 1960s, including John's Children, the Trees, and the Litter, similarly presented women as passive, dumb objects to be used, and abused, by men. Such themes became prevalent in hard rock during the 1970s, as women musicians and fans were pushed further to the margins of rock culture.

The trend of misogynist rock lyrics continued well past the 1970s, however. For example, in Lisa Sloat's analysis of male-authored lyrics for heavy metal bands of the 1980s and early 1990s, she noted three dominant ways women are portrayed, all of which suggest men's power through women's subordination: (1) women are represented as sex toys to be used for male sexual pleasure (e.g., Jackyl's "She Love My Cock" [1992]); (2) women are constructed as dangerous and in need of men's control (e.g., Black 'n Blue's "Wicked Witch" (1984)]); and (3) women are portrayed as victims of men's abuse (e.g., Faster Pussycat's "Where There's a Whip, There's a Way" [1989]). Although many early male punk bands excluded any mention of women from their lyrics as a result of punk's antiromantic ideology, several wrote songs with misogynist lyrics, including the Stranglers' "Ugly" (1977), which involves the strangling of a female lover because she has acne.

Sloat and other feminist scholars have attributed women's negative representation in male-centered rock lyrics to male songwriters' negative experiences with women, the dominance of patriarchal ideology, and the prevalence of misogyny. However, Walser encourages us to consider also how these themes may be indicative of men's compromised power, particularly after the rebirth of feminism in the 1960s. Moreover, while whiteness, patriarchy, and heterosexuality continue to be the dominant ideologies of race, gender, and sexuality in Western societies, many poor young straight men have nonetheless felt disenfranchised as a result of their marginalized class and generational status. Indeed, as a result of the achievements of people of color, women, and members of the LGBTQI community over the past few decades, rock has become a primary cultural site for young white straight men's negotiation of their frustration with the loss of power experienced by their specific demographic group.

Men have not been alone in constructing demeaning lyrical representations of women in rock songs, however. Several women songwriters have done this also. For example, "He Hit Me (and It Felt Like a Kiss" (1962), cowritten by Carole King, has received considerable criticism for suggesting partner abuse as an expression of love. A decade and a half later, Fleetwood Mac's "Gold Dust Woman" (1977), penned by Stevie Nicks, tells the tale of a heartless, drug-addicted woman who preys on a man's affections only to leave him broken and disheartened. Thus, just as we should be mindful that some male lyricists have written both misogynist and women-affirming lyrics, we should be careful not to assume that all female songwriters are necessarily celebratory of women.

Male Aggression and Violence

In hard rock styles, such as punk and heavy metal, aggression and violence are common themes that male songwriters have used to assert, or at least fantasize about, men's control and power. As noted, many feminists have decried male-authored rock lyrics' representation of women as victims of male abuse in such songs as "Where There's a Whip, There's a Way." Yet numerous rock songs construct men also as victims of male aggression. For example, in Mötley Crüe's "Bastard" (1983), the narrator fantasizes about killing "the king of sleaze" with both a knife and a rope. Often such themes of aggression in rock lyrics are connected to a working-class male subjectivity, as in Thin Lizzy's "The Boys Are Back in Town" (1976): "Guess who just got back today? / Those wild-eyed boys that had been away / Friday night they'll be dressed to kill / . . . If the boys want to fight, you'd better let them."

Given its interests in rebellion, danger, horror, and the occult, heavy metal is the rock style that has most employed themes of male aggression and violence. Black Sabbath's "Iron Man" (1971), a classic heavy metal anthem, was one of the first rock songs to explore the theme of men's power through vengeance: "Now the time is here / For iron man to spread fear / Vengeance from the grave / Kills the people he once saved." Male punk bands have written their fair share of aggression-filled rock lyrics as well. The Sex Pistols' classic punk song "Anarchy in the UK" (1976) ends with the command "Get pissed / Destroy!" Similar to both "Iron Man" and the Stooges' "Search and Destroy" (1973), Big Black's "Kerosene" (1986) makes use of the theme of technologized masculinity to tell a tale of a desperate, isolated young man who seeks out destruction as a means for feeling empowered.

As "Iron Man" exemplifies, the themes of aggression and violence often take on a supernatural or otherworldly perspective in hard rock lyrics. Typically at the center of such lyrics is a male ruler-like figure, a dark lord perhaps first personified by Mick Jagger of the Rolling Stones for "Sympathy for the Devil" (1968). As Reynolds and Press demonstrate, this persona has been referenced repeatedly in male-authored hard rock lyrics, including "Anarchy in the UK," which positions the narrator as the Antichrist. Less otherworldly but still dangerous is the sociopathic serial killer who populates such songs as Therapy's "Dancing with Manson" (1991): "The one thing I've looked for all my life / Is killing everything I ever want." Such aggressive and violent lyric themes likely have roots in rock's rebellious ethos. Yet, as Walser suggests, they also suggest songwriters' minimal opportunities for power in real life and thus their desire to construct such agency via fantasy.

Gynocentric Lyrics

Historically, **gynocentric** or women-centered lyrics have been marginalized in rock culture as a result of men's dominance of songwriting, particularly after the mid-1960s. In contrast, Charlotte Greig has noted the prevalence of women's issues in folk music, which has been more open than rock to women's perspectives. Nevertheless, numerous female lyricists have written rock lyrics, particularly during those eras when women musicians' presence has been substantial. Such lyrics commonly construct a woman-centered perspective and often take a feminist perspective on gender relations, particularly since the 1980s.

Emphasized Femininity

The women lyricists writing during the "girl group" era of the early 1960s typically constructed girlhood in relation to patriarchal heteronormativity, thus situating young women as dependent on males for love and affirmation while reproducing notions of men's superiority. For example, Carole King's "One Fine Day" (1963) portrays its female narrator as desperately seeking a male's attention: "Though I know you're the / Kind of boy / Who only wants to run around / I'll keep waiting." Such lyrical constructions align with Connell's definition of emphasized femininity, which is always subordinate to and helps to reaffirm hegemonic masculinity.

Marriage has traditionally been avoided in rock lyrics due to rock culture's prevalent antidomestic ideology. However, some women songwriters have focused on this theme, particularly during the prefeminist girl group period. For example, "Chapel of Love" (1964), cowritten by Ellie Greenwich, presents marriage as a fairytale with birds singing, bells ringing, and loneliness abated. Yet the song does not construct the bride as dependent on her soon-to-be husband. Rather it presents them both as mutually dependent: "I'll be his and he'll be mine / We'll love until the end of time." Such lyrics suggest a desire for equality in heterosexual marriage that perhaps resulted from Greenwich's own desires as a career woman, not to mention feminist discourse's reemergence at that time.

Écriture Féminine and Gender Solidarity

Despite the presence of gynocentric lyrics in other popular music styles, such as folk, it was several decades after the women's liberation movement before female rock lyricists began to write more frequently about women's experiences that did not necessarily affirm patriarchal heterosexuality. Theodore Gracyk refers to this musical approach as **gender solidarity**, wherein women bond over a shared, essential gender identity to disrupt heteronormative patriarchy. This practice is closely aligned with *écriture feminine* and the ideology of cultural feminism. We might also think here of the **Bechdel Test**, developed by artist Alison Bechdel, which requires that a work of fiction involve at least two women who talk to each other about something other than a man.

With the rise of more female and feminist rockers since the 1990s, consumers have been exposed to a variety of women's issues that had long been ignored in rock culture. For example, several female rock performers have authored songs about pregnancy and motherhood, including Chrissie Hynde, who wrote "I'm a Mother" (1994) for the Pretenders. Both Toni Childs and Sinead O'Connor created concept albums devoted to the theme of motherhood—*The Woman's Boat* (1994) and *Universal Mother* (1994), respectively. Meanwhile, some women lyricists have raised the issue of abortion in their songs, as Ani DiFranco does in "Tiptoe" (1995). Yet the best-known rock song about abortion is likely the Sex Pistols' "Bodies" (1977), whose male-authored lyrics have been widely debated because of their confusing representations of abortion.

Since the 1990s female rock lyricists have also been writing more assertively and explicitly about women's sexuality. The Yeastie Girlz "You Suck" (1988) was one of the first songs to do this. The woman narrator refutes her male lover's many reasons for avoiding cunnilingus and demands: "Now you suck, suck it hard / Go down baby / You suck, suck it hard / And move your tongue around." Similarly, Liz Phair's hit "Flower" (1993) is quite explicit in its representation of a woman's sexual pleasures: "Every time I see your face / I get all wet between my legs." Nevertheless, as often happens when a woman asserts her desire publicly, Phair's lyrics—especially "I want to be your blowjob queen"—were misunderstood by many people as simply whorish and in the service of straight men.

Given the prevalence of male-on-female abuse in patriarchal societies, it is not surprising that this theme has been raised in women's rock lyrics also, although quite differently from how it appears in male-authored songs. Recent lyrics in this vein focus attention on the victims of such abuse, revealing the emotional and physical consequences for such women. L7's "Can I Run?" (1994), for example, deals with the general fear women face living in a society where male violence against females is often tolerated: "Is he under the bed; is he in the back street? / Can I run?" Tori Amos's a cappella song "Me and a Gun" (1992) also channels such fears while expressing her first-hand experience of being raped. 7 Year Bitch's "Icy Blue" (1994) challenges women everywhere to stand up to partner abuse: "Are you gonna let him, let him love you to death? / Are you gonna let him?" Bikini Kill's "Suck My Left One" (1991) similarly argues for fighting back against male abuse, yet this time the focus is on girls victimized by incestual rape: "My sister pulls the covers down / She reaches over, flicks on the light / She says to him / Suck my left one." Bikini Kill's song also addresses mothers' common complicity in incestual abuse, thus revealing the complicated gender dynamics of such experiences.

Few male bands have explored women's sexual objectification and harassment by men from a woman's perspective. However, Fugazi's "Suggestion" (1988) received considerable attention as a result of a male musician assuming the position of a victimized woman in the song: "Why can't I walk down a street free of suggestion? / Is my body the only trait in the eyes of men?" While some feminists have objected to MacKaye's writing and performance of "Suggestion," ultimately the narrator's point of view moves from first to third person, implicating everyone for the perpetuation of our rape culture: "He touches her 'cause he wants to feel it / We blame her for being there / But, we are all guilty." MacKaye's willingness to focus on this social issue was likely due to his own progressive values, as well as his friendships with and influence by young feminists in the punk and Riot Grrrl scenes.

Troubling Gender

While gynocentric lyricists have certainly undermined the phallogocentrism associated historically with rock, the practices of *écriture féminine* and gender solidarity have done little to upset the heteronormative patriarchal sex/gender system, since they reproduce the notion that men and women are opposites and that all women (and all men) share similar experiences. Nevertheless, some songwriters have challenged these traditional gender politics by questioning gender norms and broadening the range of gendered behaviors beyond the binary formulation of masculine/feminine. These strategies are musical examples of what Judith Butler calls **gender trouble** and Gracyk refers to as **gender transgression**.

Men's Vulnerability

Several male rock lyricists have problematized hegemonic masculinity by exploring forms of manhood that do not adhere to the macho sex gods and dark lords that populate many hard rock songs. This lyrical development has not necessarily replaced phallogocentric lyrics that privilege heteronormative masculinity, however. It has merely expanded the range of masculinities represented in rock songs.

For example, let's return to the lyrics of Bruce Springsteen's "Born to Run" (1975). Despite the song's possible interpretation as validating men's superiority over women, the lyrics speak to the difficulties working-class young men face as a result of their socioeconomic status (particularly during the era of Reaganomics) and their limited options for escape. Indeed, the lines "Girls comb their hair in rearview mirrors / And the boys try to look so hard" speak directly to gender as performed and thus suggest the possibility of men failing at hegemonic masculinity. Taking a different stance on working-class masculinity, Gang of Four's "Not Great Men" (1979) draws attention to the absence of poor men from history while also asserting their essential role in society: "No weak men in the books at home / The strong men who have made the world."

While Bob Dylan is perhaps the first rocker to write explicitly about male vulnerability and thus to debunk the myth of male machismo (e.g., "It's Alright Ma [I'm Only Bleeding]" [1965]), it wasn't until the rise of punk that male vulnerability became a common theme in rock lyrics. Unlike heavy metal lyrics, which tend to depict men's hatred and aggression as directed toward others, many male-centered punk and postpunk songs focus on self-loathing, a quality more often associated with femininity. Joy Division's "Isolation" (1980) is prototypical in this regard: "I'm ashamed of the things I've been put through / I'm ashamed of the person I am." Black Flag's "Damaged I" (1981) follows suit: "Stupid feelings / Stupid illusions / I'm confused . . . / Scars for me to wear."

As Terri Sutton has noted, several male rock musicians of the 1990s, particularly those associated with alternative rock, put forth songs that pointed to male vulnerability, including Stone Temple Pilots' "Creep" (1992), Nirvana's "Rape Me" (1993), and Nine Inch Nail's "Hurt" (1993). While few of these songs contain social critiques on the subject, Pearl Jam's "Jeremy" (1991) suggests that the recent trend of American white boys turning on their schoolmates in violence is the result of family and peer abuse: "Daddy didn't give attention/ Oh, to the fact that mommy didn't care . . . / Clearly I remember picking on the boy / Seemed a harmless little fuck." Interestingly, the narrator, whose relationship to Jeremy is unclear, includes himself in the larger group of people who unwittingly "unleashed a lion."

Although male vulnerability was quite popular in 1990s rock culture, perhaps demonstrated best by the popularity of Beck's "Loser" (1994), Sutton argues that we should be suspicious of this lyrical parade of male victims. For while such songs suggest that men can be wounded and suffering, they typically deny patriarchal hegemony and thus do not acknowledge the abuse heaped on women as a result of misogyny. In other words, in failing to address the structural imbalances between men and women that leave the latter much more disenfranchised, such songs do little to subvert traditional gender politics.

Powerful Females

As a result of the dispersion of liberal feminist ideologies since the 1970s, female rock lyricists have increasingly represented powerful women outside heterosexual narratives. Helen Reddy's "I am Woman" (1972) is prototypical in this regard and quickly became a feminist anthem because of its assertion of female strength and invincibility. Since Reddy's hit, numerous contemporary feminist songwriters have written rock lyrics that present women as powerful figures. Ani DiFranco's "Not a Pretty Girl" (1995) made a significant impact when it was released, given its assertions of female strength, independence, and self-respect: "I am not a pretty girl / That is not what I do / I ain't no damsel in distress / And I don't need to be rescued." Despite receiving less airplay than DiFranco's song, Bikini Kill's "Rebel Girl" (1993) is a punk- and feminism-infused anthem to girl power: "When she talks / The revolution's coming / In her hips / There's revolution." These latter two songs take a defiant tone not found in the more popular "Just a Girl" from No Doubt (1995), whose lyrics focus less on women's power than their oppression under patriarchy.

Other female rock lyricists have similarly constructed songs objecting to the pressure they feel to conform to the traditional roles of wife and mother simply because they are women. Joan Jett's song "Spinster" (1994) is particularly potent in its rejection of these patriarchal heteronormative roles: "I'm no one's wife and I'm not your little girl / Don't tell me I'm useless 'cause I want more from this world." In striking contrast to rock's historical privileging of youthfulness, Jett proudly takes on the role of spinster in this song, reconfiguring and reclaiming it through the dual lenses of queerness and mature adulthood.

A common method for presenting women as powerful is to place them in a historically male-dominated position, often alongside masculine objects. In relation to music videos, Lisa Lewis labels this strategy **access,** since it reveals women's occupation of male roles, practices, and spaces historically off limits to them. L7's "Shirley" (1994) is a good example of lyrical access, or what Judith Halberstam would call **female masculinity**. The song is an homage to Shirley Muldowney, the first woman to receive a license from the National Hot Rod Association to drive a top fuel dragster and a three-time champion racer in the late 1970s and early 1980s. Pointing to the sexism that keeps most women out of male-dominated activities, the song includes an audio clip of a male sportscaster asking, "What's a beautiful girl like you doing racing in a place like this?" Shirley's curt response, "Winning," not only answers his question but points to the ludicrous assumptions embedded in it about appropriate female behavior and the limits of women's achievement.

Revealing Gender Construction and Fluidity

As a result of the wide dispersal of feminist and queer sensibilities over the past four decades, numerous rock lyricists have brought attention to the social construction of gender norms in their songs. Yet such themes were evident, albeit to a far lesser extent, in rock culture of the 1970s, a time of significant social transformation. Lou Reed's "Take a Walk on the Wild Side" (1972), an homage to some of the nonconformists associated with Andy Warhol, was one of the first (and few) rock songs to trouble gender performance outright by drawing attention to transgender body politics: "Shaved her legs and then he was a she / She said, 'Hey Babe, take a walk on the wild side.'"

While Reed dabbled in transgender identity for only a brief period in the 1970s, Jayne County, a trans rocker associated with the early punk CBGB scene, has regularly focused on gender trouble in her songs. For example, in her cover of the Barbarians' "Are You a Boy or Are You a Girl?" (1980), County sings: "In your bleach blonde hair / You look like a girl / Well, you may be a boy, but / Hey, you look like a girl." Her "Man Enough to Be a Woman" (1978) is more specific in its exploration of gender as a performance: "conditioned to portraying the mask of masculinity / Another blend of different shading / I am what I am / I don't give a damn." Such lyrics are all the more powerful when performed live as listeners are able to see the transgender body singing them.

Although not all gay men and lesbians fit the gender nonnormative stereotype (i.e., effeminate gay men and masculine lesbians), several gay and lesbian rock performers have taken up this theme, perhaps as a means of affirming their sexual identities. Sung by a then-closeted Elton John, "The Bitch Is Back" (1974) was one of the first rock songs in this vein and opened the door for similar themes in later songs, such as Skinjob's "Gender Bender" (2003), written by male vocalist Mitch Fury: "I don't really care what they think / Or what they have to say / Just give respect / And get the pronouns straight / That's Ms. Fury to you, boy." Meanwhile, Gina Dent's "Supergirl" (2002) comments on the gender passing that lesbians employ to protect themselves in a homophobic culture: "Supergirl lives a double life / Pretends she wants a husband instead of a wife . . . / She's fighting the scrimmage on both fronts / Trying to be two places at once."

Several other rock lyricists have commented also on the social construction of femininity, although not necessarily from a queer perspective. Perhaps the most explicit rock song to discuss emphasized femininity as a result of women's subordination to men is John Lennon and Yoko Ono's "Woman Is the Nigger of the World" (1972). Controversial both then and now, the lyrics connect women's oppression to black people as enslaved property while also drawing attention to how femininity is constructed in heteronormative patriarchal societies: "We insult her everyday on TV / And wonder why she has no guts or confidence." The Slits' "Typical Girls" (1978) similarly calls attention to women's performances of emphasized femininity, albeit via irony: "Typical girls stand by their man / Typical girls are really swell / Typical girls learn how to act shocked/ Typical girls don't rebel."

Some male rockers have attempted to problematize hegemonic masculinity by critiquing its social construction. For example, Pulp's version of "I'm a Man" questions: "I start to wonder what it takes to be a man / Well I learned to drink and I learned to smoke and I learned to tell a dirty joke / If that's all there is, then there's no point for me." Meanwhile, other rock groups, like Tenacious D, have parodied rock's heterosexual machismo in their lyrics, sometimes running the risk of honoring the object of their ridicule.

Queerness

While numerous rock songs discuss the constructed nature of gender, few actually subvert the binary sex/gender system that grounds heterosexual patriarchy. Indeed, in only crossing sex and gender identities, such songs may ultimately reify the oppositions of male/female and masculine/feminine. In contrast, queer songs blur the boundaries between these subjectivities while suggesting gender as nonbinary, fluid, and multiple in expression. In other words, in queer culture sex and gender are not aligned but exploded. Here "queer" means antinormative and resistant to dualistic forms of meaning making while also not necessarily being indicative of homosexual desire. Some rock lyrics are explicitly queer in their gender nonconformity or homoerotics. Yet many queer theorists, like Alexander Doty, would argue that queerness runs throughout mass culture and can easily be read by those who know its nonnormative codes, including gender trouble.

David Bowie's "Rebel, Rebel" (1974) was one of the first rock songs to receive considerable discussion as a result of its attention to genderqueerness: "You got your mother in a whirl / She's not sure if you're a boy or a girl." Released a half decade later, Prince's "I Wanna Be Your Lover" (1979) queered its narrator by suggesting both gender and sexual fluidity: "I wanna be your brother / I wanna be your mother and your sister, too."

While Bowie and Prince often flirted with gender ambiguity in lyrics, other rock songwriters have commented more explicitly on gender fluidity in contemporary society. Beginning with a lyric that references traditional gender politics, Joe Jackson's "Real Men" (1982) repeatedly questions: "What's a man now," thus pointing to the fluidity of gender performance and thus a disruption of the sex/gender system. Moreover, the song deconstructs the stereotypical portrayal of homosexuals as gender deviant: "All the gays are macho / Can't you see their leather shine." A decade later, Tribe 8's "Femme Bitch Top" (1995) queers its subject by noting her masculine and feminine qualities simultaneously: "Her phallic tricks are the butt of a whip / And a handful of lipstick."

Songs like "Real Men" and "Femme Bitch Top" explore queer identities yet do so with one toe still planted in a bigendered world, as can be seen with the use of terms like "man" and "she." Yet some rock lyrics subvert such binary gender logics more explicitly. For example, the Replacements' "Androgynous" (1984) comments on the fluidity of a nonbinary genderqueer world: "Now, something meets Boy / And something meets Girl / They both look the same . . . / Unisex, evolution." Despite the queer utopia suggested by the lyrics, note how the songwriter's use of "something" here suggests the difficulty of communicating about non-normative subjectivities when language often restricts us to gendered pronouns.

Some rock vocalists have queered gender politics by singing lyrics whose narrator is constructed as a member of a different gender. Genderqueer interpretations occur because listeners typically associate the gender of a song's narrator (the "I" of the song) with the gender of the person singing it. For example, Deborah Harry's performance of Blondie's "Rifle Range" (1976), Linda Ronstadt's singing of the Rolling Stones' "Tumbling Dice" (1978), and k.d. lang's cover of Steve Miller's "The Joker" (1997) disrupt the gender construction of the songs' male narrators through their vocalization, while also problematizing the women singers' relationship to femininity by taking on a masculine role.

If romance or sexuality is a theme in a rock song, and the vocalist covering it does not change the pronoun used originally to describe the narrator's lover, such performances are often interpreted as sexually queer as well as genderqueer. This happened when Joan Jett covered Tommy and the Shondells' "Crimson and Cover" (1982), Lyle Lovett performed Tammy Wynette's "Stand by Your Man" (1989), and Janet Jackson recorded Rod Stewart's "Tonight's the Night" (2000). In contrast to these lyrical transgressions by straight performers, an increasing number of queer people are writing songs that speak openly about same-sex desire, a significant change from the days when gays and lesbians closeted such desires lyrically through metaphor and connotation.

The increased presence of queer lyrics in rock culture over the past two decades is indicative of progressive change. Indeed, such lyrics suggest not only the further diversification of gender identities in rock culture but also the undermining of its historic patriarchal and heteronormative ideologies. Yet it is important to keep in mind the limited popularity and commercial viability of such songs in a much larger cultural context where queerness is still marginalized and members of the LGBTQI community are still feared and abused.

Summary

This chapter has examined rock lyrics so that we can understand how gender is constructed, negotiated, and subverted through song. Most rock lyricists have been men, which has contributed to an overvalorization of males and masculine power as well as the subordination of females and femininity in rock lyrics. Nevertheless, as demonstrated by the increased presence of feminist and queer perspectives that honor women and trouble gender, rock lyrics have evolved over the past six decades. Yet that evolution has never been linear, nor has it been necessarily progressive, despite rock culture's self-congratulatory rebellious spirit. Indeed, many male rock songwriters continue to privilege a form of sexually virile and technically powerful masculinity, and plenty of female rockers compose lyrics that affirm women's essential femininity.

At the same time, we must remember that just as some feminist scholars have struggled to reconcile their radical politics with their love of the Rolling Stone's misogynist lyrics, other rock fans must negotiate their own identities and values with their pleasure in music that moves them. In other words, lyrics alone do not determine our pleasure, or displeasure, in a song. We can make sense of such contradictory impulses only by attending also to the musical sounds in which rock lyrics are embedded. In addition to exploring gender in rock lyrics, this chapter also addressed song structure and the various methods used to study rock lyrics. Chapter 11 explores the constructions of gender in rock print media, specifically album covers.

Further Exploration

1. Study the lyrics of your top five most favorite songs

How many of these songs were written by males? How many were written by females? What kinds of representations of males and females appear in these lyrics? What methods do the songs' lyricists use to affirm traditional gender norms? What methods are used to subvert such norms?

2. Study the lyrics of the entries in *Billboard*'s current "Hot Modern Rock Tracks" (http://www.billboard.com/bbcom/charts/chart_display.jsp?g=Singles&f=Hot+Modern+Rock+Tracks).

How many of these songs were written by males? How many were written by females? What kinds of representations of males and females appear in these lyrics? What methods do the songs' lyricists use to affirm traditional gender norms? What methods are used to subvert such norms?

3. Peruse *Rolling Stone*'s list of the five hundred "Greatest Songs of All Time" (http://www.rollingstone.com/news/coverstory/500songs).

How many of these songs were written by males? How many were written by females? What does this information tell you about the gender politics of songwriting? Do you notice any gendered patterns with regard to particular genres of music (e.g., rock, hip-hop, etc.)?

4. Visit the website of the Songwriters Hall of Fame (http://www.songwritershalloffame.org).

While perusing the list of inductees, count the number of female versus the number of male lyricists who have been inducted and note the style of music written by each inductee. In what style do most male inductees write? What about the female inductees? Have these figures changed since the 1980s? What does this information tell you about the gender politics of songwriting in general and rock songwriting in particular?

5. Write the lyrics for a rock song.

Consider the different ways you can work with the song's language and form to align it with rock's lyrical traditions. Reflect on how its language and form relate to gender politics, and consider ways that you might manipulate these song components to challenge rock conventions.

Further Reading

Burns, Lori, and Mélisse Lafrance. *Disruptive Divas: Feminism, Identity and Popular Music*. New York: Routledge, 2001.

Frith, Simon. *Performing Rites: On the Value of Popular Music*. Cambridge: Harvard University Press, 1996.

Gracyk, Theodore. *I Wanna Be Me: Rock Music and the Politics of Identity*. Philadelphia: Temple University Press, 2001.

Greig, Charlotte. "Female Identity and the Woman Songwriter." *Sexing the Groove: Popular Music and Gender*. Ed. Sheila Whiteley. New York: Routledge, 1997. 168–77.

Reynolds, Simon, and Joy Press. *The Sex Revolts: Gender, Rebellion and Rock 'n' Roll*. Cambridge: Harvard University Press, 1995.

Sloat, Lisa J. "Incubus: Male Songwriters' Portrayals of Women's Sexuality in Pop Metal Music." *Youth Culture: Identity in a Postmodern World*. Ed. Jonathon S. Epstein. Malden: Blackwell, 1998. 286–301.

Sutton, Terri. "The Soft Boys: The New Man in Rock." *Trouble Girls: The Rolling Stone Book of Women in Rock*. Ed. Barbara O'Dair. New York: Random House, 1997. 527–35.

Walser, Robert. *Running with the Devil: Power, Gender, and Madness in Heavy Metal Music*. Hanover: Wesleyan University Press, 1993.

11 ON THE COVER
Rock Print Images

LISTEN: TUSCADERO, "PAPER DOLL" (*MY Way or the Highway*, Elektra, 1998). *With a special address to girls via its focus on fairytales and fashion magazines, this song critiques the effects of commercial media culture, including the marginalization of nonconformists.*

Since rock music emerged as a distinct style in the 1950s, rock culture has produced numerous forms of **visual media** in relation to it, including photographs, posters, advertisements, album covers, T-shirts, films, music videos, and websites. Such imagery has taken on an increasingly important role in rock culture since the late twentieth century as live performances have become more expensive and popular culture has become more visually mediated through such technologies as television and the Internet.

Not surprisingly, the vast majority of visual media associated with rock culture features rock musicians, because such texts function primarily as promotional devices for such performers and their art. Yet such images also contribute to our broader landscape of representation and thus establish norms for behavior used in identity formation and social relationships. Therefore, the images that circulate in rock culture are significant to anyone interested in how gender is represented in this community.

Both this chapter and the next explore rock's mediated imagery, with a focus on the gender politics involved in such texts' design and meaning. Of primary concern is media producers' reliance on established patterns of depicting men and women, patterns that have contributed to the reproduction of dominant ideologies of gender not only in rock culture but also in society at large. Nevertheless, visual artists do not always follow conventions, and many of those working in rock culture have developed representational strategies that have challenged and, in some cases, subverted heteronormative patriarchy and conservative gender politics.

This chapter explores still images in rock culture, particularly album covers and, to a lesser degree, magazine photographs. Chapter 12 looks more closely at music videos. Although a wide range of rock-associated visual texts is available for study, album covers and music videos are given special attention because of their historic significance not only to rock musicians and the recording industry but also to rock consumers and critics. Indeed, despite album covers' and music videos' considerable decrease in size as a result of technological transformations, both continue to be important mechanisms for artistic expression, product promotion, and consumer identification in rock culture.

Representation

Human beings have developed many forms of **communication** to express ourselves and interact with others. Although spoken and written languages have dominated human communication practices for centuries, since the early 1900s, most societies have become increasingly reliant on visual forms of communication, particularly those created through photography. Such imagery is primarily produced and circulated today by **mass media** (newspapers, film, television, the Internet). Yet visual media are created also by amateurs and independent artists.

Representation refers to the ways in which a particular concept, object, or person is rendered in a **medium**, such as writing, drawing, painting, sculpture, or photography. Many people evaluate visual representations based on their ability to accurately reflect that which they portray. For example, we might debate whether the representation of a rock band in the fictional film *Ladies and Gentlemen: The Fabulous Stains* (1982) authentically depicts real musicians and their experiences. Yet our material reality can never be perfectly represented, since each person perceives and communicates about it differently. Moreover, to return to the example above, no one rock band can represent all other rock bands, just as there is no one visual medium that can exactly reproduce reality. In other words, we have no way to visually clone reality, only to produce approximate simulations of it.

In light of our inability to reproduce reality, we should consider how we know it, which is through the various forms of communication humans have developed. Like spoken words and written text, visual representations help us to express thought and emotion, to document and process experiences, to explore and develop identities, to communicate and form relationships with others, and to understand and navigate the worlds in which we live. In other words, representations are human constructions that in turn shape our reality. Moreover, representations are culturally specific; the codes and conventions used to produce them are not universal but are developed over time in particular places and by particular groups of people. These are important concepts to keep in mind when considering the ways gender has been represented in rock culture.

Visual Representations in Rock Culture

Since rock is a performative musical style that relies on human bodies for creative expression, the visual representation of musicians has long been a significant component of rock culture. Typically rendered via photography (although illustrations, cinematography, and other forms of visual art are used as well), such imagery helps rock musicians to communicate about their music in ways other than sound and live performance. In turn, consumers, particularly those who cannot attend live shows, use these images to make sense of rock sounds and the musicians who produce them. Yet visual depictions of musicians serve other purposes in rock culture as well. Most significantly, because rock music is a commercial cultural form with economic ties to the entertainment industries, the visual representation of rock musicians is essential to the marketing and promotion of such performers' art.

While the expressive and economic functions of rock's visual media are somewhat easy to understand, the aesthetic strategies and ideological meanings of such images are not. This chapter focuses on analytical approaches that are used to comprehend the gender politics involved in rock-centered imagery. Some of these methods will be familiar from Chapter 10; however, the production and interpretation of visual media entail different codes and practices from those used for written language, such as song lyrics.

Analyzing Visual Media

Several methods for examining visual images are utilized today in critical media studies, including content analysis, formal analysis, semiotics and ideological analysis, psychoanalytic criticism, and poststructuralist feminist and queer readings. This chapter focuses primarily on the first four of these, as they have been most used to analyze still images. Although these approaches are used also to study music videos, Chapter 12 explores poststructuralist feminist and queer readings in more detail because of their usefulness in studying contemporary audiovisual motion media. In both chapters, the emphasis is on visual images rather than the individuals who produce them. Nevertheless, each chapter has a brief discussion of the gender politics involved in producing images of rock musicians.

Content Analysis

As discussed in Chapter 10, one of the primary methods for studying media texts is **content analysis**, which facilitates a general understanding of a text by describing its most superficial elements (e.g., words, sounds, images). All forms of textual analysis begin with content analysis. Scholars using content analysis to study rock media have typically paid attention only to the most manifest elements of such texts, and their work usually involves coding and counting the prevalence of particular phenomena in such imagery.

One of the key concerns of media scholars interested in gender is how the presence of men and women in media compares to real-life demographic statistics. For example, in the 1970s, Gaye Tuchman conducted a quantitative content analysis that compared women's presence and men's presence in U.S. media, particularly television. Her data demonstrated that women were virtually absent from media texts at that time. This data led Tuchman to argue that women were **symbolically annihilated** in U.S. media culture in comparison to men, and her work catalyzed other feminists to advocate gender parity in visual media.

Like other feminist media content analyses, gender-based studies of rock's visual media have typically begun with counting female and male bodies in a particular visual text or group of texts. For example, Mavis Bayton analyzed several guitarist magazines from three different years: 1988, 1992, and 1996. She found that the vast majority of images in such texts were of men and that the women who did appear were typically not musicians. Bayton used the data from her research to make comparisons with similar phenomena in rock culture, such as the number of male and female guitarists played on the radio.

Paul Théberge found a similar trend in his mid-1990s survey of over two hundred issues of *Keyboard*: Fewer than ten women performers were featured in the magazine's cover stories, thus contributing to the erroneous idea that women rarely play keyboards. More recently, Erin Hatton and Mary Nell Trautner conducted a content analysis of gender and sexual representation on covers of *Rolling Stone* over a four-decade period (1967–2009). Much like Bayton and Théberge, Hatton and Trautner demonstrated that men were featured on the covers of this prominent rock magazine far more often than women. Of 931 covers in their study, 651 (about 70 percent) featured only men, and 205 (22 percent) depicted only women. (The other covers depicted either no humans or a mix of males and females.) To counter the historic overrepresentation of men in musician magazines, periodicals directed toward female musicians and edited by women, such as *Rockrgrl*, *She Shreds*, and *Tom Tom*, privilege images of women (see Figure 11.1).

Like music magazines, album covers are important sites of signification in rock culture. Unfortunately, few scholars have studied album covers, and, as of the writing of this book, no content analysis quantitatively comparing the presence of men and women on rock album covers has been published. Nevertheless, given that musicians are the individuals most often depicted on such covers and that historically there have been far fewer female rock performers, we can reasonably expect that the number of men featured on rock album covers overwhelmingly exceeds the number of women. That theory is supported by a review of the list "100 Classic Album Covers," collated by Michael Azerrad and published by *Rolling Stone*. Unfortunately, this list is not representative of all album covers ever produced, is not specific to rock music, and is not up to date. Nevertheless, it contains a vast number of rock album covers designed between the 1950s and 1990s and thus provides an interesting sample for an informal content analysis of gender in rock album cover design.

Figure 11.1 *Tom Tom Magazine* 27

Tom Tom Magazine, 2016

Forty of the one hundred album covers in Azerrad's list feature men, nineteen feature men, and eight feature members of both gender. (Several do not feature human beings at all.) Much as Bayton found, many album covers for male-led rock bands feature women who are not musicians (e.g., Roxy Music's *Country Life* [1974]). Indeed, of the nineteen covers that feature women, only six include women musicians. Moreover, only four of those covers are for women musicians associated with rock: Deborah Harry, Joni Mitchell, Carly Simon, and Patti Smith.

Clearly, the low ratio of female to male images in rock media prior to the mid-1990s, as found in these studies, is understandable given the small number of women rock musicians performing during that period. Yet we should be careful not to overgeneralize about women's minimal visual representation in this culture historically. For example, if we were to compare the number of female and male images in mid-1990s rock media, that data would likely demonstrate a far larger proportion of women's representation as a result of their greater involvement as rock musicians during that period. It is crucial, therefore, to consider the specific sociohistorical contexts of rock's visual texts, as well as other elements that may have bearing on such text's representations of gender, such as genre and targeted audience.

Formal Analysis

Media producers make numerous decisions to manage the process of visual representation, decisions that demonstrate the constructed nature of media texts. Indeed, most producers put considerable time and effort into controlling the many variables that might affect their product's final rendering and thus its reception. Even documentary filmmakers must manage the reality they attempt to depict by making such decisions as when to turn the camera on and off.

Given the many decisions that contribute to the production of any one image, most feminist media scholars have moved beyond studies that only quantify men's and women's presences in texts. Such researchers are more interested in *which* bodies are depicted, *how*, and *why*. Of particular concern to these scholars is an image's ***mise-en-scène***—the composition of people and objects on a stage or in front of a camera. Qualitative media scholars often refer to the study of *mise-en-scène* as **formal analysis**, since critical attention is paid primarily to the **form** (shape, mode, or configuration) in which textual **content** appears. With regard to the formal analysis of visual media texts, scholars also pay attention to such formal components as casting, costuming and grooming, setting, character roles, and action, as well as camerawork.

As a result of the amount of materials, effort, and time required, the composition of a visual text's *mise-en-scène* is typically the work of several different individuals, including an art director, a costume designer, a set designer, a lighting designer, and a photographer, as well as assistants to such artists. If the text being created is fictional, as in a narrative music video, then a casting agent is often involved also. Gender often plays a role in such positions when producing rock-related images, with men being hired more often than women as art directors, lighting designers, and photographers. However, several women have won Grammy Awards for "Best Record Packaging" in the past decade. Who has ultimate authority over the production of the image is related to individual contracts and the larger context of the work being created. For example, Marion Leonard notes that the types of decision musicians make for photographic shoots are often related to the stage of their careers. Those with considerable status often have a reasonable amount of control over the visual images associated with their music, while those who are lesser known have little control in comparison to record producers.

Casting

The process of **casting** for visual media involves determining the gender of the person to be featured, as well as their race, age, body type, other physical characteristics, and specific talents. Although the term "casting" is typically used in relation to fictional texts, it applies also to documentary texts featuring real people (such as album covers) since all forms of media production involve decisions about who will—and who will not—be represented.

Numerous feminist studies have demonstrated that the women most often featured in contemporary Western visual texts are white, thin, buxom, conventionally attractive young adults who are well-groomed and sport fashionable clothing and accessories. Many of these characteristics are true also for the men depicted in Western popular culture today. Yet historically male media figures have not been as young or thin as their female counterparts. Instead, the media have focused on men who are successful in the public sphere, a realm dominated until recently by middle-aged men. When such casting choices are compared to current U.S. demographics, it is clear that a vast majority of Americans are not depicted in media culture. When nonnormative individuals—people of color, the elderly, the poor, and genderqueer people—are shown in visual media, it is typically to comment on their exceptionality or deviance.

To date, no published research on rock magazines or album covers has analyzed the races, ages, body types, or other physical characteristics of the men and women represented in those texts. Nevertheless, given the historic dominance of rock by young white men, we might deduce that those individuals are featured prominently in most of the visual imagery associated with this culture. Athena Elafros's content analysis of *Rockrgrl*'s representations of musicians demonstrates how its foregrounding of white women contributed to the marginalization of women of color. Were we to push Elafros's intersectional analysis further, we would likely find that most rock magazines also privilege thinness. Nevertheless, that trend has been disrupted somewhat by magazines like *NME*, which has featured musician and fat activist Beth Ditto of Gossip (see Figure 11.2).

Figure 11.2   Beth Ditto cover for *NME*
NME, 2007

The various elements affecting media producers' casting decisions are not stable. For example, in rock culture, such decisions are based on criteria specific to genre, targeted market, the medium of choice, an artist's commercial success, and the larger sociohistorical context. Thus, while we might be tempted to make a generalization about young white males' dominance of rock's visual imagery, doing so would prevent us from recognizing moments of exception, such as the mid-1950s through early 1960s, when many girls and African Americans were creating and consuming this music, and the mid- to late 1990s, when the number of women in rock culture increased significantly.

Costuming and Grooming

Costuming involves the clothing and fashion accessories selected for performers; **grooming** refers to hairstyle and make-up. The term "costuming" is typically used in relation to characters appearing in theatrical plays or fictional media. Nevertheless, even when texts represent real people, decisions are made as to how to clothe and adorn those bodies, decisions that impact how those bodies

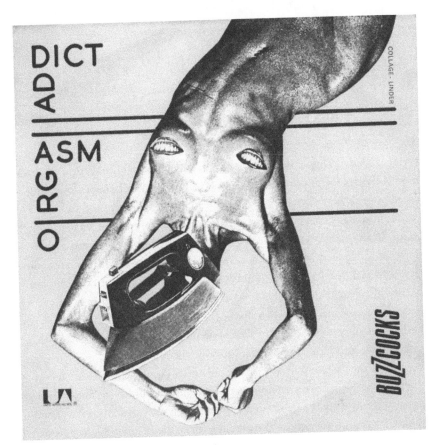

Figure 11.3 The Buzzcocks, *Orgasm Addict*
United Artists, 1977

Figure 11.4 Prince, *Lovesexy*
Paisley Park Records, 1988

perform gender. Thus, costuming choices have long been of interest to feminist media scholars. As discussed in Chapters 5 and 8, rock fashions are often influenced by genre, as well as the time period in which they are created and worn.

Traditionally, male costuming has been determined by socioeconomic status. In the early twentieth century, for example, wealthy Western men were commonly depicted wearing business suits, and working-class men were shown in less formal, resilient attire conducive to manual labor, such as denim jeans. Meanwhile, female clothing has historically been restricted to dresses and skirts, with class status marked by the value of the fabric and the style and intricacy of design. Yet since the 1970s and the reemergence of feminist sentiment, many girls and women have adopted traditionally masculine apparel, such as pants, because of their need to fit into historically male-dominated spaces. Moreover, as a result of the rise of teen culture and the counterculture in the mid-twentieth century, informality has permeated most contemporary societies, even affecting middle-class professionals, who now often "dress down" for both work and leisure. Rock fashions have followed this trend, as the common clothing items of today's rock musicians are no longer suits and dresses but jeans and T-shirts.

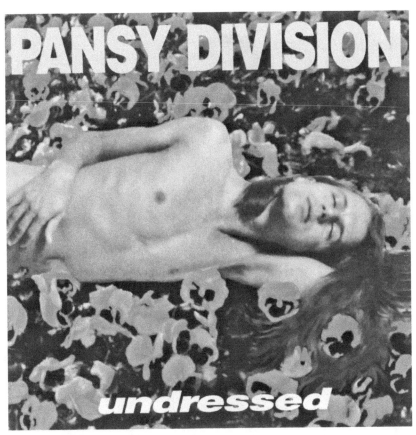

Figure 11.5   Pansy Division, *Undressed*
Lookout Records, 1993

Although sexual attractiveness has not been as important in rock culture as it has in pop, postfeminist media promote the idea that women should exhibit their agency primarily through sexually attractive bodies. Thus, in a move that harkens back to the prefeminist era, most postfeminist texts feature women who appear highly sexualized in clothing that is form-fitting and reveals the maximum amount of flesh. With the recent mainstreaming of gay male subculture, contemporary media culture has witnessed a parallel increase in men's fashions that highlight male body parts, particularly the pectoral and groin regions. This male costuming choice has been a part of rock culture for a much longer period, however, especially in phallocentric hard rock scenes.

Several scholars conducting gender-based formal analyses of rock imagery have considered costuming choices. For example, Bayton's study of gender representation in 1980s and 1990s guitar magazines demonstrated that while few females were featured, those who were shown were scantily clad and thus eroticized. Meanwhile, Hatton and Trautner's research revealed that while most men featured in *Rolling Stone* covers are not eroticized, most women are not just sexualized but hypersexualized. Although Bayton found that guitar magazines often

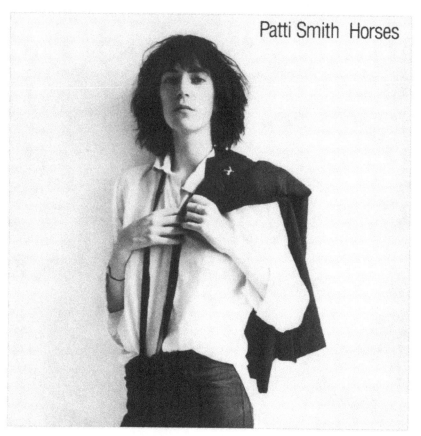

Figure 11.6 Patti Smith, *Horses*
Arista, 1975

depict male musicians as bare-chested, Hatton and Trautner's analysis demonstrated that males have rarely dressed provocatively for *Rolling Stone* covers.

To date, no content analyses focusing on costuming in rock album covers have been published. However, a review of Azerrad's list of one hundred
classic album covers reveals a similar pattern of women wearing sexualized,
revealing clothing, particularly on albums for male rock bands, as can be seen
in Scorpions' *Love Drive* (1979) and Bob Geldof's *Sex, Age & Death* (2001).
Unlike music videos, which undergo rigorous censorship reviews for television,
many rock album covers, especially for male acts, have featured nude women,
including Jimi Hendrix's *Electric Ladyland* (1968), Scorpions' *Virgin Killer*
(1977), Jane's Addiction's *Nothing's Shocking* (1988), Pulp's *This Is Hardcore*
(1998), and the Red Hot Chili Peppers' *By the Way* (2002). Some covers
designed by women artists have critiqued this practice by subverting viewers'
pleasure in such images, as in Linder's design for the Buzzcock's *Orgasm Addict*
(1977) (Figure 11.3).

In contrast to the erotic apparel (and sometimes lack of apparel) for
women featured on rock album covers, males typically appear fully attired in

Figure 11.7   Bat for Lashes, *The Haunted Man*
Parlophone, 2012

informal clothing typical of working-class male adolescents (e.g., denim jeans, T-shirts, leather jackets), as can be seen in several album covers from Azerrad's top one hundred list: the Who's *Who's Next* (1971), Bruce Springsteen's *Born to Run* (1975), and the Ramones' eponymous album (1976). This type of apparel continues to be conventional among today's male rockers also, although it has been modified at times as a result of fashion trends (e.g., the narrowing of pant legs).

In comparison to women, few men have been shown completely nude on rock album covers. John Lennon and Yoko Ono's *Unfinished Music No. 1: Two Virgins* (1968) and Prince's *Lovesexy* (1990) are notable exceptions (see Figure 11.4). Yet, in keeping with Bayton's study of guitar magazines, several album covers for male rock acts, particularly those whose gender is queered or ambiguous, feature men with bare chests, including the Stooges' *Raw Power* (1973), David Bowie's *Diamond Dogs* (1974), the Smiths' eponymous album (1984), and Pansy Division's *Undressed* (1993) (see Figure 11.5).

Because of sexualized standards set for women's depictions in Western, female rock musicians—particularly those who are of color, genderqueer, over

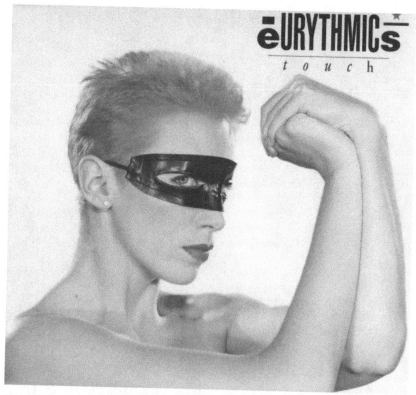

Figure 11.8 Eurythmics, *Touch*
RCA, 1983

forty years old, or disabled—have faced difficult choices with regard to how to present their bodies in visual representation. As Leonard argues, such decisions have a direct bearing on how such performers are understood by the public. Therefore, most female rock musicians, especially those in the early stages of their careers, have taken special care that their clothing is not only fashionable but communicates their band's image.

In early rock history, standards for women's respectable representations were quite high. Hence, most female rock performers were represented somewhat conservatively, wearing unrevealing dresses or skirts, as can be seen in Brenda Lee's *Grandma, What Great Songs You Sang!* (1959) and the Shirelles' *Baby, It's You* (1962). Because of loosened standards for female apparel, not to mention women musicians' historically minimal control over the imagery used to sell their music, since the 1970s many female rockers have appeared in somewhat revealing clothing—as can be seen in Carly Simon's *Playing Possum* (1975) and Lita Ford's *Lita* (1988).

As women have gained more power in popular culture, those musicians with considerable control over their careers have taken greater license with their visual portrayal, often subverting gender-based fashion norms and body politics. One of the first indications that female musicians had a broader range of clothing options to choose from when fashioning their personas was the album

Figure 11.9   David Bowie, *The Man Who Sold the World*
Mercury, 1971

cover for Patti Smith's *Horses* (1975), which shows Smith, sans make-up with
unkempt hair, wearing black pants and a white button-down shirt, a suit jacket
thrown over her shoulder (Figure 11.6).

Such practices of female masculinization through clothing increased among
women rock performers during the 1980s and 1990s, especially among those
involved in historically male-dominated subgenres. Indeed, women involved in
punk and heavy metal have regularly sported masculine attire, such as work
boots and leather jackets (e.g., Girlschool's *Hit and Run* [1981]). Lesbian rockers who identify as a butch have also worn more masculine attire for their album
covers (e.g., Melissa Etheridge's debut album [1988], Kaia's debut album [1996],
and the Shondes' *Searchlight* [2011]). As Judith Halberstam might argue, such
performances of female masculinity via fashion necessarily trouble rock's gender norms and thus the sex/gender system.

Unlike women pop performers, female rock musicians rarely appear in print
media as partially or fully nude. Nevertheless, some have attempted to portray
themselves as sexually assertive rather than merely decorative, as can be seen in
the album cover for the Slits' *Cut* (1979) and Bat for Lashes' *The Haunted Man*
(2012) (see Figure 11.7). Yet many recent images in this vein—such as the covers

Figure 11.10 Skunk Anansie, *Paranoid and Sunburnt*
One Little Indian, 1995

for Liz Phair's eponymous album (2003), Courtney Love's *America's Sweetheart* (2004), and Spinnerette's eponymous album (2009)—are arguably suggestive of postfeminist sexual subjectification, wherein women assert their power primarily through hypersexualization, which does not subvert gender norms.

Other female rock musicians transgressed the gender stereotyping of women's and men's visual representation by mixing feminine and masculine fashion accessories, a practice Judith Butler might call **gender trouble** and Theodore Gracyk labels **gender transgression**. For example, the cover for the Eurythmics' *Touch* (1983) shows singer Annie Lennox bare-shouldered but also sporting an orange crew cut and a black leather bondage mask (Figure 11.8). Along with the cover's inclusion of Lennox's muscular biceps and clipped fingernails, these accouterments suggest masculinity and power and complicate the femininity suggested by such details as her diamond earrings and red lipstick. Moreover, each of these accessories draws attention to the cultural construction of gender. A similar mix of feminine and masculine accouterments can be seen in Wendy O. Williams's portrayals for the Plasmatics' album covers.

Figure 11.11   Peaches, *Fatherfucker*
XL, 2003

In turn, some album cover art for male musicians has troubled rock fashion's traditional gender norms, as is clear from virtually all of Prince's and David Bowie's album covers, which show the musicians in various forms of feminine apparel (e.g., David Bowie's *The Man Who Sold the World* [1970]- see Figure 11.9). Several male bands have taken a more humorous approach to cross-gender costuming for album covers, as can be seen in Frank Zappa's *We're Only in It for the Money* (1968) and the Rolling Stones' *Some Girls* (1978). Nevertheless, despite exceptions like Jayne County (formerly Wayne), male rockers have rarely incorporated feminine attire into their media representations on a regular basis.

With regard to grooming, male rockers' hairstyles in visual media have ranged from bald or shaved to long locks with virtually no response from the rock community. Meanwhile, depictions of women rockers with hairstyles that are not long, and thus not in keeping with feminine beauty norms, have typically garnered attention both within and outside this culture. Perhaps the most radical form of hairstyle for a woman is the shaved head, which is commonly

Figure 11.12   Babes in Toyland, *Painkillers*
Southern Records, 1993

understood as a refusal to perform femininity and thus as a symbol of non-conformity and rebellion. The first female rocker to pose with a shaved head for a record cover was Sinead O'Connor, who did so for her debut album, *The Lion and the Cobra* (1987). Other women rockers have performed their nonbinary genderqueerness via masculine hairstyles, as Hannah Blilie of Gossip did by sporting a well-coifed pompadour for the cover of *Music for Men* (2009). Meanwhile, as noted in Chapter 8, several black female rock musicians have resisted tropes of white feminine beauty in media representations by wearing their hair in Afros or shaving their heads (e.g., Skin of Skunk Anansie, *Paranoid and Sunburnt* [1995] - see Figure 11.10).

While the growth or shaving of men's body hair rarely gains notice in rock culture, a recent trend among male rockers is the full male beard. In contrast, Western women have long been encouraged to shave or cover their body hair. Thus, those who expose it are considered rebellious and unfeminine, if not lesbian. Patti Smith was the first female rock musician to publicly reveal her armpit hair on an album cover (e.g., *Easter* [1978]), a practice adopted decades later by Beth Ditto for Gossip's *Standing in the Way of Control* (2006). Peaches,

Figure 11.13   Girl in a Coma, *Exits and All the Rest*
Blackheart Records, 2011

along with sister act CocoRosie, have taken the queering of the female body via body hair one step further, as evidenced by their facial hair for the covers of *Fatherfucker* (2003) and *Grey Oceans* (2010) (see Figure 11.11).

Despite its common affiliation with women, make-up has been used historically by both male and female rockers in performances, publicity, and album covers (e.g., Lou Reed's *Transformer* [1972] and Björk's *Biophilia* [2011]). While some contemporary male punk musicians have been known to wear eye make-up and nail polish in everyday life, most male rockers go without make-up on a regular basis and thus affirm traditional masculine body politics.

In contrast, the absence of make-up on a female body signifies resistance to conventional feminine body politics and beauty regimes and thus puts women's gender, if not sexual identity, in question. Many women rock musicians who prefer to appear without make-up in visual media are feminist, queer, and/or have connections to punk or other forms of independent music culture. Nevertheless, as a result of pressure from their record labels, which are concerned about sales, even female musicians who regularly perform without make-up sometimes feel the need to glamorize themselves for photo shoots, particularly early in their

Figure 11.14 That Dog's *Totally Crushed Out*
DGC Records, 1995

careers (e.g., Neko Case & Her Boyfriends, *The Virginian* [1997]). Meanwhile, out lesbians or bisexual women in full make-up (e.g., Beth Ditto's eponymous *Beth Ditto EP* [2011]) subvert the historical connection of femininity and heterosexuality, as well as the stereotype of queer women as masculine. Also challenging was Courtney Love and Kat Bjelland's "kinderwhore" style, which mixed signifiers of girlish innocence and mature female sexuality, including smeared make-up and babydoll dresses (as can be seen in Figure 11.12, the inside cover of Babes in Toyland's *Painkillers* [1993]).

One strategy some women musicians have used to avoid the hypersexualized appearance demanded of them for photo shoots is to insist that their bodies not appear on album covers or in interviews. For example, Martina Axen of Drain STH recalls: "we purposely didn't put photos on our CD jacket or release any to the press at first to avoid stereotypes."[1] In turn, *Tom Tom Magazine*, which focuses on female drummers, has considered publishing an entire issue without pictures to draw attention to the musicians as opposed to their gender.

Setting

Visual imagery can communicate about gender also via **setting**, the spaces in which human bodies and other objects appear. Scenic sets for theatrical plays and fictional media texts are often designed to express something about the characters and story. And even in the world of documentary filmmaking, directors make choices about where their subjects should be located. Historically, physical space has been divided by gender: the **public sphere** of education, work, and politics was associated primarily with men, while women's roles and activities were restricted to the domestic or **private sphere**. Thus, depictions of nondomestic, public spaces have typically featured men and connoted masculinity, while images of homes have usually featured women and suggested femininity.

As a result of recent transformations in gender politics, women in many societies have far greater access to public spaces, which in turn has contributed to a rise in visual imagery showing women outside the domestic sphere. A slight increase in male representation in the domestic sphere has occurred also, although images of the public sphere still predominantly feature men. Interestingly, depictions of men at home are not necessarily emasculating, since a long tradition of patriarchy exists in family life, and the idea that "a man's home is his castle" is still popular.

A review of the artwork featured in Azerrad's "100 Classic Album Covers" reveals some interesting decisions by designers with regard to space. The vast majority of covers in that grouping show male musicians in an indeterminate space that is neither inside nor outside, as exemplified by Bruce Springsteen's *Born to Run* (1975). The majority of covers featuring male musicians outdoors were designed for rock groups (e.g., the Who's *Who's Next* [1971], the Ramones' eponymous album [1976], and U2's *The Joshua Tree* [1987]). Interestingly, the number of covers featuring men outdoors (eight) is almost the same as the number showing women shot outdoors (seven), although in contrast to the men in such images, most of the women are not musicians. And in contrast to those featuring men outdoors, the external settings of covers with women are more often rural than urban (e.g., Joni Mitchell's *Hejira* [1976] and Bow Wow Wow's *See Jungle! See Jungle! Go Join Your Gang Yeah! City All Over, Go Ape Crazy!* [1981]). The number of covers that feature men indoors is also the same as the number with women indoors (four). However, only male musicians are shown in distinctly domestic settings: Bob Dylan's *Bringing It All Back Home* (1965) and Rod Stewart's *Never a Dull Moment* (1972).

Given that Azerrad's list of classic album covers was created over twenty years ago, it is useful to consider if the settings depicted on rock covers have changed since that time, particularly in relation to the increase in women rockers. A likely transformation with regard to gendered spaces in such media is the increased portrayal of female rockers in urban spaces, what Lewis would term **access** (e.g., Sleater-Kinney's *Hot Rock* [1999], PJ Harvey's *Stories of the City, Stories from the Sea* [2000], and Girl in a Coma's *Exits and All the Rest* [2011] - see Figure 11.13).

Another interesting development has been the depiction of girls in their bedrooms (e.g., That Dog's *Totally Crushed Out* [1995] and the Donnas' *Spend the Night* [2002]), a trend that emerged in the mid-1990s, likely as a result of Riot Grrrl's privileging of girlhood and marketers' increased appeals to young female consumers (see Figure 11.14). In her analysis of gender and music video, Lewis labels this strategy of privileging feminine spaces **discovery.**

Roles and Actions

Although we typically think of **roles** in relation to the social position occupied by fictional characters, real-life people also take on roles that communicate their identities, social circles, and everyday experiences. Different people occupy such roles differently, which means that the meanings attached to these roles are fluid rather than static. Nevertheless, roles are often affiliated with particular **actions** or practices as well as specific spaces and social institutions, and we learn such roles from our parents and others as we develop. In today's society, people often turn to the media also to understand themselves and negotiate social relations. Thus, fictional character roles and behaviors participate in the construction of real-life identities and social interactions, and vice versa.

Prior to the late nineteenth century, girls and women were restricted to the roles and practices associated with the domestic sphere, particularly motherhood and household labor. In contrast, boys and men were afforded roles in the public sphere of education, work, and politics. In the past half century, shifts in the economy as well as in gender norms have resulted in greater female presence in the public sphere. Yet a large percentage of women in contemporary media continue to be shown in domestic roles. In turn, young women are still often restricted to a passive, decorative function that suggests their emphasized femininity and thus subordination to men. Because of the historical association of productivity with men, media characters who are depicted as active (either through movement, labor, or aggression) are commonly thought to be masculine, while passive individuals are considered feminine. Nevertheless, such gendered meanings are not stable, and often they are inflected by socioeconomic status (as labor is affiliated with the working class and leisure with the rich).

To date, no content analyses of rock album covers have taken into consideration the roles and actions of the people portrayed in them. Yet a survey of Azerrad's list of one hundred classic album covers reveals that the dominant role occupied by the people in these texts is that of a poser, specifically someone who sits, stands, or lies passively for a photograph. Men and women take up this role equally, which is not surprising, given the promotional function of such texts and the need for consumers to identify quickly with the product being marketed. Interestingly, only men appear with musical instruments (a prop that confers on them the role of musician), and only two of those men are shown performing. Such findings would be different if we were to include album covers

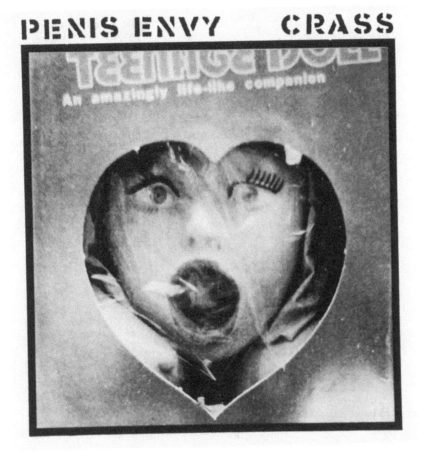

Figure 11.15 Crass, *Penis Envy*
Crass Records, 1981

designed since the early 1990s, as an increasing number of female instrumentalists have been involved in rock culture.

The Disadvantages of Content Analysis

Although quantitative and formal content analyses are useful for producing generalized data on media texts that can be used to initiate policy change,
studies that attend only to the most superficial elements of visual imagery have
drawbacks. First, such analyses are often conducted by scholars who assume that
media can reflect reality accurately. Second, such studies do not typically take
connotative content into consideration and thus present incomplete interpretations of texts. Third, by focusing on generalizable patterns, these studies often
dismiss contradictory data that, if attended to, might reveal further information about the text and complicate interpretations. Fourth, the majority of such
studies ignores both textual polysemy and reception practices and thus incorrectly assumes that all viewers read texts the same way.

PEEL SLOWLY AND SEE

Andy Warhol

Figure 11.16   The Velvet Underground, *The Velvet Underground and Nico*
Verve, 1967

When considering how gendered meanings are produced through media representations, we must remember that no one aspect of an image's design creates a gendered connotation. Instead, gendered meanings are constructed through such elements' combination in the overall composition of the image, as well as their relation to other imagery circulating concurrently in visual culture. For example, although the album cover for Crass's *Penis Envy* (1981) depicts a blow-up doll used in male masturbation, the objective in using this image was to shock viewers into an awareness women's sexual oppression, not to elicit celebration of it, as a quantitative analysis focusing on only its superficial details might conclude (Figure 11.15).

Gender-based content analyses contributed to a form of media criticism called **image studies**, which persists in much popular criticism today. The objective of such research is to evaluate visual images for their "positive/progressive" or "negative/regressive" meaning. While image studies were useful in galvanizing attention to gender representations in the 1970s, this approach has received criticism from feminist media scholars ever since because such evaluations are subjective, and the criteria used to make them vary widely. Moreover, as with other forms of content analysis, image studies tend to produce more questions than answers, particularly about how representational patterns have developed,

Figure 11.17   L7, *L7*
Epitaph, 1988

why they persist, and what they mean. To answer those questions, critical media scholars have utilized certain forms of critical analysis, particularly semiotics.

Semiotics and Ideological Analysis

First developed for analyzing spoken and written language, **semiotics**—the study of signs and signification—has proven useful also for scholars of other forms of communication, including audiovisual media. By combining Ferdinand de Saussure's theories (discussed in Chapter 10) with those developed later by Charles Peirce, contemporary scholars using semiotics have been able to analyze a vast array of signs that are multimedia in form, such as films, television programs, websites, and games.

Peirce delineates three basic forms of signs. **Iconic signs**, such as portraits of people or landscape drawings, resemble the person or object being represented. **Indexical signs** bear some existential relationship to the things they represent. For example, fingerprints are used as indexes of individuals, just as symptoms, like hives, are indexes of particular illnesses. **Symbolic signs** have

Figure 11.18 Toni Childs, *The Woman's Boat*
Geffen, 1994

no relationship to the object or person they represent; the connection between the two is arbitrary and based on convention. (In this way, Peirce's theory of symbolic signs is similar to Saussure's theory of signs in general.) Examples of symbolic signs include wedding rings, national flags, and some religious symbols, such as the Jewish Star of David.

Commercial media culture, particularly advertising, relies strongly on symbolic signs because they communicate quickly and concisely the character of a particular product or manufacturer. The media's use of symbols is perhaps most evident in stock photography, advertisements, and other promotional material, such as flyers, billboards, and album covers, which by necessity must communicate their messages with speed and efficiency to attract a large number of consumers.

The electric guitar has become the primary symbol of rock culture, despite the fact that other instruments are used to perform rock music and that the electric guitar is utilized in many other forms of popular music also. Another symbol used often in rock culture yet not specific to it is the "horns" hand gesture (from the Italian *corna*). This gesture is made by extending the index and pinky fingers while holding down the two middle fingers with the thumb. While some conservative

Christians have understood it as satanic, rockers use it to communicate fan identity, to signify community, and to express pleasure during a musical performance.

Since the 1970s feminist semioticians, such as Judith Williamson, have drawn attention to the various ways gender politics imbue signs with values and meaning, and their research has focused on how men and women are represented in commercial visual media. Grounding such scholarship is the theory that the men who dominate media production encode texts with patriarchal, heteronormative ideologies. For example, such work demonstrates that male bodies have long been used in visual media to suggest men's achievements, strength, and superiority. Consider, for example, the images of male rulers' heads on coins or statues representing male war heroes. Many album covers for male rock bands feature musicians in this heroic manner also. Yet it is not always full male bodies that are used to connote masculine power. Because of its uniqueness to male bodies, the penis could be employed as a synecdoche of maleness and men's virility. Yet, instead, visual designers wanting to avoid censorship have used the larger male crotch area to signify male power, as can be seen in the album covers for the Rolling Stones' *Sticky Fingers* (1971) and W.A.S.P.'s *Animal* (1993). Visual artists have also utilized **phallic objects** for a similar connotation, as can be seen in the Velvet Underground's *The Velvet Underground and Nico* (1967) and Led Zeppelin's debut album (1969) (see Figure 11.16).

Other objects have been used to suggest maleness and men's virility also. For example, since the rise of industrialization, men have been associated with mechanical and electric technologies used to control nature, manufacture products, and accrue wealth. Hence, visual artists often signify masculinity and male power through the representation of men interacting with such objects as cars, motorcycles, and weapons (e.g., Mötley Crüe's *Girls Girls Girls* [1987]). But the technology most commonly used to connote masculinity in rock culture is the electric guitar. As discussed in Chapter 7, the electric guitar has been gendered masculine because it has been designed and used mostly by men, and it symbolizes power because of its connection with sonic volume and distortion. As a result of these connotations, many male rockers have appeared on album covers with their guitars (e.g., Ted Nugent's *Free-for-All* [1976] and Bruce Springsteen's *Human Touch* [1992]).

Nevertheless, Steve Waksman's theory of technophallic devices suggests that both men and women can gain access to power via their engagement with technology. So it is no surprise that album covers for women guitarists have capitalized on the electric guitar's ability to symbolically confer power (e.g., Joan Jett's eponymous debut album [1980], Melissa Etheridge's *Never Enough* [1992], Bonnie Raitt's *Souls Alike* [2005]). Yet few of these album covers depict women actively playing guitars. Exceptions include L7's eponymous debut album (1988), Sleater-Kinney's debut album (1995), Team Dresch's *Captain, My Captain* (1996), and the Donnas' *American Teenage Rock 'n' Roll Machine* (1998) (see Figure 11.17).

While male bodies are used regularly in Western art to represent men's intellectual and cultural achievements, female bodies have been utilized more often to signify nature, because of women's reproductive capabilities and the gendering of the mind/body split. In rock culture this has meant that women are often shown in natural settings and without the tools of industry and commerce (e.g., Roxy Music's *Country Life* [1974]). Although rock's antidomestic ideology has kept images of pregnancy and motherhood to a minimum, some designers working with women musicians have drawn on reproductive iconography (as seen in Figure 11.18, Toni Childs's *The Woman's Boat* [1994]), thus contributing to the female-centric approach of discovery discussed by Lewis.

Historically, Western images of women have taken on one of two connotations, innocence or evil, a practice that dates back to Eve's fall from grace in the Bible. Often such images have been sexualized, thus producing the virgin/whore dichotomy that has limited female roles and behavior. Ideologies involving age and racial politics frequently come into play here also, as innocence is typically signified via a young, white girl, while older women or women of color have been used to represent evil.

Images of young and sexually attractive women appear regularly in rock album covers, typically to signify the virility of the male musicians being promoted. Often such female bodies are displayed as decorative objects, which, while having the power to attract the viewer's attention, are more commonly understood as symbols of feminine passivity and women's subordination to men (e.g., the Cars' *Candy-O* [1979]). With such patterns of signification, women rock musicians have struggled to be seen as legitimate performers. As Deborah Harry of Blondie recalls of her early career: "I wasn't looked at as being a female singer-songwriter. People weren't even generally aware that I wrote my own songs or played the piano. The media just promoted me as a female body. It's like I had to prove that I'm an artist in a female body."[2] Brody Dalle of the Distillers and Spinnerette sums up this phenomenon succinctly: "what women look like always becomes so much more important than what we have to say."[3] As noted, feminist rock musicians have responded to the patriarchal structure of signification in album covers by appearing masculine or androgynous, by privileging their feminine and sexual agency, and by refusing to be represented.

Psychoanalytic Readings

As feminist scholars first argued in the 1970s, men's historic control over the production of visual media has significantly influenced the representation of male and female bodies in such texts. Utilizing psychoanalytic theory, several feminist scholars have attempted to explain why certain gendered patterns of media representation persist by exploring how male desires and fears shape creative output.

In her pioneering theory of the **male gaze**, Laura Mulvey argued that men's combined domination of the roles of film director, cinematographer, and screenwriter resulted in classic Hollywood movies' phallocentrism, which viewers are encouraged to adopt when watching movies. Utilizing **psychoanalytic theories** of visual pleasure, Mulvey demonstrated that Hollywood films construct the male gaze in part through their representation of goal-oriented male protagonists with whom viewers are meant to identify. At the same time, the power of such characters is confirmed through their **fetishistic** gazing at passive women. In other words, in the world of film, men look and women are to be looked at. Nowhere is this male gaze clearer than in sequences that require viewers to take on the male protagonist's perspective via a point-of-view shot of a **sexually objectified** female body, as happens in *Vertigo* (1958), *Charlie's Angels* (2000), and the *Transformers* franchise (2007–14).

While Mulvey's theory explains *how* women are made into passive, sexualized objects in Hollywood cinema through specific storytelling and camera practices, she also took pains to explain *why* this representational pattern developed. Utilizing psychoanalytic theories, Mulvey noted that men find pleasure in looking at powerful male characters (especially those played by movie stars) because such images allow them to identify with an ideal figure of their same gender. In contrast, men's viewing of women is often uncomfortable, since it reminds them of the possibility of castration and women's lack of power. In Freudian theories of psychosexual development, boys believe that their mothers have been castrated, since they do not have penises. As a result, boys develop castration anxiety and sublimate their desire for their mother. Yet, as Mulvey theorized, the structures of cinema make men's gazing at female characters pleasurable. In the first place, male spectators sit at a distance from the images on the screen and therefore are allowed to be voyeurs without risk of being caught. Second, male spectators identify with male protagonists who typically "get the girl" and have control over her. Finally, male viewers can use female characters' sexualized bodies as fetish objects and thus regain a sense of power.

Not surprisingly, rock photography has seen less involvement of women than men since the emergence of rock 'n' roll in the 1950s, mostly due to the legacy of patriarchy in journalism and visual art. For example, of the seventy photographers associated with RockArchive.com, a website devoted to rock photography, only eleven are women. While more female photographers have become involved in rock photography since the 1970s, and several have achieved notoriety—particularly Jill Furmanovsky, Lynn Goldsmith, Annie Leibovitz, and Linda McCartney—the world of rock photography remains dominated by men.

Plenty of rock's visual texts, especially those created for male bands, construct a male gaze for consumers by sexually objectifying the female bodies depicted therein. As Bayton demonstrated, musician magazines often use women's objectification to confer power on the men in such images as well as the consumers of the gear being promoted. The message communicated by such images is that the male consumer will become sexually powerful and able to attract such women by purchasing the product. Designers of album covers for male rock musicians regularly use images of eroticized women also. Yet the absence of men in many of rock covers is interesting, for it suggests that male consumers do not necessarily need a male character with whom they can identify to feel powerful. They merely need to gaze upon the woman's fetishized body.

In addition to demonstrating Hollywood films' consistent use of female bodies as fetish objects, Mulvey drew attention to other aesthetic practices that suggest women's objectification and thus minimal power. In particular, she noted that female body parts, such as legs, are often shot in close-up and used as fetish objects in movies, as can be seen in the first appearance of Julia Roberts's body in *Pretty Woman* (1990). This practice, commonly utilized by the advertising industry and known as **fragmentation**, has been widely critiqued by feminists since it suggests that women are objects merely made up of parts, not complete human subjects with thoughts and feelings.

In keeping with such representational strategies, several rock album covers that include women depict only a part of their bodies, as can be seen in Black Crowes' *Amorica* (1994) and the Strokes' *Is This It* (2001). This practice of fragmentation is taken to the extreme on the Nutz's *Nutz Too* album cover (1975), where each band member is photographed individually with one female body part. Although the collection of images reveals that they are all part of the same woman, she is not "complete," since the borders of the photographs eliminate significant portions of her anatomy, including her face.

Reconsidering the Gaze

Mulvey's theory of the male gaze and women's sexual objectification in Hollywood cinema has been quite influential on feminist scholars, galvanizing thousands of research projects into women's and men's representation in media. Nevertheless, her theory is not without faults, and it has received almost as much criticism as the amount of scholarship it has inspired. In particular, Mulvey's contention that media texts always put us in the position of a male viewer, and that viewers always adopt that position, is problematic. Not only does her theory refuse to acknowledge active female viewership and the presence of female-centered media (although there was clearly less of it when Mulvey wrote her essay), she ignores the possibility of LGBTQI viewers' reception practices, as well as those of people of color.

As feminist studies of girls' magazines, women's weepies, and chick lit have demonstrated, a long history exists of media texts that subvert patriarchal representational strategies by foregrounding females, femininity, and women's culture. While clearly not all such texts are feminist, few of them rely only on patriarchal representational practices. At the same time, queer scholars, like Alexander Doty, have complicated the idea that all media texts are heterocentric by demonstrating that queerness is central in media culture and therefore that homoeroticism does not reside at some subtextual level to which only LGBTQI viewers have access. Meanwhile, critical race scholars, like bell hooks, have drawn attention to how people of color often view images created for white people in an oppositional way, thereby challenging all of us to think more critically about how the intersections of gender, race, and other identities impact our media reception practices.

The work of cultural studies scholars like Stuart Hall has shown us that media texts are polysemous, able to be interpreted in different ways by different people whose backgrounds, identities, and knowledges inflect how they make sense of culture. At the same time, viewers' physical identities (gender, race, age) do not constrain their ability to find pleasure in media characters whose identities differ from their own. Thus, we must consider the possibility that even media that seem most normative may be pleasurable to audiences other than their primary one of straight white young men.

Summary

This chapter began an examination of the role of gender in rock's visual media. With a focus on album covers, we have explored the ways men's and women's bodies have been depicted. Essential to such analyses are the concept of representation and the relationship of visual images to material reality. By surveying the approaches scholars have used to study representation, readers are able to comprehend the different strategies that have been used to depict men and women in rock culture. Content analyses demonstrate that men far outnumber women in most rock album covers. Nevertheless, such analyses provide us with little information as to why such disproportion predominates. By using other qualitative approaches—specifically formal analysis, semiotics, ideological analysis, and psychoanalytic readings—readers can develop a better sense of the conventions in gender in rock album cover art as well as explanations for why these conventions have developed. Readers can also gain an understanding of the strategies that have been used in rock imagery to resist and subvert stereotypical depictions of men and women. Chapter 12 continues the discussions of rock's visual media started here by looking at music videos.

Further Exploration

1. Analyze images of men and women on the covers of your ten most favorite albums.

How are men depicted in these covers? How are women depicted? What type of clothing do members of each sex typically wear? In what kinds of setting are the men and women depicted? What roles do the men and women occupy, and in what kind of action are they engaged? How do representations of women and men in these magazines compare when technology is part of the image? Over all, describe what differences, if any, exist between representations of women and men in these magazines.

2. Examine the text and images in magazines marketed primarily to male musicians, such as *Guitar Player* and *Modern Drummer*.

Discuss how men and women are depicted in such magazines' editorial and advertising content. What is the ratio of male to female appearances in such texts? How would you describe the diversity of men's and women's identities in these magazines with regard to race, age, class, and sexuality? What type of clothing do members of each sex typically wear? In what kinds of setting are the men and women depicted? What roles do the men and women occupy, and in what kind of action are they engaged? How do representations of women and men in these magazines compare when technology is part of the image? Overall, describe what differences, if any, exist between representations of women and men in these magazines. In addition, describe the ratio of males to females on the magazines' editorial staffs.

3. Analyze the text and images of magazines marketed primarily to women musicians and consumers, such as *Rockrgrl* and *Women Who Rock*.

Discuss how men and women are depicted in such magazines' editorial and advertising content. What is the ratio of male to female appearance in such texts? How would you describe the diversity of men's and women's identities in these magazines with regard to race, age, class, and sexuality? What type of clothing do members of each sex typically wear? In what kinds of setting are the men and women depicted? What roles do the men and women occupy, and in what kinds of action are they engaged? How do representations of women and men in these magazines compare when technology is part of the image? Overall, describe what differences, if any, exist between representations of women and men in these magazines. In addition, describe the ratio of males to females on the magazines' editorial staffs.

4. Compare the results of your findings from exercises 1, 2, and 3.

Do you notice any general tendencies with regard to how males and females are visually depicted in popular music culture?

5. Create an album cover for a rock band.

Consider what visual components you might use to express the nature of this band and its music. If you have access to the band, ask if they would like to be part of the photo shoot. Determine how you will costume and position the band members, and what activities they will perform. If you do not have access to the band, select images you might use to create the album. (Be sure to check with your instructor about copyright policies.) Reflect on how your decisions relate to gender politics and consider ways you might challenge gender norms.

Further Reading

Azerrad, Michael. "100 Classic Album Covers." *Rolling Stone* 617 (November 14, 1991), 91+.

Bayton, Mavis. "Women and the Electric Guitar." *Sexing the Groove: Popular Music and Gender.* Ed. Sheila Whiteley. New York: Routledge, 1997. 37–49.

Elafros, Athena. " 'No Beauty Tips or Guilt Trips': *Rockrgrl*, Rock, and Representation." *Popular Music and Society* 33.4 (2010): 487–99.

Gracyk, Theodor. *Rhythm and Noise: An Aesthetics of Rock.* Durham: Duke University Press, 1996.

Hatton, Erin, and Mary Nell Trautner. "Equal Opportunity Objectification? The Sexualization of Men and Women on the Cover of *Rolling Stone*." *Sexuality & Culture* 15.3 (2011): 556–78.

Jones, Steve, and Martin Sorger. "Covering Music: A Brief History and Analysis of Album Cover Design." *Journal of Popular Music Studies* 11/12 (1999/2000): 68–102.

Leonard, Marion. *Gender in the Music Industry: Rock, Discourse and Girl Power.* Hampshire: Ashgate, 2007.

Lewis, Lisa. *Gender Politics and MTV: Voicing the Difference.* Philadelphia: Temple University Press, 1992.

Mulvey, Laura. "Visual Pleasure and Narrative Cinema." *Screen* 16.3 (1975): 6–18.

Théberge, Paul. *Any Sound You Can Imagine: Making Music/Consuming Technology.* Hanover: Wesleyan University Press, 1997.

12 ON-SCREEN
Rock Music Videos

LISTEN AND WATCH: MUSIC video for Dire Straits, "Money for Nothing" (*Brothers in Arms*, Warner Bros., 1985). *The working-class male narrator in this song is dismissive of rock stars' seeming lack of work and heteronormative masculinity yet envious of their wealth and attractiveness to women. The video includes a good example of women's sexual objectification, a common trait of 1980s videos for all-male rock bands.*

Continuing the discussion of gendered images in rock culture, this chapter analyzes music videos. In the broad range of visual media forms associated with rock, music video is one of the most contemporary. Yet, because of the ubiquity of music videos since MTV was launched in the early 1980s, they have become one of the most significant sites of contemporary representation and promotion of rock music. Indeed, many consumers today "listen" to rock songs by watching music videos, and more consumers watch rock performances via videos than live shows.

Music videos have garnered significant attention from media scholars, especially during their heyday on MTV in the 1980s and 1990s. Much research in this area focused on the meaning of music video's formal attributes, such as editing, narrative, and production design. Yet the gender politics of music videos have been of concern to scholars also. Consider, for example, that of the 122 videos nominated for MTV's "Best Rock Video" award over the past twenty-five years, only 8 videos or 6.6 percent have been for bands that have at least one female member. More significant, by 2016, only one video for a female musician had won this award: Lorde's "Royals."

Since gender has been performed in numerous ways in rock videos, it is important to examine specific modes of representation when discussing individual videos. Such modes have transformed considerably over the past three decades of music video history as a result of changes in musical genres and media production, shifts in gender politics in society, and criticism from activists. Of particular concern are those representational strategies that uphold heteronormative patriarchal ideology and traditional gender norms.

Most scholars agree that a song's lyrics and musical sounds should not be ignored when analyzing music videos, since those sonic elements contribute to the overall meaning of such texts. Nonetheless, this chapter focuses primarily on the visual elements of rock videos to demonstrate the ways gender is communicated visually in motion media. Readers interested in conducting holistic analyses of rock videos that examine lyrics, music, and visuals are encouraged to review the chapters on rock sounds and rock lyrics.

Readers who have not already done so are encouraged to review Chapter 11 before reading this one, as that chapter discusses many of terms and concepts used here. Moreover, Chapter 11 gives an overview of content analysis and formal analysis, which many scholars use to study the superficial characteristics of music videos. The primary methodologies discussed in this chapter, however, are poststructuralist feminist and queer readings. In this chapter we will also explore gender in relation to music video producers.

Music Videos

Music videos are short audiovisual texts created to promote one specific song. Although ubiquitous in popular culture today, music videos were not the first type of media devised to publicize popular music; they are merely the most contemporary form serving this function. Musical artists have been featured in documentary and narrative films since the 1920s. During that decade, one-song short films emerged as a unique media form. In the 1940s, short musical films called **soundies** were developed as promotional texts to be played on Panoram visual jukeboxes. In 1960, **Scopitones** were introduced in France for similar purposes.

Like film, television has been instrumental for the promotion of popular music artists. The early U.S. television schedule of the late 1940s and early 1950s included many variety shows featuring musicians. In the 1950s several rock-based musical shows oriented toward teenagers were introduced, including *American Bandstand*, one of the longest running series in U.S. television history. Nevertheless, **MTV** (Music Television Network) has had the greatest impact on the visual representation of rock musicians historically.

It was not until the introduction of MTV in 1981 that music videos were widely seen by consumers. With the popularity of MTV, music videos eventually became autonomous commodities in their own right, either packaged together in VHS and DVD collections or sold individually via online distributors, like iTunes. Thanks to video-sharing software, web users can now browse music videos on online sites, like YouTube and Vimeo. Much like album covers, music video formats have grown smaller due to mobile digital devices.

Although some music videos have been understood as art and their directors lauded for their creative vision, the primary function of music videos is commercial: they advertise songs and performers, as well as record labels and video directors, to consumers. Another primary purpose of music videos is as visual accompaniments to musical sounds and lyrics. The images contained in such videos are used to project particular meanings about musicians and their music and thus to connect with consumers. Thus, music videos also serve as a site through which musicians and consumers can construct their identities and communities.

Analyzing Gender in Music Videos

Content Analysis

As discussed in previous chapters, **content analysis** is one of the main methodologies used to study media texts. This approach is designed to facilitate a general and objective understanding of a text by describing, and often counting, its most superficial elements. All forms of textual analysis begin with content analysis.

Given broad concerns about patriarchy in popular culture and women's symbolic annihilation in the media, several scholars have conducted quantitative content analyses of music videos to discern the ratio of male to female appearances in such texts. In one of the first of these studies, Jane Brown and Kenneth Campbell found that men outnumbered women almost six to one in music videos shown on MTV in 1984. Steven Seidman examined videos broadcast on MTV in 1987 and found that 64 percent of the characters were male, while only 34 percent were female. Joe Gow analyzed music videos from the early 1990s and found that men outnumbered women in lead character roles almost five to one. Seidman repeated his study, focusing on videos from 1993, only to find the result to be somewhat like the first: 63 percent of the characters in the videos he studied were men, and 37 percent were women. No quantitative content analysis focusing on the appearances of males and females in music videos has been published since Seidman's second study. Therefore, we have no such data on music videos produced from the mid-1990s through the writing of this book.

These content analyses provide a general impression of the ratio of males and females in music videos during the 1980s and early 1990s. However, none of these analyses are rock-specific. Moreover, few of those studies considered how the presence of males and females in videos differs across musical genres, not to mention across MTV's programs. For example, many of the network's "alternative" programs, such as *120 Minutes*, have featured women more frequently than MTV's other programs, like *Headbangers Ball*, which focused on heavy metal, a male-dominated genre.

Formal Analysis

As discussed in Chapter 11, **formal analysis** of visual media involves critical attention to elements of *mise-en-scène*. As will be shown below, several of the scholars mentioned above who used content analysis to study music videos also attended to such texts' formal characteristics. In this case, such elements as casting, setting, costuming and grooming, and character roles and action were explored in relation to gender politics.

Casting

The process of **casting** for visual media texts involves determining the gender of the individual to be featured, as well as their race, age, body type, and other physical characteristics. Attention to casting decisions in music video production has been important to scholars interested in documenting representational inequality and facilitating greater diversity among performers working in this medium. Of the eighty-seven music videos analyzed in Brown and Campbell's study, 94 percent of the people featured were white; people of color accounted for only 5 percent. Research conducted by Barry Sherman and Joseph Dominick in the early 1980s showed slightly better diversity, with 83 percent white individuals and 17 percent nonwhite. In Seidman's first study, 89 percent were white and 11 percent were not white. Likely as a result of MTV's turn toward more hip-hop programming in the 1990s, Seidman's second study found that racial diversity on MTV had altered considerably: 63 percent of the people were white, and 37 percent not white. While Sherman and Dominick's study revealed the dominant age group in music videos to be ages eighteen to thirty-four, none of the other studies discussed here analyzed the age or physical traits of music video characters, such as hair color and body type.

Costuming

As noted in Chapter 11, **costuming** decisions are often discussed in gender-based studies of music video, since fashion is utilized to communicate identity. As Carol Vernallis asserts, clothing provides a quick introduction to characters represented in videos yet also clarifies relationships between characters. Sherman and Dominick's study of early 1980s music videos revealed that roughly one-half of the women in music videos wore "provocative" clothing, compared to about one-tenth of the men. In their study of music videos from the mid-1980s, Richard Vincent, Dennis Davis, and Lilly Ann Boruszkowski found that both men and women wore fashionable clothing; yet women, because they were commonly used as decorative objects in videos, were often depicted in lingerie, bathing suits, or other forms of sexualized clothing. Similar results were found by Seidman, whose first study of music videos showed that more than a third of the female characters wore "revealing" clothing compared to less than 5 percent of males. In his second study, Seidman noted a slight difference in these figures: The number of women wearing revealing clothing decreased by four percentage points, and the number of men increased by two.

Setting

Since the positioning of human subjects in visual texts also communicates something about identity, the **setting** or location of music videos has drawn attention from quantitative scholars also. Brown and Campbell's study, for example, revealed that the institutions of work and family were portrayed with equal frequency in videos of the early 1980s. Unfortunately, their study did not explore in which locations males and females were featured most. Sherman and Dominick's analysis of music videos from the same period revealed that almost 60 percent featured urban settings and the most common locations were homes (44 percent), cars (28), workplaces (21), and bars (21). Although the other quantitative analyses of music videos' gender representation discussed above did not examine setting specifically, their data on videos' narrative situations and characters' roles and actions (discussed below) are suggestive of specific locations.

In her qualitative study of music videos of the early 1980s, Lisa Lewis found that videos addressed to male viewers commonly represent the street, which has long been understood as a primary location for the display of boyhood and youthful masculinity. She also demonstrated that music videos created for female musicians in the mid-1980s showed women accessing such public spaces and thus complicated the traditional association of females and the domestic sphere. Nevertheless, because Lewis's sample size was small, it is difficult to ascertain whether her findings were representative of music videos' gender politics at the time of her study. Moreover, Lewis's analysis is not specific to rock videos.

Roles and Actions

Most music videos are not **narrative** texts in the conventional sense (that is, they do not include a story about characters who have clearly defined goals and are transformed by the people and situations they encounter). However, such texts do have figures who perform specific **actions** and take on distinct character **roles**, which in turn connote something about their gender identities.

Many of the quantitative studies that compare male and female presences in music videos have focused on the occupational roles and actions of characters. For example, Brown and Campbell found that the lead characters in music videos—most of whom were men—were rarely engaged in traditional professional or domestic activities. Instead, they were predominantly shown performing music and engaged in social, non-work-related practices. Women, in contrast, were more often depicted in passive, solitary, nonambitious activities and rarely appeared with musical instruments.

In his first study, Seidman found that males in music videos occupied almost all of the character roles historically dominated by men (e.g., soldier, police, mechanic, scientist). Similarly, women played stereotypical roles, including hairstylist, dancer, fashion model, and telephone operator. Interestingly, males were shown in almost two-thirds of the roles Seidman defined as gender-neutral (e.g., artist, office worker). In a comparative analysis, Seidman discovered that music video role representations did not reflect the ratio of males and females in such jobs in real life. For example, more women occupy traditionally male-dominated jobs in reality than music videos suggest. Seidman's second study had similar results; however, the number of women in gender-neutral roles in music videos increased by the early 1990s such that the ratio of males to females in such roles was almost equivalent.

In a study of music videos from the early 1990s, Gow also found that men occupied the majority of lead character roles, which included artist, poser, and crowd pleaser. (The poser does virtually nothing and is mostly there to be photographed.) The primary lead roles for women were poser and dancer, while their primary supporting role was model. Gow's study also demonstrated that while women were portrayed primarily in activities that emphasized their appearance, male activities were more varied and did not call attention to their bodies as much as their skills.

Brown and Campbell did not find significant differences between males and females with regard to displays of aggressive or sexual behavior. However, Sherman and Dominick discovered that men accounted for 84 percent of aggressive acts in the videos in their study, while women constituted only around 16 percent. In turn, both of Seidman's studies demonstrated that females were portrayed as more affectionate than males. A study by Vincent, Davis, and Boruszkowski found significant differences in music video representations of sexual and aggressive behavior among males and females.

Qualitative Studies of Rock Videos

As discussed in Chapter 11, content analyses often leave questions about how a text's content relates to other social phenomena unanswered. As a result, scholars trained in **qualitative analysis** have relied on other approaches for interpreting the specific characteristics and qualities of visual texts, such as music videos. For example, **psychoanalytic theory** has been used to understand the psychological reasons for the persistence of the male gaze and women's sexual objectification in music videos. In turn, **semiotics** has allowed scholars to explore the connotative meanings of music video imagery as well as the ideologies associated with such connotations.

For scholars interested in analyzing in depth how gender representation works in music video, **poststructuralist theories** have been especially useful. Poststructuralist theory contends that much of human reality is socially constructed and argues against the use of binary social categories, such as male/female, which limit human identities and experiences to only two possibilities. When used to critically analyze media texts, poststructuralist theories provide a means for understanding the construction of the dualistic sex/gender system as well as determining representational strategies that disrupt hegemonic ideologies of gender.

In the following sections, we will utilize the three approaches noted above to understand the primary strategies that rock music video directors employ to represent gender. Because media texts are complexly constructed, few qualitative scholars make use of only one methodology when analyzing them. Thus, the readings of music videos that follow entail a somewhat eclectic mix of methods suggested by the texts and representational strategies at hand.

Affirming Gender Norms

Phallocentrism and Hegemonic Masculinity

Many feminist scholars have used Laura Mulvey's theory of the **male gaze** and women's **sexual objectification** in Hollywood cinema to understand gender representations in other forms of media. Indeed, several scholars, including E. Ann Kaplan, have done so in relation to music videos. Such researchers have specifically drawn attention to the phallocentric and heteronormative nature of most rock videos (especially those in the hard rock genres). Scholars theorize this representational trope in relation to men's historic domination of music video production and the need to attract MTV's targeted audience of male youth.

Perhaps as a result of their training in film schools or work in commercial advertising, many male music video directors have adopted Hollywood's classical paradigm of gender representation by featuring the members of male rock groups as powerful. The most prominent method for achieving this connotation is to depict band members performing their music. Interestingly, with the exception of Linkin Park's "Shadow of the Day" (2008), Lorde's "Royals" (2014), and Fall Out Boy's "Uma Thurman" (2015), every video that has won MTV's "Best Rock Video" award since 1989 has prominently featured performances by male musicians. Although most videos' performance sequences show band members playing together and "plugged in," sometimes they perform without an audience or electricity, requiring viewers to suspend disbelief about the authenticity of the performances on display. Some performances are portrayed even more abstractly, with individual band members (often the vocalist) performing alone and in an undefined space. Yet, regardless of the manner in which such performances are depicted, these video sequences confer masculinity and power on the men in them via their command of the camera's attention, their occupation of the role of rock musician, their engagement with instruments and technology, and their typically active, if not frenzied, performance style. (As a result, such videos allow male viewers to narcissistically identify with powerful, talented male musicians.) By comparison, most women musicians depicted in rock videos are vocalists, and in general they do not have the powerful presence communicated by male instrumentalists.

Another prominent representational strategy for connoting male power in rock videos has been associating men with sexually objectified women, much as Mulvey found in classical Hollywood movies. During the second half of the 1980s, this strategy became a dominant technique for portraying women in rock videos, largely as a result of MTV's emphasis at that time on heavy metal, a genre that constructs masculinity and male power through the presence of eroticized women. Moreover, once this trend developed, it took some years before it received enough criticism from activists for alternate practices to be developed.

Although categorically dismissed as offensive by many feminists, the sexual depiction of women in rock videos seems appropriate when they serve to visually represent lyrics about women's sexuality, a common theme in rock songs. Consider, for example, the videos for John Mellencamp's "Hurts So Good" (1981), Mötley Crüe's "Girls, Girls, Girls" (1987), and Warrant's "Cherry Pie" (1990). Nonetheless, women's sexual objectification is prevalent even in videos for songs whose lyrics are *not* primarily about female sexuality. Although dated, the music video for the Romantics' "Talking in Your Sleep" (1983) reveals some strategies music video directors have used to communicate male power through women's objectification. Therefore, it works well as an introduction to gender-based music video analysis.

"Talking in Your Sleep" begins with a young white woman disrobing in a series of close-up shots of fragmented body parts (her leg, ankle, and shoe-covered foot). These shots are followed by her removal of the top of her dress, which drops to her ankles. The camera then depicts the woman from the waist down, revealing her bare legs and bikini underwear. In the next shot, she removes her black bra, and the back of her naked torso is revealed. Shortly after the woman disrobes, she puts on a see-through nightgown. In the next shot, the young white male band members appear and begin performing their song. Like the woman, the men are depicted in an indistinct indoor space.

As the "Talking in Your Sleep" video continues, two scenes foregrounding the men are interwoven. The first depicts the musicians performing, while the second shows them walking through a group of women in negligees who, although supposedly sleeping, are standing up. In the mix of these parallel scenes, a young white woman appears in isolation from the others, and the camera fragments her body into fetishized parts (shoes, stockings, and garter). The other parts of her body, including her face, are never shown. The insertion of this scene is strange and confusing, as the woman's clothing is dissimilar from that of the woman at the start of the video, suggesting that they are two different people. Another isolated scene shows the band's lead singer approaching yet another young white woman who is wearing a white, nonrevealing nightgown and clutching a teddy bear. As he touches her face, she suddenly takes on the appearance of Marilyn Monroe, her innocent, girlish appearance now sexualized in an iconic and consumerist manner via a blonde wig, shoulder-less gown, and pouty red lips.

While some viewers might argue that the video's images merely represent the song's lyrics, it is interesting to consider those lyrics and what other images might have been selected. The story told by the lyrics is of man who listens to a woman, who, while sleeping, speaks of her secret love for him. Although we might interpret the man as the subject of this story, given that he sings about the situation and has access to the woman's unconscious, it is also possible to understand the lyrics as constructing the woman as the active agent in the story. In other words, *she* controls their narrative, not him. In the video, however, these positions of subject/object are reversed. Rather than representing the woman's secret love, the video shows only *the man's* sexual desires, which the lyrics never discuss. Only by positioning the narrator (and his bandmates) as the subject of the lyrics do its strange, isolated moments of eroticized women make sense.

Four men appear in the video, and all are young and white and wear considerably more clothing than the women. All the men appear in black leather jackets and pants, common signifiers of masculinity and hipness in rock culture during the early 1980s. Although one man is not wearing a shirt, his bare chest further suggests male virility. The men's primary actions in the video are performing music and walking among the sleeping women. The flashlights the men use as they "tour" the sleeping women suggest their enhanced ability to see in the dark. Combined with their musical abilities and free movement among the women, the flashlights suggest that the men have far greater power than the women. Indeed, while the men have the ability to communicate, all of the women are silent, which further renders them passive and in opposition to the male agency on display.

The sexual objectification of women in male-centered rock videos like "Talking in Your Sleep" has received considerable attention from activists and scholars, including Sut Jhally, who has made several documentary films about this topic. As a result of such criticism, some directors of music videos have struggled to find new modes of representing masculinity without utilizing sexually objectified female bodies. Yet this traditional practice persists, although arguably not in the blatant manner of 1980s videos. Consider, for example, the videos for Megadeth's "Moto Psycho" (2001) and Queens of the Stone Age's "Go with the Flow" (2002). Primarily focusing on the male band members in performance, both videos include images of eroticized female bodies. While it could be argued that the women are acting "naturally" by dancing, close-up shots of their breasts, buttocks, and crotches belie any defense of unintentional sexualization.

Some videos for contemporary male rockers have attempted to make fun of this representational trope through the use of **parody**, as can be seen in the video for Fountains of Wayne's "Stacy's Mom" (2003). As the lyrics tell the tale of a boy who desires his girlfriend's mother, the visuals show several scenes where the boy gazes upon Stacy's mom: wearing a short tennis dress while picking Stacy up from school; undressing near her bedroom window while he watches from outside; receiving a back massage in her yard as he mows the lawn; and bending over to clean the kitchen floor while wearing a cleavage-revealing dress. Interestingly, the rest of the video is devoted to depictions of Stacy, the boy's undeveloped preteen girlfriend, who is shown in her bedroom and poolside interacting with media depicting Fountains of Wayne's members. (As seen in Figure 12.1, the musicians appear in posters on Stacy's wall, on magazine covers, and on her television set.) While she is sometimes put in the same positions as her mother, particularly at the pool, the video does not sexually objectify Stacy's body. And although she wears Lolita-like sunglasses, she is no tease. Indeed, the video portrays Stacy as more mature than her boyfriend, whose exhibitions of sexual desire are awkward and laugh-provoking.

If viewers are unable to understand the video's parodic take on the media's conventional strategy for depicting women, that point is driven home in a fantasy sequence of Stacy's mom as a scantily clad pole dancer, a sequence that seems lifted almost shot for shot from the video for Mötley Crüe's "Girls, Girls, Girls" (1987). Another fantasy sequences shows Stacy's mom dripping wet and emerging slowly

Figure 12.1   Fountains of Wayne, "Stacy's Mom"
S-Curve Records, 2003

from a swimming pool, à la Phoebe Cates's character in *Fast Times at Ridgemont High* (1982). Yet, as much as the video seems to be poking fun at the prevalence of sexual objectification in earlier media culture, as well as the awkwardness of preteen boys' sexuality, it relies on viewers' cultural competence not only to "get the joke" but also to understand those links as parodic. Moreover, the video risks reinforcing this sexist strategy of representing women (as well as the ideology that drives it) by focusing repeatedly on Stacy's mom's voluptuous and fragmented body parts. Rosalind Gill has linked such knowing, ironic cultural moments to the postfeminist sensibility, in that the producers of such texts appear to take criticisms of female representation to heart yet ultimately deny them in a way that reinforces heteronormative patriarchy. In other words, they attempt to have it both ways, that is, simultaneously feminist and sexist.

Emphasized Femininity

Few studies have analyzed the presence of the phallocentric representational mode in videos for *female* rock musicians. Yet this practice is common in the world of rock video. Given that women musicians have historically had little power in the recording business and that men continue to be the dominant market for rock, it is not surprising that some female rockers have agreed to be portrayed in sexually objectifying ways in their music videos. Such representational practices seem appropriate when the lyrics of a song are specifically about women's sexuality. Nevertheless, plenty of music videos for female performers sexually objectify women even when their lyrics do not address sexuality. By relying on strategies that have long been used to construct the male gaze, these representations ultimately produce a heteronormative patriarchal gender politics grounded in women's sexual objectification. (Whether lesbians might find such images pleasurable is a question addressed below.)

Context is important here, for as with male-centered videos that use this strategy, the trend of sexually objectifying female musicians was most dominant in rock videos of the 1980s, when heavy metal was being promoted regularly on MTV. The video for Lita Ford's "Kiss Me Deadly" (1988) is an excellent example. Ford is well known for her talents as a guitarist, but her body is privileged in this video far more than her musical skills. The beginning of the video shows her first in close-up singing into a microphone, then in full-body silhouette gyrating against a microphone stand, and finally in a well-lit medium shot where her bustier accentuates her cleavage and bare shoulders. Such imagery works to construct Ford as a vocalist and a spectacle, both of which affirm her femininity for viewers potentially threatened by her musical skills. While the video does depict Ford playing her guitar, the most memorable scenes are those of her wearing skintight clothing meant to show off her curvaceous figure and of her crawling sensuously across a floor. Indeed, as much as the video's *mise-en-scène* attempts to reaffirm Ford's powerful performance style, that connotation is repeatedly undermined through shots that foreground and fragment her body.

Given feminist criticism of music videos that sexually objectify women, such portrayals have decreased somewhat since the 1980s. Nevertheless, this representational strategy is still prevalent in music video culture, even in texts for women artists. This is likely due to the rise of postfeminism, which suggests that women's power lies in their heteronormative sexuality. Liz Phair's "Everything to Me" (2005) is a good example. The camerawork and production design adopt stereotypical strategies for emphasizing feminine sexuality, including close-ups of Phair's red lipstick, windswept blonde hair, low-cut minidress, and bare legs. Moreover, as the band is belted by rain, she becomes drenched, and her wet clothing further accentuates her curves. While the video depicts Phair with an electric guitar, her playing of it is minimal, and her role as beautiful vocalist is highlighted, both of which diminish her musical agency.

Exscription

In addition to noting the prominent sexualization of women in music videos for male hard rock bands, Robert Walser has discussed the representational strategy of **exscription** in some of these texts, particularly those related to heavy metal. In this mode, only men are featured and women are absent entirely, a practice that suggests the primacy of men, masculinity, and male bonding and thus affirms patriarchal ideology.

Judas Priest's "Heading Out to the Highway" (1981) is a good example of exscription in rock videos. The primary scenes of this text focus on the all-male band performing on a set made to look like a desert highway, a location that immediately connotes masculinity. While the highway also suggests travel and an escape from everyday (domestic) life, the desert symbolizes an unconquered, harsh frontier. The band members' costuming and accessories—black leather biker jackets and pants, as well as metal-studded wristbands—are suggestive of aggressiveness and power. (Secondary narrative sequences depict the band members in jeans and T-shirts participating in a drag race.) Masculine power is also produced through the camera's focus on the instrumentalists' musical talent, as well as the lead singer's commanding performance style. Since no women appear in the video, a homosocial atmosphere is present from the start. For those who might be threatened by the video's possible slippage from homosocial to homoerotic, the tough masculinity signified by the imagery (and sounds) works to shore up the band member's heterosexuality. Nevertheless, Judas Priest's lead singer, Rob Halford, is gay, and he has often drawn from the gay male leather subculture for his performance aesthetics.

Another 1980s music video that utilizes the mode of exscription is Bruce Springsteen's "Born in the U.S.A." (1984). Like most of Springsteen's work, this video is an anthem to working-class American men; this time he focuses on Vietnam War veterans. Although two images of women are included, neither depicts women soldiers or workers, a representational choice that allows the other images to construct both the military and working-class professions as male. Nevertheless, in contrast to the Judas Priest video, Springsteen's does little to suggest that men are all-powerful: it shows them unemployed and troubled, thus complicating conventional notions of both manhood and masculinity.

Also offering an alternative view of manhood and male homosociality, several music videos for gay and queer bands have used exscription, including Extra Fancy's "Sinnerman" (1996), Pansy Division's "Manada" (1997), and Hunx and His Punx's "Cruising" (2012).

Discovery

Videos for female rock musicians have used exscription also, although in these cases it is men who are absent. Lisa Lewis refers to this mode as **discovery**, in that it works to privilege women, femininity, and female bonding over men and heterosexuality, which is in keeping with the requirements for the Bechdel Test discussed in Chapter 10. Similar to Hélène Cixous's *écriture féminine* and what Theodore Gracyk labels **gender solidarity**, discovery is related to cultural feminism's celebration of women and femininity in response to their denigration in patriarchal society. While early music videos utilizing the discovery mode, such as Cyndi Lauper's "Girls Just Want to Have Fun" (1984), typically relied on nonmusical spaces, objects, and actions to construct femininity, recent videos produced for all-female bands are better able to incorporate musical performance as part of the "women's world" they honor.

An interesting example of the discovery mode is the video for Babes in Toyland's "Sweet 69" (1995). The music video begins in black and white with a crowd of teenage girls screaming wildly, an image made iconic by Beatles' fans in the early 1960s. Yet when the music starts, the image cuts to three women colorfully attired in hippie wear and playing rock instruments. The mere juxtaposition of these two short scenes undoes the stereotypical portrayal of female rock fans as male-centered and heterosexually oriented, not to mention that of women musicians as only vocally talented. As the video continues, the band appears in different outfits associated with specific time periods of rock history. For example, in a later sequence, the musicians wear 1960s formalwear and dance on a small platform surrounded by dancers (Figure 12.2). Shot from above, the style is Busby Berkleyesque—a colorful spectacle of female bodies moving together as a unit. Sending home the message that rock is no longer a boys-only club, the final sequence is shot documentary style with the band performing to a crowd of enthusiastic women (Figure 12.3).

Figure 12.2 Babes in Toyland, "Sweet 69"
Reprise, 1995

Figure 12.3 Babes in Toyland, "Sweet 69"
Reprise, 1995

Although "Sweet 69" is clearly homosocial, it does not announce itself as being about lesbianism. In contrast, some music videos for lesbian rock performers have used the discovery mode to foreground a queer subjectivity and erotics, as can be seen in the videos for k.d. lang's "Just Keep Me Moving" (1993) and for Melissa Etheridge's cover of Joan Armatrading's "The Weakness in Me" (1995).

Troubling Gender

Women-centered music videos featuring the discovery mode have certainly troubled the historically male-dominated terrain of rock imagery, just as gay male bands' use of exscription has. Yet such videos, by associating women with traditional feminine activities, roles, and costuming, run the risk of possibly reproducing the heteronormative sex/gender system. Thus, women-centered music videos are more progressive when they problematize the notion that females and femininity are naturally aligned. Videos that subvert the traditional conflation of males and masculinity are similarly progressive.

As discussed in Chapter 2, a key concept in contemporary feminist and queer studies is that gender is socially constructed through human behavior and interaction rather than naturally connected to biological sex. Queer scholar Judith Butler contributed significantly to this approach, arguing that for femininity and masculinity to accrue meaning in society, the roles and behaviors associated with them must be repeated over and over again. The flip side of this concept, of course, is that gender can be deconstructed via disruptions of this repetitive cycle. Butler refers to this process as **gender trouble**; Gracyk, a popular music scholar, calls it **gender transgression**. Butler's theory of gender trouble has been enormously influential for feminist media studies, since that field has long explored how hegemonic masculinity and emphasized femininity are portrayed while also calling attention to representational strategies that disrupt that process.

Over the past two decades, several rock video directors have used techniques that challenge patriarchal heteronormative forms of representation and, in some cases, subvert traditional gender norms.

Role Reversal/Access

One of the primary ways media producers have challenged patriarchal gender representation is **role reversal**, that is, depicting women involved in roles typically occupied by men, and vice versa. While the objective of this strategy is to suggest that women can do things men have traditionally done, and vice versa, often such reversals work to reproduce rather than subvert a gender stereotype. This is clear in some rock videos for all-male bands where men cross-dress in female **drag**, such as Aerosmith's "Dude (Looks Like a Lady)" (1987), Nirvana's "In Bloom" (1992), and U2's "One" (1992). Some scholars argue for drag's progressive contributions to gender trouble, since the parodic performance of a particular gender (e.g., femininity) by a body whose characteristics are not associated with that gender (e.g., a beard) calls attention to gender's construction. Yet male drag in rock videos tends to be relatively brief and a means of humor, thus doing little to upset the power dynamics of traditional gender politics. Freddy Mercury's female drag for Queen's "The Show Must Go On" (1991) is likely interpreted differently from those mentioned above, since he was known to be gay. It might be better to compare it with performances by female impersonators in such videos as the Knife's "Pass This On" (2003) and Perfume Genius's "Queen" (2014).

Since most male rockers are invested in the power gained from their dual positions as men and rock musicians, few have been willing to have that power compromised by appearing for long periods of time in feminine roles, attire, and spaces. Thus, videos like Weezer's "Island in the Sun" (2001) and OK Go's "White Knuckles" (2010), which depict men with small animals, could be read as simply ironic and reproductive of gender norms. Meanwhile, as discussed below, videos that feature effeminate males, such as those for Sigur Rós's "Viðrar Vel Til Loftárása" ("Good Weather for an Airstrike," 2001), call into question the common conflation of manhood and masculinity and thus trouble the sex/gender system.

In contrast to the relative dearth of representations of male femininity in rock music videos, many female musicians have taken on men's roles and masculine attributes in videos as part of their larger struggle for recognition in a male-dominated industry and society. Lewis refers to this representational mode as **access,** since women have historically been excluded from male roles, activities, and spaces. The female access mode, therefore, is associated primarily with liberal feminism. Perhaps the simplest form of access appears at the level of clothing, with women wearing men's clothing, as can be seen in early music videos for Suzi Quatro, Joan Jett and the Blackhearts, and the Pretenders. Yet it was arguably Annie Lennox of the Eurythmics who most popularized via music video women's use of men's clothing, as can be seen in "Who's That Girl?" (1983) and "Sweet Dreams" (1983). Nonetheless, this practice no longer reads as subversively as it did a few decades ago, since women's use of male fashion items has increased since the 1980s.

An interesting twist on the access strategy is to present female musicians objectifying men and thus reversing the traditional gender dynamics of the gaze. This practice is used in music videos more often for women musicians who do not perform rock, as can be seen in Shania Twain's "Man! I Feel Like a Woman" (1999), Keri Hilson's "Turnin' Me On" (2009), Jennifer Lopez's "I Luh Ya Papi" (2014), Maddie & Tae's "Girl in a Country Song" (2014), and Ingrid Michaelson's "Girls Chase Boys" (2014). Nevertheless, these role reversals via male sexual objectification do little to upset heterosexual gender politics, since femininity is not simultaneously troubled in these music videos. In contrast, the Donnas' "40 Boys in 40 Nights" (2002) does upset the sex/gender system by combining male objectification with images of talented women musicians performing a historically male-dominated style of music.

Any video that includes representations of female instrumentalists is utilizing the access mode, since more men have occupied that position and most women rockers are vocalists. A classic example of this form of access appears in the video for Joan Jett and the Blackhearts' "Bad Reputation" (1981). Jett, the only woman in the band, is repeatedly shown being thrown out of places dominated by men, including bars and record label offices, where she is told to "come back when you're dressed like a lady." (She appears in jeans and a leather jacket.) Despite such rejection, she and her bandmates decide to launch their own record label, eventually becoming such a sensation that multiple labels attempt to sign them—a dramatization of their real story). Unlike the many female rockers who only sing, Jett is able to fully exploit her role as a guitarist in this video, perhaps the most dominant indicator that she has accessed the boys' club of rock culture.

The video for the Donnas' "Take It Off" (2002) is less fictional than those discussed above, and it is perhaps the video's realism that makes its message of access that much more powerful. "Take It Off" begins with an image of a school theater's doors adorned with a "Battle of the Bands" poster. Appearing in various guises, the members of the Donnas perform as both all-male and all-female bands (see Figures 12.4 and 12.5). In contrast to most real-life situations like this, however, the boy bands receive neither applause from the audience nor high scores from the judges. Instead, the girl band walks away with the main prize at the show's end, a welcome change in rock's gender politics.

Figure 12.4   The Donnas, "Take It Off"
Atlantic, 2002

Figure 12.5 The Donnas, "Take It Off"
Atlantic, 2002

Revealing Gender Construction and Fluidity

Since the early 1990s, several rock videos have challenged the supposedly natural state of patriarchal heteronormative gender politics by demonstrating femininity and masculinity as socially produced. Interestingly, unlike many of the role reversal videos discussed previously, none of these videos construct a heterosexual gaze, and some even go so far as to challenge that convention and invite queer readings by suggesting the fluidity of both sexuality and gender.

One of the first rock videos to comment on femininity's construction was PJ Harvey's "Man-Size" (1993). In stark contrast to the glamorous women who typically appear in music videos, Harvey appears unadorned. In the first scene, she wears a T-shirt and pants, with her hair pulled back in a bun. With a long-stemmed rose between her teeth, she holds a ruffled dress to her body, moving about as if modeling it (see Figure 12.6). Subsequent to this scene, she appears with wet, shoulder-length hair in a printed T-shirt and slightly too-large white underpants, singing directly to the camera and confronting viewers with her stark, natural beauty.

Annie Lennox's "Why" (1992) takes the message of femininity's construction one step further by revealing the labor involved in the female beautification process. Beginning with an unadorned Lennox in front of a mirror, the video shows not only each step of her make-up process, but the multiple poses the singer must endure for the camera to capture a good image. Hole's "Violet" (1994) also foregrounds the construction of femininity, as well as girls' socialization to attract the male gaze. In a series of vignettes, the video shows girls and women on display as beauty pageant contestants, erotic dancers, and models for artists (Figure 12.7). The video also depicts men watching such performances, thus suggesting

Figure 12.6 PJ Harvey, "Man Size"
Island, 1993

Figure 12.7 Hole, "Violet"
Geffen, 1995

and critiquing connections between the male gaze, female objectification, and the construction of heterosexual masculinity.

While the videos mentioned so far feature white musicians, Tamar-kali's "Boot" (2006) focuses on two black figures—a young girl protagonist and the

Figure 12.8 Tamar-kali, "Boot"
OyaWarrior Records, 2006

performer (see Figure 12.8). The video foregrounds the intersections of gender and race through the girl's physical transformation from conventional femininity into a masculine performance involving boots, a denim jacket, an afro, and her assertive stance and active body. Tamar-kali's complicated display—which includes facial piercings, make-up, contained hair, and leather wristbands alongside masterful electric guitar playing—further suggests the multiple possibilities of women's gender performance.

Relatively few rock videos have foregrounded masculinity's construction, either by men or women. One of the first to do so was the video for the Beastie Boys' "Sabotage" (1994). Modeled after television police dramas, the video foregrounds how masculinity is produced in such texts via physical aggression, martial arts, street-oriented locations, and fast-paced editing involving moving bodies and automobiles. Moreover, each of the men in the video wears a wig and fake facial hair.

The Odds' "Heterosexual Man" (1993) also makes use of fake hair to comment on the social construction of masculinity (and femininity). The video begins with a skit based on the topic "heterosexual men" in the format of a "rock video." As the Odds play in the background (singing "I want to make every woman I see"), comedians perform as heterosexual men in the audience, wearing long sideburns and flannel shirts while rocking out with beers in hand. This juxtaposition calls attention to how easily masculine power is ascribed to male rock musicians. Yet the masculine identity of the audience and band members becomes more unstable as the video continues, leading to questions about the gender and sexuality suggested by the song's lyrics. For instance, on looking in a bathroom mirror, one of the male audience members realizes he is wearing make-up (Figure 12.9). His horror quickly dissipates, however, when his next glimpse shows a masculine visage. Nevertheless, the band members begin a

Figure 12.9 The Odds, "Heterosexual Man"
Zoo Entertainment, 1993

gender transformation, appearing in make-up, wigs, and dresses. Meanwhile, the women in the audience move to the foreground in the frame, revealing that they, too, are men dressed as women.

A more recent rock video that complicates the construction of masculine identity is Orianthi's video for "Highly Strung" (2009), which features Steve Vai, a well-known guitarist. As a minimalist text meant to foreground Orianthi's instrumental talents as much as Vai's, the video depicts the musicians in an empty space with only their guitars and amplifiers. The scene cuts between Orianthi performing, Vai performing, and the two musicians performing together. The chords they play echo and riff off of each other, ultimately blending together. Because of the historical association of both the electric guitar and guitarists with manhood and masculinity, Orianthi's presence as a highly skilled woman shredder disrupts the video's affirmation of Vai's masculinity as much as it complicates viewers' understanding of her femininity. The video thus implies that masculinity can no longer be assured in rock via one of its primary mechanisms: virtuosic performances of the electric guitar. Nevertheless, Orianthi's long, bleached-blond hair, tight-fitting jeans, high heels, and painted nails (highlighted in close-up shots meant to foreground her skills) still work to confirm her femininity and to differentiate her gender from Vai's.

Queerness

Most rock videos that explore gender construction comment on only one form of gender identity—that is, either femininity or masculinity but not both concurrently. Moreover, the majority of these videos feature cisgender bodies and rarely include transgender or genderqueer bodies. Hence, such videos may not be fully effective in affirming feminist and queer gender politics and in subverting the binary sex/gender system that supports heteronormative patriarchy. In contrast, several recent rock videos have attempted to deconstruct traditional sex/gender associations and have made more room for an overtly queer sensibility in rock culture.

Garbage's "Androgyny" (2001), for example, begins with two identical-looking people groping each other. As one leaves, Garbage's vocalist, Shirley Manson, walks through the other person, who looks like a woman. Yet when Shirley emerges on the other side, her long locks have been shorn into an androgynous, asymmetrical haircut and her cleavage-revealing top has been replaced by one less sensual. The video has many similar scenes that confound our sense of "man" and "woman," including one that depicts androgynous people moving between bathrooms labeled "boys" and "girls." We also see both "men" and "women" applying make-up, and a female-looking person creates fake breasts from bathroom tissue. The video's peep-show effect, offering only brief glimpses of bathroom stall occupants, recalls the video for Madonna's "Justify My Love" (1990), which similarly explored gender confusion and queer sexuality.

Another rock video to trouble the gender binary is Arcade Fire's "We Exist" (2014). The narrative focuses on a young person who is exploring a feminine transgender identity. As the video begins, she shaves her head, puts on a bra, dons make-up and a wig, and tries on different tops, thus revealing both the performativity of gender and the struggle for transgender expression. Once her feminine look is complete, she heads out to a bar, only to be ridiculed and attacked by some of the straight, cisgender men there. Yet she ultimately finds herself through music and dance, which she shares with four other feminized

Figure 12.10 Arcade Fire, "We Exist"
Merge, 2014

men in a dreamlike sequence. In the video's conclusion, which is meant to signify her self-acceptance and self-pride, she joins Arcade Fire onstage during a live performance (Figure 12.10). Many viewers appreciate the video's (and song's) exploration of gender performance and transgender identity. However, other people have criticized the video for reproducing transgender stereotypes as well as featuring a straight, cisgender actor (Andrew Garfield) rather than a transgender actor.

The music video for Perfume Genius's "Hood" (2012) also subverts traditional expectations for performances of gender. The video begins with a close-up of Michael Hadreas (Perfume Genius) singing to the camera. As the camera backs away from him, it reveals that he is somewhat petite in stature and being held like a baby in the arms of a much larger and more muscular man, gay porn star Arpad Miklos. As the video progresses, Miklos is depicted as caring for Hadreas by brushing his hair and applying lipstick and eye shadow to his face (Figure 12.11). Presented together, the two men complicate normative views of gender as well as sexuality. As enacted by multiple bodies, the gender fluidity and -queerness on display in "Hood" are evident also in the butch and femme performances that often appear in videos for queer women bands, like God-des and She's "Love Machine" (2011).

Another rock video to foreground genderqueerness is Gossip's "Listen Up" (2002). The video plays with viewer expectations for the representation of both men and women, as well as the display of heterosexuality and same-sex attraction. While two main performers in the video appear to be in drag, shots of these individuals' living spaces reveal that the cross-dressing on display is not a singular, extraordinary performance but a lifestyle choice. Moreover, by exposing the labor that goes into such performances, the video refuses the notion of gender's naturalness. The video for the Magnetic Fields' "Andrew in Drag"

Figure 12.11   Perfume Genius, "Hood"
Matador, 2012

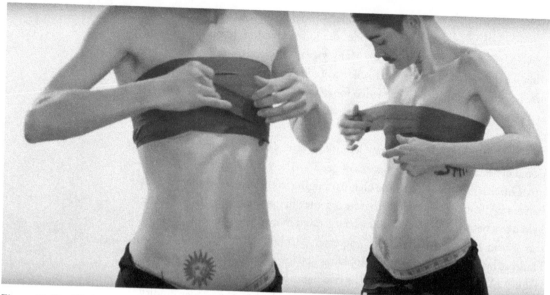

Figure 12.12   The Magnetic Fields, "Andrew in Drag"
Merge, 2012

(2012) similarly comments on gender's construction and fluidity by showing the body routines of a drag queen and king (Figure 12.12). Yet here the song's lyrics further foreground and queer that theme.

Gender in Music Video Production

Despite the greater presence of rock video images that move away from and, in some cases, directly challenge the phallocentrism and sexual objectification central to early rock videos, the music industry continues to promote rock artists who are primarily white, young, male, and heterosexual. Unfortunately, these characteristics also describe the vast majority of music video directors, who often have more control over the representational politics in rock videos than musicians do. Indeed, only five of the videos mentioned in this chapter were directed by women. Less than 10 percent of music video directors in the United States and Canada are female, and that number is not likely to rise anytime soon. Another indicator of video directing's gender norms, is that only one woman, Valerie Faris, has received a "Best Direction" award for a rock video since 1984 when MTV began honoring directors at its annual Video Music Awards celebration. Such skewed gender politics in music video production has as much to do with gender bias in film schools as with men dominating the music industry.

Yet the ongoing patriarchy of rock video production does not mean that all male directors working in that field are necessarily sexist, which would be just as false to say as that all female directors are feminist. Nevertheless, many male music video directors continue to rely on traditional representational strategies for promoting straight, white, young men as powerful and heroic, often through the exclusion or stereotypical representation of women. Moreover, as Vernallis reminds us, most video directors must comply with the demands of record label executives, who are also often beholden to more traditional approaches to gender representation.

The historic domination of music video production by male directors affects more than just how performers are depicted, however. For example, of all the music video directors featured in Palm Pictures' Directors Label series, not one is a woman, which means the collection does not include all the videos produced for some of the musicians highlighted in the series. More attention to gender by media professionals would help to create better gender equity in the hiring and promotion of video directors, as well as in the representational strategies used to create music videos. In the meantime, successful women music video directors, such as Nancy Bardawil, Valerie Faris, Liz Friedlander, Mary Lambert, Sophie Muller, and Floria Sigismondi, deserve greater recognition for their achievements.

Summary

This chapter continued our exploration of gendered representations in rock's visual landscape, this time focusing on music videos. While studies employing quantitative and formal approaches are surveyed, this chapter primarily utilizes poststructuralist feminist and queer reading strategies to examine methods used to depict men and women in rock videos. In particular, we explored the dominant use of the phallocentric mode, which constructs male musicians as powerful and reaffirms hegemonic masculinity yet also minimalizes women's presence and portrays them as passive, sexual objects. Also discussed were the practices of exscription and discovery, which exclude members of the opposite sex and thus affirm homosociality. Greater attention is paid here to the strategies of gender trouble in rock videos, including the reversal of sex roles, the foregrounding of gender construction, and the adoption of a queer perspective, wherein gender is presented as nonbinary and fluid. The gender politics of music video production was also discussed, thus providing a context for the dominant patterns found in rock video culture. Chapter 13 begins Part V and examines the roles consumers and fandom play in the gender politics of rock culture.

Further Exploration

1. Conduct a content analysis of a music video.

Focusing on casting, costuming, setting, roles, and actions, analyze the gender dynamics at work in a music video. Do these affirm or subvert the sex/gender system? Do they affirm queerness?

2. Conduct a qualitative analysis of a music video.

Discuss how the visual components in this video either affirm or subvert patriarchal ideology through attention to how gender is performed and constructed. Is patriarchal ideology affirmed? If so, how? Does the video engage in gender trouble? If so, how? Is queerness explored or affirmed? If so, how?

3. Compare the careers of one male and one female music video director.

With which musicians and bands has each director worked? Are those musicians predominantly male or female? How would you describe the gender politics of each director with regard to how they represent males and females? Does each director affirm or subvert the sex/gender system? Does each affirm queerness? What kind of awards and public recognition has each director received?

4. Make a music video.

Review the lyrics of the song and consider what visual components you might use to express their meaning. If you have access to the band that composed the song, ask if they would like to participate in making the video. Consider how you will costume and position the band members or other actors and what activities they will perform. If you do not have actors, determine what still or moving images you might use to convey the song's meaning. (Be sure to check with your instructor about copyright policies.) Reflect on how your decisions relate to gender politics and consider ways you might challenge gender norms.

Further Reading

Beebe, Roger, and Jason Middleton, eds. *Medium Cool: Music Videos from Soundies to Cellphones*. Durham: Duke University Press, 2007.

Brown, Jane, and Kenneth Campbell. "Race and Gender in Music Videos: The Same Beat but a Different Drummer." *Journal of Communication* 36.1 (1986): 94–106.

Goodwin, Andrew. *Dancing in the Distraction Factory: Music Television and Popular Culture*. Minneapolis: University of Minnesota Press, 1992.

Gow, Joe. "Reconsidering Gender Roles on MTV: Depictions in the Most Popular Music Videos of the Early 1990s." *Communication Reports* 9.2 (1996): 151–61.

Lewis, Lisa A. "Being Discovered: The Emergence of Female Address on MTV." *Sound and Vision: The Music Video Reader.* Eds. Simon Frith, Andrew Goodwin, and Lawrence Grossberg. New York: Routledge, 1993. 129–51.

Lewis, Lisa A. "Form and Female Authorship in Music Video." *Gender, Race, and Class in Media: A Text-Reader.* Eds. Gail Dines and Jean M. Humez. Thousand Oaks: Sage, 1995. 499–507.

Lewis, Lisa. *Gender Politics and MTV: Voicing the Difference.* Philadelphia: Temple University Press, 1992.

Seidman, Steven A. "An Investigation of Sex-Role Stereotyping in Music Videos." *Journal of Broadcasting and Electronic Media* 36.2 (1992): 209–16.

Seidman, Steven A. "Revisiting Sex-Role Stereotyping in MTV Videos." *International Journal of Instructional Media* 26.1 (1999): 11–22.

Sherman Barry L., and Joseph R. Dominick. "Violence and Sex in Music Videos: TV and Rock'n'Roll." *Journal of Communication* 36.1 (1986): 79–93.

Vernallis, Carol. *Experiencing Music Video: Aesthetics and Cultural Context.* New York: Columbia University Press, 2004.

Vernallis, Carol. *Unruly Media: YouTube, Music Video, and the New Digital Cinema.* New York: Oxford University Press, 2013.

Vincent, Richard C., Dennis K. Davis, and Lilly Ann Boruszkowski. "Sexism on MTV: The Portrayal of Women in Rock Videos." *Journalism Quarterly* 64.4 (1987): 750–55.

Walser, Robert. "Forging Masculinity: Heavy-Metal Sounds and Images of Gender." *Sound and Vision: The Music Video Reader.* Eds. Simon Frith, Andrew Goodwin, and Lawrence Grossberg. London: Routledge, 1993. 153–81.

V

Rock's Other Players

Consumers and Critics

13 TEENYBOPPERS AND HEADBANGERS
Rock Consumers and Fandom

LISTEN: HELEN LOVE, "JOEY RAMONEY" (*Radio Hits*, Damaged Goods, 1993). *A good example of fans as prosumers (producer-consumers), this pop-punk song reveals not only the passion of fans' infatuation with their idols but also the creativity with which some fans poach from favorite tunes to create their own music.*

For any community to develop and sustain itself as a music scene, it must involve not only musicians but also people who consume music. Here "consume" means "to take in," not necessarily "to purchase," although much cultural consumption today involves buying commodities. For most people, listening is the primary means of engaging with music. However, numerous activities are associated with musical consumption, including dancing and attending live performances. **Music consumers** are defined as those individuals who enjoy music and listen to it on a regular basis. **Music fans** are those consumers who have a greater than average social, emotional, and economic investment in a specific music culture. They are also consumers who produce art and media texts related to their object of interest, such as blogs.

During the first decade of rock 'n' roll, consumption of this music and participation in its culture did not necessarily require attending live shows or purchasing musical recordings. Many of rock 'n' roll's early fans listened to it on the radio or jukeboxes and watched rock musicians featured in movies and television programs. Indeed, such media were necessary to establish interest among consumers who did not have access to live performances due to age, class, or geographic location. With the commercial development of rock culture, music consumption became increasingly associated also with attending concerts and purchasing records, as well as bands' other forms of promotional material, such as posters and T-shirts.

When many people think of a stereotypical rock consumer, they imagine a teenager. More than any other, this demographic group has been associated with rock consumption throughout this culture's sixty-year history. As discussed in

Chapter 3, the commercial entities promoting this new style of music in the late 1950 specifically targeted teenagers. Although many contemporary rock consumers (and musicians) are well beyond their teenage years, all privilege the youthful spirit long associated with rock culture. This characteristic of youthfulness is important to keep in mind when considering the reasons some individuals invest in rock music.

North Americans and Britons dominated rock's audience during its first two decades. Yet rock consumers, as a result of this music's global dispersion via media and international tours, can now be found in virtually every country on the planet. Many people of color have been rock consumers, and their number equaled, if not rivaled, the number of white consumers during the early rock 'n' roll era. Nevertheless, as rock became increasingly affiliated with white musicians and fans in the mid- to late 1960s, Latinos and African Americans were marginalized in the scene. When hip-hop emerged from black and Latino communities in the mid-1970s, rock became more firmly associated with white people.

Since the mid-1960s the media have represented rock as boys' music, while girls are more often depicted as pop fans. Nevertheless, such constructions elide the history and diversity of rock consumers. Numerous girls and women have been drawn to rock music since its emergence, and during some historical periods, such as the early 1960s and mid-1990s, females have been a large part of rock's consumer market. In turn, a significant number of LGBTQI consumers have become a visible part of rock culture since the 1990s as a result of the growing presence of queer musicians as well as the mainstreaming of the LGBTQI community.

The study of music consumption has taken many forms in the past few decades. Some scholars are interested in how listeners interpret specific lyrics and musical sounds, while others are more concerned with how music impacts people emotionally and contributes to their construction of self-identity. Some scholars have focused on the psychological dimensions of star/fan relationships, while others analyze the social and economic practices of musical consumption, including collecting. And some scholars focus on the technologies used in musical consumption, while others study the cultural texts that fans themselves produce, such as fanzines. This chapter analyzes rock consumers and their myriad practices through the lens of gender. In particular, we will explore how gender politics have shaped musical tastes and forms of consumption in rock culture, providing consumers with different opportunities for engaging with rock music and musicians.

Musical Consumption and Technology

For much of history, listeners consumed music in immediate proximity to the musicians creating it, and often the boundary between these two groups was blurry. While live performance is still privileged by most rock consumers, since the mid-twentieth century, music has been most consumed via sound recordings. As discussed in Chapter 4, musical recordings have been produced in numerous formats, including records, tapes, CDs, and MPEG or MP3 files. In turn, musical recordings have been delivered to consumers via a variety of mass media technologies. Radio broadcasts long served as the primary method for listening to recorded music for free. However, cable television, particularly MTV, changed that dynamic in the 1980s. Today consumers can pay to stream or download music via online services, like Spotify, Bandcamp, and iTunes, or they can consume it for free via such platforms as Pandora, SoundCloud, and YouTube. The amount of free music online has helped to reenergize popular music culture, especially among younger people, who have little disposable income.

During rock 'n' roll's first decade, consumers with phonographs listened via 45 rpm records. Between the late 1960s and the early 2000s, the sixty-minute album (whether materialized as a record, tape, or CD) became the recording format most privileged among rockers. Although vinyl 33 1/3 rpm LP records continue to be celebrated among rock collectors, digital MP3 singles have eroded album sales. Many rock connoisseurs have home stereo systems with separate components, including phonographs, CD players, receivers, amplifiers, and speakers. Yet most rock consumers have also long used mobile technologies—transistor radios, car stereos, personal cassette players, MP3 players, and smartphones—to carry music with them and to sonically shape their environments.

Music Consumption and Taste

As Tia DeNora's research on music consumers demonstrates, human beings use music in their everyday lives for numerous purposes. Chief among those is their exploration and construction of identity. In addition, music often plays an affective role in managing emotions, as well as a disciplinary role in structuring our bodies, experiences, and relations with other people. DeNora's work prompts us to ask questions about the power of music in consumers' lives, that is, how music matters and also how it helps to constitute consumers as individuals and members of specific groups.

Music consumers demonstrate their **taste** or preference for a particular genre through listening to and buying music. While many are omnivorous in their musical consumption, listening to a wide variety of musical styles, some focus more specifically on a singular genre. Those with limited tastes often become fans through their allegiance to a genre and participation in the community that supports it. While some people feel that they are "naturally drawn" to certain musical styles, musical tastes—like preferences in food and fashion—are socially constructed. The development of such tastes often changes over time. The activities of developing, demonstrating, and discussing one's musical tastes are practices of **distinction**, as they reveal our categorization, preferences, and dislikes.

As Pierre Bourdieu has demonstrated, human beings often use taste to express their identities and to establish community with others, thus affirming their particular social status. While much of Bourdieu's research in this area focused on taste preferences among different socioeconomic classes, we can use his theory to understand, for example, how people have used rock music over the past sixty years to express their identities as youthful. More particularly, we might note that rock culture has most attracted white male youth whose preference for rock music is also used to signify their values of rebelliousness, bohemianism, and homosocial bonding. Such young men affirm their taste for rock music as well as their status in rock culture by sharing with others their **cultural capital**, in this instance, their knowledge of particular bands as well as other information and skills specific to this musical scene. Historically, girls and women wanting to participate in rock culture have had a difficult time, largely because girls are not encouraged to have a taste for rock music and therefore do not have the same opportunities as boys to accrue the cultural capital necessary to establish credibility in rock scenes.

Rock Fans

Rock fans are people with significant knowledge about, as well as emotional, social, and financial commitments to, rock culture. As Lawrence Grossberg argues, fans have a particular affective sensibility for the cultural artifacts in which they invest, a feeling of absorption that guides the construction of their identities. Yet music fans also lose themselves by participating with others in fan groups whose members agree to specific rules and rituals. Through their involvement in a fan community and engagement with particular products associated with it, fans are able to maintain an oppositional identity that separates them from other consumers. These practices align fan communities with what Bourdieu calls **cultures of distinction** and Herbert Gans refers to as **taste cultures**.

Fans are essential to rock **scenes**—geographic communities organized around a particular musical genre, a group of musicians, and a cluster of musical venues. As Dick Hebdige has demonstrated, because of their often-spectacular practices, including fashion style, many rock scenes have become interesting to the media industries and other commercial entities and have expanded beyond their original physical boundaries to become **subcultures**. Since the emergence of rock 'n' roll in the mid-1950s, numerous rock scenes and rock-based subcultures have sprung up in the United States and abroad. While many of those communities have been formed and maintained by rockers themselves, the recording industry has been enormously supportive of fan activities, given fans' ability to generate huge profits for labels.

Rock fans, particularly those in nonurban areas, have relied on various forms of communication to network with each other and to maintain community beyond live musical events. For several decades, newsletters and **fanzines** were the dominant form of media created by rock fans. More recently, rock fans have embraced the Internet as a means of sharing their tastes, knowledge, and experiences with each other. In the process, such fans have complicated the material boundaries of rock's local scenes and global culture. Fan blogs, chatrooms, and social media platforms are especially attractive to diehard fans because they offer new ways of interacting directly with musicians. While some performers regularly post to online fan forums, many contemporary rock bands have their own websites through which they can distribute their music and communicate with fans.

As Matt Hills notes, fans in general must consistently balance their tendency toward anticommercial ideologies with the fact that many of their practices are facilitated by capitalist consumer culture. This is true of rock fans as well. Historically, heavy metal has been the most beloved rock genre, and its broad popularity is likely the result of its excessive commodification. The stereotype of the rock fan is based largely on "metalheads" and "headbangers" because of their ubiquity in popular culture at large over the past fifty years.

Nevertheless, several styles of rock music, including punk and folk rock, have privileged an anticapitalist stance that has necessarily led to reconfigurations of rock celebrity and fandom. For example, punk rockers have long championed amateurist, authentic, and anticommercial values that have contributed to increased interaction between musicians and consumers. Indeed, perhaps more than any other rock style, the punk scene encourages its consumers to also be producers by championing a DIY ethos. Punk **prosumers** significantly complicate the conventional oppositions of production and consumption in music cultures.

Studying Musical Consumption and Fandom

Prior to the 1980s, many scholars of popular culture, including popular music studies, engaged primarily in the interpretation of cultural texts, such as song lyrics, and often the only people discussed in such research were cultural producers, like songwriters. As a result of new forms of criticism informed by Marxism, psychoanalysis, and poststructuralism, scholars of popular culture began to advocate in the 1980s for more attention to the ways readers, viewers, and listeners use and make meaning of cultural artifacts, like songs. Recognizing the subjective and often idiosyncratic nature of academic analysis, such scholars were interested in how consumers extend their practices beyond interpretation. Focusing on consumers, such work helped to form what is known today as **reception studies** or **audience studies**.

This shift in critical focus from texts and authors to consumers is often attributed to Roland Barthes. Writing provocatively about the "death of the author," he challenged literary scholars to see readers as responsible for a text's meaning and therefore to analyze the practices of reception to understand a text's significance. In other words, he encouraged us to understand readers as active producers rather than passive recipients of literary meaning.

During the 1980s, scholars interested in film reception were still predominantly invested in psychoanalytic theories that constructed an ahistorical and universal film spectator. However, at that same time, television and cultural scholars began paying considerable critical attention to TV audiences along with consumers of other forms of popular culture. Stuart Hall was one of the first scholars to explore how media consumers **decode** the various ideologies that producers **encode** in texts. Recognizing that not all consumers interpret texts the same way, he theorized that television viewers accept, oppose, or negotiate the ideologies embedded in texts by their producers. In particular, Hall was interested in how the socioeconomic class of TV audience members impacted their response to particular texts and ideologies.

David Morley helped to push Hall's theory in new directions by arguing that viewers' decoding practices are not related to their class status alone. Instead, Morley theorized that individual consumers bring unique sets of skills and knowledge, or **cultural competencies**, to their practices of media consumption. Those competencies are based on one's identity (e.g., sex, race, class, age) as well as one's background, one's experience, and the context of one's media consumption. In addition, he argued that consumer practices cannot be deduced from texts via scholars' close analyses; instead, researchers must observe and talk with consumers, practices long associated with the fieldwork of anthropologists (discussed below).

By moving away from close textual analysis and attending to the specificities of consumers' identities and backgrounds, as well as their actual consumption habits and experiences, Morley and other scholars studying readers, viewers, and listeners have produced greater comprehension of the multiple and often contradictory forms of cultural consumption. In particular, the work of Michel DeCerteau has helped us to understand how consumers make use of the cultural artifacts that they read, watch, and hear, often deviating from such texts' intended uses and sometimes "poaching" from them to produce new texts that are more pleasurable and meaningful.

A vital area of audience studies today is **fandom**, the culture of fans. Emerging alongside scholarship on movie stars and other cultural celebrities, research on fans explores their excessive interest in certain cultural objects and performers as well as their creation of communities. Such scholarship takes fandom seriously and has thus helped to subvert stereotypes of fans as dysfunctional and possibly dangerous individuals.

A key concept in the psychoanalytical approach to fandom is **identification**. Fan identification is associated with a desire either to be intimately involved with one's idol or to be like one's idol. Jackie Stacey distinguishes between **identificatory fantasies** and **identificatory practices**. The former happen during a consumer's engagement with a cultural text, such as listening to music, and include escapism, worship, and a desire to become like the featured performer. Identificatory practices happen after one's engagement with a text and involve imitating an idol's behavior or appearance. Despite some scholars' emphasis on fans' desires to have or to be like a star, multimedia narrative texts, such as music videos, offer numerous sites for fans' engagement and thus make interpretations of fan reception practices difficult to unravel.

John Fiske expanded fan studies in new directions in the 1980s by moving it beyond a psychological perspective. Interested in the productive practices of cultural consumers, he analyzed the **shadow cultural economy** that fans develop through activities like collecting and media production. Many other contemporary scholars, including Henry Jenkins, have pursued investigations of how fan communities blur the boundaries between consumption and production via such **participatory practices** as zine making and bootleg tape collecting.

While scholars interested in reception practices often conduct close textual analyses to make sense of how consumers' interpretations and uses of cultural artifacts, other scholars gather data using procedures associated with **ethnography**. Ethnographic practices, which were originally developed to study indigenous cultures, include observation, surveys, and interviews. In addition to these methods, cultural scholars using ethnographic approaches to fandom have increasingly turned to material produced by consumers themselves, such as diaries, letters, and online posts.

The field of musical reception and audience studies has grown substantially in the past two decades, in part because a long tradition of ethnographic study exists in musicology. Referred to as **ethnomusicology**, this field focuses on the social and cultural aspects of music. An increasing number of popular music scholars have used ethnographic practices to explore the activities, roles, and relationships of individuals associated with specific rock fan communities, as can be seen in Paul Hodkinson's *Goth*, Jeffrey Arnett's *Metalheads*, Erika Doss's *Elvis Culture*, and Daniel Cavicchi's *Tramps Like Us*, which focuses on fans of Bruce Springsteen. Meanwhile, scholars like Tia DeNora are examining the experiential phenomenological effects of rock music on consumers via ethnographic methods.

Gender and Consumption

How production and consumption are conceived and practiced in rock culture has been strongly influenced by traditional gender politics. Culturally productive practices have been affiliated with men and thus masculinity since the ancient Greeks. As discussed in Chapter 4, this connection is largely the result of patriarchal societies' privileging men's paid labor in the public sphere over all other forms of work, including women's unpaid domestic labor. During the nineteenth century, as rural home production decreased and manufactured consumer goods increased, bourgeois women were encouraged to engage in shopping for themselves and for their families. As a result, consumption became increasingly associated with females and femininity.

Figure 13.1 *Detroit Rock City*
New Line Cinema, 1999

The historical gendering of production as a masculine practice continues in contemporary rock culture. In fact, most individuals assume that it is primarily men who produce rock music. While that notion is largely true, it has contributed to the many challenges women musicians face when trying to find work and legitimacy in this cultural field. Interestingly, the practice of consumption has not been as feminized in rock culture as it has in many other cultural sites. As suggested, the vast majority of people would likely respond "male" if asked "What is the dominant gender of rock consumers?" Many forms of popular culture perpetuate this gendered stereotype, as can be seen in movies like *Detroit Rock City*, whose narrative and paratexts (e.g., posters, DVD covers) promote the rebellious masculinity of its rock fan protagonists (see Figure 13.1).

The gendered stereotyping of rock consumers has resulted from the male dominance of rock audiences throughout much of rock history. Male rock consumers have been most associated with harder styles, like metal and punk, and the male **headbanger** (or **metalhead**), as noted, is perhaps the most dominant rock consumer stereotype today. Nevertheless, girls and women have long been rock consumers also. As explored below, several stereotypes of female rock consumers exist, particularly the **teenybopper**, who enjoys upbeat rock music (commonly referred to as "pop" to distance it from rock culture), and the **groupie**, who typically prefers hard rock styles. In popular discourse, female teenyboppers and groupies are presented as desiring to *have* rock musicians, who are always presented as male in such constructions, rather than to be *like* rock musicians.

Needless to say, such gendered stereotypes of rock consumers ignore female fans who actively identify with and want to be like the musicians they admire, as much as they deny any romantic or sexual desires on the part of male fans. In other words, both male and female rock fans can want to *be like* the musicians they admire, just as both male and female rock fans can want to *have* rock performers. Moreover, both women and men can be rock musicians, so female-female and female-male musician/fan relations are possible and must be considered also.

Collecting: Connoisseurship and Hipness

Because consumption has been feminized, male rock consumers have often had to negotiate difficult gender dynamics when engaged in musical consumption. Such consumers have used two primary strategies in this regard. First, as a result of strong identification with their idols, some male rock consumers develop a desire to play rock instruments. Often such desire translates only into playing air guitar, but some males gain access to instruments and start their own bands as a result of such identification. By connecting their fandom and desire to the realm of cultural production, such consumers keep at bay the possible feminization of their consumption practices.

Typically the first songs performed by new bands are covers of favorite songs already in circulation, a practice that allows fans to extend their devotion and identification in new directions. **Tribute bands** are a further extension of this practice, as the members of such groups are fans who physically embody their adoration of performers through fashion, make-up, hairstyles, and musical performance. Although such copying tends to be associated with girl fans in other realms of popular culture, some female bands that impersonate male groups, such as Lez Zeppelin, work to subvert the conventionally homosocial dimension of this practice via parody.

The second and perhaps more dominant strategy used by male rock consumers to negotiate the common feminization of consumption is to participate in **record collecting**. As Will Straw argues, this form of consumption allows males to affirm their masculinity since it involves several practices long associated with men. For example, since rare records are more costly than those that are new, and record collectors tend to value expensive home sound systems, collecting requires considerable disposable income and thus the type of purchasing power associated with professional men. In addition, collecting is a practice that privileges ownership, an identity historically associated with wealthy men. Shopping is commonly feminized, but women typically purchase items that are consumed readily either by themselves or their families. In contrast, collectors purchase items that are used to display social status and become permanent fixtures in their lives. Record collecting also requires disposable time, since it is often difficult to locate treasures. Because fandom is linked so strongly with desire, record collecting also allows male rock consumers to displace their emotions for the music onto the material objects by which it is communicated. Vinyl records are prized possessions and are often cared for better than the rest of the collector's material goods.

As Straw discusses, record collectors privilege **connoisseurship**, a particular form of knowledge and communication that has been associated historically with male elites. The connoisseur is a person who knows a great deal about a subject and thus is able to make evaluative judgments of it. Record collectors—like collectors of guitars, automobiles, and baseball cards—typically operate within a community that allows them to exchange their knowledge of such goods with other people. The exchange of this cultural capital happens much like the exchange of goods and money, bestowing on those involved a particular status and power. Record collectors use their knowledge of and preferences in rock music to police the boundaries of their group, as can be seen in the film *High Fidelity* (pictured in Figure 13.2). While record stores and garage sales used to serve as dominant sites of record collecting, the Internet now allows collectors to overcome geographical barriers and to communicate with others well beyond their home communities.

Figure 13.2 *High Fidelity*
Buena Vista Pictures, 2000

Because the knowledge privileged in record collector culture is not learned in school, Straw argues that this form of connoisseurship connotes **hipness**, an identity typically aligned with young men and highly valued in rock culture. Yet the connoisseur, to appear hip to others, must not display the effort and time it takes to accumulate knowledge and goods. Such practices must seem effortless, as if the collector has always known the most obscure trivia about the most obscure band.

While record collecting can help men affirm their masculinity, as Straw suggests, that process is not an easy or guaranteed one. Indeed, the hip record collector must be wary of appearing too nerdish, privileging his love and accumulation of facts and rare vinyl over everything else in his life. He must develop tactics for refuting criticisms that his knowledge is worthless outside rock culture and that he is socially, emotionally, and sexually immature or dysfunctional. The stereotype of the pathological male fan—consistently referenced in pop culture texts—haunts hip record collectors' practices and relationships.

Because of record collecting's historical association with ownership, knowledge, and technology and therefore males, most people do not consider women to be actively involved in this cultural practice. Yet rock culture has a history of female collecting dating back to the genre's earliest years, in part because of girls' considerable involvement as fans at that time, as well as the inexpensiveness of the commodities and technologies originally involved in collecting rock music. In particular, the development of 45 rpm singles and portable phonographs during the postwar era made collecting far more accessible to young rock fans of both genders than it had been previously. Nevertheless, as rock bands of the 1960s began to privilege LP albums, a format that required better and more expensive sound systems, collecting rock records became affiliated with young men.

The reemergence of feminist sentiment and reconfiguration of national economies since the 1960s resulted in an increase in female involvement in the paid workforce, which in turn has meant that contemporary women have more disposable income than previous generations to spend on cultural products, like records. Thus, by the end of the twentieth century, women record collectors were no longer seen as much as anomaly in rock culture. Indeed, many female rock fans have been able to parlay their love and knowledge of records into not just musical performance but also other jobs that require such connoisseurship, like record store clerk, disc jockey, and music critic.

Teenyboppers and Groupies

Because fandom is linked to passion, desire, and excess, this form of cultural consumption is commonly sexualized when the performer and the fan are of different genders. For example, if the cultural producer being idolized is male, female fans are assumed to desire romantic or sexual relations with him rather than to be interested in the artifacts he produces. Given that men have long dominated the role of producer in rock culture, this heterosexual dynamic is regularly used to understand female consumers' interest in rock culture. Popular culture has helped to maintain this stereotype. One of the most iconic moments in rock's visual history is of teenage girls screaming and crying while watching the Beatles perform at a London concert in the early 1960s. Because this moment was part of the band's first and most popular film, *A Hard Day's Night*, which

Figure 13.3 *A Hard Day's Night*
United Artists, 1964

was distributed broadly, it helped to concretize the stereotype of the hysteric young female rock fan while also to solidify the celebrity of the Fab Four (Figure 13.3).

The Beatles' concerts weren't the first time girls had responded to rock musicians in this way, however. (And it wasn't only girls who reacted enthusiastically to this band.) Television appearances by Elvis Presley garnered similar high-spiritedness among young females in the mid-1950s. Yet even before the emergence of rock 'n' roll, girl consumers had attracted media attention for their adoration of crooners like Frank Sinatra. This phenomenon was part of a significant increase in commercial attention to white, middle-class teenage girls during the mid-twentieth century.

Journalists have often explained the phenomenon of girls' fandom via pop psychological theories and thus constructed fans as afflicted by conformity and mass hysteria. Sinatra fandom, for example, was dubbed "Sinatrauma," while Beatles fandom was labeled "Beatlemania." In contrast, some feminist scholars have connected girls' rock fandom to feminist identity and politics. Barbara Ehrenreich, Elizabeth Hess, and Gloria Jacobs, for example, contextualize Beatles fandom in relation to the sexual repression of females during the Cold War period. In particular, such scholars theorize female Beatles fans as exhibiting protofeminist behavior through their embodied, public, and mass expressions of sexual desire for somewhat androgynous male musicians whom they would never marry and likely never meet. Moreover, female Beatles fans problematized what it meant to be white, middle-class girls, since their objects of adoration were part of a culture associated with rebellion against mainstream values.

As Simon Frith and Angela McRobbie demonstrate, by the 1970s teenyboppers were largely associated with the realm of pop, a discursive strategy that has worked to sustain the male domination of rock culture in the sectors of both production and consumption. (In a later project, McRobbie explored the role of dance for teen girls, thus helping to shift conversations about music fandom in a new direction by focusing on the body and affective experience.) Focusing on the young female fans depicted in rock criticism and television shows like *The Monkees*, Norma Coates has critiqued the common pathologizing of teenyboppers specifically for the way it constructs such fans as the feminized abject of rock's ostensibly all-male culture. Coates also explores the other dominant and similarly negative stereotype of women in rock culture during the 1960s and 1970s: groupies.

Typically counterposed to teenyboppers, groupies exist at the other end of the heterosexualized spectrum of female rock fan stereotypes. Unlike teenyboppers, who are assumed to fantasize about romantic relationships with male musicians, groupies are constructed as female rock fans who actively pursue intimate, sexual relations with rock stars. Just as teenyboppers have been theorized as emerging in response to the sexual repressiveness of the mid-twentieth century, groupies have been connected to the **sexual revolution** of the late 1960s and

1970s. The birth control pill was released on the consumer market in the early 1960s, thus facilitating women's reproductive and sexual liberation. As a result, many young people came to understand sexual experience as linked not to reproduction but rather to pleasure and transcendence. Hippies, who saw sexuality as a natural and spiritually powerful part of human behavior, promoted

Figure 13.4   Pamela Des Barres's *I'm with the Band*
Beech Tree Books, 1987

"free love," which contributed to a societal shift away from puritanical sexual morality as well as an increase in sexually explicit media texts.

It was in this particular context that the groupie stereotype emerged in rock culture. As a result of her sexual relationships with numerous male rock stars during the 1960s and 1970s, Pamela Des Barres, known then as "Miss Pamela," is the best-known groupie from this period, in part because she has written so much about her experiences in books like her best-seller *I'm with the Band* (see Figure 13.4). Cynthia Plaster Caster, another female rock fan associated with late 1960s and early 1970s rock culture, became famous for making plaster casts of famous male rock stars' genitalia, thus contributing to the sexual connotation of groupies.

Since the 1970s, numerous individuals have derided groupies as a result of their sexual relations with male rock stars. For instance, many feminists see groupies as reproducing patriarchal gender ideologies and the oppression of women. Yet it may be more productive to understand groupie behavior in its specific sociohistorical context. That is, we might understand groupiedom as an attempt by young women to achieve power and independence at a time when very few avenues existed for them to do so, especially if they were not wealthy. By associating regularly with rock stars, groupies were able not only to rebel against bourgeois feminine norms, especially the roles of wife and mother, but also to gain status in an alternative culture they valued.

Moreover, it is important to consider the emergence of groupies in relation to the limited opportunities for female participation in rock culture during the late 1960s and 1970s. While rock historians now valorize the work of Janis Joplin, Joni Mitchell, Grace Slick, and Tina Turner, rock culture became increasingly male and inhospitable to women during that period, in part because of its valorization of hard, loud, guitar-driven aesthetics. (It is no surprise that the vast majority of women rockers back then were singers, not instrumentalists.) In addition, music critics of that period consistently opposed rock to pop, which was commonly discussed as feminine, as well as inauthentic and overly commercial. In other words, "real" men liked rock. Pop was for girls.

Recently several groupies have attempted to rearticulate their previous fan behavior in ways that suggest their empowerment rather than objectification. Some, such as Des Barres, have discussed their power as muses for male rock musicians, while others have focused on their independence and sexual assertiveness. Thus, some groupies suggest that they developed their own sense of freedom via rock culture and outside the official women's liberation movement. Nevertheless, women's sexual assertiveness remains one of the most contentious points among feminists today. For although most feminists agree that women should be able to use their bodies however they see fit, many note that there is no guarantee that men will relate to those bodies in respectful ways.

Rethinking Rock Fandom

Several writers have complicated the gender-specific and heterocentrist nature of most writing on rock consumption and thus the stereotypes associated with rock consumers. In a short fanzine article published in the early 1980s, Lori Twersky critiqued the myths that exist about female rock fans. In particular, she noted that many female fans do not condone the hardcore rock lifestyle, that female desire for male attention isn't the same as sexual desire, that girls' desire to form relationships should not be confused with their desire to have promiscuous sex, and, most powerfully, that many female rock fans desire to *be* the rock star rather than to have sex with a rock star.

Twersky also argued that some female rock fans do not care as much about the music and musicians as they do about human interactions in particular rock scenes. Other scholars focusing on girl rock fans have focused on homosocial camaraderie rather than patriarchal, heteronormative devotion. Since a desire to have romantic or sexual relations with musical stars is not primary among all rock consumers, the pleasures of same-sex bonding helps to explain other forms of rock fandom also, including that of heterosexual males.

Sue Wise, one of the first feminist scholars of rock fandom, argued that her devotion to Elvis Presley was not the result of heterosexual desire for this male performer (she identifies as lesbian) but rather because she saw Presley as a friend and companion she could rely on in good times as well as bad. Wise thereby disrupts the heterosexual narrative rock critics have constructed for Presley and his female fans, as well as the masculinist representation of Presley's fans as primarily male.

More recently, Arlene Stein has commented on the attraction of rock culture to female music consumers who resist the ideal of heteronormative femininity. She argues that rock culture, because of its ideology of rebellion and antidomesticity, offers a place for girls and women to subvert gender norms and explore alternate identities. In particular, Stein's work helps us to understand how female fans—including lesbians like herself—are attracted to the empowered, rebellious form of masculinity long privileged among, and identified with by, male rock musicians and consumers.

Susan Fast has conducted ethnographic research on female heterosexual rock fans, particularly those interested in Led Zeppelin and similar hard rock bands. Like Wise and Stein, Fast subverts the male/rock and female/pop binaries that have long circulated within and outside rock culture, including rock scholarship. In addition to demonstrating girls' and women's considerable interest and participation in hard rock culture, she highlights the great degree to which such fans invest in and appropriate male rock stars' phallic power, as much as the reluctance of many in the rock community, including feminist scholars, to appreciate such practices and their troubling of the sex/gender system.

As suggested, much of the research on female rock fans has explored those consumers who follow male rock stars and bands. In comparison, little attention has been given, even by feminist rock scholars, to female fans of women rock musicians. Lisa Lewis's analysis of the young female "wannabes" devoted to Madonna and Cyndi Lauper in the 1980s is one of the few extended studies of girl fandom focused on women musicians, and her work helps us to better understand Stacey's theories of fan imitation and copying as applied to young female rock consumers. With a focus on middle-aged women, Laura Vroomen's study of Kate Bush fans problematizes conventional stereotypes of both rock fans and female fans at large, while also revealing some of the ways individuals negotiate online fan communities, an increasingly rich area of study.

While considerable research on Riot Grrrl has focused on specific activities engaged by girls in this community, particularly zine making, little of this scholarship analyzes members of these communities as *fans* relating to musicians, likely because more attention has been paid to such individuals' productive, rather than consumerist, behaviors. Nevertheless, research on lesbian rock fans by scholars like Gill Valentine and Angela Wilson helps to expand our understanding of how such consumers interact with rock music, musicians, and each other at live shows and in everyday life, helping to construct for them both queer identities and queer spaces.

Although rock history is riddled with incidents of male rock fans forming romantic relationships with or sexual attachments to male rock stars, that topic is absent from most research on male-dominated rock genres, as well as scholarship on both teenyboppers and groupies. As an exception, Robert Walser has discussed gay male metalheads' fondness for gay male musicians as well as metal culture's tendencies toward homoeroticism in its common exscription of women. Yet few scholars since have touched on the potential for male homosociality to blur into male homosexuality in rock culture. Such avoidance of this topic has a much to do with the heterocentrism dominant in popular music studies as with the continued prevalence of homophobia in rock culture and society in general.

Along with popular films, like Todd Haynes's *Velvet Goldmine,* recent scholarship on queercore has helped to raise public awareness that teenage boys' and young men's music fandom can operate in the realm of desire just as much as that of girls and women. Hopefully, with the rise of queer music studies, more attention will be paid to homoerotic fan attachments in rock culture. In the meantime, little discussion, either academic or popular, has focused on male fans of female rock musicians, an unfortunate consequence of how both male fandom and female musicianship have been understood traditionally.

Summary

This chapter has moved beyond the roles, practices, and texts of rock musicians to consider how gender impacts rock consumers and practices of consumption. Although many people see performers as central to rock culture, careful consideration of rock consumers and their activities demonstrates their profound importance to this community. After all, without an audience, rock music would fail to circulate beyond its moment of performance. Nevertheless, as many studies of music fandom have revealed, rock consumption does not just entail listening to rock music. Rock fans engage in numerous practices that allow them to explore their identities, connect with others, and assert their pleasure in the music. Because of this, it has been necessary to move beyond those methodologies typically used to analyze texts and representation and instead to adopt ethnographic approaches used to study culture and communities.

Although young men have long dominated rock fandom, girls and women have been a vital presence in rock culture since the emergence of this unique popular style. Gender has played a major role in facilitating certain modes of rock consumption. This is perhaps most clear in star/fan relations. While boys and men tend to look to male rock stars as role models through which they can fashion their own identities, girls and women have commonly been encouraged to see such musicians as objects of romantic fantasy or sexual desire. In other words, while rock fandom affirms male homosociality, female rock fans have necessarily had to negotiate not only the patriarchal dynamics of this scene but also its heterocentrism.

The gender dynamics of rock consumption impact more than star/fan relations, however. As Straw's work on musical connoisseurship suggests, rock fandom also involves fan-to-fan relations in which consumers accrue and exchange cultural capital through such practices as record collecting. Unfortunately, this type of fan behavior has long been connected with males, and girls and women have found it difficult to negotiate the world of rock connoisseurship as a result.

While more attention to rock fans and their various practices, especially record collecting, zine making, and cover bands, has provided us with a better understanding for how rock consumers participate in and negotiate rock culture, what needs further exploration are those consumers who have been consistently marginalized within it, particularly members of the LGBTQI community. Only when the homoerotic identifications and practices of rock fans are more broadly studied will we have a better sense of how gender operates in this particular musical culture. In Chapter 14 we will consider more closely the last major site of gender construction in rock culture: rock criticism.

Further Exploration

1.   Consider your own music-based consumer practices.

What in particular draws you to particular performers or bands? Do you gravitate toward any particular genre of music? If so, does gender have anything to do with that pull? Do you avoid certain types of music? If so, does gender have anything to do with that avoidance? Has your music consumerism changed over time? If so, how and why?

2.   Consider your own music-based fan practices.

Of which performer, band, or genre of music are you a fan? In which fan activities do you engage? In which do you not engage? How has your gender influenced your music fandom? Has your fandom changed over time? If so, how and why?

3.   Study the fans of a band.

Attend the live performance of a band and observe the fans. (Be sure to check with your instructor first about your institution's guidelines for human subjects research.) In what activities do these fans engage, and how do those practices relate to gender politics? What are the gender dynamics of this fan community's relationship with the band members, and how do those dynamics compare to those historically found in rock culture?

4.   Examine fan websites.

Visit a website devoted to facilitating dialogue among music fans, such as a Tumblr page for a musician or band or those linked to http://www.fanasylum. com. What types of fan interaction does this site facilitate? What types of performer/consumer interaction does this site facilitate? How does this site construct fans with regard to gender? Do such fan constructions affirm or subvert stereotypical notions of music consumers?

5.   Watch the first ten minutes of *Detroit Rock City*.

Consider the identities of the rock fans depicted, and discuss the various practices of rock consumption related to these characters. How do these individuals avoid the feminization of fandom and consumption so as to affirm their masculine identities? How is rock's masculinity opposed to pop's femininity in this sequence?

6.   Watch the film *High Fidelity* or read the novel on which it was based.

Which characters are involved in the culture of connoisseurship represented in the film/novel, and in what practices of connoisseurship do they engage? How does the film/novel associate gender and musical connoisseurship? What films do you know that focus on female record collectors? How do those films differ from *High Fidelity*?

7.   Watch the film *Velvet Goldmine*.

How does the film complicate the traditional construction of rock fans as heterosexual? Does the film problematize the stereotype of rock fans as male? If so, how? If not, why not?

Further Reading

Arnett, Jeffrey Jensen. *Metalheads: Heavy Metal Music and Adolescent Alienation*. Boulder: Westview Press, 1996.

Cavicchi, Daniel. *Tramps Like Us: Music and Meaning among Springsteen Fans*. New York: Oxford University Press, 1998.

Coates, Norma. "Teenyboppers, Groupies, and Other Grotesques: Girls and Women and Rock Culture in the 1960s and Early 1970s." *Journal of Popular Music Studies* 15.1 (2003): 65–94.

DeNora, Tia. *Music in Everyday Life*. Cambridge: Cambridge University Press, 2000.

Doss, Erika Lee. *Elvis Culture: Fans, Faith, and Image*. Lawrence: University Press of Kansas, 1999.

Ehrenreich, Barbara, Elizabeth Hess, and Gloria Jacobs. "Beatlemania: Girls Just Want to Have Fun." *Re-making Love: The Feminization of Sex*. Garden City: Anchor, 1986. 10–38.

Fast, Susan. *In the Houses of the Holy: Led Zeppelin and the Power of Rock Music*. New York: Oxford University Press, 2001.

Frith, Simon, and Angela McRobbie. "Rock and Sexuality." *Screen Education* 29 (1978–79): 3–19.

Hebdige, Dick. *Subculture: The Meaning of Style*. New York: Routledge, 1979.

Hills, Matt. *Fan Cultures*. New York: Routledge, 2002.

Hodkinson, Paul. *Goth: Identity, Style and Subculture.* London: Berg, 2002.

Lewis, Lisa. *Gender Politics and MTV: Voicing the Difference.* Philadelphia: Temple University Press, 1992.

Stein, Arlene. "Rock against Romance: Gender, Rock 'n' Roll, and Resistance." *Stars Don't Stand Still in the Sky: Music and Myth.* Eds. Karen Kelly and Evelyn McDonnell. New York: New York University Press, 1998. 215–27.

Straw, Will. "Sizing Up Record Collections: Gender and Connoisseurship in Rock Music Culture." *Sexing the Groove: Popular Music and Gender.* Ed. Sheila Whiteley. New York: Routledge, 1997. 3–15.

Twersky, Lori. "Devils or Angels? The Female Teenage Audience Examined." *Trouser Press* (April 1981): 27–9.

Weinstein, Deena. *Heavy Metal: A Cultural Sociology.* New York: Maxwell Macmillan International, 1991.

Wise, Sue. "Sexing Elvis." *On Record: Rock, Pop, and the Written Word.* Eds. Simon Frith and Andrew Goodwin. New York: Pantheon Books, 1990. 390–98.

14 EVALUATION AND INTERPRETATION
Rock Criticism

LISTEN: THE JAYHAWKS, "LET the Critics Wonder" (*The Jayhawks*, Bunkhouse, 1986). *With obscure and disconnected lyrics, this song resists the practices of interpretation regularly performed by critics. Poking fun at the world of rock criticism, the band encourages listeners to be mindful of the slippage that often occurs between the performance of music and its analysis and evaluation.*

Another site in rock culture that is influenced by gender politics is **criticism**—written and verbal discourse produced from an informed perspective that interprets or evaluates a cultural phenomenon. In the case of rock culture, songs, albums, videos, and live performances are the texts being critiqued. The majority of music listeners engage periodically in some sort of critical dialogue, either sharing their favorite songs with friends or disparaging others' tastes and interests. Yet many individuals are regularly engaged in written forms of **music criticism** also. Numerous forms of amateur and professional written music criticism exist, from zines and blogs to commercial magazines and newspapers to trade publications and scholarly journals.

This chapter examines the gender dynamics of **rock criticism** in its written forms. We will begin by considering specific types of criticism associated with fans, the commercial market, and the academy. We will then explore the involvement of men and women in these practices, particularly professional rock criticism and rock scholarship, and will analyze the ways gender-inflected tastes affect such critical discourse. In turn, the chapter will consider gender's impact on accessibility to different written formats. Since men have long dominated both rock criticism and rock scholarship, we will explore the strategies that female critics have employed to get their voices heard and respected in rock culture.

Types and Functions of Rock Criticism

Four sites of criticism exist in contemporary rock culture: fan criticism, popular criticism, trade criticism, and academic criticism. Critical discourse by the most invested consumers of a particular cultural text is known as **fan criticism**. As discussed in Chapter 13, fan communities operate as what Herbert Gans calls **taste cultures** and Pierre Bourdieu refers to as **cultures of distinction**. In music taste cultures, fans regularly use critical discourse to make distinctions between music and musicians they think should be valued in their community and those they believe should be disregarded. While most fan criticism happens verbally, more engaged fans tend to put their evaluations into writing via **fanzines** (independently produced magazines created for pleasure, not profit) or digital media texts, like blogs. Online chatrooms and customer reviews are other sites of rock fans' written critical discourse.

When most people hear the term "music criticism" they think of the written reviews of songs, albums, and shows that appear in commercial magazines, newspapers, and online forums. Such reviews are classifiable as **popular music criticism** and are part of a much larger field known as **popular music journalism**, which includes not only critical reviews of musical texts and performances but also interviews with performers, reviews of music videos and music-oriented books and films (both documentary and fictional), and photographs and other news-oriented discourse meant to inform the public about popular music culture. Dave Laing distinguishes between the popular music criticism that appears in general periodicals, like newspapers, and that which appears in specialist magazines devoted to particular musical genres. This chapter will focus on the latter when discussing rock criticism.

Popular music critics regularly offer interpretations of songs that help listeners understand their meanings. Yet such reviews are produced also to help consumers in their buying practices and include criteria that can be used when deciding on purchases. Thus, popular music critics function as **cultural intermediaries** between musicians, audience members, and the recording industry. Use of the term "popular" with regard to this form of critical discourse is up for debate, therefore, as critics do not necessarily reflect widespread sentiment about a song or album as much as they help to produce it, typically by privileging artists and musical styles they prefer while criticizing or ignoring those they don't.

The recording industry has its own type of music criticism, which appears in **trade publications**, such as *Billboard*. Such periodicals are produced for industry professionals interested in the production, marketing, and sale of recorded music. In particular, readers of these magazines are invested in musicians' commercial potential and economic success, especially in relation to their recordings and concert tours. Although such readers may be fans also, as businesspeople they have less concern about the meaning of a group's music or performances.

Academic criticism is a form of critical discourse that is produced through scholarly research and analysis grounded in theory. Music-based academic criticism can be divided into two categories: **musicology** and **popular music studies**. Academic rock criticism typically falls into the latter category, which is more concerned with musical performance, reception, and culture than musicology, which focuses primarily on written compositions. Unlike popular criticism, which is often meant to facilitate consumers' buying practices, and fan criticism, which is typically subjective and evaluative, the goal of academic criticism is to provide in-depth, critically informed analyses of music, musicians, and the recording industry and thus to promote a better understanding of popular music culture.

It should be noted that in contemporary rock culture, many people engage in at least three of these forms of criticism concurrently. Most popular critics and academic critics are fans. In turn, many rock scholars also write music reviews as fans and popular critics. Moreover, researchers have regularly relied on popular critics for interpretations of songs, albums, and musicians, as well as histories of particular music scenes. Perhaps the easiest way to discern what type of rock criticism one is looking at, therefore, is to consider its publication venue, which also suggests its intended audience. Fan criticism usually appears in fanzines or blogs and is primarily consumed by other fans within a particular music scene. Most popular criticism appears in commercial print magazines and online sites, as well as books published by popular presses. This type of criticism is broadly available to anyone interested who has the time and money to access it. Trade criticism is usually confined to industry periodicals. Academic criticism typically appears in journals, monographs, and anthologies published by scholarly presses. Less accessible than popular criticism due to its minimal reproduction and commercial promotion, academic criticism is most often consumed by professors, students, and others with considerable education and interest in musical analysis.

History of Rock Criticism

Popular Criticism

Popular music criticism, now largely a journalistic practice, has its roots in art criticism, which emerged in the eighteenth century during the Enlightenment and gave rise to critical dialogue about European classical music. Such forms of critical discourse focused on **aesthetics** and determining whether a piece of music was beautiful, structurally holistic, and culturally significant.

Popular music criticism developed with the rise of recorded music. While critical evaluations of musical aesthetics have been important in this realm also, popular criticism often functions to provide consumers with mechanisms for discerning worthy products distributed by the recording industry. The recording and popularity of jazz music in the early twentieth century led to the introduction of several jazz-oriented magazines, including *Melody Maker* and *Down Beat*. These periodicals were the most successful of all popular music magazines until the emergence of rock music.

Although rock 'n' roll was addressed in the 1950s by popular music newspapers, like *Hit Parader*, as well as the trade journals, like *Billboard*, rock criticism did not develop in earnest until the late 1960s, when some music journalists began to promote rock as a more authentic form of popular music than pop. Most Americans think of *Rolling Stone* when they think of early rock criticism, yet the field was largely developed in England before U.S. periodicals appeared. *Melody Maker*, published in England since 1926, was the first British magazine to take rock seriously. Launched to cover jazz, *Melody Maker* was at first resistant to rock music. Yet, with its rival *New Musical Express* attending to rock from 1952 onward, *Melody Maker* eventually privileged rock as its primary genre. *Melody Maker* was often understood as the more conservative of the two British magazines, while *New Musical Express* was understood as more progressive. They merged in 2000 under the latter's title, commonly shortened to *NME*. The magazine launched its associated website, NME.com, in 1996.

U.S. rock magazines were introduced in the 1960s in the midst of the development of rock 'n' roll into rock as well as the rise of the hippie counterculture. As hippies attempted to subvert mainstream society, they introduced numerous underground newspapers and journals that contained their alternative values. Although rock magazines of this period did not have such a radical approach, they helped to promote some hippie values as well as rock culture. *Crawdaddy!*, introduced by Paul Williams in 1966, was the first U.S. rock magazine. As discussed below, *Crawdaddy!* started as a fanzine yet became popular and transitioned quickly to become like other mainstream magazines, with subscriptions and paid advertisements.

Despite its popularity, *Crawdaddy!* was quickly overshadowed by upstart *Rolling Stone*, launched in 1967 by Jann Wenner. For many rockers, *Rolling Stone* remains the pinnacle of popular rock criticism. Millions of contemporary readers consult its music reviews in print and online, and appearing on its cover is considered to be one of the greatest honors a band can receive. *Rolling Stone* has been home to numerous influential rock critics, including Michael Azerrad, Cameron Crowe, Anthony DeCurtis, Jon Landau, and Greil Marcus. Most *Rolling Stone* writers have been men. Yet perhaps the best photographer associated with the magazine is Annie Leibovitz, who served as its chief photographer and took many iconic images of rock stars during the first decade of her career, including John Lennon's last photograph.

While *Rolling Stone* has maintained its dominance in the world of popular rock criticism for fifty years (in part by launching a companion website in the late 1990s), several other magazines have emerged to challenge that hegemony.

One of the first and most successful was *Creem*, founded in 1969 by Barry Kramer and Tony Reay. Like *Rolling Stone*, *Creem* employed numerous rock journalists who became famous in their own right, including Lester Bangs and Dave Marsh. Lisa Robinson, Jaan Uhelszki, and Ellen Willis, among the very few women rock critics in the 1960s and 1970s, also wrote for *Creem*. First established in Detroit and thus known for its "outsider" status, *Creem* is often lauded for being the first rock magazine to publish work about new rock genres, such as punk and heavy metal.

Since *Creem* ceased publication in the late 1980s, the magazine most competitive with *Rolling Stone* (at least before the Internet) has been *Spin*, which has never focused on rock exclusively. Launched by Bob Guccione, Jr., in 1985, *Spin* gained notoriety in the 1990s for featuring many lesser-known bands, while *Rolling Stone* was understood by many at the time as favoring "classic" 1970s rock. Like its older peer, *Spin* now has an online presence that includes music videos, songs to download, and other interactive components not available in its print version.

College Music Journal (*CMJ*) was launched in 1978 as a trade magazine for college radio stations. Eventually changing its name to *CMJ New Music Report*, the magazine contained programming lists of U.S. college stations. It helped bring about a particular style of noncommercial radio programming, as well as a rock genre commonly referred to in the 1980s as "college rock." For consumers, *CMJ* also published *New Music Monthly*, which was closer in orientation to *Spin* and *Rolling Stone* and offered band interviews and album reviews. Each issue of *New Music Monthly* included a CD sampler of new music, thus connecting consumers more directly with upcoming bands and performers. *CMJ New Music Monthly* ended publication in 2009; however, *CMJ*'s online site, launched in the late 1990s, continues to offer consumers reviews of new rock music.

In an effort to bring rock critics into conversation with one another, Robert Christgau, then writing for the *Village Voice*, introduced the Pazz and Jop Poll in 1971. Still in existence today, the periodical's annual February issue publishes hundreds of music critics' "top ten" lists of songs and albums. Numerous rock-oriented fanzine editors have taken up Pazz and Jop's strategy, publishing their own lists of favorite songs, albums, and musicians.

In addition to writing newspaper and magazine reviews, many popular rock critics have published books. Greil Marcus's *Mystery Train* was among the first. Since its publication, rock critics have regularly produced surveys of particular performers, genres, scenes, and historical periods associated with rock culture. Ellen Willis's *Beginning to See the Light* was the first collection of rock criticism penned by a female critic (Figure 14.1). The first book of popular music criticism to focus specifically on women artists, *Signed, Sealed, and Delivered*, was written by Sue Steward and Sheryl Garratt (Figure 14.2).

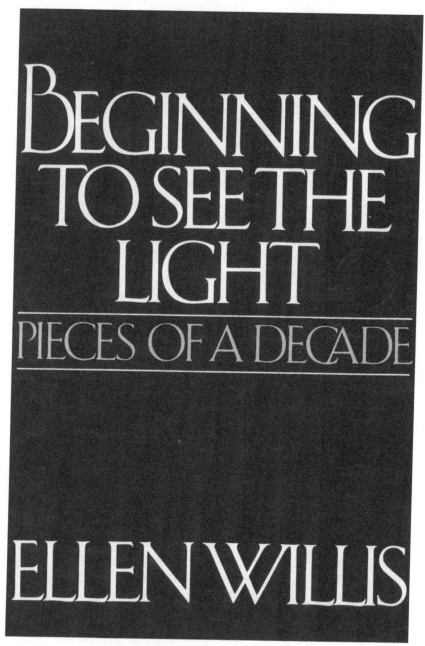

Figure 14.1 Ellen Willis, *Beginning to See the Light*
Wideview Books, 1982

With the expansion of the Internet, the world of popular music criticism has broadened substantially. All of the existing print publications focusing on rock criticism, including *Rolling Stone* and *Spin*, now have online versions, although those websites must now compete with a wide array of others that also offer music reviews, such as Pitchfork and Pop Matters. In turn, online archival sites, like Rock's Back Pages, allow readers to access to decades' worth of rock

Figure 14.2 Sue Steward and Sheryl Garratt, *Signed, Sealed, and Delivered*
South End Press, 1999

criticism. Nevertheless, as a result of consumers' greater accessibility to media production and distribution via the Web, the greatest amount of contemporary critical discourse about rock comes from fans, not professional critics.

Fan Criticism

One of the primary forms of fan criticism in rock culture is the fanzine, a specific type within the much broader category of **zines**. The history of fanzines is often traced back only as far as 1970s punk culture, when such periodicals became a prominent component of rock scenes. Nevertheless, these self-publications have a longer and more complex history in a variety of subcultures, including science fiction fans of the late 1930s and the Beat poets of the 1950s. Prior to the late 1990s and the rise of the Internet, many rock critics began their careers by writing for fanzines. Rock fanzines typically consist of reviews of new albums, interviews with bands, song lyrics, and photographs or illustrations of favorite performers.

Most contemporary zinesters are teenagers and young adults who feel alienated from dominant society and commercial culture. Zines are an attractive medium for such youth because they require minimal education and technical skill to produce and their main materials (paper and writing implements) are inexpensive. In keeping with the antiindustrial, anticommercial ethos of countercultural production, zines are typically created via relatively unsophisticated means: handwritten or typewritten text, hand-drawn illustrations, snapshots, and photocopied text and images appropriated from commercial media texts. Unlike the professional magazines that dominate the publishing industry, zines typically are created at home, independently from commercial publishers.

The independent, DIY ethos privileged by zinesters has important connections to the antiindustrial, anticapitalist practice known in France as *la perruque*. Zine producers often rely on illicit means of producing their texts, using office time, equipment, and supplies, as well as postage and photocopying services, to create, reproduce, and distribute their texts. Other zinesters "scam" the means of zine production from commercial photocopy houses. Zinesters also freely appropriate text and images that have been mass-produced by the media industries, refusing to adhere to policies meant to protect intellectual and artistic property. Yet such text and images are rarely reproduced in their original forms, as zinemakers reassemble such materials to produce new meanings (a practice alternately called *bricolage* and *détournement*).

The first popular fanzine associated with rock culture was *Crawdaddy!*, which was introduced by Paul Williams in 1966. Yet, as noted, it quickly transitioned to become a commercial magazine. Other early rock fanzines include Greg Shaw and David Harris's *Mojo-Navigator Rock and Roll News*, founded in 1966, and *Who Put the Bomp?* (later shorted to just *Bomp!*), which Shaw launched in 1970. *Bam Balam*, *Eurock*, and *Flash 1972* are also associated with this period of rock. Often incorporating the psychedelic aesthetics commonly found in comic books at that time, these fanzines helped to develop the style, format, and production process relied on by future generations of zine editors.

Despite their early history in rock culture, rock fanzines are primarily associated with the punk and metal genres. The first punk fanzine created in the United States was *Punk*, founded in 1975 by Legs McNeil, John Holmstrom, and Ged Dunn. It originated as a means of communicating fan admiration for the Dictators, a protopunk garage band in New York. A British fanzine linked with early punk culture is *Sniffin' Glue*, started by Mark Perry in 1976. Fanzines became quite popular in the early punk community, which valued both independent media production and critical dialogue about mainstream society.

Fanzine production continued to be strong in punk culture throughout the 1980s and 1990s. Perhaps the most popular punk-oriented fanzines of this era were *Maximumrocknroll*, started by Tim Yohannon in 1982, and *Punk Planet*, introduced by Anne Elizabeth Moore and Dan Sinker in 1994. Meanwhile, fanzine production became quite popular among U.S. heavy metal fans during this period also, in part because of the influence of hardcore punk on metal musicians. One of the longest lasting metal zines is *Metal Core*, started by Chris Forbes in 1986.

Various groups of fans commonly disenfranchised in rock culture, especially women and queer people, became interested in creating zines in the late 1980s and early 1990s so as to carve out safe and supportive spaces where they could review bands, share personal stories, and communicate with each other. The queercore and Riot Grrrl scenes that developed during this period were instrumental in inspiring the production and distribution of numerous fanzines. Popular 1990s zines associated with these two groups include *Chainsaw, Girl Germs, Jigsaw, Bikini Kill, J.D.s, Homocore*, and *Outpunk* (see Figure 14.3). Many of the creators of these texts emphasized their personal experiences in rock culture, including as performers.

With the broad expansion of the Internet since the mid-1990s, many people thought fanzines would disappear as a primary site of rock fan discourse. While zine culture is not as vibrant today as it was twenty years ago, many rock fans who oppose the commercial and governmental dominance of the Internet continue to create paper fanzines. Nevertheless, the Internet's ability to quickly connect numerous human beings in different places has made it a primary tool for the contemporary fanzine community. Indeed, many fanzine editors who still value paper texts often produce their zines via computer software and trade or sell their zines via online distribution services, or **distros**. In turn, many rock fanzines have been archived online via such sites as Zine Library Dot Info and the Queer Zine Archive Project.

Meanwhile, the Web has offered other rock fans numerous opportunities for engaging in critical discourse. Indeed, the Internet has become a primary forum for rock fan discourse, and a multitude of fan-run rock blogs and websites now exist online. Perhaps the most popular today is Pitchfork, which focuses on independent music and was started by rock fan Ryan Schreiber in 1995. In turn, many rock fans use their social media accounts to comment on and post photos of their favorite music and performers. One of the Web's most significant advancements over other media is that it allows users to link to numerous sites. Thus, when rock fans embed links to their favorite band's MP3s and music videos in blogs, Twitter, and Instagram posts, they help to speed considerably the process of familiarization necessary for other users to make determinations about musical interests.

As with zines, queer and female rock fans often see the Web as a valued space for airing their opinions about and tastes in music and musicians without

Figure 14.3 *Homocore* 4
Homocore, 1989

fear of dismissal or censorship. It should be no surprise, therefore, that many women and queer fans are now blogging about rock on sites like The Girls Are (TGA) and Feminist Music Geek. By linking their websites to each other, such bloggers are able to create geographically diverse communities that not only help to circulate reviews and information about music and performers but also serve as a support system for marginalized music fans.

Academic Criticism

Music-based academic criticism can be divided into two primary camps: musicology and popular music studies. The differences between these two fields were discussed in Chapter 1. More significant to the current chapter is the development of academic forms of *rock* music criticism and that field's particular gender politics. **Rock scholarship**—academic critical discourse about rock music—owes a huge debt to the scholars who have focused on older forms of popular music, especially jazz and folk. Yet, while many musicologists have accepted jazz as worthy of study and ethnomusicologists readily embrace American folk music alongside other indigenous musical styles, rock was a relative latecomer to musicology.

Meanwhile, outside traditional music studies, rock music and culture have been of interest to scholars in literature, sociology, cultural studies, and media studies for some time. Each of these disciplines has brought its unique theories and methodologies to bear on popular music studies, although the dearth of attention to details commonly analyzed by musicologists, such as sound aesthetics and structures, has resulted in unbalanced interpretations of musical texts. For example, many literary scholars have studied rock lyrics, often by applying theories and methodologies used to analyze poetry. Yet traditional approaches to literary criticism are not adaptable to the study of musical sounds.

Simon Frith is almost single-handedly responsible for expanding rock scholarship beyond its original lyrics-based analyses. As a sociologist trained in critical theory, as well as a rock fan cum critic, Frith takes a cultural studies approach to rock music and is interested in how performance, pleasure, and power are negotiated in rock culture. His first book, *The Sociology of Rock*, was published in 1978 and was then revised as *Sound Effects* in 1981. Frith is prolific in his music scholarship, and one of his most recent books to influence rock criticism is *Performing Rites*.

Other rock scholars to emerge in the late 1970s and early 1980s include Reebee Garofalo, whose *Rock 'n' Roll Is Here to Pay* (coauthored with Steve Chapple) was published in 1977. One of the first academic books to address rock culture, it provides a political economy analysis of the U.S. recording business as well as a history of rock music that attends to both gender and race. Another well-known academic study of rock culture is Dick Hebdige's *Subculture*, published in 1979. Hebdige's book helped to expand rock studies beyond a lyrical focus by exploring punk style and its relation to reggae culture in Britain during the mid-1970s. Despite Hebdige's use of sophisticated critical theory, like semiotics, *Subculture* has been widely read outside of the academy.

By the mid-1980s, the increased popularity of music videos led to an influx of media scholars into popular music studies, thus expanding academic rock criticism to encompass issues of visual representation, celebrity, and postmodern aesthetics. With identity as a primary site of critical inquiry in media studies, scholars interested in race, gender, and sexuality were drawn to rock videos also.

Many single-authored academic books on rock culture have been published over the past two decades. Yet to date there is no scholarly journal devoted specifically to rock criticism. Instead, rock scholars tend to publish in the periodicals devoted to popular music studies, *Popular Music and Society*, published since 1971, *Popular Music*, in print since 1981, and the *Journal of Popular Music Studies*, published since 1988 by the International Association for the Study of Popular Music (IASPM). The only journal specific to issues of gender in music is *Women and Music*, which has been published since 1997.

Few universities and colleges have departments devoted to popular music studies. Therefore, most scholars who study rock music and culture do not have degrees in popular music and instead are affiliated with traditional academic disciplines, such as media studies. Nevertheless, most rock scholars are also members of the IASPM, which is an interdisciplinary organization that maintains a listserv for dialogue and networking among popular music researchers at large. In 1996, a group of rock scholars formed Rocklist, a listserv for researchers studying rock music and culture. As will be discussed in more detail below, several feminist scholars formed their own listserv for a brief period in the late 1990s as a response to the sexism and male domination they experienced as members of Rocklist.

Gender and Rock Criticism

When considering the effects of gender politics on rock criticism, we might explore not only the identity of rock critics and their primary readers but also the gender dynamics ascribed to the musical texts such critics discuss. Also worthy of consideration here is the impact of gender on the discourses and rhetorical strategies that critics use when writing reviews and analyses of rock music and its performers. It is important to note that the broader fields of cultural criticism and scholarship have been dominated historically by wealthy men, as a result of most women's and poor people's lack of education and literacy and thus their exclusion from the professional realms of journalism and academia. Although **rock journalism** emerged in the 1960s, a time of considerable social change, this field continues to reveal its patriarchal and classist legacy, one that can be found as well in academic research on rock culture.

Fan Criticism

Since the majority of rock fans have historically been white males, it is not surprising that the earliest fanzine producers were members of this demographic group. Unfortunately, despite women's increased involvement in rock culture since the latter part of the twentieth century, boys and men continue to dominate rock-based zine culture, especially that associated with the heavy metal genre. This phenomenon can be understood in relation to boys' and girls' different socialization with regard to cultural connoisseurship. Males are socialized to be far more invested than females in the type of critical discourse that is privileged among music fans, especially those committed to fanzine production.

Nevertheless, since the late 1970s an increasing number of women have become involved in producing zines. Punk culture has had a major influence on this trend because of its privileging of amateurism and the DIY ethos. While male-edited zines like *Punk* and *Sniffin' Glue* are repeatedly mentioned in the histories written of early punk fanzines, several female punks were active in zine making also during the late 1970s and early 1980s, including Wendy Blume of *Let It Rock*, and Crystal Clear, Vinyl Virgin, and Sarah Shoshubi, who coedited *More-On*. Like other punk periodicals of that period, most zines produced by these women functioned primarily as fanzines, privileging interviews with punk musicians and reviews of shows and recordings.

During the mid- to late 1980s, a significant number of zines produced by teenage girls and young women, including Laura MacDougal's *Sister Nobody*, Donna Dresch's *Chainsaw*, and Tobi Vail's *Jigsaw*, began to privilege autobiographical writings alongside fan discourse, thus helping to develop the genre now known as "personal zines" or "perzines." This style of zine, first associated with the queercore movement, was later privileged in the Riot Grrrl community also and can be seen in such zines as *Bikini Kill, Girl Germs*, and *Riot Grrrl*. Given the progressive gender and sexual politics of fans associated with these two music styles, women musicians and LGBTQI performers have likely received more attention in Riot Grrrl and queercore zines than they have via popular or academic rock criticism.

Meanwhile, most of the fanzines in heavy metal culture tend to be produced by males. Since such zines also focus, sometimes exclusively, on male bands and privilege such themes as horror, violence, and the occult, they tend to reaffirm the masculinist perspective commonly associated with this rock genre and thus discourage female involvement at both the fan and musician level.

Popular Criticism

A quick perusal of the names listed in the current **mastheads** of commercial rock magazines, such as *Rolling Stone,* reveals men's continued domination of contemporary rock journalism, especially with regard to editorial and senior writing positions. Moreover, the common assumption among individuals working for these magazines is that their readers are young males and it is that group's tastes that must be kept in mind if money is to be made. This phenomenon has continued unabated for decades, despite the long history of women's interest in rock culture, as well as increased popularity of feminist ideologies over that period.

Until recently, little popular attention has been given to the patriarchal and other regressive values that have structured rock criticism. In a recent interview for Pitchfork, Björk criticized journalists for giving male collaborators more, or sometimes sole, credit for their work with women artists, a criticism that builds on other female musicians' critiques of sexism in music journalism. In turn, several feminist critics have brought attention to this field's nonprogressive gender politics by sharing their own experiences. For example, Ann Powers has commented that the male homosociality of rock culture can be off-putting to female music fans, who have a more difficult time than men breaking into rock criticism. In turn, Lucy O'Brien has described the tendency for magazine and newspaper editors to offer male critics opportunities to write longer articles, while women are relegated to shorter reviews, often of music from lesser-known bands, and interviews with female performers. This problem has been exacerbated by the dominance of editorial positions by men, many of whom started as critics and have thus been offered more opportunities for advancement than their female colleagues. To date, Sia Michel of *Spin* is the only woman to have edited a major rock publication in the United States, and she did so only for four years. By comparison, Jann Wenner has been editor of *Rolling Stone* since 1967, half a century. Meanwhile, women have historically predominated in low-paying administrative positions for such periodicals.

Alongside female rock musicians and critics, several academics have considered the gender dynamics of popular music criticism in terms of both labor and rhetoric. For example, Kembrew McLeod discovered in his study of the *Village Voice*'s Pazz and Jop polls that only an 8 percent increase in the number of female rock critics had occurred between 1978 and 1998, with women making up only 15 percent of the roughly five hundred critics who contributed in 1997 and 1998. Yet that figure wasn't specific to just Pazz and Jop. McLeod found that only 15 percent of the Rock and Rap Confidential/Addicted to Noise Writers' Poll was female. These figures are reflective of the gendered nature of magazine staffs. For instance, in 1999, 15 percent of *Rolling Stone*'s and 20 percent of *Spin*'s editorial and senior writing staffs were female, figures similar to other rock periodicals at that time. While the percentage of women writers and editors at such magazines has risen over the past two decades, such increases have not resulted in gender equity. The editorial and writing staff members of rock periodicals published in the United Kingdom and the United States are still predominantly white young men.

The reasons for the historic male domination in rock journalism are somewhat complex and have deep roots that are difficult to untangle. In the 1960s, when rock journalism was first taking off, rock culture was, despite its self-proclaimed revolutionary nature, both sexist and misogynist, and thus exclusionary of and off-putting to many women. By the early 1970s, rock journalism was also racist and homophobic, at once romanticizing earlier African American blues musicians, like Robert Johnson, and privileging blues-influenced white male rock, such as that produced by the Rolling Stones, Eric Clapton, and Van Morrison, while denigrating the multiracial and substantially gay culture of disco. Although the black power movement was flourishing during this period, few African Americans contributed to rock journalism after the early 1960s.

Meanwhile, patriarchal gender politics were still the norm in the 1960s, with few women attending college and even fewer college-educated women pursuing careers. As a result, there was a dearth of female journalists in the 1960s and early 1970s. Feminists involved in the women's liberation movement largely rejected the rock culture of the 1970s. However, rock journalism saw a rise in female, and sometimes feminist, criticism during that decade, as journalists like Jaan Uhelszki and musicians like Patti Smith began to write reviews and interview musicians, while photographers like Annie Leibovitz and Lynn Goldsmith contributed to rock's photojournalism. The success of these female writers and photographers, as well as the respect afforded them, helped to inspire more women to take up rock criticism.

Many women rock critics have started their careers at small, local publications before obtaining jobs at more traditional publications. Ann Powers, for example, got her start writing for the *Rocket*, an independent, biweekly newspaper focused on the Seattle rock scene, before writing for such mainstream publications as the *New York Times*. In turn, some female rock fans, like Julie Burchill, have been able to turn their amateur fan criticism into paid positions at commercial rock publications. In an effort to honor women critics and to insert their voices into the commonly male-authored histories of popular music criticism, Evelyn McDonnell and Ann Powers collected over sixty essays by mostly American female critics for the book *Rock She Wrote*. Journalist Liz Evans followed a few years later with a British collection of women's rock criticism, *Girls Will Be Boys*.

Despite the rise of female rock journalists since the 1970s, it is important to note that such critics have to navigate a rock culture that has consistently been constructed as a predominantly male and masculine scene. As much of this book has demonstrated, male rock fans and musicians regularly participate in forms of discourse and camaraderie that help to shore up their masculinity while preserving their scene's homosociality. While some female critics claim that being women has helped their careers in rock journalism, since their gender brings them greater attention in a mostly male arena, many female critics and photographers recall being "othered" by their male colleagues and readers and thus made to feel peripheral and delegitimized in their work environments and, at times, rock culture. Indeed, many women rock critics and photographers have reported being given bad assignments by their editors, a practice that works to contain their ambitions and the threat they pose to male journalists. Not surprisingly, several female rock critics use writing about women, gender, and rock criticism as a way to negotiate their frustration and pain over such marginalization. Meanwhile, others have attempted to promote rock criticism as a career option for women by downplaying its negative stereotypes and discussing the considerable amount of influence journalists can have on promoting musicians.

In the realm of academic music criticism, several scholars have drawn attention to the sexism and other regressive ideologies that have historically pervaded rock journalism. For example, McLeod demonstrates that male rock critics maintained a discursive environment through the late 1990s that worked to marginalize and deprivilege not only women critics but also women performers, feminine performance styles, and women's musical tastes. By focusing primarily on male performers and celebrating performance styles associated with phallic masculinity, male critics have created a somewhat exclusive boys' club of rock journalism.

This phenomenon is directly related to an ideological perspective in rock journalism that has come to be known as **rockism**. To be rockist is to value the blues and spin-off genres, like punk and hard rock, which similarly privilege the authenticity and emotional honesty of live performance and performers. Via rockism, rock is constructed as the norm against which all other popular music forms are critiqued and found inferior. Key to the rockist perspective are male musicians who display raw, natural talent but are not brown or black, as well as those who are in touch with their emotions but are not feminine or gay.

Analyzing 587 reviews of albums appearing in the Pazz and Jop polls between 1971 and 1999, McLeod demonstrates the prevalence of the **phallogocentric** rockist perspective among critics writing for *Spin*, *Creem*, *Rolling Stone*, and *Crawdaddy!* He notes that the adjectives used by such critics to describe "good" music are connected to nine themes, all of which have been aligned historically with men and masculinity:

Aggressive intensity: compulsion, savage, roar, tough, powerful, angry, desperate
Violence: murderous, violent, switchblades, holocaust, gunfire, barrage
Rawness: primitive, rough, crude, basic, garage-rock, unvarnished
Simplicity: lack of adornment, direct, classic
Personal expression: honesty, sincerity, from the heart, nakedness
Seriousness: intelligence, gutsy, mature, sophisticated, substantial
Traditionalism: ability to reference musical roots
Authenticity: real, genuine, primitive, substantial
Originality: experimentation, inventiveness, disregard for formula, imaginative.

Meanwhile, the adjectives used by rock critics to describe "bad" music coalesce around seven themes, all historically associated with women and femininity (and "pop"):

Softness: soft, weak, light, wimpy, sweet, insipid, wispy, castrated
Slickness: overproduced, fluffy, vapid, gloss, inoffensive, formula

Blandness: boring, middle-of-the-road, menopausal, sanitized
Vapidity: stupid, trivial, dumb, dim-witted, banal, insipid
Commercialism: appealing to masses, brain-killing entertainment, corporate,
  hitmakers
Formulaic unoriginality: pedestrian, clichéd, shopworn, formula, rehash,
  play-it-safe
Sweet sentimentalism: sappy, mawkish, mush and sap, weepers.

Like McLeod's project, Helen Davies's study of the contemporary British rock press demonstrates that patriarchy has guided the system by which male rock critics evaluate musical texts. There, good/serious/credible music has been regularly aligned with male musicians and masculinity, and bad/silly/unacceptable music has been consistently associated with women musicians and femininity. Male critics' consistent privileging of male performers, affirmation of machismo, and assumption of a predominantly male audience has helped to produce rock culture as a men's preserve unwelcoming of femininity and off limits to women.

At the same time, however, we might understand male critics' celebration of phallic masculinity and disparagement of females and femininity as attempts to shore up rock journalism's fragile patriarchy in the face of challenges to rock culture by women and queer people over the past two decades. Indeed, many male critics attempt to lessen the threat of women artists to rock's male homosociality by ignoring them and their work, constructing them as inconsequential in comparison to male musicians, or representing them as women first and foremost, commonly by focusing on their bodily appearance.

In addition to looking at the gendered rhetoric that rock critics use when reviewing albums, scholars have studied the questions that journalists ask female interview subjects. For example, Brenda Johnson-Grau has shown that rock journalists tend to ask women musicians about their personal lives (e.g., parents, partners) more than their music. If their art is addressed, female performers are often forced to defend their talent, since journalists will often question their songwriting, instrumental, and/or producing skills. Bayton has noted that while critics typically ask male musicians about their musical influences, skills, and technology, they often do not query female performers about their development as musicians or the equipment they use. Avoidance of these topics suggests that rock critics often assume that women musicians are technophobic, possess little skill or talent, and have only female role models. The latter strategy is commonly used to homogenize all women performers and to ghettoize them in one group that is set apart from "normal" (i.e., male) rock musicians.

Over the span of rock's history, women rock critics have often attempted to subvert the phallogocentric discursive patterns noted above. As Evelyn McDonnell notes, whether through their own volition or because of their editors' demands, female journalists typically cover "women's issues" for their magazine or newspaper, and this translates to being responsible for interviewing women musicians and reviewing their work. While male publishers and editors have used this practice to keep women writers and topics at a safe distance from "hard" and "serious" news, such ghettoization has also held advantages for female journalists and their subjects. Indeed, as the number of women rock critics has increased, so has the number of women-centered bands focused on by the media. A writer's feminist consciousness only increases the chances that they will cover female artists.

Some women writers, like Louise Bruton, have drawn attention to the sexist ways critics represent female rock musicians by parodying their approach in fake descriptions of male rock stars (see Figure 14.4). Meanwhile, other women rock critics frustrated with the male hegemony of rock criticism have launched their own independent rock-themed periodicals, typically starting with fanzines. For example, Lori Twersky edited *Bitch*, whose subtitle was "The Women's Rock Mag with Bite," from 1985 to 1989. (This zine is different from the contemporary magazine *Bitch*.) Although published for only four years, *Bitch* was enormously influential in encouraging young women to see rock journalism, not to mention rock musical production, as a viable pastime and career.

Carla DeSantis Black introduced *Rockrgrl* in 1995, a time of considerable energy for feminists in rock culture, largely as a result of the signing of several women performers and female-powered bands to major labels, as well as the influence of the Riot Grrrl community. As a musician, DeSantis Black was frustrated with how mainstream music magazines treated women performers and wanted a place to publicly voice such criticisms while also bringing more positive attention to women musicians. Beginning as a zine, *Rockrgrl* developed into a magazine replete with color, glossy pages, and advertisements (see Figure 14.5).

In addition to editing the magazine, DeSantis Black organized several conferences under the *Rockrgrl* banner, bringing together women musicians, critics, and industry professionals for conversation and networking. DeSantis Black also cofounded *Women Who Rock*, published by Cherry Lane and introduced only a few years after *Rockrgrl*. Unfortunately, both magazines folded in the early 2000s, largely as a result of the troubled economy and the growing popularity of the Internet. In the meantime, however, two new magazines for women rock musicians have been launched: *Tom Tom Magazine*, for female drummers, and *She Shreds*, for women guitarists.

In light of the dearth of reporting on earlier generations of women rock musicians, several women writers have built a female-centric history of rock that fills serious gaps in male-authored rock histories. This is the project of Gillian Gaar's *She's a Rebel*, Lucy O'Brien's *She Bop*, Gerri Hirshey's *We Gotta Get Out of This Place*, and Barbara O'Dair's collection *Trouble Girls*. Several of these

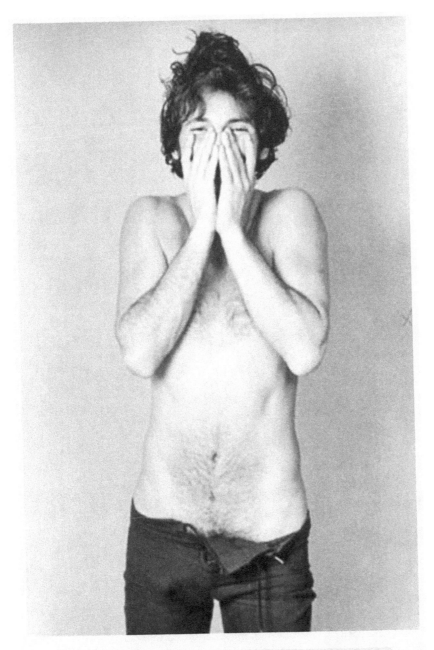

Bruce Springsteen flaunting his curves in his trademark barely-there jeans ★ 2

Figure 14.4 Louise Bruton's parody of Bruce Springsteen photo
HeadStuff, 2015

Figure 14.5　*Rockrgrl* 29
Rockrgrl, 1999

books have been reprinted, which indicates the considerable desire on the part of musicians, consumers, and scholars for further information about women rock musicians. Documentary films like Stephanie Bennett's *Women in Rock*, Beth Harrington's *Welcome to the Club: The Women of Rockabilly*, and Morgan Neville's *20 Feet from Stardom* have also contributed to this historical reclamation by focusing specifically on women rock musicians.

Given the rise of women's rock journalism in recent years, it is not surprising that McLeod and several other scholars have noted a progressive (albeit slight) change in the gender dynamics of popular rock criticism over the past decade. Indeed, there are more women critics and magazine editors today than ever before. Moreover, as a result of feminist ideologies permeating our society, many contemporary rock journalists are more aware of their gender-based biases than those working several decades ago when this practice first emerged. In turn, editors and readers no longer tolerate sexist discourse to the extent their forebears did in rock's early years.

Academic Criticism

Just as popular rock criticism has been male-dominated and masculinist over the past thirty years, so, too, has academic rock criticism for the most part. This ideological framework has been well served by the academy, which, despite a great influx of female scholars since the 1970s, continues to hire and promote male academics at a greater rate than their female peers. Nevertheless, in contrast to women journalists, who continue to battle the age-old patriarchy of the music and publishing industries, female scholars have been able to carve out a viable, international support system that ensures that their voices are heard broadly: the field of women's and gender studies.

Nevertheless, several women scholars have documented the regressive gender politics that persist in academic rock criticism. For example, Norma Coates has analyzed the patriarchy and sexism that she and other women rock scholars experienced on Rocklist, an academic listserv devoted to rock studies. Coates demonstrates how women who broached the topic of gender were often ignored or had their comments trivialized by male list members. In addition, the male list members often wrote lengthy posts filled with obscure rock trivia that tended to foreclose discussion. Although not consciously deployed by the men on Rocklist, such strategies constructed a male-homosocial virtual space unwelcome to women, much like offline rock scenes.

Marginalized within a site they helped to create, several women Rocklist members (including this author) formed a group where questions about rock's gender politics were central. We named it Clitlist in response to the original listserv's phallocentrism. Like other separatist feminist ventures, Clitlist provided us with a supportive site where our scholarly interests were taken seriously and respected as valid. Unfortunately, Clitlist lasted only a short time, as several of the women finished their graduate degrees and moved on to other academic projects. Some, like Coates, became involved with IASPM, which has been more welcoming of women researchers and gender studies in recent years.

The effects of feminist rock scholarship since the late 1990s have been extensive. In addition to many book chapters and journal articles, several influential books about women rockers have been written by feminist rock scholars, including Mavis Bayton's *Frock Rock*, Sheila Whiteley's *Women and Popular Music*, Lori Burns and Mélisse Lafrance's *Disruptive Divas*, Helen Reddington's *The Lost Women of Rock Music*, Jacqueline Warwick's *Girl Groups, Girl Culture*, Mimi Schippers's *Rockin' out of the Box*, and Marion Leonard's *Gender in the Music Industry*.

Robert Walser's *Running with the Devil*, published in 1993, was the first book by a male scholar to focus on masculinity in rock, and Freya Jarman-Iven's recent collection *Oh Boy! Masculinities and Popular Music* carries that project forward, albeit with scholarship by both men and women. Women still lead the way in analyzing gender in rock culture. Yet male researchers' interest in rock's gender politics has experienced a significant rise in the past decade, in part due to women scholars' demands for more attention to this topic, as well as the further proliferation of feminist and queer theory in the academy and rock culture.

The rise of gender-based rock scholarship in the larger realm of critical discourse about rock culture has also contributed to more attention to LGBTQI issues in rock culture, as evidenced by Doris Leibetseder's *Queer Tracks* and Curran Nault's *Queercore*. Unfortunately, the same has not been true in popular forms of rock criticism. Like patriarchy, homophobia still structures that field to a great extent, so that critics who are queer find it difficult to express their identities to fellow writers, much less mainstream audiences. Yet nonmusic LGBTQI publications, like *Out*, sometimes publish popular rock criticism. Meanwhile, more queer-centered rock criticism appears in fanzines and blogs, discursive sites where writers have far more legitimacy and control over their audience.

Summary

This chapter has examined the broad world of rock criticism with a particular eye on the role of gender in it. Although some scholars have analyzed the gender politics of popular music criticism, this discursive site deserves far greater attention, particularly since it significantly impacts musicians' comprehension of how their work is publicly received, as well as consumers' tastes, musical selections, and social relations. As such, music criticism also has a profound impact on the recording industry.

Through a survey of popular, fan, and academic rock criticism, we have considered many trends discussed elsewhere in this book. In particular, men have historically dominated all three forms of rock criticism since the emergence of rock 'n' roll. Nevertheless, whether relegated to writing about women performers by male editors or freely choosing to do so because of shared gender status or cultural tastes, women critics (and women-centered rock criticism) have posed a significant challenge to rock's historically phallocentric critical discourse. Moreover, by insisting that gender matters, women rock critics have challenged all those who evaluate and interpret rock culture to consider gender as an always already significant factor. Hopefully, with the tools for analyzing the gender dynamics of rock culture now in your hands, you, too, will contribute to the growth of gender-based rock criticism via your own research and writing.

Further Exploration

1. Analyze album reviews.

Find a few album reviews each for a female-centered band and a male-centered band performing in the same rock genre (e.g., metal or punk). Note the adjectives used by different critics to describe these two bands' music. How would you categorize such adjectives with regard to gender? What reasons might exist for the ways in which these reviews are gendered? How might the gendering of the bands' music be related to the performers? To the genre of music? To the critic writing the review? To the review's targeted audience?

2. Study shifts in popular rock criticism.

Examine the names and deduce the sex of *Rolling Stone* editors and writers in issues of the magazine published in 1967, 1977, 1987, 1997, 2007, and 2017, one for each year. What is the ratio of male to female editors and writers at the magazine for each of these years? What changes have occurred with regard to gendered employment at the magazine over this forty-year period? Has there been progress for female employees in any area over this period?

3. Examine an online forum for music criticism.

After considering multiple entries on the site, discuss the gender dynamics of the forum's participants. How many are male? How many are female? Is the moderator male or female? Do you notice any differences in the language style of the male and female participants? If so, what might account for those differences? If not, what might account for similarities?

4. Compare fanzines or blogs.

Review several fanzines or blogs produced by male and female editors. How does gender impact the name and design of each fanzine or blog? What bands are reviewed in each? What style of music is privileged in each? What does the gendering of the zine's or blog's name, design, reviews, and privileged genre tell you about the gender of its targeted readers?

5. Analyze shifts in popular music scholarship.

Examine the names and deduce the sex of scholars whose work is published in the *Journal of Popular Music Studies* in 1990, 1995, 2000, 2005, 2010, and 2015, one for each year. What is the ratio of male to female editors and authors in this journal for each of these years? What changes have occurred with regard to the gender of editors and authors in this journal over this twenty-year period? Has there been progress for female scholars over this period?

6.   Interview a popular music critic.

Discuss with the critic their experience in reviewing music. (Be sure to check with your instructor first about your institution's guidelines for human subjects research.) Focus on the critic's selection of music to review, criteria for evaluation, and the relation of both to gender politics. Compare your findings to some reviews written by the critic.

7.   Write your own song or album reviews.

Select music to review. Listen several times, each time paying attention to a different component of the song (e.g., lyrics, sound, form). Reflect on what words come to mind to describe these various components, as well as the overall meaning of the song. As you write, consider how your own language and evaluation of this music relate to gender politics, especially with regard to the genre of the music, its performers, and your intended audience.

Further Reading

Brooks, Daphne A. "The Write to Rock: Racial Mythologies, Feminist Theory, and the Pleasures of Rock Music Criticism." *Women and Music: A Journal of Gender and Culture* 12.1 (2008): 54–62.

Bruton, Louise. "If Male Musicians Were Described the Same Way as Female Musicians." HeadStuff, July 15, 2015. http://www.headstuff.org/2015/07/if-male-musicians-were-described-the-same-way-as-female-musicians/.

Carson, Mina, Tisa Lewis, and Susan M. Shaw. *Girls Rock! Fifty Years of Women Making Music.* Lexington: University Press of Kentucky, 2015.

Clifford-Napoleone, Amber R. *Queerness in Heavy Metal Music: Metal Bent.* New York: Routledge, 2015.

Coates, Norma. "Can't We Just Talk about the Music?: Rock and Gender on the Internet." *Mapping the Beat: Popular Music and Contemporary Theory.* Eds. Thomas Swiss, John Sloop, and Andrew Herman. Malden: Blackwell, 1998. 77–99.

Davies, Helen. "All Rock and Roll Is Homosocial: The Representation of Women in the British Rock Music Press." *Popular Music* 20.3 (2001): 301–19.

Duncombe, Stephen. *Notes from Underground: Zines and the Politics of Alternative Culture.* London: Verso, 1997.

Elafros, Athena. "'No Beauty Tips or Guilt Trips': *Rockrgrl*, Rock, and Representation." *Popular Music and Society* 33.4 (2010): 487–99.

Evans, Liz. *Girls Will Be Boys: Women Report on Rock.* London: Pandora, 1997.

Fenster, Mark. "Queer Punk Fanzines: Identity, Community and the Articulation of Homosexuality and Hardcore." *Journal of Communication Inquiry* 17.1 (1993): 73–94.

Grier, Miles Parks. "Said the Hooker to the Thief: 'Some Way Out' of Rockism." *Journal of Popular Music Studies* 25.1 (2013): 31–55.

Johnson-Grau, Brenda. "Sweet Nothings: Presentation of Women Musicians in Pop Journalism." *Pop Music and the Press.* Ed. Steve Jones and Kevin Featherly. Philadelphia: Temple University Press, 2002. 202–18.

Kruse, Holly. "Abandoning the Absolute: Transcendence and Gender in Popular Music Discourse." *Pop Music and the Press.* Ed. Steve Jones. Philadelphia: Temple University Press, 2002. 134–55.

Leibetseder, Doris. *Queer Tracks: Subversive Strategies in Rock and Pop Music.* New York: Routledge, 2016.

Leonard, Marion. "Feminism, 'Subculture,' and Grrrl Power." *Sexing the Groove: Popular Music and Gender.* Ed. Sheila Whiteley. New York: Routledge, 1997. 230–55.

McDonnell, Evelyn. "The Feminine Critique: The Secret History of Women and Rock Journalism." *Rock She Wrote: Women Write about Rock, Pop, and Rap.* Eds. Evelyn McDonnell and Ann Powers. New York: Delta, 1995. 5–23.

McDonnell, Evelyn, and Ann Powers, eds. *Rock She Wrote: Women Write about Rock, Pop, and Rap.* New York: Delta, 1995.

McLeod, Kembrew. "Between Rock and a Hard Place: Gender and Rock Criticism." *Pop Music and the Press.* Ed. Steve Jones. Philadelphia: Temple University Press, 2002. 93–113.

NOTES

Chapter 4

1. Lara Baker, "Women in the Music Business: Mind the Gender Gap," *Huffington Post*, June 20, 2013, http://www.huffingtonpost.co.uk/lara-baker/women-in-the-music-business_b_3472612.html.
2. Baker.
3. Helienne Lindvall, "Behind the Music: Where Are the Female A&Rs?," *Guardian*, July 23, 2009, http://www.theguardian.com/music/musicblog/2009/jul/23/behind-music-female-a-rs.
4. Quoted in Carla DeSantis Black, *GrlTalk: 231 Memorable Quotes from ROCKRGRL Magazine* (Austin: MEOW, 2013), 44.
5. Quoted in Barbara O'Dair, ed., *Trouble Girls: The Rolling Stone Book of Women in Rock* (New York: Random House, 1997), 439.
6. Quoted in Mimi Schippers, *Rockin' out of the Box: Gender Maneuvering in Alternative Hard Rock* (New Brunswick: Rutgers University Press, 2002), 167.
7. Quoted in Mavis Bayton, *Frock Rock: Women Performing Popular Music* (Oxford: Oxford University Press, 1998), 132–33.
8. Quoted in Lucy O'Brien, *She Bop II: The Definitive History of Women in Rock, Pop and Soul* (New York: Continuum, 2002), 169.
9. Quoted in Bayton, 166.
10. Quoted in Bayton, 168.
11. Quoted in DeSantis Black, 44.
12. Quoted in Bayton, 37.
13. Quoted in Gillian G. Gaar, *She's a Rebel: The History of Women in Rock & Roll* (Seattle: Seal Press, 1992), 197.
14. Quoted in Bayton, 6.
15. Quoted in O'Brien, 450.
16. Quoted in O'Brien, 412.

17. Lorraine Ali, "Exiled in Guyville," *Rolling Stone*, October 6, 1994, 57–58.
18. Quoted in O'Brien, 440.
19. Quoted in Schippers, 127.
20. Quoted in O'Dair, 437.

Chapter 6

1. Information on Grammy nominees and winners can be found on the Grammy website: https://www.grammy.com/.
2. Quoted in Mavis Bayton, *Frock Rock: Women Performing Popular Music* (Oxford: Oxford University Press, 1998), 37.
3. Quoted in Carla DeSantis Black, *GrlTalk: 231 Memorable Quotes from ROCKRGRL Magazine* (Austin: MEOW, 2013) 47.
4. Quoted in Bayton, 18.
5. Quoted in DeSantis Black, 65.
6. Quoted in DeSantis Black, 67.
7. Quoted in Bayton, 49.
8. Quoted in Bayton, 15.
9. Quoted in Lucy O'Brien, *She Bop II: The Definitive History of Women in Rock, Pop and Soul* (New York: Continuum, 2002), 128.
10. Quoted in Bayton, 15.
11. Quoted in DeSantis Black, 88.
12. Quoted in DeSantis Black, 89.
13. Quoted in DeSantis Black, 85.
14. Quoted in Mimi Schippers, *Rockin' out of the Box: Gender Maneuvering in Alternative Hard Rock* (New Brunswick: Rutgers University Press, 2002), 72.

Chapter 7

1. Quoted in "One Drummer One Question: Janet Weiss," *Tom Tom Magazine*, November 11, 2009, http://tomtommag.com/one-drummer-one-question-janet-weiss/.
2. Quoted in Clare Longrigg, "Not Bad—for a Girl," *Guardian*, January 29, 2004, http://www.theguardian.com/music/2004/jan/30/gender.popandrock.
3. Quoted in Zaneta Sykes, "Why All Women Should Play Percussion," *Tom Tom Magazine* 8 (Winter 2011/12), https://issuu.com/tomtommagazine/docs/issue8kidsissue/40.
4. Quoted in Longrigg.
5. Quoted in Gina Arnold and Shawn Dahl, eds., "Chicks with Picks," *Trouble Girls: The* Rolling Stone *Book of Women in Rock*, ed. Barbara O'Dair (New York: Random House, 1997), 435.
6. Quoted in Arnold and Dahl, 436.
7. Quoted in Arnold and Dahl, 438.

8. Quoted in Mary Ann Clawson, "When Women Play the Bass: Instrument Specialization and Gender Interpretation in Alternative Rock Music," *Gender & Society* 13.2 (April 1999), 200.

9. Quoted in Leslie C. Gay, Jr., "Acting Up, Talking Tech: New York Rock Musicians and Their Metaphors of Technology," *Ethnomusicology* 42.1 (1998), 90.

10. Melissa Bobbitt, "I'm Sick of Running Into Misogyny at Guitar Shops, So I Did an Experiment," *xojane*, August 24, 2015, http://www.xojane.com/issues/misogyny-at-guitar-shops.

11. Quoted in "Steve Hillage," *Guitar Player* 44.9 (September 2010), 62–4.

Chapter 8

1. Quoted in Mavis Bayton, *Frock Rock: Women Performing Popular Music* (Oxford: Oxford University Press, 1998), 127.

2. Quoted in Bayton, 4.

3. Quoted in Carla DeSantis Black, *GRLTalk: 231 Memorable Quotes from ROCKRGRL Magazine* (Austin: MEOW, 2013), 49.

4. Quoted in DeSantis Black, 113.

5. Quoted in DeSantis Black, 105.

6. Quoted in Barbara O'Dair, ed., *Trouble Girls: The Rolling Stone Book of Women in Rock* (New York: Random House, 1997), 439.

7. Quoted in Bayton, 8.

8. Quoted in Bayton, 132.

9. Quoted in Bayton, 16.

10. Quoted in Bayton, 15.

11. Quoted in Megan Seling, "The Warped Tour's Woman Problem," *Wondering Sound*, June 16, 2014, http://www.wonderingsound.com/feature/warped-tour-woman-problem/.

12. Quoted in Bayton, 37.

13. Fiona Sturges, "Where are the Women to Rock the Music Industry?" *The Independent*, June 25, 2010, <http://www.independent.co.uk/arts-entertainment/music/features/where-are-the-women-to-rock-the-music-industry-2009515.html>

14. Quoted in DeSantis Black, 106.

15. Quoted in DeSantis Black, 25.

Chapter 11

1. Quoted in Carla DeSantis Black, *GRLTalk: 231 Memorable Quotes from ROCKRGRL Magazine* (Austin: MEOW, 2013), 47.

2. Quoted in Gillian G. Gaar, *She's a Rebel: The History of Women in Rock & Roll* (Seattle: Seal Press, 1992), 223.

3. Quoted in DeSantis Black, 109.

INDEX